Walking with Houyhnhnms

A true adventure story along the Roman Military Way, in the shadow of the Wall, told by three ponies – Roamer, Thorn and Solo

With contributions to the narrative from experts, from artists aged 15–18 years and from interviewers and storytellers aged 4–11 years

Shadow of the Wall

WALKING WITH HOUYHNHNMS

D A Murray

WALKING WITH HOUYHNHNMS

Copyright © D A Murray 2017

A catalogue record for this book is available from the British Library.

First published in 2017 by
HOUYHNHNMS PUBLISHING

ISBN 978-0-9955824-0-8

Address enquiries to the author at
http://www.shadow-of-the-wall.co.uk.

Printed and bound by
www.printondemand-worldwide.com
Peterborough, England

All paper used in the printing of this book has been made from wood grown in managed, sustainable forests. This is a print-on-demand book.

To Mora

Contents

Introduction   1

Suddenly training for a grand expedition   3

   16th June – Lincoln   3

   9th July – Stoney Gill Farm, Shap, Cumbria   4

   19th July – Heathlands Farm, Carlisle, Cumbria   6

   20th July – Stoney Gill   7

   6th August – Lincoln Common   9

The meeting of three ponies   13

   12th August – Stoney Gill   13

   17th August – Stoney Gill   14

   30th September – Stoney Gill   21

   1st October – Stoney Gill   21

   11th October – Stoney Gill   23

Sea and city traffic: stranded in the dark   26

   *12th October – Tynemouth Castle and Rising Sun Country
Park*   26

A broken gate, dangerous roads and children   36

   *13th October – Segedunum Fort, Carville School and
Ouseburn Farm*   36

The River Tyne: a forced detour and a long climb   49

14th October – Newcastle, Black Row Riding Centre and Heddon-on-the-Wall   49

A missing boot and stuck on the Military Way   57

15th October – Vallum Farm   57

Attempted escape   64

16th October – Errington Arms   64

Panic and gales   74

17th October – Codlaw Hill   74

Another lost harness and a raging river   81

18th October – Greencarts   81

19th October – Greencarts, rest day and satellites   88

Marsh and rocks   98

20th October – Sewing Shields   98

21st October – Housesteads Fort and Bradley Farm   105

Steep hills, bogs and a successful escape   115

22nd October – Cawfields   115

23rd October – Walltown Crags, Great Chesters Roman Fort and Thirlwall Castle   126

Crossing the Irthing   138

24th October – A golf club and Chapel House   138

25th October – Gilsland, Willowford, Birdoswald and High House   145

Baskets, barding and a quarry: the re-enactment   156

26th October – Combe Crag and Quarry Side   156

Waterlogged ground, frightened cows and a blown-away tent   173

27th October – Lanercost Priory and Howgill   173

28th October – Newtown   186

29th October – Bleatarn   192

Families, donkeys, busy roads and another school   198

30th October – Walby Farm Park   198

31st October – Tarraby, Stanwix School and Linstock Castle   203

Obstacles along the Eden   223

*1st November – Rickerby Park Memorial Bridge and
Knockupworth*   223

Inquisitive cattle, kissing gates and a strange fence   240

2nd November – Grinsdale, Kirkandrews and Beaumont Hall   240

A ford, more mini-humans and knee-deep mud   257

*3rd November – Burgh-by-Sands School, Dykesfield and
Drumburgh Castle*   257

The last school: Wall's end   271

4th November – Bowness-on-Solway School and North Plain   271

Freezing fog, fireworks, birds but no water   296

5th November – Campfield Marsh Nature Reserve   296

A frozen tent, seaweed and more fog   304

6th November – Eastwards to Drumburgh   304

7th November – Drumburgh Nature Reserve   314

The final trek and then homeward bound   324

8th November – Dykesfield and Beaumont Hall   324

Veterinary check-up: a long rest   332

9th November – Stoney Gill, Shap   332

Revisiting   346

10th November – Stoney Gill, Carville School and Newcastle   346

ix

Reunion before the final parting   350

    13th November – Stoney Gill   350

    14th November – Stoney Gill   358

Epilogue: reflections   363

Illustrations   366

Itinerary maps   387

Acknowledgements   393

References   396

About the author   400

Introduction

Roamer:

I am Lathomdale Roamer, a Fell pony. You may call me Roamer. We might have met. Here I chronicle my quest with another Fell pony – we are natives of Britain – alongside Hadrian's Wall. At the beginning, I doubted whether we would accomplish anything.

During our journey, we learned countless facts, made fascinating discoveries and beheld unusual sights and sounds. In addition, wildlife and equine experts along the way identified imminent dangers facing England's native ponies. Furthermore, we solved a puzzle: scientists, farmers and other conservationists helped us to understand why humans need our assistance to protect wild plants and animals.

How far did we stroll altogether? I dare say it wasn't a trifling distance, on reflection, for a four-year-old. We hope you will enjoy reading about our exploits, and that our previously secret thoughts and feelings will entertain you.

Thorn:

Recently I participated in an expedition with my companion, Roamer. We and another dear friend, Solo, were helping our man, who wants to save the world's wild ponies from extinction. By the way, my name is Huntsmans Blackthorn. Do I have a story for you!

We attempted to hike from coast to coast, east to west. Can you guess which of us led the way? For reasons we shall divulge, I wore what our man described as a Roman packsaddle. Roamer sported a traditional British Army packsaddle. During our travels, knowledgeable persons enlightened us about our ancestral history,

1

Roman packhorses and the Military Way, the Wall's archaeology and other intriguing Wall facts, and we learned about our living relatives. We also met hundreds of young mini-humans, who quizzed our man about the quest.

Did we reach the Wall's western extremity? We reveal all through our diaries.

Solo:

I am Thornbeck Solitaire. The packhorseman nicknamed me Solo, I suppose mainly because I am a loner. Honestly, I quite like it – the name, I mean. I would love to tell you about *Shadow of the Wall* from my perspective.

With human assistance, Thorn and Roamer recorded many of their numerous encounters and deeds. Among other things, my pals aided the packhorseman in carrying out archaeological research: they were stars in a possibly unique re-enactment.

Our story begins at a time when we were all contented ponies, living free. Wandering about in a Fell herd, grazing undisturbed in virtually natural countryside, able to savour a landscape still only partially tamed by humans, is possibly the finest experience on earth. This, we believed, was our destiny, until something extraordinary happened.

It was a momentous time, as you shall discover . . .

Suddenly training for a grand expedition

16th June – Lincoln

Roamer:

ONE mild, cloudy, dreamy afternoon, I am relaxing in Lincoln, an ancient Roman colony by a pool. I see two men advancing towards me. One, young and fair-haired, is Mark, my keeper. The other, older, dark-haired human is holding a halter and double-looped lead rope in his right hand. What is he doing here on my land?

The unknown visitor slowly, carefully, places the halter over my nose, secures it behind my ears and then leads me to a small paddock. "Hai-ai-ai-ai!" I nicker, but he ignores me. "Please go away," I tell him, but he's not listening.

The stranger begins training me. Walking alternately on my left and right, he leads me up and down the paddock a dozen times.

"Stand" and "Walk on" and "Stay" he continually orders.

Next, he entices me to trot in a circle on what he refers to as a lunging rein. I prefer going anticlockwise.

"Ha-ha," I chuckle. "This is fun."

I am remarkably good at playing his games. At least, he and Mark reckon so. However, why is he doing this?

"A cavesson" – whatever that is – "isn't required," decides the stranger. "Roamer has settled down quickly. He will do the job. I foresee he will be easy to school for the expedition."

I have no idea what the outsider is talking about. To what job is he referring? What does he mean by "expedition"?

Now those humans are assessing my back's shape, length and width. I soon realise their intention: the stranger places a weighty saddle onto my back. It fits comfortably but restricts my full range of movement: I've never had a girth strap under my belly before.

Straight away, they present to me two large, oblong, canvas saddlebags I observed them unloading earlier from a vehicle. Each bag has an internal back and bottom made of wood, I deduce.

"Pfft," I snort, shaking my head. "Keep those away from me!" I beg, but again they seem to take little notice.

The stranger, who is moving slowly and talking quietly, calms me. He shows me one bag close up, which I sniff. It has been on another equine previously, I can tell. He carefully attaches it to my saddle by means of two brass rings – I guess they are 40 centimetres apart – hanging from the bag's back. He places these over two steel hooks located on the saddle's left-hand side. Next, he attaches the second bag to my saddle's right-hand side. What a weird sensation!

"Oi-oi-oi-oi!" I whinny, as any untamed pony might.

Mark leaves abruptly: he must attend to unrelated, urgent matters. I am alone with the mysterious visitor. He stays with me for the rest of the afternoon. I can't yet estimate human time, but that is too long in my opinion. Although I delight in his attention, I must endure an exacting, bothersome ordeal. He tests me severely, enticing me to execute all manner of dexterous manoeuvres whilst carrying his saddle and bags. I'm glad when it is over.

9th *July – Stoney Gill Farm, Shap, Cumbria*

Thorn:

Stoney Gill, a rocky, narrow ravine, is my home. It's a perfect hideaway. Usually, nobody pesters me. Today, something's wrong. Another man is entering my field with Bill, my owner. This unwelcome visitor is here not merely to stroke me: I can sense it.

"Na-ah," I murmur.

I don't recognise the visitor. Therefore, I am wary. I trust only one human – Bill.

"Why won't they leave me alone?" I ask myself as they approach.

They'll not throw a halter over my head without appetising food to entice me. Okay, Bill has food. Even so, I'll not give in to him too easily.

My owner leads me to a small paddock. What's up?

A human – the unwelcome newcomer I have just met – caresses my body for the first time in my life. He runs his right hand over my neck and back. I can cope. Strangely, it is soothing. Ah-ha, that's divine, much better than I imagined.

He is brushing me firmly yet gently. Heh, heh, it tickles; it's like rolling in soft, spring grass. Wait! He begins to brush my legs. Nobody may touch my legs! I prance about, hardly bearing it. I suspect, falsely, he will give up soon. He perseveres, but I can avoid him all day if necessary. I am winning.

Next, the invader leads me about the paddock using a slender, cotton rope. I won't allow myself to wheedle close to him, but at least I can relax.

We stop walking. He begins to brush my mane.

"Nay," I squeal inaudibly. "Keep away from my head, especially my ears! Nay, leave my ears alone!"

I shake my head twice. I shy away.

Eventually, I'm calmer. He rests a hand at the top of each leg in turn. I hate this. Now he slides his left hand slowly down my left foreleg towards my fetlock. You've no chance, whoever you are, I decide: as I said, nobody touches my lower legs.

Though I try to think clearly, it's impossible. I'm confused. I back off, panting, nostrils splayed. He tries to pick up my left forehoof. I back off further. He tries once more. I attempt to pull away, yet he holds tightly onto my head collar.

"Good boy. Steady, boy," this man gently reassures, but he's not fooling me!

"What is he planning to do next?" I ask myself.

5

I look straight at him, snorting contemptuously, warning him. Come near me with your leather bridle and I'll be off, I decide spontaneously. He can see the whites of my wide, wild eyes.

My thoughts are almost deafening as I attempt to gather composure. Okay, I silently reason, I'll be calm if you stay away from my legs and ears.

I let the invader bridle me. His head harness smells of brand-new leather. Bill adjusts the bit-straps. Now, together, they offer me a training bit. I don't want it, but I have no choice: the invader slides it cleverly into my mouth. I attempt to eject it but fail. Two lightweight, silvered, hinged pieces of ultra-smooth, tasteless, cold metal sit uncomfortably over my tongue; I'll never get used to them.

Thankfully, hundreds of paces later, after leading me about the paddock by his pesky bridle to which is attached that horrible bit, my owner's companion gently removes the metal from my mouth.

"That will do for now," he states cheerily.

Do for now? What else have they in mind? Haven't they upset me enough?

"Yes, he has performed brilliantly," replies Bill.

They release me. I gallop without hesitation down to my stream, as far away from cramped paddocks as possible. Warm sunshine laps gently across my back. I am overjoyed: my torment has ended.

19th *July – Heathlands Farm, Carlisle, Cumbria*

Solo:

On a glorious, balmy, midsummer evening, Michael, my owner, is conversing with another male human. All of a sudden, my world turns upside down.

"Here's a young Fell pony," enthuses Michael, gesturing in my direction. "He might be suitable for your expedition."

The foreigner bridles me, places what he describes as "a British

Army packsaddle" on my back and then attaches two unquestionably custom-made saddlebags, one to each side of the saddle. Next, accompanied by Michael, he manipulates me about the farm.

"Walk on!" and "Trot on!" and "Back up!" and "Stand!" the foreigner repeatedly commands as he leads me around trees and other natural obstacles, between gateposts and along farm tracks.

"He'll be perfect," proclaims my trainer nearly three hours later, just before the sun disappears.

I'll be perfect for what? I should like to know. Leave me to graze quietly, please.

By and by, Michael releases me into the field where my friends, three older Fell ponies, are grazing. This nightmare's over, or so I believe.

20th July – Stoney Gill

Thorn:

Yesterday, unexpectedly, the same, unwelcome human I met 11 days ago placed a peculiar-looking object on my back. He described it as a packsaddle. Why, however, was he harassing me with it?

"We made it using archaeological evidence found partly in the vicinity of Hadrian's Wall," he told Bill. "An expert saddler helped me to reconstruct the steel pommel and cantle from an iron pommel discovered in southern England. He then attached these to a beech wood 'tree'. This sits on each side of the pony's back. We've padded the frame with horsehair covered by thick leather."

"The iron pommel, an archaeological expert has suggested, was part of a Roman packsaddle," added Bill's visitor. "Of course, this interpretation is debatable: some archaeologists suggest that metal pommels were first incorporated into saddles during the medieval period, which would have been not before the fifth century at earliest – after the Romans left Britain."

"Unfortunately," explained the visitor as he attached the human-

7

made device to me, "you can't adjust the saddle easily: quite likely, it was made originally for a specific pack animal. Luckily, it fits Thorn's back. Roamer's back rises more steeply at the withers: the saddle's pommel might rub slightly against his neck."

Who was Roamer? What had he to do with my predicament? All I knew was that the visitor's so-called "Roman saddle" felt unstable, which vexed me. It seemed likely to fall sideways at any moment: only a cotton strap under my girth held it precariously in place. I shuffled about with this unnatural contraption on my back for ages, which I didn't enjoy.

Today, Bill and his still unidentified visitor are training me even harder with their saddle.

"Let's put his harness on now," recommends my uninvited guest.

I begin to panic.

"First, take him inside," suggests Bill. "He'll be calmer there."

The intruder marches me quietly into a sizable wooden shed, where he manages to soothe me. He then guides a thick, leather strap around my breast before buckling its ends to the saddle's front. Next, he places a second, similar strap around my buttocks and attaches it to the saddle's rear. Slickly he buckles thinner, looping straps, attached to this harness, around my neck and rump.

Such unfamiliar cowhide, though soft against my skin, irritates me exceedingly. Okay, straps do stabilise this saddle: it's becoming an extension of my body. Nevertheless, so many fittings and fastenings aren't a good omen.

"Hold him steady, lad," warns Bill, "while I put on the crupper."

Oh, no, no, I conclude. I'm having no strap under my tail. I've had enough. I'm off!

I struggle, unsuccessfully, to break free, dancing about for several minutes in the shed. At last, the intruder manages to calm me. However, I am still overwrought, wide-eyed. I don't enjoy anybody messing about with me.

As I am watching the intruder warily, Bill tricks me. He sneaks up behind me. Without warning, he grabs my tail firmly! The crupper is in place before I can react. Although it isn't uncomfortable, I disliked being tricked.

I relax, but only temporarily. The intruder, who is still holding my lead rope, runs his right hand down the back of my right foreleg; he attempts to pick up my hoof. I shy away. He tries again, this time focussing his attention on my right hind leg. I back away again, agitated. He should give up! Instead, he caresses only the top part of each leg. Okay, I can handle that. We strike an uneasy truce.

My unsought, new-found human companion leaves me alone; I can recover from my tribulation. Before long, however, I must accompany him on long rambles, initially across fields and then up and down a cart track alongside aggressive motorway traffic. Fast cars passing close by don't concern me – I have seen and heard their whining engines for weeks – but I still can't accept my saddle easily. Humans, who generally are unable to read ponies' minds, wouldn't perceive my reticence.

What is going on now? This same, persistent human one-third fills each of two large, empty, hessian bags with red sand. Afterwards, he securely ties them with reef knots to opposite ends of a one-metre piece of stout, three-strand rope. Next, he and my owner place the rope over my saddle, letting one bag hang on each side. Oh, I get it: I must stride out with these bags dangling. This is dead easy, no bother at all, for a strong, sturdy, strapping Fell pony.

"Let's call it a day," advises Bill.

"He has done marvellously," responds his accomplice.

The intruder unsaddles and brushes me. He opens my field gate and removes my head collar. I am free!

6th August – Lincoln Common

Roamer:
The mysterious stranger has returned to teach me further clever tricks. This time, he has brought a young man, Alex, with him, who follows us everywhere with a black cine-camera.

I practise using a British Military packsaddle and two lightly loaded saddlebags. These specially made saddlebags are wide, apparently: it's hard to steer safely through slender, confining openings unless you are quick-witted and skilful. During training, I nimbly twist between and around chairs, traffic cones and other obstacles, and I stride alongside hedges. I turn around in cramped spaces, trot figures of eight around trees and change direction instantly. Then I practise everything backwards! However, why am I learning to do this?

"Roamer must be able to judge the width of any gap to within half a centimetre," reasons the trainer. "He will need to negotiate narrow gateways."

"Perhaps that's asking a bit much at this stage," suggests Mark, who has been monitoring my improvement.

"He is capable of doing it," believes the trainer.

Of course I am. We Fell ponies are extraordinarily gifted; at times, we are more intelligent than humans.

The trainer leads me, still carrying wide saddlebags, to the stable yard's doorless opening. He controls me using a red, two-metre, cotton rope attached to my bridle.

"Stand!" he orders as he tries to line me up with the middle of a gap hardly wider than my pack.

Now he commands, "Walk on."

I hesitate because I don't trust him absolutely. Ultimately, I go for it. My pack scrapes against an old, iron door latch. I squeeze through, just. It's simple.

He slides the palm of his right hand briefly along the side of my neck towards my withers and then gently but firmly pats my left shoulder with his fingers, praising me: "Good boy, Roamer."

Nothing much rattles me. The trainer repeatedly leads me through the doorway. I usually stay calm and in control, managing not to touch anything: I could do it in my sleep.

I go through another field onto Lincoln Common, my favourite spot since I moved south from Cumbria: what a lovely, open space this is. Cumbria, the territory of the Cumbri, of the Welsh, where men of the same country reside, is my original home, of course.

Look! Other Fell ponies, similar in appearance to me, live on the common. Three youngsters chase me because they're my friends. They miss me, naturally, and are anxious to discover what I'm doing. One pure black, two-year-old colt nuzzles up to me.

"Roamer has quite a following," remarks the trainer.

Each of my pals is two years younger than I am. I'm permanently in charge on my common; every free-living pony here accepts it.

The trainer decides to interview Mark. I've no idea why. Alex carries on filming.

"Tell me about the ponies on Lincoln Common," says the trainer.

"About 50 equines – including a small herd of Fell ponies – are registered on West Common. It's roughly 360 acres in area. Every inhabited household within the city boundary has grazing rights for one horse or pony. Grazing rights stop developers from encroaching upon the common. Development is a constant threat."

"What do you do on this common?"

"I look after the herd of Fell ponies, including one pony I own. It's a full-time hobby really."

"What was Lathomdale Roamer like when you first got hold of him?"

"Apart from having had a little bit of basic handling, he was fairly wild."

"What do you think of him now we've done about six hours training?"

"This pony is a quick learner."

I do figure things out quickly, of course!

"This is the first time we've had a pack on him," says the trainer. "We've done about a mile and a half so far. He hasn't wrecked the pack, and he's a pretty fast walker."

"Nothing fazes him," replies Mark enthusiastically. "He's typical of the Fell breed."

"Do you reckon he'll be ready in time?"

Will I be ready for what? I'd like to know.

"I think he'll be fantastic," replies Mark. "From the day we bought him, you could tell that he was going to be a star."

Shall I become a star? I don't think so.

As we leave the common, my three friends instinctively tag along, but Mark cleverly dissuades them from pursuing us beyond a gateway. They trot off, snorting and whinnying. I am disappointed not to be playing with them. Instead, the trainer leads me up and down steep grassy embankments, across roads, by parked cars, among more trees and through mature summer grasses and shrubs.

Back at the stable yard, the trainer and Mark converse intently.

"He is progressing well," claims the former.

"I'll do bits of extra training on the common with Roamer to keep him trim and aware," promises Mark.

Why Mark also would want to instruct me is mystifying; even my pals are intrigued. What a nuisance! I hope these workouts don't become regular occurrences: they could spoil my fun.

The meeting of three ponies

12th August – Stoney Gill

Thorn:

I meet Solo for the first time: what a staggering surprise! We soon become inseparable friends, strolling, cantering and grazing essentially everywhere as one. Solo relies upon me to protect him: he's much younger than I am, and this isn't his home.

Even though Solo insists on forcing me to kneel from time to time, it's just a harmless game; I don't object. Of course, no human could persuade a Fell pony to perform such a trick in mere seconds!

Solo:

Recently, Michael moved me from Heathlands Farm, wonderful, hidden land overgrown with heather. I couldn't understand why.

Today, he transports me from Gretna, a town located on a grassy, gravelly hill just north of the Scottish border. In my new, unfamiliar, English surroundings, a short distance southwards, over 30 unrecognisable, untamed Fell ponies live.

Soon, without a care, I am running and grazing freely with another black Fell pony on a steep, tantalisingly green hillside.

"Hi, who are you?" I inquire casually as we gallop, panting, towards a sheltered valley.

"I'm Thorn," confides the other pony. "What are you doing on my range?"

"I'm not sure," I reply. "It's not my idea."

We play alongside each other, untroubled, throughout the day.

Our favourite game is tag; we canter backwards and forwards in chase upon chase.

I was the dominant male back home: any pony there will tell you. Now I want to take charge at Stoney Gill. I like to nibble Thorn's neck gently. Occasionally, I also nibble his forelegs to make him kneel. Even though he is twice my age and, therefore, is stronger and wiser, I am taller and, I admit, a bit too bossy. Yes, I realise it's his territory, not mine. Still, he doesn't convey any impression of minding my antics. I'm no threat, really.

By day's end, Thorn and I are getting on exceptionally well together. I hope we shall become close friends.

17th August – Stoney Gill

Thorn:

Bill and the unidentified intruder are back. They entice Solo and me with tasty, unusually shaped, dry food. Somehow, Bill's visitor no longer alarms me.

This morning, the two humans are training us in concert, which should be enjoyable. Wait a minute. They are placing the Roman packsaddle onto Solo. Oi-oi, that's mine!

Now the unidentified man, today dressed in black, is leading Solo out of the paddock into an adjoining field. They begin tramping across the hillside, alongside a hedge, leaving me standing with Bill and tied to a wooden rail. I yearn to be closer to my new friend; no human has any right to keep us apart. I'm not putting up with it. I easily pull free from the rail, rear and then, with one flick of my powerful, muscular forelegs, kick down the paddock fence separating us: the fence was feeble. Na-ah! Bill lunges for my halter, grabbing me before I can escape.

The man returns with Solo.

"How is he?" asks Bill.

"First class," replies the intruder, "except that he hasn't learned every command yet. How did Thorn manage to demolish your fence?"

"He had an uncontrollable urge to join Solo."

It's true: my desire to be with him is irresistible.

"Is he hurt?" queries the intruder, alarmed.

"No, lad, he's fine, in perfect condition, but I'll need a new fence!"

This isn't fun. They are taking Solo – he's wearing my packsaddle loaded with saddlebags – onto a grassy track alongside the motorway. Even a slim, bearded man who is filming everything with a moving-image camera, though don't ask me why, has waltzed off with my friend. I am not quite alone, however: a kind, softly spoken woman named, I think, Barbara, who is visiting Bill today, has taken charge of me. Nonetheless, I remain infuriated. I repeatedly stomp my left rear hoof loudly on the concrete ground, but nobody seems to be listening.

Ten minutes later, Solo is back. They remove his saddlebags. Perhaps they have realised we shouldn't be parted, even temporarily. Oh, no, that's not what I had in mind! The unidentified intruder, who appears to be in charge of our training, is tying me to Solo.

"Stop it, will you?" I protest, snorting, but he ignores me.

First, he clips a small, shiny, brass coupling chain to both rings of my bridle bit. Then he attaches one end of a roughly one-yard-long, one-inch-wide, brown, leather strap to a smaller ring in the chain's centre. Simultaneously, Bill attaches the other end of this connecting harness to the rear left-hand D-ring of Solo's saddle.

"This coupling chain should ensure equal tension on each of Thorn's bit rings, giving him a much gentler, untroubled experience," explains the intruder to Bill. "The connecting strap has two quick-release buckles. In emergency situations, I am able to separate the two ponies swiftly by pulling on either Thorn's chain buckle or Solo's saddle buckle."

"That's not a bad idea, lad," responds Bill.

What does "emergency situations" imply? I don't fancy the sound of that. Although I did not wish humans to separate Solo from me, I wasn't expecting them to chain us together. Are we prisoners?

"My saddler made two straps," continues Bill's accomplice, "so I can lead from Solo's right-hand side when necessary – in traffic, for example."

"This could prove interesting," maintains Bill, a tiny hint of sardonic amusement in his voice.

"Our set-up hasn't been tried before," confesses the intruder. "It had better succeed; otherwise, we shall have a serious dilemma!"

What possible serious dilemma could there be? I am alarmed anew as the intruder leads Solo from my pal's left-hand side. I must follow, also on Solo's left, across the hillside.

"Woo, lads!" I wail, which roughly means, "Stop! Release me. I don't desire human-made problems, thanks all the same."

Mere seconds into our test walk, this arrangement isn't working: I am dangerously close to Solo's hind legs, and I'm on his wrong side, his right-hand side, by mistake.

"Nay, nay, Solo!" I shout, but it's too late.

I accidentally nudge his flank. Here it comes! He bucks; his hind legs lash out wildly. Because I am vigilant, quick, nimble and athletic, I swerve away just in time. Disturbed air rushes past my face. The intruder urgently releases the buckle on Solo's saddle, freeing us. At least the buckle works.

The intruder places a comforting hand on Solo's neck. Hang on! Who's comforting me? It was I who almost required veterinary hospital treatment, and merely because two foolish humans harnessed me behind Solo. Though Solo kicked out frantically, it was unpremeditated: he didn't intend to hurt me; it wasn't his fault.

Those humans are definitely to blame. When, a few weeks ago, the trainer estimated the connecting strap length with a shepherd's rope and toggle, I was testing the Roman saddle. He assumed that the same setup would work if Solo wore it and I walked behind. He miscalculated. Solo's torso is longer: the strap is too short. Only I should wear this particular saddle. Besides, I am a born leader.

"We could easily adjust the strap's length," frets the intruder. "It's constructed in two halves. However, I fear that's not the solution: Solo refuses to lead and Thorn's not yet assured as a follower."

"Aye," agrees Bill. "Let's swap them around."

Finally, they are thinking clearly. They unsaddle Solo, place his

Roman saddle onto me and then reattach our connecting harness, putting me in front. I am in heaven. What's more, Solo is plodding behind me contentedly; there are no tricks. Life is altogether quieter.

Half an hour later, they have led us across a field, along a farm track beside the motorway and in grand clockwise and anticlockwise circles. No hitch or dispute has befallen us. Ye-ee-ee-ee-eh!

"What an unbelievable difference!" declares Bill.

"We've discovered something extraordinary today," confides his surprised accomplice.

They've reached conclusions that were obvious to Solo and me from the beginning. In future, they must ensure that I lead, or else.

"I think we've done enough for today," figures Bill.

After seven hours, who could face further coaching? I hope Cameraman, who has remained silent during much of our ordeal, has managed to capture each training episode on film: I refuse to go through more torment today for anybody.

They release us. Before you can blink, free of all inhibition, we are cantering through a vast field towards a secluded corner by a stream. Natural, unbridled exercise is best.

Solo:

This Roman packsaddle smells of new wool and brown cowhide. It is an odd, well-nigh indescribable shape. Four iron rings, two on each side of the saddle, each about five centimetres in diameter, protrude from the shiny leather. Together, the rings form corners of a rectangle. I've no idea what their purpose is. The saddle's soft, woollen base sits comfortably enough, but nerve endings are firing off, telling my brain that my back itches: nothing man-made has rested on my muscles before.

An hour, give or take, passes. I am acclimatising to this saddle, and the harness – I'm strapped up like baled hay – isn't bothering me particularly.

The same foreigner who trained me at Heathlands Farm is leading me briskly up a grassy track parallel to and close to a busy motorway. He is considerate and sympathetic, but I am a reluctant participant.

Bill, Thorn's owner, is driving a scary motor, his quad bike, about 10 metres behind me. It worries me constantly. I repeatedly glance back nervously. Even though the foreigner gently admonishes me, I continue to be wary.

"Don't be afraid, Solo," he reassures, successfully managing to hide what must be his justifiable concern.

Where is Thorn? I can't see him anywhere. Minutes ago, he smashed down a wooden fence whilst trying to reach me; I was training with the foreigner in an adjoining field. I heard the fence cave in, collapse and clatter to the ground: it was old and rickety. Thorn and I become unsettled, occasionally angry, whenever humans keep us apart for very long.

Countless muddled thoughts race through my mind as I continue walking. Virtually all new situations bewilder me, but I am persevering; I advance even when motorway lorries scream at me.

We make it back to the paddock safely. Thorn and I are reunited. There, Bill attaches Thorn's bridle to the rear of my Roman saddle via a brand-new, metre-long, thin, leather strap.

The foreigner leads us across a sloping field. I'm in front; Thorn follows. I hate it. Thorn barges into me each time I halt or change direction. He is continually rubbing against me. I can't stand anybody, even Thorn, near my hind legs.

Thorn keeps crowding me. I've no choice. I instinctively buck, kicking out wildly with both hind feet, narrowly missing Thorn's face.

"Na-ah!" yells Thorn. "Take it easy, Solo. Calm down."

The foreigner, aided by Bill, rapidly unbuckles me from Thorn. I didn't desire to injure him – Thorn is my closest friend – but he was invading my space.

"Did you get all that on film, Alan?" inquires the foreigner.

"Yes," replies a bearded man who has been pointing a strange invention at me. "Mind you, everything happened so quickly."

Now Thorn is wearing my Roman saddle. They have locked me inside a separate field, away from him. The foreigner is teaching him clever tricks. I strain my long, black, velvety neck to peer over the hawthorn hedge. Repeatedly I try to jump it to be near him. Bother! It's unreasonably high.

Where is Thorn going without me? I gallop back and forth wildly, tracking him up and down the hedge line until I am too tired to continue.

"Na-ah," I wail. "Come back! I am frightened on my own."

Those humans ignore my neighs and whinnies, keeping me waiting alone for ages. Much later, however, I am happy to be toddling behind Thorn, attached to him with their leather harness. We've swapped saddles: now I'm wearing the British saddle, which I cope with easily. I have solved how to advance safely behind Thorn, to his side. I'm not annoying him and he isn't irritating me!

"Brilliant!" utters Bill.

I sense that Thorn is a born leader; I'll follow him anywhere. Nevertheless, I'm mightily relieved when our schoolings – you might call it "attempted domestication" – are over.

Now what's happening? Oh, I see. The foreigner wants to interview Bill. Thorn and I must stand still with the humans while the bearded man positions an elongated, fur-covered object on a three-footed metal stand two metres away.

"Speak into the microphone," orders the bearded man, "but look at the camera."

"Bill, how long have we been training these two ponies?" asks the foreigner.

"We've done seventeen-and-a-half hours."

"Seventeen-and-a-half hours," repeats the foreigner, "from off the hill; that's not bad. They're standing quietly at the moment, but they've destroyed a fence and given us the run-around this afternoon."

Bill laughs. Why is he amused?

"We're just about winning, though," adds the foreigner.

"That's what he thinks," whispers Thorn to me.

"Bill, tell me," continues the foreigner. "How many ponies do you have?"

"With the foals this year, there are about 70," explains Bill.

"I understand that Fell ponies are in decline. Is that right?"

"Very much so."

"What might be the reason?"

"Well, they want them off the commons: they reckon the commons are overgrazed. Plus, people who keep them are getting older."

"These ponies live on the mountains, moors and marshes of Cumbria and also in parts of Northumberland, Lancashire and Durham," continues the foreigner. "That's their stronghold?"

"Yes," replies Bill.

"I guess people are forcing them off of the commons for several reasons?"

"Yes. There's nowhere for them to live."

"How long do you think it will be before we see the last semi-wild herd in Cumbria if we don't do something about it?"

"In my own mind, I can see there won't be more than 100 ponies left in 10 years' time."

I'm too young to understand what they are talking about, I'm thinking. What has this to do with me?

"So, basically, we've got to do something about it?" concludes the foreigner.

"Absolutely," replies Bill. "We must if we want to keep them on these commons."

"Roughly how many breeders keep them on commons?"

"About a dozen breeders have more than half a dozen ponies."

"Do we need an incentive?"

"Aye, we need an incentive for the young ones to keep 'em," concurs Bill earnestly.

"Do you believe we'll get Thorn and Solo ready in time?"

"Aye, definitely," insists Bill. "They've come on in leaps and bounds."

"They have," agrees the foreigner, nodding. "They're standing quietly with us now; two weeks ago, they would have been dragging us around this field."

Will we be ready in time for what? I'm worried and even more confused.

30th September – Stoney Gill

Roamer:

Mark marches me from Lincoln Common this early morning. He aids a waiting horsebox driver to load me into a monstrous carriage. Another equine – I sense a mare – hides inside a separate compartment of the carriage. I hear but cannot see her stomping about this unfriendly, manufactured, metal contrivance that smells strongly of unfamiliar horses. Where are we going? Somebody help me!

Although no windows exist in my lorry horsebox, I can hear the engine's frantic roar. We travel at a frightening speed throughout the morning, pausing only briefly en route to pick up a third equine passenger.

It's afternoon when we eventually halt alongside a noisy motorway. A friendly farmer, appreciably older than Mark, is waiting nearby. He transfers me to a smaller, single-stall horse trailer before driving me to a colossal hillside field in the middle of a vast nowhere. I am thoroughly bewildered. Where am I?

"Hai-ai-ai-ai!" I shout repeatedly, realising that I am alone and afraid.

1st October – Stoney Gill

Roamer:

Today, in my new home near Shap in Cumbria, the site of a prehistoric stone circle, I remain apprehensive.

The air is cooler here than on my common. Hey! This terrain isn't exactly flat, either: large, water-soaked, rolling hills surround me. Westwards I spy enormous mountains. They remind me of my birthplace, yet I've never been here before.

I am shuffling warily in unfamiliar countryside when I spy another gelding Fell pony. He is silky black and handsome, as am I. We call loudly to each other. His name is Thorn. He introduces me to his friend, Solo. Perhaps life isn't so bad here after all, though I pine for my old friends in Lincoln.

Thorn:

One cool, breezy day – humans call this time of year autumn – I am exercising alone in woodland near my gurgling stream. Unexpectedly, I meet another pony.

"Who are you?" I gasp, astonished.

"Call me Roamer," he purrs softly.

"Hello, Roamer. I've heard of you," I tell him excitedly.

"How could you have heard of me?" he asks, startled by my unanticipated response.

"I'll explain," I say. "Would you care to strut alongside me through these woods?"

"Yes, I would love to!" he replies.

"Where have you sprung from?" I ask.

"It's a complicated story," he confides. "Basically, a mysterious human taught me various clever skills. Eight weeks later, two other strangers transported me here. I had no warning."

This afternoon, Roamer and I become better acquainted.

"Shall I introduce you to my closest friend, Solo?" I ask as we are ambling harmoniously side by side.

"Where is he?"

"Hiding behind those ash trees in the distance, I expect," I tell him.

"Ye-ee-ee-eh!" whinnies Roamer, in delighted anticipation. "Let's find him straight away!"

Though I've heard Bill mention Roamer's name, I'm unsure why my latest comrade has arrived here. Nevertheless, I am thrilled to meet another relative. Now there are three of us: three young, black, well-built, gelding Fell ponies sharing the same spacious hillside and the same marvellous adventure. Somehow, however, I have a hunch this tranquil, idyllic life won't last for ever.

11th October – Stoney Gill

Roamer:

Bill, an upland farmer, is Thorn's owner. He and the man who trained me at Lincoln Common are instructing all three of us in unison. Thorn, Solo and I are practising techniques and skills together, rationalises my trainer, because we are "suitable" Fell ponies.

For what are we suitable? I would like to know. Solo and Thorn are equally mystified.

I am wearing that Military saddle again. The men harness me behind Thorn, who is wearing a strange-looking saddle: it has horns. My trainer then leads us across fields, along the sides of hedges, up and down a long, narrow farm track, onto roads and close to a motorway where thousands of vehicles scream. Walking whilst tied behind another pony is rather an interesting experience; it takes some getting used to. Fortunately, I'm easygoing: I don't mind. Besides, Thorn and I are becoming close friends these days.

"We have put up with hours of this," moans Thorn as dusk approaches. "Why?"

Solo's not happy either. It has been a tiring, eventful day.

"Training's finished," announces Bill. "They are ready."

"I'll soon find out whether you're right," answers the other man.

"I'm glad today's over," I tell Thorn.

"What was the point of it all?" wonders Solo, who, being the youngest, is the most anxious of us.

The humans chortle on, but I can't be bothered to listen to their blah conversation. Instead, I close my eyes and attempt to rest.

"Thorn, what were Bill and the other man discussing?" I ask a short time later, after they have released us.

"Allegedly, we shall be walking along the entire length of an ancient, man-made monument called Hadrian's Wall," proclaims Thorn matter-of-factly. "Don't ask me where it is."

"Which wall?" inquires Solo, not quite believing Thorn. "I know of no long walls. It sounds far away. Must we cross boggy ground?"

"Yes, presumably," retorts Thorn. "Which reminds me: Bill's accomplice mentioned that he has additional employment for us during the walk."

"What did he say?" I ask, considerably perplexed.

"We ponies must carry kit."

"W-w-why must we carry kit along the Wall?" I stammer, shocked. "What are they thinking of?"

"Don't you realise, Roamer? Now we are pack ponies!"

"Oh, I suppose it's true," I admit, overwhelmed by Thorn's blindingly obvious observation.

Instantly, I comprehend that the other man must be somebody called Packhorseman, a human I have heard of before. I never suspected his intention: I have been preparing for a special purpose, without realising it, for what seems a lifetime. In fact, however, barely 20 hours since I commenced training, I am "sufficiently well coached" according to Packhorseman.

Thorn's latest news, when we are relaxing by a stream this evening, is that I must wear quite a heavy pack on my back. He is adamant: I shall be carrying many unusual, curious objects and hiking a lengthy distance. What does he mean by "lengthy"? Is it 10 kilometres or 50 kilometres? Who knows? Will the pack make me unbearably sore? Even worse, I shall wear no shoes on my feet: our supposedly wise trainers have decided we don't need horseshoes; it's something to do with our tough, blue-horn hooves. Possibly, those humans assume correctly. Nevertheless, I am uneasy.

Thorn:

Finally, we have completed our training. I am a rapid learner, my owner concludes.

Somebody has made a decision. Evidently, I am one of a purportedly lucky trio chosen to hoof it alongside a wall called, I believe, Hadrian's Wall. An emperor, who hailed from a place called the Iberian Peninsula, wherever that is, built it 19 centuries ago. Yes, I shall be trotting off to Hadrian's Wall, though I've no inkling when this might eventuate. From now on, the man in black is our new guardian, at least temporarily; I guess he's our man.

Solo:

Earlier today, Thorn overheard Bill talking to the stranger who trained me. Sometime, soon, we shall begin a titanic trek.

I believe I shall carry a gigantic backpack. What will that pack contain? It may prove to be excruciatingly difficult for me to carry a human's belongings as I tread next to their so-called Wall. I worry: my hooves might hurt; the load might damage my back or it could do much worse; I groan at the mere thought of carrying such a load. This expedition, I have decided, could prove to be physically too demanding, even mentally unbearable. I'm too young to die.

Why should humans force us ponies to visit a Roman ruin? I don't care who made it; I'd rather not contemplate historic relics. Frankly, it's just a wall, an old wall, what's left of it, which, in my opinion, can't be much. Old, decrepit buildings aren't worth fussing about. Are they?

Will Thorn be the leading pony? I hope so. I hate to lead: I almost injured him during training, you will recall.

All at once, life is terribly unpredictable.

Sea and city traffic: stranded in the dark

12th October – Tynemouth Castle and Rising Sun Country Park

Roamer:

WHERE am I going so early this morning? Why is Packhorseman, accompanied by another man, leading me from our field?

"I expect we are embarking on our journey to the Wall," declares Thorn as our new acquaintance, Bill's brother, leads me into his equine transporter. "Maybe we will soon begin our long-distance slog."

"How much time will Wall slogging take?" I gasp.

"About a week, I'd say," warns Thorn – he has no idea really – as the horse trailer door slams with a heavy, metallic thud, blocking most of the daylight.

Hours later, we disembark onto a lofty grass verge outside an antiquated building whose signpost displays the words "Tynemouth Castle". Behind this solitary structure, a castle at the outfall of the river flow, I glimpse a watery expanse – sea, I presume – spreading eastwards to the horizon. At this moment, I long to be a baby horse: I could have stayed with Solo.

Industrious, bustling activity ensues as Packhorseman, assisted by Bill's brother – I've ascertained his name is Ernie – and John, Ernie's son-in-law, prepares us for travelling on foot.

"Unfortunately," explains Packhorseman to Ernie, "we can't use the castle grounds to load up the ponies."

"Why not?" inquires Ernie, surprised by this revelation.

"English Heritage senior representatives wouldn't permit entry. Months ago, I requested access, but to no avail."

"So the castle's usually open to the public – unless you happen to have pack ponies in tow," observes Thorn dryly.

I am too preoccupied to answer him: today, right now, I must bear two bulky packs on my back, one against each flank. Each contains a stack of luggage. I've learned that there are groceries inside, for instance. At least we won't go hungry!

My saddle and harness don't represent a trifling weight, either. Packhorseman, who shall accompany us on our journey, informs Ernie and John that British Army saddlers "constructed the saddle from fine-grained leather, beech wood and steel" several decades ago. He says another expert, a master saddler from southern England, renovated it according to precise Army "General Service Modified" specifications, using the finest materials, 12 years ago.

Who cares about saddle making? I do, when the harness allows humans to transport a sizeable load. Thorn believes I must wear this saddle and harness and these oversized saddlebags for at least 100 miles. I hope he's wrong. I daren't imagine how far that is, but it sounds a long, long way. My situation appears worse than that of a Cumbrian hill pony habitually carrying a load of wall stones, though I've never carried any.

The men begin loading gear into Thorn's Roman saddlebags. He seems unperturbed, relaxed, as he soaks up the tepid afternoon sun. In truth, standing on only three legs, resting his left rear hoof, eyes half closed but ears forward, he is always gathering information. It's comforting to know that Thorn is with me: our challenge is less daunting. I really like Thorn, which is just as well since we are now working so closely together.

Slowly I'm becoming used to my first full load; I am more optimistic; perhaps roaming with bags won't be so bad after all.

"I must admit, some equines might be flattered if Packhorseman chose them for his *Shadow of the Wall* expedition," I whisper to

Thorn. "Anyway, I've decided: in future, I shall call him simply 'Pan'."

Thorn is not listening: by now, he's more interested in the human conversation.

"My owner's brother has asked our man to explain what we'll be doing," announces Thorn eventually. "Guess what, Roamer? During our long hike, we'll be visiting schools; apparently, children are eager to meet us and find out about us."

There's no time to contemplate Thorn's proclamation: we instantly start walking with the man who tirelessly trained us. I am nervous but also exhilarated. This is it – the real thing!

Scarcely have we begun when my earlier doubts return: Pan has packed so much into my saddlebags that the load's size is troubling me; it is ginormous. Will I cope? I am agile and powerful, but how shall I triumph over unusually narrow gateways? Training was easy: the pack wasn't so wide. Probably I should trust in Pan, but I remain concerned.

"He must have checked the pack's width," I mutter repeatedly, attempting to console myself.

We walk and walk . . . and walk. It's late: the air is becoming colder, the way darker. I pine for home.

According to Pan, we have travelled eight tentative kilometres. He decides to camp prematurely, but there's no safe place to sleep. Our horsebox returns. Ernie and John ferry us to Rising Sun Country Park, so named to honour an old, now extinct, coal-mining pit.

"Ye-ee-ee-eh!" I nicker, more than slightly confused.

Pan converses with the park owner, who anticipated that our arrival would be much earlier.

"I'll happily sleep in your Celtic roundhouse," confesses Pan. "I'm exhausted, too tired to pitch my tent, tonight."

"Help yourself to a cup of coffee," offers the park janitor. "Feel free to use the kitchen if you wish to cook anything. I won't be locking up for another hour."

What exactly is happening? I stand at the park's garden gate much of this first night, wondering where Pan is. Thankfully, he frequently comes to check that everything's all right. Perhaps he is fearful we might slip out of the garden and wander about. We might. Who could blame us? We were living a free life yesterday. A single indisputable fact gnaws at me: I am profoundly insecure, unsettled, so far from home.

Thorn:

Where are they taking me now? Why must I walk into this box on wheels? Ah, I get it: we must be heading to the Wall. Oh, there's fresh hay here. How lovely. Wait. The door is closing. I'm in the dark.

"Hai-ai-ai-ai-ai!" I call, but no human answers.

Three hours later, somebody – I don't recall who – leads me, blinking, into daylight. Where am I? Who is that other pony? Oh, okay, it's Roamer.

"Where are we?" asks Roamer, bewildered. "Where is Solo? Why are we standing beside an unfamiliar castle?"

"Hello again," I say calmly, still blinking. "They have left Solo at home. This is why they have been training us. Don't be afraid, Roamer."

Our man, the same human who instructed us, first saddles Roamer and then saddles me. Next, he unloads several plastic boxes and other curious items of equipment from the four-by-four and begins to place each item laboriously, precisely, box by box, piece by piece, into one or other of our saddlebags. Two men, who ferried me here, assist him. Roamer stares: initially he is unwilling to believe what is happening.

"I'm guessing everything will fit in," declares our man. "I have tested the expedition packing procedure previously, but only without the ponies. I've decided, more or less, which saddle should carry which gear."

Now is not an occasion for guessing, I suspect. I count 15 boxes and waterproof bags in total, plus other equipment, to load onto us.

"Each pack must be balanced," continues our man. "If left-hand-side and right-hand-side weights are not equal, a saddle will slip. I'll attach my tent separately to Thorn's saddle."

29

"He'll never figure out such a complicated mess," I advise Roamer an hour later. "We could be here tomorrow."

Luckily, I am wrong. How he successfully packs each expedition item, I fail to fathom. We are suddenly ready. Meanwhile, a photographer, a young, slim man who works for a local newspaper, has been waiting patiently throughout the cramming process, camera ready. He efficiently snaps about a dozen shots of Roamer and me fully laden. Roamer enjoys posing, but I'm agitated, desperate to get moving.

"Your ponies will feature in tomorrow's edition," hollers the photographer as he hurriedly leaves.

I wonder: is he late for his next assignment?

"Come on, boys," encourages our man. "Let's go!"

Right away, with no other warning, we are striding towards Hadrian's Wall, though I still don't appreciate why.

"Hai-ai-ai-ai!" I wail. "What's that 'beep . . . beep' noise? Look at those cars!"

"Lots of luck," shouts Bill's brother. "We'll telephone you later to check how things are going."

To our left is a locked castle surrounded by grass-topped cliffs. Beyond, 100 feet below us, is a wide, empty, deep green wetness ready to engulf us. It is what humans call the North Sea, a flat, unruffled expanse beneath a grey, uninviting sky. Where has so much water come from? A seagull cries twice, forbidding our entry into her parallel world, where few equines would choose to be.

At last, our expedition has commenced, but Roamer and I are disappointed because our man is forcing us to carry full packs. We aren't keen on lugging gear for miles: quickly we could become extremely weary.

As expected, he has chosen me to wear his Roman saddle.

"Thorn's back is better shaped to fit it," he told Bill, during training at Stoney Gill.

Never mind what our man thinks. In reality, the saddle already bothers my back. Perhaps that's because I'm unused to bearing any load, but why must I carry it? Besides, though I realise I am conveying our man's shelter, so far I have no detailed impression of the pack's contents.

Roamer is unhappy for another reason: his pack is even bigger and more intimidating than mine. He sports an Army packsaddle.

As we tentatively turn a clifftop corner, I glance back apprehensively. The horsebox hasn't moved. Those two men, who ferried us here from Stoney Gill, are studying a map intently; I presume they are lost. So am I.

It is late afternoon. Roamer and I are alone with our man in a strange, unwelcoming place. We are tramping along a cycle path adjacent to and high above the ocean. I lick my breeze-battered, salt-encrusted lips. I have never seen or tasted sea before. I am beguiled yet simultaneously fearful of this wild, watery unknown. Our man keeps ordering us to hurry up. Is he oblivious to our discomfort? To be honest, I'm tired already. My feet are becoming sore. No, I am not exaggerating!

Three stressful though trouble-free miles later, countless vehicles confront us at a quayside in the locality of Chirton, a village with a church once belonging to monks. Some of these iron monsters are motionless, but others move rapidly. Our man has taught us to dodge stationary objects nimbly and to be unafraid of hectic traffic, but this is a severe, premature test. I am leading; Roamer is behind. We encounter our first busy road. Although we are alert and wary, we'll not panic: we usually like people, and we are frightened of nothing, well, practically nothing, despite everything being so new, so unfamiliar. However, our man had better be certain of what he is doing.

After climbing up an extraordinarily steep road, we leave the seaside at Chirton Dene Quays, a deep, wooded valley, and head through a quiet park of vibrant, still blooming gardens with neatly laid out cycling and walking trails. We emerge at Percy Mains, where, a century ago, pit men mined the High Main coal seam. Our joy is fleeting: dozens of cars are speeding. They approach from several directions. We must cross two teeming major roads at dangerous roundabouts. Less than two hours has elapsed since we left the coastal castle, but my mind and muscles have fooled me into believing we have been hiking for days. We can't relax for even a second.

Under a darkening sky, our man switches on elegant, compact, rectangular flashing lights attached to the pommels and cantles of our saddles, white in front and red behind. He is wearing a yellow waistcoat fringed with red and blue squares. On its back are six large, white letters that spell POLITE, followed by four black-lettered words: NOTICE – PLEASE SLOW DOWN. I am wearing a yellow band over my breast harness. Roamer and I also sport yellow leg bands. Drivers can spot us easily. Even so, it will be too difficult to see where we are going shortly. Why don't we halt? Where will we end up? Can't we go home now?

Our man is worried. He telephones his accomplices who brought us here.

"Hi, Ernie," he begins. "Where are you? . . . Still in Newcastle? . . . I'm sorry that you are having difficulty getting home! . . . Please, I need your help if you aren't too far away. . . . Are you able to turn around and pick us up? . . . We will fail to cover the last two miles to our prearranged campsite before nightfall. We left Tynemouth too late. . . . Okay, we'll meet you there. Thank you."

We head briskly for a shopping centre two-thirds of a mile away. A friendly local man, returning home from work, guides us across a dangerous roundabout. Moments later, our horse trailer turns up.

"We've been waiting for you nearby," says the senior ferryman. "We watched you arrive."

Roamer and I are pleased to see transport: we cannot wait to relinquish our backpacks. Our man, who also seems relieved, unsaddles us. The younger ferryman, who was driving, leads Roamer first, me second, into the horsebox.

Daylight has gone before we reach a reconstructed Celtic village, our destination within a peaceful country park, away from deafening vehicles.

The senior ferryman switches on his vehicle's headlights at the campsite: he and our man are able to unload and store our gear more easily. Shortly afterwards, the horsebox is gliding away; only a single torch pierces the village's darkness.

Our man brushes and feeds us. Oh, bother! It's impossible to drink water from his collapsible green buckets: they are too slender for our noses. Fortunately, the human responsible for overseeing the park lends our man two clean, plastic buckets. Though chemical-laden tap water is unappealing to Fell ponies, it tastes surprisingly refreshing after today's ordeal.

"There's a quarry on the far side of the village gate. They could graze there," suggests the park manager.

"They would adore that," acknowledges our man, "but it has markedly steep sides: tomorrow morning, how would I ever catch them?"

"They may stay in the Celtic village's garden if you prefer. They'll be safe there."

"Your last suggestion sounds better. I can't risk them escaping."

Yes, give me one chance, please. I'll be off faster than a not quite cornered fox.

Having checked its perimeter fence, our man lets us loose in a tiny, visitor's garden containing a pond. At least, I perceive it to be minuscule.

Our man decides to sleep in a Celtic roundhouse situated just outside the garden. The wooden roundhouse is an authentically reconstructed ancient building, strangely shaped, with wattle-and-daub panels and conical, thatched roof. Earlier, he stored saddles, harnesses and packs inside this draughty shelter: its two fashioned doorways are open, doorless, almost opposite each other. I hope he doesn't expect a warm, peaceful night's rest.

"Why is he sleeping there?" I ask Roamer.

"Most likely to keep both eyes on us!" he replies. "Besides, where else could he sleep? He's tired, and he's probably thinking it's too late or too much trouble for him to erect his modern roundhouse."

I'm glad Roamer is here with me: I don't relish extraordinary situations whatsoever. This bizarre night, we take scant rest. We are looking for an escape route. I hunger for home; I thirst for our enticing, tranquil hillside.

33

Solo:

This fine, autumn morning, I am relaxing not far from Stoney Gill.

"Let's load up and then get going," shouts a human whose voice and face I don't recognise, though I suspect he is Bill's brother.

A second, younger unknown man appears. Assisted by Bill's brother, he places four white, plastic boxes, innumerable small, bulging, waterproof bags and a longer, heavier, waterproof bag – somebody describes it as "the tent" – into the rear compartment of an impressively pristine, shiny vehicle. What is happening?

I trot to the yard gate. A short while later, Thorn and Roamer saunter up.

Bill and a fourth man, who is dressed in black, are in conversation about 10 paces away. They are preparing to saddle us up, or so it seems.

Abruptly, to my astonishment, Bill's brother, who is now leading Thorn by a halter rope, pats my neck and whispers, "Bye, Solo."

"You've made the correct decision," says Bill to the man in black, whose face I recognise to be that of the human who recently trained me. "Solo would serve you best as your reserve pony."

"Yes, I may enlist Solo urgently," stresses the other man. "He's trained well enough. I'll call upon him if either Thorn or Roamer becomes injured or unfit. Please would you explain to Michael?"

"Aye, lad," promises Bill.

"Nay, nay!" I yell. "I want to go with the others!"

I charge frantically about the paddock, looking for Thorn and Roamer. They have wrenched my new friends from me. They have snatched them away, leaving me alone and lonely. I never suspected their intentions: there was no chance to say goodbye. I am in shock.

"Forgive me, Solo, but you are too young, not quite mature enough, to handle a whole expedition," the trainer confides.

No, I'm not too young! Well, okay, I am just three years old. Why should age matter? I am annoyed, never mind terribly sad, to observe my friends going adventuring without me.

"You are extremely important, though," he continues. "I shall need your help whenever either of your friends requires a rest.

Meantime, look after yourself."

He strokes my head and neck firmly several times, turns smartly away and then climbs into his spotless, blue car.

"Hai-ai-ai-ai!" I whinny loudly as the horse trailer trundles out of sight. "Good luck Thorn and Roamer. Don't forget me! Hai-ai-ai-ai!"

I hope that my newest companions shall not become ill or injured and that we shall reunite very soon.

A broken gate, dangerous roads and children

13th October – Segedunum Fort, Carville School and Ouseburn Farm

Roamer:

AT about six o'clock, not yet time for me to awaken fully, Thorn tries to escape into the quarry. He breaks down our enclosure's holding gate made of willow branches, startling me. There is a deafening crash as the gate tumbles into pieces. My monocular vision takes over, but I stay calm: it's nothing to do with me.

Pan, who hears the rumble, appears at the gateway seconds later, blocking Thorn's escape exit just in time. Thorn stares at him, contemplating whether he dare try to charge the gateway, but Pan, who holds his ground, succeeds in containing him within the garden. Pan then constructs a makeshift barrier across the gateway; he stretches a lead rope – normally it attaches to Thorn's head collar – between a smooth, metal rail and the still intact gatepost. Meanwhile, Thorn races uncontrollably about the garden, exasperated that his escape bid has failed. He's being stubborn.

Pan can't entice Thorn with food. Both man and pony intend to win a vital game. Thorn desires freedom. Pan must strike camp immediately. Who will win? Thorn isn't happy. I, on the other hand, already cherish my changed life.

Before we recommence our odyssey, we need breakfast. I am about to sample, for the second time since we left Tynemouth, special, pellet-shaped pony food I have been carrying. Pan measures the pellets into a brown leather nosebag. One of his saddlers has fashioned it specifically to fit my head. I instantly adapt to it. Hmm, those pellets taste subtly yeasty and very slightly salty; their delightful perfume reminds me of summer's hillside herbs. Morning feeds could become an agreeable habit!

What humans refer to as "about an hour" has rolled by since Thorn began his amusing caper. A stubborn, moody pony, he has thwarted every attempt by Pan to catch him, jumping a shallow, ornamental pond and hiding amongst the garden's tallest bushes each time Pan has tried to corner him. His antics have partially destroyed the vegetation. Now, noticing that I'm happily eating breakfast, he pauses.

I look straight at him, binocular vision taking over, as Pan removes my nosebag.

"Come on, Thorn," I reason. "There's only one way we're getting out of here: with the help of our keeper. Settle down, eat your breakfast and then we can leave."

Thorn understands: he isn't stupid. He has spent so much energy playing daft games that he is now extremely hungry; apprehension prevented him from eating much last evening, and a breakfast food trail, which Pan laid earlier to catch him, was so meagre that he wasn't tempted.

"Okay," he murmurs, nodding impulsively.

My friend has decided to cooperate. He lets Pan entice and collar him. Finally, Pan manages to feed him properly.

"Well done. That's better," I say. "Let's wait for the right moment to escape."

"I desperately wish to break out of here; this isn't my idea of fun," he reiterates mournfully before gulping down remaining morsels of his breakfast pellets. "Mind you," he adds mischievously, "I won our game, didn't I?"

Later, as Pan saddles us up at a modern, metal gateway to the quarry, I overhear him talking to the park manager.

"I'm sorry about your gate. What do I owe you?"

"Nothing: it's easily repairable," replies the sympathetic gatekeeper. "Don't upset yourself."

Pan thanks him for being so tolerant but remains duly concerned.

"Thorn has been giving me the run-around," he adds. "He kept refusing to be haltered. Now I've no time for breakfast."

I glance at Thorn. He is relaxing, utterly unperturbed by his escapade: he doesn't have to apologise or fix anything.

Pan continues his preparations. Final adjustments to our loads take longer than I estimated: on our first full day of trekking, into the city called Newcastle, he prepares meticulously.

Off we go! Initially, we take a quiet packhorse trail, what Pan refers to as the Waggon Route, plodded by uncounted, dedicated pack ponies over a century ago. Before long, however, we are meandering purposefully through the back streets of Newcastle, a settlement which Roman invaders originally called Pons Aelius, the bridge of Aelius. Please let Pan's sense of direction prevail.

As we gradually approach a bustling city centre, I listen anxiously. Why is there clamour from two directions simultaneously? I look. Why are noisy, mystifying, newfangled machines whizzing alarmingly past my sensitive ears? Why don't they ever cease? Thankfully, Thorn is behaving impeccably. He had better, or else.

We arrive at Wallsend and the remains of what was once an extensive fortification; Romans named it Segedunum, I learn, possibly referring to a strong fort. Here, we meet several teachers and most of the children from Carville – the house on the rock – Primary School.

"Oh, look, ponies!" squeals an excited boy who suddenly appears, running from seemingly nowhere.

These mini-humans aren't a loud bunch; on the contrary, they are extremely mindful of our nervousness. I am uneasy, a little frightened, but mostly elated. It's simply that I've never encountered so many youngsters together. In fact, I've never met any before. Two female teachers soothe me by stroking my neck; their caring hands caress gently. Of course, agitated Thorn dances about, trying to hide, but Pan quickly calms him.

Children are inquisitive, I decide: they continue looking at us and begin asking umpteen questions. Pan chats with every one, describing how, through this expedition, we are trying to save the homes of ponies living outside in wide-open spaces. Afterwards, I have a slightly better notion of why Thorn and I are here, but I'm still bewildered.

Eventually, we must leave those children and the fort. Segedunum, built on the northern shore of a 90-degree bend in the River Tyne, the flowing or dissolving river, is compelling to behold even today. Apparently, the fort covered an area of 138 by 120 metres; in equine language, that's 4 acres. From this vantage point, Romans could see clearly southwards, upstream, and they could observe the Tyne's flow eastwards, downstream.

"No doubt, this offered a strategic advantage," remarks Pan. "In the third and fourth centuries," he recalls from a previous visit to the museum, "a unit of cavalry and infantry, the Fourth Cohort of Lingones, lived here. Four cavalry troops stabled their horses in four barrack-blocks. Each barrack-block housed 30 horses in 10 rooms, each room accommodating just three troopers and their horses."

Pan is also aware that Romans demolished and rebuilt the stable barracks during the third century.

"What were our Segedunum ancestors like?" wonders Thorn.

"One thing is clear," I reply. "They shared living quarters with cavalry. This intrigues me."

Acres of ruined buildings, excavations worthy of exploration, may provide ancestral clues, but Pan daren't linger here much longer: we're in a hurry. Besides, Thorn and I are becoming impatient.

The Military Way begins or ends, whichever you prefer, at Segedunum's west gate, I gather. Innumerable Roman horses – or perhaps they were ponies – entered and left the fort here. At about midday, we must depart too.

We follow the Way's line as closely as possible, a route approximately 90 metres south of the Wall at Tumulus Avenue. Pan has already discovered that Romans built the Way, a road of some kind, from river cobbles and sandstones here. We are marching smartly past modern buildings. I see children at a window.

"Hai-ai-ai-ai! Any idea where we are?" I inquire, puzzled.

"Where do I conclude we are?" taunts Thorn, pointing with his head. "See that sign? Isn't that Carville Primary School's emblem?"

"Oh, I loved meeting everybody from Carville earlier," I tell him. "I bet it was a treat for you too! Didn't those children behave surprisingly well?"

Thorn, who is now concentrating on traffic, doesn't respond.

Our first, now non-existent, milecastle is Stotts Pow, once the site of a marshy, ditch-like stream that horses frequented. In bygone days, this was a wet place. From here, via Stotts Road, we strike out for Fossway, a Wall ditch road, the main thoroughfare. We are on a charge. We continue speedily past the location of a second fortified gate, also lost, opposite Brough Park Stadium at Walker – the marsh by the Wall. The Wall ditch guides our route to Byker Hill, so named because it was a Viking village near the marsh several centuries ago.

"North of the Wall," Pan enlightens us, "Romans dug out this substantial, usually V-shaped, ditch along the Wall's entire length except where crags, natural barriers to invasion, existed."

Now we are truly shadowing the line of the Wall.

"Generally, the Wall ditch is roughly 8½ metres, 28 feet, wide and about 2¾ metres, 9 feet, deep," continues Pan, "but exceptions exist. In some places, for example, they failed to dig it to its intended depth."

Already I realise that this human likes to recite imperfect facts to nobody: I call it "thinking aloud".

"I wonder whether they found the rock too hard to excavate in places," suggests Thorn, which, I admit, is a practical consideration.

"Those Romans who dug the ditch placed dig-out to the north of the ditch to fashion another barrier, a mound," mutters Pan, now deep in thought. "And they built pits with stakes on the berm – the flat distance from the ditch to the Wall. The Stone Wall's berm is roughly 6 metres, 20 feet, across. The berm of the eventually demolished Turf Wall, west of Harrow's Scar, is usually about 2½ metres, 8 feet, wide. Nevertheless, variations from less than 2 metres to 12 metres exist. What do you think of that, boys?"

"I wouldn't have risked crossing the Wall here, or anywhere for that matter," observes Thorn. "It would have been too dangerous."

Surely, no invaders would have been silly enough to try to cross the berm? I suddenly feel tremendous sympathy for those horses involved in any attempt.

Alas, however, Thorn and I have little time to dwell on such feelings. This sunny afternoon, as we trot cautiously along a wide, busy, city street, I stretch and, on occasions, strain every sinew of my legs. Mostly, worrying thoughts occupy my mind. Will hard, rocky roads easily tire Thorn and me because we don't wear shoes? And why am I frightened of vehicle-laden highways? It occurs to me that human speed machines often travel too swiftly; I dislike their loudly purring, droning, occasionally screeching noises as they shoot by. Horseless chariots that emit deafening, sometimes inharmonious sounds of singing voices intermingled with played instruments also unnerve me: such vibrations resonate harshly in my sensitive ears.

We turn into a less used, minor road parallel to and south of Shields Road, a major highway, close to where Romans built the Wall about 2⅓ metres wide.

"Shields Road was a busy turnpike road that linked Newcastle to North Shields," announces Pan. "Long ago, North Shields was merely a fisherman's hut north of the River Tyne."

"Why is he giving us a history lesson today?" asks Thorn, perplexed. "Does he suspect we understand what he's saying?"

"I don't think so, but who else can he talk to?" I reply.

Presently we plunge from atop Byker Bank towards a city farm. Our descent is excessively steep, too steep for most heavily laden ponies to handle, especially on day two of an expedition, but we manage.

Whether Ouseburn Milecastle once was located on the eastern or western side of Ouse Burn's rushing water near Byker Bridge is unclear, but one thing is certain: here we have tasted the route our ancestors would have trodden regularly. Pan recounts that dozens of Roman working ponies must have stayed at Segedunum Fort, which also harboured chickens, sheep, pigs, lambs and goats.

We promptly turn away from noisy Byker Bank, taking an old

packhorse trail through quiet, valley woodland beneath a towering, multi-arched, main road bridge stretching 50 metres above us. Shortly afterwards, upon crossing an eighteenth-century, squared sandstone packhorse bridge located on the main north-south packhorse route through Ouseburn Valley, we find ourselves at Ouseburn, a tranquil, hidden oasis close to Newcastle's pulsating heart. People who run this pocket-sized, energetic, urban farm welcome Thorn and me warmly. One adoring woman hugs Thorn repeatedly; I suspect he secretly revels in her attention.

This starry night, we are relaxing in a severely sloping field containing an immense variety of edible plants, including grasses, thistles and nettles, sublime rough grazing for Fell ponies. Normally, goats live here. On this occasion, unwittingly, they have given up their home for us! Around our field, bright, yellow, neon lights burn perpetually, creating an eerie, confusing daylight.

Pan measures out our pellets – they undoubtedly keep us going – before constructing his temporary green shelter: he sleeps in a tent. Thorn and I have no shelter; we prefer sleeping outside, anyway. We particularly relish nibbling fresh grass; occasionally, we even lie or roll in it.

From time to time this early evening, Pan leaves his shelter to spend precious moments with us and to inquire how we are faring. Later on, when he fails to reappear, we decide to hang about his tent: somehow, we feel more secure.

Next morning at about five o'clock – Thorn says he can guess time accurately by the sky's brightness and, as in this instance, by how long ago the sun set – we are munching within two strides of Pan's guy ropes. Unexpectedly, he climbs out of his tent, approaches us, strokes me considerately and then quietly commands us to leave.

"Go on, you two," he orders. "Grab some rest. I need uninterrupted sleep."

We must have woken Pan up. Nonetheless, Thorn and I refuse to budge: we dare not lose him. Otherwise, how would we get home? Where are we exactly? Only he knows. Where will he take us later today? A reassuring zip, closing the tent's flysheet, interrupts my urban-edge thoughts.

Thorn:

I wasn't happy last evening. Cramped Celtic gardens aren't to my liking: I am a free-living pony.

I've an urge to explore. Not long after daybreak, I kick down the garden's insubstantial, wobbly, willow gate. I almost get away with it. Roamer and I are about to sneak out when, annoyingly, our man blocks the open gateway, thwarting us. I won't cooperate until I've played about in the garden; I jump the pond whenever he tries to corner me. Eventually, hunger overcomes me. We must wait for another chance to escape.

We arrive unannounced at Segedunum on a sunny, dry day – perfect trekking weather. The car park is empty. Gardens of archaeological remains are deserted.

Our man quizzes the museum's cheerful male assistant assigned to look after us.

"Excuse me. Have you seen my cameraman?" he asks casually.

"He was here 15 minutes ago," replies the assistant. "He went looking for you, so I understand."

"That makes no sense," responds our man, startled by this discovery. "He is supposed to be here to film schoolchildren meeting my ponies. We organised it with Segedunum staff six months ago. Something's wrong."

Let's carry on regardless, without Cameraman, I'm thinking. Otherwise, we'll be here all day.

The helpful assistant shows us to our designated meeting place, behind a white, corded rope placed close to a fence. The rope will separate us slightly from mini-humans, I suspect. Presumably, this arrangement is a safety precaution. Obviously, some people think it is necessary: they may be correct.

The assistant fetches Roamer and me a bucket of water each, a kind, thoughtful gesture. Meanwhile, our man, who is uneasy wondering where Cameraman might be, hurriedly swigs down a cup of tea as Carville children, accompanied by four teachers, join us. They were waiting patiently inside the museum, anticipating our arrival.

"How tall are the ponies?" politely asks an enthusiastic girl.

"I believe Roamer is fractionally over 13¼ hands, that's 134.6 centimetres or 53 inches, from ground to withers," he responds. "The withers is composed of several small bones in the back between the pony's shoulder blades. These bones are the highest non-variable point of the skeleton: they don't move. Thorn is a little taller, fractionally under 13½ hands, which is 137.2 centimetres or 54 inches."

"How wide is an average adult hand?" whispers Roamer to me.

"By my reckoning, it is four inches," I reply in a higher pitch and lower volume than any human, even a child, can hear. "I suppose that's how they measured ponies' heights in ancient times."

"How much do Thorn and Roamer weigh?" inquires a boy aged about eight.

"No one has weighed them," says our man, "though it could be done. We can't be sure without recording scientific measurements; based on their heights, a vet' and I estimate Roamer weighs roughly 265 kilograms and Thorn weighs roughly 305 kilograms – so avoid their feet!"

How true: I mustn't squash tiny toes.

A seven-year-old boy – I can guess ages – ponders how strong we are. Put it this way: no human could hold me back single-handedly.

"Incredibly strong," insists our man. "Thanks to their thick-boned legs and well-developed, muscular loins and shoulders, they can carry and pull a considerable load. Humans have bred Fell ponies over more than a century for their strength and endurance. These two will live outside on the hills all year round, even in snow. If they chose to leave me, I would have difficulty preventing them, even with bridle control. You must win their trust."

"What were Fell ponies used for in the past?" wonders the youngest boy of all.

"They originally carried lead, copper and iron – fairly high-density metals – from mines to factories. They also carried wool, milk and the post. Roman stonemasons likely employed some British wild ponies, not unlike Fell ponies in several particular respects, to carry stone uphill from quarries to the Wall."

"Do Thorn and Roamer have a mum and dad?" asks another eight-year-old boy.

"Yes. Their fathers, the sires, are stallions. Their mothers, the dams, are mares. Roamer, Thorn and my reserve pony, Solo, are all geldings: they are males, boys, but they can't have foals."

I didn't realise that we aren't able to sire foals, and neither did Roamer.

"It's a shame," he murmurs. "On the other hand, perhaps our man selected us to represent the breed because we're geldings."

"For how long can Fell ponies live?" queries an older girl.

"Over 30 years, if you treat them properly," claims our man.

"Are the ponies afraid of anything?" inquires a girl aged about seven.

"Yes, they become anxious in situations they haven't met before, though they rapidly calm down. They aren't afraid of cars. Why? Well, they trained within 60 metres of a motorway."

It's true: we could cope with heavy traffic yesterday and again this morning. Nevertheless, I'm constantly wary and alert. On vehicle-crammed roads my adrenalin pumps. I have discovered how a rabbit, continually hunted by a fox, feels: she has only a vague idea of when and where the fox might strike.

"What happens if the ponies are injured during the journey?" asks a courteous 10-year-old boy.

"Good question," admits our man. "We will ferry the injured pony speedily home. A horse vet' will take care of him. We'll bring in Solo, our reserve pony. He will deputise until the injured pony has recovered. So far, they have sustained no injuries, mainly because they are exceptionally fit, phenomenally intelligent and possess calm personalities."

True, Roamer and I are fit, and we have tremendous brainpower, believe me. We don't intend to become injured, which reminds me:

how is my dear friend, Solo? Dare I speculate what he is doing? Almost certainly, he is untroubled, grazing contentedly in a small, cosy valley not too far from lucky Stoney Gill ponies.

A younger boy, concerned about our man, asks, "What would you do if you had an injury?"

"I'd summon help using my mobile 'phone," he reasons. "And, as a safety precaution, I usually notify someone, explaining where I am going each day: it's a basic rule of survival."

"What do you eat on the expedition?" inquires a 10-year-old girl.

"I eat dry, dehydrated and some tinned foods mostly, including oats, pasta, rice, different types of fruits and nuts, tomatoes, beans, fish, oatcakes and biscuits. Soups, coffee, tea and drinking chocolate are also essential. Additionally, I reserve a couple of ready-made meals for emergencies. Of course, I eat fresh fruit when it's available. I cook on a compact, gas-cylinder stove. My stove, cooking pans and plastic, recycled cup and plates are all collapsible: they pack into tiny spaces."

"Oi-oi-oi," objects Roamer. "No wonder my pack is so hefty: it's all the food I am carrying – especially Pan's."

What an entertaining assortment these smiling children are: they think of such fascinating questions for our man to answer. There's no stopping them!

"What made you train the ponies?" asks a girl aged eight.

"After training them, I can appreciate exactly their habits, strengths and weaknesses," explains our man. "It's easier to anticipate what they might do in any situation."

"Which pony was easiest to train?" asks an older girl.

"Roamer was easiest: his Lincoln keeper had handled him four weeks before we commenced training. Nobody had handled Thorn beforehand, and he's six. Solo was also less easy to train: he's so young."

Yes, it's true: initially, I was a rebel.

"When you were training them, did you ever get hurt?" inquires yet another eight-year-old boy.

"No, though there were a couple of close calls," admits our man.

"And, so far during the expedition, Alan – my cameraman – and I have remained injury free."

At this instant, remarkably, no hands are raised skywards, prompting a teacher to announce spontaneously, "It's time to go back to school for lunch."

Our man hurriedly snaps a group photograph. In three blinks of my eyes, every child has disappeared. Were they a dream or a mirage? Did I imagine it?

We are alone. Cameraman still is missing. Now an opportunity arises for our man to telephone him. The 'phone's loudspeaker is on.

"Hello, Alan. What happened?" asks our man.

"As I began setting up my camera at the fort," explains Cameraman, "an on-duty museum official informed me that I wasn't allowed to film there. The official said, 'We have children here, so it's out of the question.' "

"Did you point out that you were part of an approved expedition and that filming was agreed weeks ago?"

"Yes," replies Cameraman. "I explained that the children were expecting me, but a staff member asked me to leave, so I decided to head back to Carlisle."

"I can understand why you would have been disappointed," sympathises our man. "You drove over 150 miles for nothing, and we have lost a rare chance to obtain precious footage. I am very sorry, but don't worry: I'll rectify this situation later. See you at the next designated filming location."

"We mustn't be discouraged by frustrated recording plans, however crucial they might be," mutters our man, attempting to console himself as he replaces his 'phone in its waist holster.

Perhaps our man is disgruntled because he promised, months ago, to film Carville children, but he cannot afford to dwell upon misunderstandings and failed arrangements. He must concentrate fully on the bigger plan. Come on, I'm thinking: we should proceed at once. Besides, standing about has made me restless.

"Thorn and Roamer, stern tests face you ahead," warns our man quietly before we leave Segedunum. "Please be prepared."

He describes to the friendly museum guide our intended route, which commences with a straight, typically Roman, main road: "We shall be walking along Fossway towards the city centre, adjacent to the Wall line, a dangerous excursion. Dozens of cars might not slow down. Afterwards, we'll head downhill, along the first part of a tortuously steep bank, Byker, a super-fast traffic road, to Ouseburn. We must be careful and vigilant."

The guide appreciates our man's caution.

"There will be no police to rescue us," divulges our man. "I requested assistance, but they are unable to escort us: these days, they have no legal remit to accompany horses. I also wrote a letter to Newcastle Council, asking for temporary road closures at a couple of the busiest junctions. Unfortunately, it couldn't accommodate us either."

Never mind. We shall deal with traffic easily, I convince myself. Though I have never been so far away from home, I am unafraid. Rather, I am looking forward to unusual, sweet-tasting herbs and grasses and to new, stimulating trail perfumes.

I am a strolling pony. Here I am, strolling down Newcastle streets. People stare when we pause to allow a small child, little older than me, to pat my pal several times, but I remain calm. Deafening cars and trucks don't bother me, either. When our man commands, "Stand!" at red lights, crossroads and roundabouts, I am unflinching, impeccable, watching out for everything. I am beginning to trust him.

Before we met our man, Roamer and I were virtually wild ponies. Even so, our man never refers to us as "wild" because humans have always owned us. Furthermore, he laments, few authentic wild places remain in Britain. Nevertheless, I believe that I was truly wild, untamed, not even slightly domesticated, when I was born. Suppose humans hadn't trained me: I'd be roaming far afield, even now; I wouldn't be interested in people; they would be unable to handle me. Before last summer began, before our man thrust upon me his world, no human could control me. Though I am exceedingly glad to be travelling with Roamer on our expedition into the unknown, I shall remember my wild roots always.

The River Tyne: a forced detour and a long climb

14th October – Newcastle, Black Row Riding Centre and Heddon-on-the-Wall

Roamer:

ALAN, the camera operator, materialises. Pan, beaming, is visibly pleased to see him in view of yesterday's misunderstanding.

Alan begins to film a conversation with Mandy, who oversees Ouseburn Farm.

"What an interesting packhorse bridge we crossed approaching the farm yesterday," declares Pan.

"Yes," confirms Mandy. "It's one of the oldest bridges in Newcastle. This site was originally a lead works."

"I guess lead would have been brought here from the mines and the spoils then gathered into heaps?"

"Yes, that's right."

"What's the link between Fell ponies and lead?" inquires Pan.

"They helped remove lead ore from mines and transport it about the country. There are historical photographs of Fell ponies working on a tip further up the valley."

"How exciting," I remark to Thorn. "Some of our ancestors worked here a century ago."

"It must have been awfully hard work," suspects Thorn. "I bet their packs were heavier than ours. I hope humans looked after those ponies properly."

"Lead is poisonous. How did you decontaminate this site?" asks Pan.

"A team of workmen took off a metre of contaminated topsoil across the whole site prior to capping it with a layer of clay 1½ metres thick," explains Mandy. "This cap sealed in any remaining contamination: it's safe for children now. They added poor-quality soil on top. Lots of adults, schoolchildren and whole families come here every day."

"Have native Fell ponies come to your farm straight from the hill before?"

"No, never," admits Mandy. "This is a first."

"Most people in Newcastle would not appreciate the close connection of Fell ponies with Newcastle," supposes Pan.

"No, they wouldn't," agrees Mandy. "And until you identified the pony on the tip in a photograph as a Fell pony, we didn't know about this link."

"People shouldn't forget what mining ponies have achieved in the past for humans," contends Thorn. "It is part of our history."

He's dead right.

Departing Ouseburn on the second leg of our far-flung Wall journey, we are a kilometre from the city's urban epicentre. Below us, the Tyne glistens and glints, bathed generously in warm, autumnal sunlight.

Although, with luck, I shall wander in the future company of other ponies, I have decided already that Thorn is special. As you are aware, he and I are not merely friends: we are becoming an efficient team. However, why are we participating in this walk?

My conflicting feelings about our situation, which humans have forced upon us, are of annoyance and excited curiosity. I still fail to understand why Pan is compelling me to carry such a bulky, burdensome load. And where are we heading exactly?

Despite my misgivings, I have persuaded myself that I shall complete this challenge successfully – whenever that might be. Why must I persevere? Firstly, noble beasts never give up: that isn't our way. Secondly, my temporary guardian is a tender-hearted human, I have decided, who will allow nothing awful to befall me. Already, in my mind, I have pledged my allegiance to this man. Whatever difficulties present themselves, I shall keep my promise.

As a scorching afternoon wears on, we two Fell ponies yearn for a relaxing stream to cool us down, but there isn't one. Instead, we skip along a little-used country road before trudging north over more tarmacadam, up a remote, rambling, energy-sapping hill. Somebody, please comfort me! My legs are painful with fatigue and my stomach's empty: I've walked an astronomical distance today.

We turn up at modern stables as the light is fading. Seven or eight ridden ponies live here. I tuck into a net full of fresh, dry hay left for me by a kind girl, the stable manager. Another young female gives me a cool drink from a bucket. Here could be an agreeable place to live.

Hang on a moment! A ridden pony is kicking his stable door repeatedly. What a racket. Each time he bangs, I'll bang back.

Now he is banging relentlessly; I am becoming distressed. I had forgotten that I hate stables at the best of times, and this is possibly the worst. I refuse to put up with his din all night. Let me out of this chicken coop, please; find me a silent field. Pan arrives to calm me temporarily.

After several sleepless hours, my noisy neighbour ceases. I feel sorry for him. Perhaps he, too, hates being indoors. Silence finally reigns and I can slumber undisturbed. No doubt, tomorrow Pan will blame me for being mischievous.

Thorn:

Today, at Ouseburn Farm, we are acquiring new food supplies. Our man takes three days' rations out of a cardboard box that he posted here two weeks ago. He places these into a white, plastic box marked "Human Food". Afterwards, he scoops from a three-foot-high, brown, paper bag our specially made pony pellets and empties them into a similar plastic box marked "Pony Food". He places both full boxes into Roamer's pack, balancing the load. I'm grateful that I'm not carrying them, but I'll not tell Roamer: he may complain even more.

Leaving the farm, we soon veer away from a line where originally the Military Way existed.

"We have no choice," our man informs Cameraman. "This direction's also safer. We can rejoin the Military Way beyond Tyne Bridge."

Our man remarks that Tyne Bridge is an inspiring riverside landmark, though I'm unsure why. Does he admire the bowed suspension shape or its glittering, criss-crossed metal struts? Alternatively, is this particular bridge simply a magnificent, iconic symbol of a bygone era, an almost forgotten age, our breed's triumphant age?

At the bridge, we climb steeply away from the river towards the city centre. Cameraman matches our pace, filming as we go. Intrigued locals occasionally turn their heads, amazed to behold two such elegant equines striding amongst the bustle of Tyne life; others ignore us, perhaps implying, falsely, that quayside ponies are still an everyday occurrence.

We pause to catch our breaths. Traffic plagues our man.

"Northumbrian Police advised me to keep off city roads," he confides to Cameraman. "Last year, an official expressed the view that it was unacceptably dangerous for horses to use Newcastle roads in this day and age."

Just wait a minute! Weren't we equines here first? We have a greater right than cars to be on British roads. For centuries, we forged highways, not forgetting byways, purely to help humans. Without us, Britain likely would have unsatisfactory, even pathetic, road systems.

Luckily, most drivers are surprisingly considerate today. We turn left from Dean Street into Mosley Street, eventually coming to Saint Nicholas Cathedral. Cameraman's moving-image recorders – he has two – stare at me. I perspire nervously. Later on, when we leave the city, I shall begin to wonder whether they were cameras or simply black boxes resembling cameras. Surrounded by so much unpredictability and unrecognisable technology, who can be certain?

I'm confused. Which direction do we take from here? Months ago, Newcastle police officers informed our man that he couldn't follow the Military Way's line beyond the cathedral.

"From here, it's a one-way traffic system," I tell Roamer, "though I wish I understood exactly what 'one-way' meant."

"I was listening to Pan," chimes Roamer. "From the fort, Westgate Road follows the Wall line west-north-west out of Newcastle, but cars may be driven only in the opposite direction. Humans don't allow equines to walk against the traffic flow, either: apparently, we are traffic. This means we would have a tough, if not impossible, job snaking through dozens of side streets to vaguely follow the Vallum."

"All right, Roamer, you're quite clever, I suppose," I admit.

"Oh, I didn't mention," he blurts. "The Vallum commences in Newcastle."

Roamer is confusing me even more. What is this Vallum exactly?

"It's a Roman earthwork," he adds quickly, "a turf frontier behind the Wall, so it must be south of the Wall."

Is he a mind reader?

Skirting around the side of the cathedral, we are onto an ancient, cobbled, confining laneway that leads steeply downwards to Side Street and Quayside. These stones may cause my feet to become sore. Mind, I suppose I'm shoeless for my own safety: steel shoes could easily slip on steep, metalled roads; I might easily hurt myself.

"Our route runs close to Castle Keep, south of the cathedral," remarks our man, "underneath which is buried Newcastle Upon Tyne's Roman fort, Pons Aelius. The fort refers to a Roman bridge bearing the Emperor Hadrian's family name, a name shared by Hadrian's successor. More accurately, therefore, the fort's name may be Pons Aelii. The bridge's exact location is unknown; about 18 centuries ago, Romans built it between streams emptying into the Tyne."

Hastily we leave Newcastle's hectic heart. Before long, we are onto a quiet, carless quayside, where Cameraman surprises me: he waves goodbye and then begins walking back towards the clamour.

We three follow a modern, signposted, brick-paved cycle path. We are marching purposefully, steadfastly, by the Tyne, a flowing, sunbathed canvas of transient, twinkling emeralds.

"Let's go, boys. Walk on," our man keeps encouraging. He is giving us no rest.

Crossing a major road, I can cool my feet on a grassy stretch through a peaceful park. Afterwards, along a timeworn track, tracing an old drovers' route, we are steering imperceptibly towards Hadrian's Wall, which we shall rediscover at Heddon, a hill covered with heather.

Roamer is convinced that our Wall journey to come will be trying and epic. He says he is prepared to face all eventualities. I, too, have given up wondering when our ordeal might be over. If I am tired, I must keep going; if my head says I should give in, my heart will tell me to press on, to reach out and grab success. Such is the life of an explorer pony, or of any working equine, I imagine.

From the river, we have climbed north via an ancient track to the edge of Tyne Riverside Country Park. Now we are heading west again. At Throckley Pond Nature Reserve – Throckley is a hill where people used to cut beams, oblong timber pieces used for building – Cameraman turns up without warning. He is 200 yards ahead, filming at the terminus of a slender, tree-lined track. How did he find us? What clever map reading!

After a considerable trek up an old, winding drove road on an arduously steep hill, we stop outside Saint Andrew's School, Heddon, too late to meet children: this afternoon, they began their half-term holiday. What a calamity! Now I understand why our man was hurrying. We have covered quite a few tricky miles today: he can't blame us.

We amble across the drove road, halting 15 or so paces later – a pace is the distance between successive falls of my left front hoof, about 56 inches I guess – to converse with a handful of very tiny children. Haven't these mini-humans seen a live pony before? They gawp, astonished, from the safety of their nursery lawn.

Our man addresses the female adult in charge: "Last year, so that your children could meet Thorn and Roamer, I promised to say hello when we passed by."

"By the way, what's a turret," I ask Roamer while our man is introducing us.

"Why do you want to know?" he replies, perplexed.

"Somebody mentioned the word yesterday," I explain. "I've been meaning to ask you all day. Have we seen one?"

"No, I don't think so, not yet. Turrets are less than 6 metres, about 19 feet, square."

His memory and sudden expertise amaze me.

"Pan reckons they were observation platforms," he continues. "Romans could control the frontier more easily by watching out for invaders. How tall they were is uncertain."

Leaving Heddon, we cross the main road directly east of Heddon West Turret.

"From Newcastle to our present location," guesses our man, "the Military Way lies on a line between Wall and Vallum for much of its length. Annoyingly, so far, we have been unable to follow that line."

Now that we are within sight of the Way, he relaxes, happier: we are on his preferred course.

As we continue at a furious pace via a narrow, snaking country lane, a frisky, reddening sun is setting. Will our man never give up walking today? I am contemplating our urgent need of a prolonged rest when, around a bend, we halt abruptly at Black Row Riding Centre, a name describing the roofs of old farm buildings.

"Hai-ai-ai!" shouts Roamer, who is discernibly relieved; so am I.

Curiosity overcomes my defensiveness. Three young women are busy dealing with our distant, ridden cousins. I count at least eight equines. They aren't Fell ponies: some are well-groomed half-breeds – mixtures of at least two different breeds.

One girl, younger than 20 years and wearing wellingtons, fetches Roamer and me each a bucket of water.

"Would they like hay?" she thoughtfully asks our man.

Without doubt, we would! Even though we are carrying pellets, I'd be insane to refuse good quality hay wherever there's no grass available. I rarely say "No, thanks" to food, in fact.

"We've no spare field for your ponies," admits another girl ruefully. "Instead, they can stay inside. Would you like to camp in a stable beside them?"

"Must I sleep inside?" I plead, but no human understands me. "I've never slept in a stable. Please, can't I stay outside, where I belong?"

"I'll put fresh bedding into three stables now," promises the second girl as she pushes away a wheelbarrow to gather straw and hay.

Our man consoles us: "Keep calm you two; I'll be with you all night."

Okay, it's nearly dark. Let's do it. Hey, this stable is quite roomy, with fresh hay and water. Wait. Something's wrong. No, no, I hate this! I'll not roll. Other equines have slept here before me. Free-living Fell ponies are exceptionally particular.

Roamer begins to kick his metal stable door after dark, to let everybody hear how much he hates being inside. A ridden horse in a stall around the corner is also banging his door repeatedly. What a clatter!

"He does it habitually," explains the stable manager.

Our man has decided that pitching his tent isn't worth the required effort. Instead, he lies on my black, pristine, waterproof raincoat, which he places on top of fresh straw. It's unlikely he or we shall sleep easily or cosily tonight.

A missing boot and stuck on the Military Way

15ᵗʰ October – Vallum Farm

Roamer:

ON a warmish, dry morning, I am carrying a monster pack; it is cumbersome; I ever wonder what's in it exactly. I am flagging already. Aside from that, just in front of my withers my neck occasionally brushes against my saddle's pommel, which irritates me. I wish Pan would adjust the load. Worse still, my back itches, but the saddle prevents me from rolling. Though I'd rather relinquish my saddle and load instantly, I am resigned: I must bear them.

From Black Row, we retrace our steps across Bays Leap Farm, so named as the place where a fugitive jumped his horse over a crag and died. I imagine his horse perished too.

Nobody is about. At the farm's entrance gateway, we turn north-east onto a track leading to a bridleway running alongside a railway line. The bridle path is slim, straight, flanked by hedges and easy going. It's time to stride out.

From the milecastle at Rudchester Burn, we are back on course, arrowing west and to the right of the Military Road. We are heading towards Rudchester Village, a modern-day hamlet whose name refers to a Roman fort, Rudda's Fort, probably the "rough camp" or "red camp": nobody is certain. Evidence indicates that a fire burnt some of the fort's stones long ago. Romans originally called this fort Vindobala, which, Pan presumes, means "bright peak" or "white peak" or "white strength". The fort covered an area of 117 by 157 metres. That's 4½ acres; I prefer to think in acres.

"There were cavalry horses at Vindobala," reveals Pan, mumbling loudly.

"Did you hear?" I ask Thorn. "Some of our ancient ancestors lived near here."

"Such a life might have suited me," he replies, "though I would have resented being in a stable."

Before reaching the milecastle at March Burn, a boundary stream, our twisting passage demands a temporary detour north-east of the Wall. Thus, we steer around Hollins Hill, where holly once grew. Fortunately, at the next track, Pan is able to navigate south, towards the road, allowing us to return to where he believes the Military Way coursed.

Regaining our position south of the Vallum at High Seat, near a milecastle where sheep and cattle would have sheltered in bad weather, we are travelling approximately west over rough terrain. We zigzag across wide fields, squeeze through natural gaps in hedges and intermittently backtrack, which keeps us off perilous, thunderous, lorry-cluttered roads. During these slick manoeuvres, unexpectedly and initially imperceptibly, my saddle slips. Quickly the load becomes dangerously unstable, threatening to pull me sideways. Pan manages, barely in time, to rebalance the weight before the saddle can slip under my belly. I trust he realises how to avoid similar mishaps in future.

Beyond a turret, we recross the highway of speeding cars and continue gently past another turret towards Harlow Hill. Here Pan pauses to let us rest. We chew on shiny, uncropped verge grass wherever possible, our favourite daytime preoccupation. He doesn't mind us nibbling when no moving vehicles are about: this offers him a chance to check his map, which he carries in a transparent case suspended by yellow cord slung over his head and left shoulder. On this occasion, he studies his map for a protracted time: either his pre-planned route is difficult to interpret or we are lost.

"Boys, getting between fields isn't simple," sighs Pan presently.

"Access gates are frequently tricky to locate."

He often talks to us, as you will have realised.

"That's not our problem," whispers Thorn as I carry on grazing voraciously. "Even so, I'd hate to be off course," he adds, the afterthought of a pony who values self-preservation.

Skirting northwards around Harlow Hill, we are slightly north of the Wall. Here, a claustrophobic footpath alongside the main road offers protection from traffic; very high hedges flank its sides. We head downhill, by two further turrets, towards Whittle Dean Water Course, a string of irregularly shaped, prettily situated ribbon reservoirs stretching either side of the road.

Where a minor road crosses this glassy, azure spectacle at right angles to our present path, we come to an embarrassing, unpredicted standstill. Ahead of Thorn is a gateway narrower than our packs. Wedged tightly between two walls, we cannot move forwards, turn around or reverse: we are stuck!

Keep calm, I am thinking. Let the human figure it out.

Without deliberation, he flags down a passing motorist.

"Please could you lend a hand?" he begs the young woman driver.

"Certainly," she answers, unperturbed by our farcical situation.

"Could you hold onto Thorn's lead rope while I remove their packs?"

Constraining Thorn isn't necessary: he is going nowhere. He isn't amused.

Finally, minus packs, we squeeze through the gateway. Pan now must repack us, a painstaking operation in severely restricted space. We're not complaining: we savour all unscheduled rests. Half an hour later, we are ready to continue. Pan thanks the kind woman for her valuable, timely help and then confirms our location. Ahead, on the south-western horizon, is medieval Welton, a village by a natural spring.

Still we are following the Wall line, north of the Military Way. Thorn has just about convinced me that our tribulations are over, at least for today, when we hit another snag. At East Wallhouses, a stile blocks our exit from an enclosed footpath, preventing access to the road. Fortunately, during his reconnaissance Pan did predict this setback: a landowner, whose property flanks the footpath, has constructed a gateway – you might call it a doorway – in the fence line. He greets us enthusiastically.

"Thanks a lot for finishing your gate in time for our arrival," acknowledges Pan, shaking the landowner's hand firmly.

Obviously, being able to anticipate obstacles is advantageous. Nevertheless, the new doorway poses a trifling predicament: Thorn scrapes through, but the gap's too narrow for me. Pan, who wasn't so clever after all, has no choice: he removes my pack again. This could become a bad habit, but I desperately hope not: it's off-putting.

After recrossing the road and Wall, we follow the Way. Traversing a field between Vallum and Wall, we arrive at Vallum Farm, tonight's destination. Those last two kilometres have taken well over an hour; soon it will be dark.

This evening, Pan reduces my pack volume by ditching reserve maps, spare lead ropes and surplus harness. Will his streamlining make much difference to my width? I doubt it.

"Would you mind hanging on to these spare items for the time being?" he begs the farm's owner, Peter. "I'm trimming the volume of gear carried."

"You can store whatever you wish in the shed, which is usually locked," replies Peter, pointing to a small, newly constructed wooden building little more than a dozen human strides away, down several wooden steps.

Pan thanks the farmer for his kindness: "If I need anything in an emergency, I'll arrange courier transportation from Vallum Farm."

On a moonless night, Thorn and I busily graze lush, uncut grass in a flat, roomy meadow. Meanwhile, Pan puts up his tent in a nearby, three-sided barn. Unfortunately, though the open side faces us, the barn has no artificial lights: we must rely on sound and smell to pinpoint his whereabouts. Yes, that's right: our sense of smell is many times greater than that of humans; our brains can identify pheromones a considerable distance away. Whenever I sense his presence, my nagging insecurity disappears; I can relax. Of course,

Pan keeps an eye on us. The happiest times of my evening are when he visits us to reassure himself that we are all right.

The farmer has loaned Pan an admittance key to Vallum Farm's cosy tea room. There, before bedtime, our leader may be studying his maps in comfort. Perhaps he is checking tomorrow's precise route.

Thorn:

Roamer usually carries our man's spare pair of walking boots. This early morning, as our man finishes loading Roamer, he realises that one of these new, leather boots is missing.

"Where could it be?" he ponders. "I must find it: I may need it for winter-like weather or rougher terrain lying ahead."

After searching the stables, yard and even kitchen frantically, unsuccessfully, our man convinces himself that somehow he has packed the boot without noticing: he hasn't. He should have paid attention. I observed where it went: the riding centre's dog sneaked up and stole it. He doubtless has hidden it by now. We leave Black Row without it.

Today marks our first trek over farming country – alongside hedges and fences, around late crops, through fields of rough grazing and across moorland. Disconcertingly, my Roman saddle keeps slipping: our man hasn't quite figured out how to balance my pack perfectly, and he is still uncertain of my most efficient harness lengths. I suppose experimentation, trial and error, is essential.

Not much less, I wager, than four strenuous hours after leaving Black Row, I am becoming weary. Naturally, though it is a privilege to be contributing towards our quest, I would welcome even a brief rest. After completing our initial training, Roamer and I never imagined that carrying a full pack would be so demanding. Our man doesn't appear fatigued; of course, he carries hardly anything on his back.

Miraculously, we attain this night's destination uninjured, where Roamer and I speedily recover. However, I suspect we are facing a sustained haul ahead. We are, I convince myself, up to the challenge.

Now and again, I still doubt my desire to continue – until Roamer reminds me that we are doing this to help prevent our virtually free-living race from becoming extinct. What's more, I must not forget that my immediate brothers, sisters and cousins, born and to be born, are most important. I shall help to save my present and future relatives from disaster; they will be proud of me, unquestionably. I don't intend to fail Roamer or our man, either. I am relieved because this human is trying to protect us. Above all, I must have faith that, through this quest, many humans will learn about and better understand our breed's plight. We few, we happy tribe of natives, shall prevail.

Solo:

Are Thorn and Roamer okay? I'm missing them terribly; I yearn for their friendship.

Last night, I dreamt of a pony's life at Hadrian's Wall. Romans had enlisted me, were compelling me, to build their Wall.

In my dream, it had been raining for five days. On the sixth day, I woke up to the clatter of pony hooves. Auxiliaries eventually opened the doors of my stable. My friends and I cantered out into a dazzling sunrise; the chill from an exhilarating breeze fought unsuccessfully against my woolly fur.

Minutes later, the auxiliaries led us to a quarry. There, they tied us to wooden boards laden with hewn rocks, which we pulled for miles as we climbed towards a distant, snaking earthworm.

Their awe-inspiring Wall was before my eyes. It seemed to go on forever eastwards. Over 20 ponies stood mere yards from the Wall, not moving, waiting for other humans to carry away transported stones and place them diligently onto a partly built section.

We toiled endlessly. At sunset, I could barely stand up any longer.

On the following, exceedingly cold, midwinter day, I was well-nigh exhausted as a soldier tied me to his board. Until I commenced pulling my new load, I did not notice that snow lay everywhere.

An erupting blizzard cast upon my friends and me. I could not see what I was doing. I became spooked. I reared, broke my shackles and galloped off!

A burning chill ran through me. Eventually, my ears, mane and tail were on the brink of becoming frozen. I was disoriented, without sense of direction. I decided to keep moving forwards.

Much later, nearly dead from fatigue, I stumbled upon a village. There were no oil lamps burning, no signs of life. I trotted over to a deserted farmhouse, searching for food and warmth, and found a bale of hay in an abandoned stable. I settled down on the stable floor and slept.

In the middle of the night, a peculiar scratching noise woke me. I looked around, but I could see only blackness. I eventually managed to ignore the noise and fell into an even deeper sleep.

I awoke again at sunrise and resolved to set out on a journey to a town where I could find a human who would feed and look after me. I walked, trotted, cantered and even galloped, hoping to meet a friend.

May I describe the last part of my extraordinary dream on another occasion? Please be patient: I must pause to eat some grass and to think about my companions.

Attempted escape

16th October – Errington Arms

Roamer:

PAN stored everything, including our latest food and other supplies, in a wooden shed overnight. This morning, it takes ages for him to reorganise our packs. I hate standing about, but it's unavoidable, I suppose, on supply days.

Peter's three-year-old daughter, Phoebe, helps Pan brush and feed us. She is cute. Pan gives her a fleeting, stationary ride on my back before he loads the packs. I don't mind, even though few humans have pressed against my body previously. I hardly notice this slight weight. She loves it!

Vicky, Peter's wife, runs Vallum Farm Tea Room and Ice Cream Parlour. Before we leave, she cooks Pan a deliciously aromatic vegetarian meal, which he is about to dispatch seated comfortably on a spacious veranda. At this moment, a woman and her male companion alight from a vehicle. They observe Thorn and me, loaded up, ready to trek.

She politely asks Pan, "What is it all about?"

"I'm endeavouring to ensure that semi-wild, extensively grazing Fell ponies don't become extinct," he says.

Thorn deduces that the woman is a TV features writer. She offers to write a story about us.

"It will be excellent publicity," she suggests.

Say, "Yes, I accept," I am thinking.

Pan pauses to consider.

"Here's the deal," he says thoughtfully. "If you can get the expedition 20 seconds of TV news coverage, I'll give you a story."

"I can't promise anything," she replies warmly.

The writer heads for the tea room. Perhaps Thorn and I will be famous, though I doubt it: I don't understand why we should be.

His meal break over, Pan discusses his route with Vicky. It is already midday as we set off westwards, hugging the Vallum's southern edge. At first, along a wide, grassy causeway through a lush field, we steer close to the line of the Military Way. We are south of where Hadrian's Wall was and still is, though we can't spot it: 17 centuries of agricultural activity have hidden all clues.

Pan, who is no longer a stranger to me, continually rambles on to passers-by about our route along the Wall.

"The Vallum is a Roman earthwork south of the Wall," he explains to a mildly interested Wall visitor, "beginning at Newcastle and finishing at the Wall's westerly tip. It is greater than 35 metres, 117 feet or 120 Roman feet, wide and is composed of a flat-bottomed ditch, often about 3 metres, 10 feet, deep, and two roughly 5-foot-high mounds with 20-foot-wide bases, one to the south and the other to the north of the ditch. The top of the ditch is roughly 20 feet wide; the bottom is up to 8 feet wide. Between each mound and the ditch are 30-foot-wide flat areas, the berms. That said, dimensions vary a lot."

"So the Military Way is between the Vallum and the Wall here?" suggests the visitor.

"Yes, I believe so," replies Pan. "It lies north of the north mound. They made the mounds from ditch material."

"I'm baffled," I tell Thorn. "What was the Military Way exactly?"

"Not listening properly Roamer?" he replies sarcastically. "That's a first! During training, our man and Cameraman discussed the Way. It's a Roman Army road that lies south of the Wall, along the top of the Vallum's north mound in lots of places, mostly within 100 metres of the Wall, however far that is. In other locations, especially westwards from the River Irthing, a river with an old, obscure, possibly Welsh meaning, it runs between the Vallum and the Wall."

"Yes, I'd realised that much, but what was its purpose?" I persist.

"I'm not sure, but I also overheard our man talking with Bill," he continues. "Romans made it, possibly in the second century, mainly from large stones and gravel. It's about 20 feet wide, and they built it up to a height of about 18 inches. What's that in metres?"

"That would be 6 metres wide and 46 centimetres high," I reply after carefully calculating. "I bet Romans designed it for horses and ponies, and perhaps for infantry, but not for carts."

"It would have been too steep for carts," estimates Thorn. "I can see a crag from here: gradients of about one in three exist. It looks as though we might have to climb up markedly steep, rocky slopes ahead. Only vigorous, mighty packhorses and pack ponies could have made it where we're going."

Perhaps Thorn is mistaken. Personally, I have one concern: our present route, whether shadowing the Military Way, Vallum or Wall, had better be reasonably flat, easy walking.

Soon we are trekking across open countryside about 100 metres south of the Wall and a dangerous main road. We are north of the north mound, practically on the line of the Military Way.

"I've been wondering about the well-preserved Wall ditch at East Wallhouses Milecastle," declares Pan. "It's up to almost 3 metres, 10 feet, deep and about 13 metres, 43 feet, wide, but why is it U shaped?"

Frankly, we're not much interested in more archaeological facts just now: Thorn and I are concentrating, attempting, safely and rather laboriously, to avoid boggy patches.

We halt. Pan studies his map briefly.

"Right, boys," he announces. "We will soon reach Wall Houses, where ruined buildings existed earlier in history. "There, we must turn south-west onto a quiet country road. Then, a few hundred metres later, we follow field edges past secluded Piers Plantation."

"Why should his route concern me unduly?" I tell Thorn. "I'm no navigator. Assuming he's confident of the direction, I'm content."

Near Halton Shields, the farmstead at Lookout Hill, we temporarily detour to the road to avoid unusually aggressive cattle. This unplanned, evasive action suits me: I'm carrying a heavy load so prefer a quiet, non-confrontational life. Past Downhill – meaning "hillside" – Quarries and Halton Red House, Pan reluctantly detours further, bypassing Stagshore – "stag wood" – Kennels, though I doubt whether a pack of noisy, raucous, yelping hounds would unnerve us!

We reach the visible platform of Halton Chesters Fort. Romans named this camp Onnum, which could refer to a nearby stream, Fence Burn; alternatively, it might signify the rock on which the fort stood, supposes Pan. He verifies we are definitely on the Military Way. It coursed from the fort's minor, east gate.

"There's not much of the fort left, as is customary," notes Thorn scornfully. "Lazy builders have robbed it badly," he adds, ever observant.

"Boys, did you know?" ventures Pan. "A cavalry regiment of 500 men lived here. Stables existed."

Why would we know? Anyway, half a thousand horses is a far larger number than I can picture.

Ahead, in the distance, Portgate Milecastle is vaguely discernible as a platform. Soon, less than 200 paces west of the milecastle's location, we encounter a modern road roundabout. All is strangely quiet at this major crossroads.

"Approximately here," muses Pan, "the clearly defined north-south Roman road, Dere Street, allowed the carriage of goods and people across the Wall at Portgate, a military gateway. The gateway began about 12 feet in front of the Wall and probably ended 12 feet behind it."

Pan shall later discover that Dere Street may refer to Deira, a sixth-century Anglian kingdom. Nowadays, it seems, heavily loaded trucks passing along this busy road often travel between Newcastle and Corbridge, the bridge over Cor Burn in Celtic Corchester, which Romans called Corstopitum.

After crossing Dere Street little more than 50 paces south of the roundabout's centre, we arrive at tonight's campsite, Errington Arms Public House, a name referring to people who came from the bright burn. Here, buried somewhere beneath the car park, lies part of Portgate's remains, where Dere Street actually intersected the Wall.

Instinctively, something other than history now occupies my

mind: I can't wait for a scrumptious evening feed.

Thorn:

We check in at our designated stopping place, Errington Arms, as nightfall descends. The inn's owner is standing outside his front door, about to lock the premises: today is early closing.

"Hello there, Nick," begins our man.

"I had no idea you were arriving today!" explains a distinctly surprised landlord.

"Didn't you receive my assistant's telephone message?" asks our man, visibly alarmed.

"No," affirms the landlord. "Where will you put them?"

He's talking about us.

"Where do you recommend?" replies our man.

"Can they be tethered on the wide grass verge?"

"Well, I possess tethering stakes, ropes and chains. However, tethering's a last resort: I haven't trained them adequately yet."

If our man attempts to tether me, I shall be off within two shakes of my head, dragging his gangling, steel stake behind me, exactly as I did in training. I'll definitely break free. I bet Roamer will, too.

"I suppose they could stay in the back garden if the girls agree," suggests the landlord. "It's their garden. They live in the flat above the inn."

The landlord introduces our man to his two young, female tenants.

"You were extremely lucky to catch me," he remarks. "I'm off home. Hope it goes well."

Our man agrees: we might have been stranded. He thanks the landlord, who departs, leaving us with two soft-spoken hosts.

"Of course they may stay in the garden," instantly utters a blond-haired girl – Roamer says her name is Lil – upon appreciating our man's dilemma.

"We hold considerable affection for ponies," admits the other, dark-haired girl named Dominica. "I work with horses at the place you are heading for tomorrow."

"Oh, you mean Codlaw Hill?" reasons our man.

"Yes. The owners told me you would arrive shortly."

I'm glad they've settled our camping arrangements because, honestly, waiting about here is making me sleepy. Remove my pack and dish out our food, please.

Our man inspects the garden.

"I'm deliberating whether they might jump over your rear wall," he confesses to the girls. "I'll never catch them if they break out."

"What are your thoughts?" I ask Roamer. "Can we escape from this oversized back yard?"

"No bother," whispers Roamer, already planning his strategy.

"Look!" I urge him, gesturing with my head. "What inviting space, what tempting grass, is waiting for us over there, on the other side of the wall."

"I'm looking. I'm definitely looking," he retorts cheerily.

"I need to fortify your garden," insists our man.

"We'll help you," reply the girls enthusiastically and almost in unison.

Our escape might prove to be more difficult than we imagined.

"I'll find some string to attach to the fence and trees," continues the girl who first welcomed us as she exits the garden.

"And I'll unpack my tethering chains and ropes," adds our man as the same girl begins climbing the stairs to her flat. "We'll require every restraint we can muster."

The other girl offers to hold our lead reins. At least we now have permission to graze the lawn.

"I apologise: they'll mess up your grass," warns our man.

"Never mind. It doesn't matter," she responds, holding tightly onto us.

Both girls are extraordinarily thoughtful and obliging, I conclude, but I wish everybody would please hurry up! We are hungry: it's well past our suppertime.

The sun has gone. A nearby roadside lamp dimly illuminates the inn and its immediate surroundings, a solitary visible building within a black, deserted landscape.

Our man hastily removes our saddles and bridles.

"Where may I store the tack?" he asks tentatively.

"Just inside the back porch," advises the second girl. "Could you grab three wooden benches while you're there? We'll fashion them into a barricade."

The first girl returns with much string and a plastic bucket brimming with cold water. Roamer is thirsty; he slurps happily. I prefer to play with the bucket, as you guessed. Unluckily, our man is on guard. He smartly removes it from my grasp before I inflict mayhem. What a shame.

Using his steel-headed mallet, our man bangs two tethering stakes into hard, sloping ground. He methodically stretches a sturdy, natural-fibre tethering rope and attached chain, 22 feet long altogether, between one stake and the garden fence. He then tightly secures another rope and chain between the second stake and a tree.

"I carry all those iron links," protests Roamer indignantly. "No wonder my body aches."

At last, we have proper food, which settles me down. While we occupy ourselves dealing with nosebags, the first girl ties her string from branch to branch along the edge of an elevated clump of small trees and bushes. Her friend wedges heavy outside tables between the garden's low, rear wall and the lawn's perimeter.

"Do they believe weak string will hold us?" I scoff when I have finished eating.

"No hope of that," mutters Roamer, pausing between mouthfuls.

Nearly an hour later, they have secured their garden, or so they judge. I reckon Romans, masters of impregnability, might have safeguarded us better: they knew precisely what they were doing. Naturally, we have spotted an exit. Roamer and I head promptly, unseen, between two trees and up a bank adjacent to a high, wooden side-fence. Here, in this corner, the wall is merely two feet higher than the ground.

"Go on. Jump it!" urges Roamer.

For several seconds I seriously contemplate whether to accept his dare. It's too late! I am about to execute my escape plan when our man charges through bushes to bar my exit, throwing his body between the wall and me.

"Could someone please give me a hand to lead them down the bank safely?" he shouts.

Our freedom bid has pinned us tightly between the fence and bushes; we cannot move. With the girls' assistance, our man carefully guides us through thick, woody undergrowth onto the lawn; the trampling of manicured vegetation is unavoidable.

He appeals to the girls: "What shall we try now to contain them?"

From their cellar, the girls grab a dozen empty, shiny, stainless steel beer barrels, each about two feet high, which they place around the perimeter. In double quick time, using more string, they have bound tables and barrels to tree branches and fencing. Meantime, our man relocates one of his tethers, tying it across our earlier escape route.

"Don't you dare try anything else," he warns.

Our urge to explore shouldn't surprise him: foremost, we are free-living ponies; we won't stay in this cramped enclosure.

"All right, let's make a cup of tea and something to eat," announces the first girl.

Our man nods, beginning to relax. Yet again, he falsely concludes he has securely ensconced us.

"Sounds like a great idea," he declares.

"Everybody has gone," I whinny to Roamer, a short while later. "It's dark. This is our chance."

The relocated chain doesn't stretch far enough: a slender gap remains. It takes us only minutes to negotiate any obstacles. We push down four barrels. We are free, happily grazing an unusually wide verge. This is tastier grass.

"They've escaped!" yells our man from somewhere upstairs, several minutes later.

All three humans rush outside to herd us back into the garden. We can't understand the fuss and excitement: we're not about to bolt.

"How did they manage to sneak out?" wonders our man.

That's our eternal secret: we're not telling.

"Don't worry," consoles the girl who handles horses regularly at Codlaw Hill. "I have telephoned a friend. She is bringing stouter rope. We'll sort this out. Relax. Finish your tea."

"I've already caused you too much trouble," agonises our man apologetically, still worried, inevitably, that we'll run away.

"I don't mind," she replies. "In fact, I'm quite enjoying the challenge."

How industrious those girls are, unfortunately for us. In no time, they have made it practically impossible to re-escape, although Roamer and I intend to try when everybody is soundly asleep. Wait a minute! I hadn't noticed: the second girl has brought us some tasty hay from Codlaw Hill; she has spread it over the lawn. This is more like it. Hay rules, okay!

The first girl offers to cook our man a meal. "We'll be able to keep an eye on them from the lounge upstairs," she reassures him.

Supper's over, I presume, when our man returns with a piercingly bright, light-emitting diode torch. The first girl has unselfishly donated it to his cause; none of his three new, black, metal torches functions properly. He peers over the high, wooden side-fence, his newly acquired beam searching us out.

"So there you are, boys, glinting eerily in this blackness," he confirms softly. "Let's have no more pranks, you green-eyed troglodytes. Understand?"

Those girls undeniably know a thing or two about tying knots. We must wait for another opportunity to break free. There will be such occasions. Wait and see! It's tolerable here, I decide, but for tonight only. Roamer and I can chew hay without being disturbed, and, in case we desire extra sustenance, there are bushes to nibble.

"Good night, Thorn and Roamer," adds our man. "Stay put, please. Quit giving me a hard time, will you?"

Off he ambles to pitch his tent on a wide grass verge in front of the public house, by an old, single-horse trap that is now a show cart. He'll not be sleeping much tonight, so close to a roundabout. Lorries will thunder past irregularly until late, and that towering neon lamp will glare. On top of everything, our solitary sentinel of the gateway will be fretting in case we escape again.

"Perhaps he should have found time to train us properly with tethers," reasons Roamer.

"Possibly he suspects we would simply yank the stakes out of the ground," I reply. "I've already done so, easily, during training."

At least we are safe here.

Panic and gales

17th October – Codlaw Hill

Roamer:

L AST night, Thorn and I were stuck outside in a cramped beer garden. I was so bored I decided to demolish a temporary fence and escape. It was fun: I enjoyed exploring under cover of darkness. However, though it felt natural, I agitated Pan slightly before he tucked himself away in his warm, cosy roundhouse. Oh, well!

This morning, no doubt, Thorn will attempt to convince Pan, Lil and Dominica that I was entirely responsible for pushing down night-time barricades, but he was as bad.

The fact is that boredom occasionally overcomes me because Thorn leads continuously. Throughout our mission, I must bring up the rear, must follow my friend, as our master can rely upon only me to walk behind, obviously. However, my desire to be in front is unquenchable. Who knows? Perhaps, I shall have an opportunity to lead before our expedition ends.

Walking behind Thorn demands clever tactics. Fortunately, Pan is growing accustomed to my habits. Admittedly, I might nibble grass from a pristine roadside verge if we pause, but this antic rarely unnerves him. En route, however, I sometimes cannot see him or the way ahead, so I become anxious. My remedy is to attempt to walk alongside Thorn. Although my friend doesn't mind, Pan is quietly annoyed whenever Thorn and I are too close together on a metalled road. To be fair, I suppose parallel walking along roads could be dangerous under most circumstances, but Pan is especially concerned

– don't ask me why – whenever I opt to walk on an available verge. Grass is softer and, therefore, gentler on my feet: as you know, I am not wearing shoes.

Today's progress along the Vallum to Wall Fell Farm has been steady and uneventful. Now, at the corner gateway of a field leading to a quiet laneway, life becomes exciting. Thorn accidentally treads on his lead rope. Pan releases it to pick up Thorn's left foreleg. My pal senses his opportunity, rears, turns around and begins to gallop without hesitation back across the flat, grassy meadow.

"Hey, what's going on?" I shout. "We-ee-ee-ee, here we go!"

I mimic Thorn's actions. I have no choice: our one-metre, leather connecting harness forces us to behave as conjoined twins. Unluckily, he has turned to his right, whereas Pan has harnessed me to Thorn's left-hand side, a dangerous situation if I don't catch up quickly. We are galloping flat out. I'm as fast as Thorn any day, providing I anticipate his moves correctly. What impish prank will he try next?

Pan hurriedly discards his rucksack. Then he chases. Nay, nay, he sprints in pursuit. He catches up a minute and roughly 200 metres later, at another gate. We are standing quietly, getting our breaths back. Miraculously, our connecting harness remains intact. Our short gallop was fun, you might think, but Pan's not smiling. I suppose he's distraught, surmising we might have injured ourselves; he might have failed to catch us single-handedly; we might have damaged our saddles; his expedition might have been ruined.

Pan approaches Thorn gently, casually, determined not to startle him. He is within a single stride, but Thorn hasn't finished yet. Impetuously, he turns and gallops off anew. Oh, no, Thorn's panicking now! We are charging from field to gateless field. Pan has no prospect of grabbing us.

Another 100 metres further on, by a hedge, Thorn halts.

"Cut it out!" I order. "I've experienced enough unanticipated excitement today, thank you."

Thorn's Roman saddle has slipped badly from his back; the pack hangs precariously. Even he accepts this game's over. The connecting harness tugged his pack sideways during our second gallop. This was inevitable: I was galloping on the wrong side, that is to say, his right-hand side.

Pan arrives again, hastily releasing the harness attached to my bridle chain. He heaves and groans, mustering reserves of strength to centre Thorn's saddle and level the sideways-leaning pack. Having righted the saddle, he checks us for injury; we're fine, naturally. He's intensely relieved and relaxes. Thorn has tried to trick me and hoodwink Pan. My pal sometimes thinks he is a comedian. However, honestly speaking, I am not particularly amused on this occasion. My joking is better, much less bothersome, I decide.

"Where's my rucksack?" worries Pan, disoriented by the chase.

He scours the ground for several minutes, sweeping backwards and forwards, Thorn and me in tow, eventually spotting it. Rucksack retrieved, we return to that troublesome gate.

We've had two incidents, two near accidents, in a day; that's two more than I prefer to cope with. Despite these setbacks, we are back on course, on schedule, albeit only temporarily. As we continue to negotiate Military Way gates skilfully, what I perceive to be a hurricane, though it isn't, stealthily creeps upon us. Strong winds don't usually affect Fell ponies used to living on unsheltered mountainsides. Today is an exception. The blast gradually increases in intensity, finally howling angrily enough to spook us.

Life's quite dangerous all of a sudden: Pan cannot stand up easily and we are distressed. He senses our agitation; without hesitating, he leads us from exposed hillside onto a valley road cushioned from weather extremes by the Vallum. We head downwards towards a riding centre at Codlaw Hill, a bag-shaped hill, where sheltered conditions might prevail.

Sally, who owns the riding centre, is pleased to see us. A kind, helpful woman, she greets us warmly but daren't tarry: she is extraordinarily preoccupied securing flapping and banging gates, doors and windows for what is about to come.

"They will be safer inside a stable tonight," suggests Sally.

At our present altitude, the blast probably wouldn't worry us, but Pan's not arguing with her: he's taking no chance.

Dan, Sally's husband, locates our needed food supplies, which is good news! We can never eat enough of those crunchy pellets. Meanwhile, Pan is attempting to settle down beside us in another stable. Thankfully, he can put up his tent on immaculately clean straw.

A fierce, gale-force storm lashes down all night. Thorn and I take it in turns to attack metal stable doors with our hind hooves: as you may have discovered, we dread enclosures with walls. Stables might suit domesticated ponies who are no longer free spirits, but they don't suit us. We aren't at ease: Pan knows this. From time to time, he checks that we aren't too distressed. His sleep, too, is intermittent and uneasy. Should we have risked it outside?

Thorn:

It is late morning when we depart, 11.30 precisely according to our man's black, waterproof chronograph. This watch, by the way, also accurately predicts the weather, a useful practical feature for humans but generally irrelevant to us.

An initial, relatively untroubled, 800-yard Vallum stroll ends smartly: to avoid a locked field gate ahead, we must detour via Portgate Farm. Momentarily, we are heading south, away from the Wall, past sleepy cows. At the farm, the farmer is conversing privately with two suit-clad, city strangers some 75 paces away. Our man waves to the trio. The farmer reciprocates as we head through a gateway onto a grassy track taking us back to the Wall and our intended course.

We soon regain the Vallum, continuing past Stanley Milecastle, visible as a gentle mound, towards the edge of a dense Scots pine forest called Stanley – stony meadow – Plantation. West of this milecastle, our route unfalteringly borders the line of the Military Way, which runs along the north mound nearly up to Planetrees Milecastle, three Roman miles further on. In case you were wondering, Roamer tells me that a Roman mile or milliarium, 1000 Roman paces, was roughly 4,854 British feet, 426 feet shorter than a

British mile. He's probably right.

Here we are with our man, who is no longer a stranger, plodding towards Stanley Plantation. Roamer says John Stanley Errington originally owned land here, though don't ask me who he was or how Roamer knows.

What outstanding luck: we enter the plantation successfully via a narrow, woodland gate. Moments afterwards, an intoxicating, rosemary-like scent of Scots pine needles, intermingled with the primeval aroma of damp, acidic, heather-enriching soil, invades my nostrils.

Almost immediately, we encounter a thicket of conifers roughly 800 yards wide. Progress is painfully sluggish along a twisting footpath barely wide enough for packs. Our man vigilantly leads us around mature trees and amongst dense undergrowth. Unpredictably and unfortunately, less than 40 paces east of this forest's exit, Roamer and I choose directions on opposite sides of a tall pine specimen that partially blocks our path.

"I estimated in a flash that the gap was insufficient for my pack," divulges Roamer later. "I was determined to avoid becoming stuck."

Roamer pulls against the tree. The leather harness connecting us tears lengthwise through its midline, beginning at the buckle pin, ripping as easily as an opened, brown paper bag of pony pellets. It falls to the ground. Fortunately, quick-release buckles have done their job: they easily detached the strap from my saddle and from the central ring of Roamer's coupling chain, which remains clipped to his snaffle.

I realise instantly, before our man becomes aware, that Roamer and I are uncoupled. Trees on either side hem us in, so I halt, stand and wait. I'm not stupid: during training, to prevent injury, I learned to remain stationary and perfectly still under hazardous circumstances. Roamer is also motionless, transfixed. Since he and I began this expedition, we have frequently discovered that panicking rarely improves any situation.

"At least those buckles still work," assesses our man ruefully. "But now we're in a fix: I can't turn you two around to search."

Our man scours thick undergrowth within a 10-yard radius, but he fails to procure the detached connecting harness.

"This is a waste of time," he murmurs, a few, near-frantic minutes later. "It could have catapulted anywhere."

I agree. It's equivalent to looking for a free-living Fell pony on a Cumbrian mountainside. Even worse, his two brand-new, pristine, white walking poles are missing. Something – a gate, tree, fence or the undulating terrain – somehow has dislodged them from my pack since we left camp, possibly since we began trekking through Stanley Plantation; I didn't feel or hear them fall.

"Now what shall we do, boys?" he asks, conceding defeat. "We need at least one fibreglass pole to prevent open gates from swinging against you."

"I've no idea," I mutter. "Don't blame me."

"In future, Pan should secure his gear better," concludes Roamer.

Unable to retrace our steps, we must continue forwards. Fortunately, our man has a spare connecting harness, which he attached earlier to the right-hand side of my saddle. Now, however, he has no poles, a scenario that should prove fascinating.

Just before we continue our woodland walk, I ask Roamer, "Why did our man choose us for this quest? Were we simply unlucky?"

"Perhaps we were lucky," he counters, as optimistic as ever.

"Doesn't your back ache even slightly from plodding?" I ask.

"No, but it is beginning to sweat beneath my saddle."

"Right now I hanker to be as free as our wild cousins of long ago," I tell him. "Wouldn't you love a long gallop, or even a canter, the cool breeze against your back, blood gushing through your arteries?"

"I would," he insists, "but I refuse to think about it. Tonight we may get an opportunity to canter freely."

At this moment, I can't even trot. I am, therefore, relieved when we reach a clearing: at least a wide, grassy track beckons.

By early afternoon, despite the absence of poles, we are progressing satisfactorily, but our man is about to make a mistake. Approaching the next farm gate, my lead rope hangs too slackly; I accidentally pin it under my left front hoof, which startles me. The rope jerks out of his hand. Now's my chance: it's time to run away with Roamer. I rear and simultaneously turn around. Roamer and I bolt off. We are free! Will our man ever catch us?

Oh, no, what's happening? As we are galloping back the way we came, through a long, lush field, my load suddenly is unbalancing me; my saddle, which has slipped badly, hangs loosely at my right side. I strive to shake it off, a futile activity. Unsettled, I must be patient: I must wait for the human to rescue a perilous predicament. He straightens the saddle with a single, mighty heave. Immediately, I am much happier, but my latest antics have failed to impress Roamer.

Tonight, a fierce, uninvited storm rages; a treacherous wind screams and whistles; seemingly endless, unsettling rain cascades from an angry sky.

During the storm, Roamer repeatedly kicks his stable door. What a din! He certainly can be boisterous. Perhaps an hour elapses; he hasn't ceased. Is he frightened or merely having a bad dream? Somehow, I can't imagine he is afraid or asleep: he simply hates anything or anybody hemming him in. I, on the other hand, am unassuming and usually behave myself in confined situations. Anyway, that's my story.

Another lost harness and a raging river

18th October – Greencarts

Roamer:

W̱ALL weather might be stunning, or it might be wild and wet. A savage wind, the considerable vestige of last night's gale, roars unabated today. Of course, Thorn and I constantly treasure our encounters with the elements, but this gust's prevailing strength alarms me as we descend smartly from an open, exposed elevation.

Pan separates us – he detaches our connecting harness from my coupling chain – before leading me on his left, Thorn on his right, steeply downhill, a tricky manoeuvre. At a wooden, bottom field gate, as we meet a lane approximately opposite Saint Oswald's Church, he realises that somehow, during the separation process, he has unintentionally dislodged the connecting strap from Thorn's saddle. Pan has lost it somewhere on the hill.

We wait patiently. Ultimately, Pan succeeds in flagging down a passing motorist, which isn't easy, I'd say, when both hands are occupied holding onto pack ponies' lead ropes. His situation is not quite desperate.

"Could you please help?" implores Pan, pointing to our travel line. "Would you mind walking uphill, through that field, to look for a long, thin, leather strap? You should be able to spot it easily: it has two shiny, metal buckles."

"I'll be happy to assist," answers this kind stranger as he parks his van.

The stranger, who normally recovers broken-down vehicles, climbs to the bottom field gate. There's no sign of any leather.

"Please try looking in the previous field," shouts Pan. "It may have become dislodged as we came through a joining gateway."

Anxious minutes pass; the recovery man is returning. I can see he has retrieved it. He-ee-ee!

"This is the only undamaged connecting harness I carry," confesses Pan, visibly relieved.

We're off again, though not for long. Just east of Planetrees Farm is a long axis milecastle, where the distance between north and south gates is considerably greater than that of short-axis milecastles. Leaving the main road near Planetrees, a place where you would have found platanus or plane trees with thin, pale, scaly bark, we turn into the private driveway of a large house alongside the Wall. A young, smiling woman is busily cleaning the dwelling. Pan interrupts her, begging water for Thorn and me. She obliges unhesitatingly, pausing from her labours further to give us half a bucket of small, sweet, juicy apples to munch. They are luscious! She offers Pan a cup of tea. He politely refuses – we are behind schedule – but he gratefully accepts a can of beer instead, placing it into his rucksack to savour later.

Pan requests the woman's brief assistance down a grassy, cow-littered slope alongside a section of impressively visible, intact Wall from Planetrees Milecastle towards High Brunton Turret.

"Here," he observes, "a section of the Broad Wall, which we have followed from the east, joins a very narrow, less than average width, section of the Narrow Wall, which stretches 15 or so metres westwards. Throughout the Stone Wall's length, the Broad Wall's average width is roughly 290 centimetres, close to 10 Roman feet, and the Narrow Wall reportedly is about 230 centimetres wide, not quite 8 Roman feet, though these dimensions vary."

During our journey, Thorn and I shall learn that archaeologists have identified different Stone Wall foundation gauges between Wallsend and Harrow's Scar Milecastle. Usually, the Broad Wall's foundation is roughly 320 centimetres wide, whereas the Narrow

Wall's foundation seems to be always less than approximately 270 centimetres wide.

So many numbers baffle me. Why does the Stone Wall become suddenly much narrower here? And why is this so-called Narrow Wall resting upon a very broad foundation? It seems that, at Planetrees and elsewhere between Newcastle and the River Irthing, Romans built much of the Narrow Wall upon a Broad Wall foundation. Perhaps, originally, they intended a Wall width of 10 Roman feet along the whole monument. Why, then, did they change their plan? Was it to save time? Were some building materials, or even pack animals, in short supply? This puzzle is too complicated for two, admittedly clever, Fell ponies to resolve.

As we descend immediately to the left of the Wall, our new acquaintance kindly deters frisky beasts from upsetting us, which delights Pan; though Thorn will take on cows any time, any place, Pan and I try to avoid confrontations. Not long afterwards, objective accomplished, this caring, happy woman, still smiling, is retracing her steps.

Soon we are meandering through the tranquil, heavily wooded grounds of Brunton House, a settlement by a river.

A young man materialises unannounced and proclaims calmly, "This is private property."

"Hello. Yes," acknowledges Pan. "George – I'm guessing he is your father – is aware that I would be passing by today. He has given me permission to use this route to the river."

"All right," responds the man, disarmed by Pan's feasible explanation of our presence.

"George was kind enough to contact my assistant yesterday," continues Pan. "He warned me that under no circumstance should I attempt to ford the North Tyne today, as it is notably swollen with rainwater: any crossing would be exceedingly dangerous for the ponies. I suppose we must use the road bridge instead. Please would you thank him for warning me?"

"Your easiest option is by road to the river," recommends the man earnestly, who then wishes Pan good luck and retreats as unexpectedly as he emerged.

Pan is grateful for this advice but is also manifestly disappointed. He has spent 2½ years meticulously planning his route, including a North Tyne traverse at the ruined site of the original Roman bridge at Chollerford, the ford in a gorge. It seems that this bridge once linked the river's eastern bank with Chesters Fort on the far, western bank. The Military Way coursed over the bridge; when Pan reconnoitred the river crossing at the gorge last year, he could see exactly where the Way linked the bridge's western abutment with the fort's east gate. The fort's remains constitute a considerable part of Chesters Museum these days. Pan is also aware that Romans named the fort Cilurnum, the cauldron pool.

Pan further contemplates the river's present state, wondering, "Does this cauldron pool really refer to the Inglepool – which definitely existed south-west of the fort until two centuries ago – as some scholars suggest? Or, after all, does it refer to the North Tyne?"

Who, if anybody, can verify the facts? There's one certainty: right now, this river's bubbling like a cauldron!

George, I have learned, owns the fishing rights at this river location: he can read the river intimately and, therefore, can ascertain the easiest crossing place. He had offered to guide Pan across this gorge today. More recently, Pan had liaised with Kielder Reservoir managers to ensure engineers did not open the dam's sluice gates upstream shortly before we crossed: any sizeable volume of water released from the reservoir into the river certainly would have rendered a traverse impossible regardless of rainfall; a dam surge could have swept us away easily, as though we were driftwood.

Although today's setback has annoyed him, Pan dare not become oblivious to pitfalls that may trap the unwary.

"I should realise," he tells himself. "Prevailing weather and seasonal effects will often thwart precise planning."

Thorn:

We briskly cross the narrow, single-lane vehicle bridge at Chollerford, but manage, nevertheless, to hold cars up behind us at traffic lights. Fleetingly unimpeded, I can observe the river as it flows past the site of Chesters Fort.

"Hey, Roamer," I shout. "Does that resemble a cauldron pool?"

"I can see quite a scattering of white, foaming rapids," he retorts. "Nevertheless, if we weren't loaded we could handle them easily."

"True," I say. "But it's not worth risking today, is it?"

"No," he agrees.

"We should have crossed this river during calmer, summer weather," I contend.

"But didn't you hear what Pan said?"

"No," I answer. "I was busy munching grass."

"He said he would have preferred to arrive here in mid-August, not mid-October, but saddlers couldn't complete reconstruction of the Roman saddle in time: it was an exceedingly complex business. Additionally, there were last-minute insurance complications: his policy wasn't adequate; he was compelled to guarantee three million pounds indemnity – though don't ask me what 'indemnity' is – against us causing damage to property or injuring people. Fortunately, two sponsors came to his rescue. Oh, and don't forget: he spent considerably greater time than he had anticipated in acquiring the most suitable expedition ponies."

"Well, he made the right decision there," I conclude. "We are the best in every respect. Furthermore, we won't injure anybody, at least not deliberately."

According to our man, the first cavalry regiment residing at Chesters Fort called itself ala Augusta ob virtutem appellata, which is beyond me, an equine with sparse Latin knowledge, to translate! He thinks it means "Augusta for Valour".

"Later," relates our man enthusiastically, "the Second Cavalry Regiment of Asturians lived at Chesters for over 200 years. It was quite a large fort, having six gateways and covering nigh-on six acres. There's a lot of archaeological evidence."

English Heritage won't allow us ponies to look around the fort or visit the museum, which baffles Roamer.

"How ironic," he points out, "especially since many of our Roman ancestors frequented the fort daily. Some supposedly helped to build it. One horse, at least, occupied this spot for about 1,700 years: Pan says his bones were found outside a bathing room!"

"That's the point, Roamer," I say. "The fort's present-day guardians must protect it so that future human generations may learn about our ancestors. Mind you," I grumble, "twenty-first-century humans frequently fail to recognise our bygone endeavours; they too easily forget. Roman pack ponies, in particular, have no place of honour."

"They should have, though!" storms Roamer.

"We shall restore honour through our expedition, definitely," I vow.

"But the river is too hazardous to ford," laments Roamer, "which is infuriating. Romans crossed here; so should we."

"Children would forgive us for using the road bridge," I point out. "And their views count."

Tonight's overnight camping spot should be on the North Tyne's western bank, as our man arranged with local farmers named Stephen and Lorna. Now, understandably, he's in no mood for dallying: there's daylight left. Besides, Chesters Museum, which leads to the fort's north gate, remains closed during weekdays at this time of year: it's something to do with spending cutbacks.

"Let's go on, boys," he decides. "On condition that you carry on to Greencarts, you shall have a day off tomorrow. It may be your last holiday for quite a while."

A whole day sounds superb. We'll have plenty of time to eat, play and rest.

"Come on," I encourage Roamer. "Let's get moving. We don't want to strand our man between two campsites at nightfall."

We pause briefly at Chesters Fort before pushing on urgently to Greencarts Farm, located on grassy, rocky moorland. Crossing the road, we are, by necessity, north of Hadrian's Wall and north-east of Walwick Milecastle. We head swiftly across Cowper Hill, possibly a horse dealer's hill in days gone by, through fields of tall, coarse, resisting grasses. Navigating behind Walwick Hall, a farm by the Wall, we climb across Rye Hill, where rye was traditionally cultivated, through further swathes of tufted, unkempt grass. This is tough trekking so late in the afternoon.

"Hello! You've made it," utters the surprised Greencarts farmer's wife. "I thought you might have given up: you planned this a while ago."

"Give up? Never!" responds our man. "How are you, Sandra?"

"We are fine. David will show you where your ponies can graze."

Tonight's allotted field, beside an old quarry and away from vehicles and habitation, is rangy, flat and peaceful.

"They should be safe in there," proclaims the friendly, helpful farmer, "but check fences for holes. If they gallivant into the quarry, you'll never retrieve them."

"Good idea, David," agrees our man. "Thanks for looking after us."

Our man is leaving nothing to chance. He keeps us waiting while he stalks the field's perimeter, closely inspecting every foot of wire fencing.

"A two-metre section abutting the road is missing or down in one corner," he reports to the farmer. "It's difficult to discern which, due to dense, flattened grass."

As darkness gradually engulfs our hideaway, the farmer sits atop a tractor. Assisted by our man, he drags up the flattened section of wire. Fencing nails and a hammer do the rest. What bad luck! We might have escaped into that quarry.

"Don't worry," commiserates Roamer. "This meadow suits us: it's perfect for cantering."

"Would you rather sleep in a camping barn tonight?" offers the farmer's wife. "It will be warmer: we are expecting a frost."

Our man is grateful.

"I could do with a peaceful night's sleep," he admits, "and I'll be able to sort out food supplies and fix my presently non-existent internet communication more easily tomorrow."

Roamer and I face a still considerable journey ahead, but I am cheerful because we are adventuring side by side. Well, we're almost side by side.

"Can our man really do anything – with your and my assistance of course – to help protect us Fell ponies?" I ask my friend this evening.

"We mustn't doubt it," reassures Roamer. "If we aren't successful, who knows what might happen to our brothers, sisters and cousins who inhabit the wildest sanctuaries?"

19th *October – Greencarts, rest day and satellites*

Roamer:

Sun pours from a cloudless sky this sharply cool morning. We are taking it easy, grazing contentedly in our meadow adjacent to an empty, pleasantly situated, walkers' campsite.

Pan inspects us. I am pleased to see him, but when he begins chatting with Sandra, I quickly realise that today there will be no load carrying; we can unwind, as he had promised.

"The weather forecast is excellent," she warns him. "You are losing a perfect travelling opportunity."

Pan recognises the seriousness of her observation. Nevertheless, he requires time to reorganise.

"My ponies deserve a rest," he responds. "And I must repair broken equipment, wash clothes, clean harnesses, plan ahead and re-establish an absent internet connection."

"There's a washing machine in the drying room where your gear is stored, next to the camping barn," she kindly offers.

He thanks her and then vanishes from view, presumably to begin his list of chores.

Thorn and I are relaxing when, a while later, my owner arrives at our field gateway. Her name is Judy. Yes, that's right: I have a Lincoln keeper and an owner from Leicestershire, the district of the people called Ligore. She is visiting me. However, her sudden, unpredicted appearance is surprising, especially since she lives over 350 kilometres away. At least, Pan mentioned that distance. Nicholas, her husband, is with her.

Judy checks me over. Evidently, I have lost weight slightly since the expedition began. Wouldn't you shrink if you carried a heavy Military saddle and harness, not to mention two full packs, on your back? Admittedly, though, my muscles are stronger, more powerful, than they were before we began training. Call me "super fit".

"Roamer's in supreme condition," Pan informs Judy. "His behaviour has been impeccable in traffic. He is shaping up nicely."

"How's Roamer getting on with Thorn?" inquires Judy thoughtfully.

"They perform well as a team. Roamer's at the back: going through tight gateways, I trust his judgement completely."

Tell me something new, please! Mind you, guess who nearly trips me up on numerous occasions? Yes, that's right – Thorn. He gives me little warning of his or Pan's intentions, repeatedly stopping and starting abruptly at inopportune moments. Nonetheless, despite my occasional annoyance, I am very fond of Thorn. He is probably the finest cousin you could wish for, more like an older brother, somebody you can admire. We are, you might say, as compatible as two worker bees in a hive. We are terrific friends.

Time passes gently. It is late afternoon. Since Judy and Nicholas left, Pan has been checking our supplies. I hear voices drifting on a lazy breeze.

"Come on," I tell Thorn. "Let's discover what the fuss is about."

We casually wander to the gate.

"Oh, our man's recording a telephone conversation on his voice tracer," observes Thorn.

"Let's listen," I suggest.

"He is talking to a veterinary scientist, Stuart, from Liverpool University," figures out Thorn seconds later. "They're discussing a disease that may affect Fell ponies. I don't fully understand their scientific talk."

"Listen," I repeat. "I expect everything will make sense."

"Local veterinaries in Cumbria were saying some Fell ponies were dying," recalls Stuart. "They couldn't explain it. What was killing these foals? We found that out: the immune system and blood supply were failing. It was a genetic problem. We spent four years trying to identify the responsible genes. We found out what the mutant gene was, which meant we could get rid of this disease."

"Isn't the disease called Foal Immunodeficiency Syndrome?" asks Pan.

"Foal what?" gasps Thorn.

"It was called Fell Pony Syndrome initially because we found it exclusively in Fell ponies," admits Stuart, "but it exists in at least two other breeds. The disease probably started in the Fell pony and then spread, but that would be hard to prove. About 45 per cent of Fell pony adults are carriers."

"I don't understand what a carrier is," complains Thorn, "but I'm glad scientists could reduce the suffering of our cousins."

"What exactly caused this disease?" asks Pan.

"If you put 100 people in a room," says Stuart, "once you have learned their names you can identify each as being different. That doesn't mean any are abnormal. We all have genetic differences. This is true of all animals. It may not be obvious to you, but ponies will recognise other ponies as being different."

"You and I aren't quite alike; I see that," I tell Thorn.

"No, I'm the good-looking one," he jests.

"Spontaneous change happens all the time," reveals Stuart. "Now and then, it's possible that a spontaneous change may affect not merely hair colour, leg length or tail length: it may lead to something harmful. That's what happened here. A spontaneous genetic change, probably about 60 years ago, actually caused a small change in a single gene. Using the latest technology at Liverpool University, we could design a test to identify breeding animals that carried this rogue gene."

"What caused the rogue gene to appear in the first place?" asks Pan, obviously eager to dispel myths.

"You'll never work out what causes spontaneous changes. Many are happening at every breeding cycle."

"If a pony carries this gene from its dam or stallion, will it live a normal, healthy life?"

"Yes. It's as with human babies," confirms Stuart. "A foal will receive half of its genes from its mother and half from its father. If any pony inherits a copy of the rogue gene from only one parent, it will be entirely normal except that it will carry the rogue gene. You can't tell any difference unless you carry out a scientific test for the gene's presence. However, if you breed two carriers together, and the foal that is born has two copies of the rogue gene, that foal will be dead within 12 weeks, I'm afraid."

"I understand," insists Thorn, "though I'm no scientist, and it's quite complicated!"

"Okay," says Pan, "so it's possible to determine whether a pony is a carrier of the faulty gene. What does this test involve exactly?"

"You pull some hairs from the neck or the back of a horse," explains Stuart. "There will be enough genetic information in those to do a simple test. The hair sample is sent to our laboratory at Newmarket."

"Are you a carrier, Roamer?" asks Thorn.

"No," I retort. "One day, Judy yanked hairs from my mane and had them tested."

"Did it hurt?"

"Not a bit," I tell him. "She pulled them one hair at a time. Are you a carrier, Thorn?"

"I'm not absolutely certain, but I don't believe I am."

"Should all Fell stallions be tested?" asks Pan.

"On a pure animal welfare basis," replies the veterinary scientist, "I would say, 'Yes,' but someone has to pay for each test. However, if people don't test their animals, those animals will be less popular for breeding purposes."

"If untested stallions aren't used in breeding programmes, could useful genetic characteristics be lost from the Fell pony population?"

"No," insists Stuart, "because they've tested most breeding animals. It's okay to carry on breeding from carriers, but don't breed two carriers together. It's a clever way of maintaining the gene pool and avoiding disease at the same time. If you breed two carriers together, there is a one in four chance you'll produce a sick offspring. You should not limit your breeding to a few favoured stallions. Animal welfare is of greater importance than show characteristics: we must eradicate this disease in future."

"Has your research prevented ponies from dying?"

"I gather no syndrome foals have been born since testing started," says Stuart. "It would be gratifying to confirm whether this is true. It's vital that people want to maintain the breed as a population. Breeders were worried for 15 years about bad press; that people would say, 'I'm not going to buy a Fell pony: they die.' Today, we've cracked this problem."

"Ye-ee-ee-eh!" I whinny to Thorn. "What cheering news. I wouldn't wish another pony to be born with this disease, ever."

Thorn enthusiastically agrees.

"Is it likely that specific characteristics, essential to the breed's make-up, may disappear completely due to any particular breeding strategy?" wonders Pan.

"Most breeders are attempting to ensure they don't lose specific characteristics," perceives Stuart. "I hear breeders have become much more aware of general issues around selective breeding. I would try to avoid losing any breed line by not overemphasising some."

"Laminitis, sweet itch and grass sickness occasionally affect specific Fell ponies," suggests Pan, changing the subject. "Are such illnesses related to the pony's genetic characteristics?"

"If you put 100 people in a room, and you spray in a cold virus, about 40 will catch a cold because 40 will be slightly different genetically from the others. That would be true of any disease in any animal. However, an awful lot of research needs to be done."

"I don't understand what equine malaises are," announces Thorn. "I've not encountered illness."

"No, me neither," I reply. "We are robust and hardy. Therefore, we don't get ailments. Is our healthiness due to our unusual genes or because we grew up living freely?"

"Maybe it's a combination of genes and environment," surmises Thorn.

"Would it be possible to compare the genetic characteristics of free-living, extensively grazing Fell breed-lines with those of non-extensively grazing, domesticated breed-lines?" asks Pan.

"You would need information for each individual pony to carry out a study," argues the veterinary scientist. "You could compare extensively grazed with non-extensively grazed populations directly using our gene analysis approach. You would compare 20 or 30 from each group. You simply obtain DNA using hair or blood samples, which you send off to a company that will do the testing."

"Would it matter whether remaining free-living breed lines were lost, providing we retained domesticated Fell ponies?"

"Don't lose any breeding lines. That's my advice!" replies Stuart.

"Come on, Roamer," pleads Thorn impatiently. "I've studied enough science for one day."

At this point, we trot off to the furthest boundary of our paddock to graze, leaving Pan to continue his deep conversation with a ghostly telephone voice.

Thorn:

This fine morning, we are relaxing within a quiet refuge. Our man has kept his word: Roamer and I have a whole day off. Without a pack, my body's as light and free as wispy, midsummer, cirrus clouds over lowland wildflower meadows.

Our man is striving, forlornly, to organise a new satellite connection for his 'phone when a man and his wife, two strangers to me, arrive unannounced at the campsite gate. They are visiting Roamer.

"Oh, it's Judy, my owner," proclaims Roamer gleefully as they approach us.

Our man has spotted the pair's arrival. He needs the woman's assistance urgently, as it happens.

"I've lost one connecting strap and the other's damaged," he relates purposefully. "Please could you visit my saddle maker in Leicestershire? Ask him whether he can manufacture two new straps as soon as possible. Would he post them to a place called Quarry Side? My assistant will give him the address. If my old strap becomes further damaged, we may not be able to carry on easily – unless I abandon one pony temporarily."

"No way is he splitting us up," I tell Roamer. "I hope his chosen saddler puts together that harness at once, though why our man can't improvise with a piece of stout rope and a few clever knots beats me."

"Or he could repair the damaged strap himself," ventures Roamer, which is another common sense, pragmatic solution.

Roamer's owner is in polite conversation with our man.

"They are talking about us," I enlighten Roamer, who is energetically munching grass.

"What about us?" he murmurs casually, between mouthfuls.

"Your owner asserts that the traditional Fell pony is stocky, solid, strong and between 13 and 13½ hands in height," I inform him.

"Describes us precisely, I'd say," mumbles Roamer.

"During the last 30 years," continues Roamer's owner, "ponies I have bred have been used for driving, riding, carrying food to other animals on farms, harrowing, rolling and even forestry work. Several were acquired for trekking."

"That's a great deal of exertion!" declares Roamer, who is now listening attentively.

"By the way, what is 'harrowing'?" I quiz Roamer. He is well acquainted with technical terms.

"I've heard Judy mention it before. You pull a heavy frame with iron teeth over land that you have ploughed, which breaks up enormous clods of earth. And rolling is where you roll a field flatter after you have sown seed in it or ploughed it, I presume."

"Okay, you know something that I don't," I admit, reluctantly.

"Well, you did ask!"

"If Fell ponies did such strenuous work a century ago, they must have been as sturdy as us," I suggest.

"Exactly!" storms Roamer. "Where would humankind be in this twenty-first century without our allegiance in decades gone by?"

He has a point.

"I approve of a pony breed being capable of several jobs," remarks Roamer's owner. "For example, in olden days, miners demanded Fell ponies."

"Yes, they couldn't transport lead without us," recalls Roamer. "Mandy said so."

"We've carried packs a fair stretch since leaving Ouseburn Farm," I point out. "And isn't it amazing? We are still going!"

"That's because Pan is protecting us from overexertion," asserts Roamer before continuing to graze as if he is starving.

Roamer's owner begins discussing our value.

"There's no profit for breeders who sell one-year-old foals," she says. "Breeders keeping their foals for two or three further years, until they grow fully, possibly could make money. Using young, grazing ponies to help conserve wild animals and plants would provide ponies with jobs before they are sold."

"She talks sense," I tell Roamer.

"We are conservation experts," he reminds me, "practised at eating a wide variety of vegetation – but not usually wildflowers – to create ideal homes for quite a few wild species. We do this naturally."

"Is the hill Fell pony's future assured?" wonders our man.

"Where there are no youngsters to take over hill herd breeding in northern England, those herds will die out," argues Roamer's owner. "Other herds may lose their living areas if people are more devoted to saving bugs and beetles from extinction than saving ponies. The Fell Pony Society might promote hill ponies better and could provide more support for older hill pony breeders. Some breeders are losing heart; they won't bother carrying on. It's the ponies' long-term future that we are striving to protect."

"How valuable is a grazing Fell pony's role in conserving wildlife?" asks our man.

"In this respect, the pony has an admirable role, particularly in its own habitats and area of origin," she replies. "In Cumbria and the north-west, Fell ponies should be employed in preference to Exmoor ponies, which should be grazing in the west of England, and even in preference to Polish Konik ponies. Breeds allocated to their own areas will serve those areas far better than bringing in foreign grazers."

"I like Exmoors and Koniks," I splutter. "So does our man. Isn't there enough room for all of us?"

"Yes," concedes Roamer. "They are our distant cousins, but the point is this: professional land guardians requisition only a finite number of ponies to graze Britain's northern semi-wild areas, and we do it best. I imagine our ancestors have lived and grazed here for at least a millennium; this is our original British home. Supposing we don't find grazing jobs here, where shall we obtain them? If nobody employs us, we could die out. Pan said so."

"I sort of understand, but it's complicated," I say.

"It's extremely complicated, Thorn, especially since we've not even finished our schooling yet."

"I would prefer ponies to be regarded and treated the same as other agricultural animals," advocates Roamer's owner vigorously.

"Would this encourage younger farmers to use their commons grazing rights to graze Fell ponies?" suggests our man.

"Yes," she replies. "Over the last 30 years, many farming families have lost grazing rights when breeders have either died or retired. Often, when someone decides to sell a herd, it is split up. It ceases to exist where it originated."

"That's unfair!" observes Roamer. "No equine family should be split up. Every working pony treasures where she or he was born. I suspect we all dream of an opportunity to return home, one day."

"Which genetic characteristics of the semi-wild Fell pony are worth protecting?" asks our man.

"Hardiness," replies Roamer's owner. "Fell ponies will thrive on simple forage. They also have a lovely character and are easy to manage and handle, and they can carry a child or an adult quite happily."

"Is saving Fell herds here in northern England crucial to the survival of the Fell pony breed and Fell Pony Society?" wonders our man.

"I would envisage so," she responds. "No scientific research has been carried out. I have consistently supported high hill breeders."

"Judy proposes that the Society employs a Scientific Officer," says Roamer.

"Before our journey began, I wasn't aware that hill herds within our breed faced any problems," I confess.

"Positive publicity's the answer," insists Roamer. "We must persuade adult humans to appreciate how difficult life is for our kind."

"It's too much for you and me to worry about right now," I point out. "First, we've an expedition to complete. Come on. Let's ferret out fresh grazing."

We trot away, leaving the humans to ponder further the mess their kind has created for native Fell ponies. When we return, Roamer's owner and her husband have left.

Much later this afternoon, we observe our man sitting on a bench outside the camping barn, clutching his 'phone and studying intently his portable computer's screen.

"Hello, is that my contact in India?" he asks.

Evidently, he is talking by telephone to a technical adviser who is miles, possibly thousands of miles, away.

"I can't receive or send signals by satellite. . . . I must be able to communicate by email urgently. Can you help? . . ."

Perhaps two hours after his initial 'phone conversation, as darkness approaches, our man cries out, shivering, "Thank you: I have a signal at last!" whereupon, he switches off his 'phone, closes his computer lid and retreats to the camping barn's relative warmth.

This evening's air is discernibly cooler than when we left Tynemouth. We aren't apprehensive: within a couple of weeks, our winter coats will grow faster. I adore this season; undeniably, tomorrow will be a demanding, exacting but invigorating day.

Marsh and rocks

20th *October – Sewing Shields*

Roamer:

IT is roughly ten o'clock, I suppose. As we are about to leave an empty, roomy barn where, for the last hour, Pan has been preparing thoroughly for today's hike, Judy's husband, Nicholas, arrives. I eventually realise he intends to travel with us.

"I don't want to hold you up," he tells Pan almost apologetically.

"Don't worry. You won't!" replies Pan. "On the other hand, inquisitive cows might; you'll be able to keep them at bay and close the gates. Truthfully, I'm pleased you are here: I'm anticipating an easy day. Let's go."

Initially, progress is rapid. Already, less than half an hour after leaving Greencarts, we are travelling smoothly across waterlogged ground approximately 150 metres north of rough and rocky Tower Tye Milecastle.

Past Black Carts, a heather-clad, rocky moor, the humans expect a beguiling, open route alongside a clearly observable Wall. Before long, however, frustration greets them: straight ahead is a chained and locked gate. Pan and Nicholas search vainly for any alternative access to the Wall across the Vallum.

"My impression was clearly false," Pan tells our guest solemnly. "I believed landowners had verified, two days ago, that all of today's en route gates would be unlocked. This setback is exasperating."

To reach Limestone Corner Milecastle, Pan and Nicholas realise they must backtrack to the nearest road gate, which means passing closer to Tower Tye. Luckily, Pan has memorised where access gates exist: he reconnoitred his whole route on foot last November and December. Upon that occasion, allegedly, a snowy, foggy, mind- and body-numbing blast engulfed the Wall.

Dragons – locked gates – force us to reroute repeatedly via the road, a disappointing reward for careful planning. Returning to the roadside on the third occasion, we are 100 metres west of Limestone Corner, a location name without geographical significance. Somehow, humans have accepted this name through common usage. Pan says the rock is, in fact, dolerite.

"Here we can spot the Military Way easily on the ground," explains Pan to Nicholas. "From a milecastle near Limestone Corner, it runs westwards for less than 100 metres, and then it crosses the road beneath where we are standing before following the Vallum's north mound to Carrawburgh Farmhouse. Unfortunately, our only feasible and accessible route is closer to and sporadically north of the Wall."

Temporarily, we navigate to what was the Military Road, where cars whizz past, single-file, from two directions. Our guest, following three paces behind, manages to slow down all traffic, which calms me. I am mastering my fear of severely frenzied vehicles during my walks with Thorn. Before our quest began, I was frightened of anything that travelled rapidly along a highway. This fear worried and annoyed me.

Even now, I much prefer soft grass verges to hard tarmac any time. As I mentioned, Pan occasionally scolds me mildly when I purposely avoid a road, but he shouldn't blame me. Fast cars aren't entirely responsible, either: I have resolved to protect my unshod hooves; a grass-topped Way is noticeably kinder to my feet.

Onto High Teppermoor – moorland with an obscure Celtic name whose translation is beyond a pony of limited education – the ground is soft. Well, actually it is extremely waterlogged. Pan has taken this route to avoid terrifying, hurtling traffic. However, High Teppermoor is marshy, dangerous terrain for ponies carrying loads at this time of year. We must cross a stream at the moor's lowest point, our means of passage to a gate and track 1½ kilometres away. Pan surveys the moor from a high vantage point for several minutes, endeavouring to figure out his optimal route. He knows there's a solitary safe crossing place.

"My recommended crossing is marked as a ford on the map, but it is difficult to locate this ford exactly on the ground," he informs Nicholas. "It took almost an hour for me to negotiate this moor safely last November, even without ponies."

"So we should take it steady!" cautions Nicholas, acutely aware of lurking peril.

Free Fell ponies, unencumbered by packs, easily manage to avoid bogs when cruising open valleys. Today, however, right now, we've no choice. Our heavy loads will make escape from marsh difficult if either of us becomes stuck. If one makes a mistake, if he places a hoof wrongly, he will inevitably drag down the other. We could both sink. Those quick release buckles had better work. I must stay alert. Even so, I trust Pan and Thorn: I trust they will not lead me astray.

We begin a careful, tricky traverse. Luckily, soon afterwards, the occupier of a nearby isolated cottage joins us. He is wearing high-fitting wellingtons.

"I'll help you across," volunteers this local stranger. "I think I recollect the safest route."

Where our safety is at stake, certainty rather than guessing is required. The stranger walks ahead, relying upon precise or perhaps imprecise human memory. Nicholas treads directly behind the stranger, checking marsh depth with Pan's newly acquired walking pole, which a sponsor posted to him urgently.

"What's it like?" shouts Pan repeatedly to Nicholas. "How deep is the bog there?"

We cautiously advance to the moor's epicentre. Deep, stinking, squelching, black mud surrounds us, threatening to swallow Thorn and me; we must backtrack twice. Several fraught minutes later, unexpectedly, we have conquered this valley's lowest point and are onto firmer ground.

"From here, you can strike out for the fence gate safely," guarantees our guide as he points north-west.

Pan thanks him wholeheartedly as the cottager begins to retrace his steps.

Why I am decidedly relieved, upon reaching the farm track, is puzzling. Sheep die helplessly in quagmires, and thoroughbred horses easily break legs. Fell ponies, on the other hand, are powerful and cunning: bogs won't trap them.

From the track we have gained, even Pan dare not venture across waterlogged moorland at Northumberland National Park's south-eastern extremity.

"Last November," he tells Nicholas, "thick, black, peaty rainwater at the only exit gateway was half a metre deep and five metres wide."

Instead, we detour to the road west of Carrawburgh Fort, which, I glean, was originally a group of fortified rocks that Romans named Brocolitia.

"Likely of Celtic origin, the name possibly refers to an enclosure or a sharp peak rather than a place infested by badgers," hypothesises Pan. "Exceptionally, Romans built Brocolitia across the Vallum. They also erected a temple here to Mithras, god of light."

Speaking of light, will we have enough to conclude our expedition before border weather deteriorates too much? Praying to Mithras may not suffice. Equines are in touch with nature: we sense acutely that each new day delivers less light than its predecessor.

At the rocks of Carraw, we regain our pre-planned route along the ditch north of, and near to, the Wall. Pan ascertained, two years ago, that fences without gates render the Vallum inaccessible here. This irritating truth briefly takes us away from the Military Way.

We deviate around bogs and thick rushes towards a gate 200 metres north of our leader's preferred route, navigating prudently through a herd of scattered black cows at a walled field boundary. I'm glad we're taking no unnecessary risks: I occasionally dread truculent creatures, especially cows. Who knows why? Arguably, it's because I hadn't met cattle before this expedition. This purebred, native herd seems benign enough, of course, but genetically changed breed lines can be unpredictable, to say the least, according to Pan.

Safely past those cattle, their gate behind us, we virtually retrace our steps, but on the opposite side of the field wall, towards the Wall ditch and Wall. Being north of the road, we merely glimpse Carraw Long Axis Milecastle. Here, the Wall ditch and Vallum mounds are running parallel to each other and close together, an imposing sight. Straight ahead of us, in the distance beyond Carraw West Turret, I can spot faint crossing points in the Vallum ditch. Legionaries, all Roman citizens I understand, supported by auxiliaries hailing from frontier provinces, built their Military Road on the north mound. I imagine how proud and eager Roman ponies might have felt in this country.

The Wall stretches arrow-like before us to a distant horizon. This is more like it: we are making steady progress over open countryside north of the Wall. We pass close to Carraw West Turret and steer north of a meagre hump, the milecastle of Shield-on-the Wall, where originally a mere hut existed. We cannot yet access the Military Way: awkward fences flourish. Nearly as good, we hug its perimeter. High ground gives us unobstructed views. By my reckoning, we are presently atop a mound that is about 11 metres, 36 feet, wide. Pan believes that Romans dug an average-sized Wall ditch – wider than 8 metres and a bit less than 3 metres deep – adjacent to the Wall here.

Two kilometres later, we are persevering alongside and north of the Wall, whose remains presently appear only as a very slight mound. No holidaying walkers are about, which suits me admirably.

At this time of day, in anticipation of testing journeys ahead, Thorn and I long to sample exotic path-side grasses to keep our strengths up. We cannot. We wish we could slurp refreshing water from extremely infrequent burns. Unfortunately, we dare not: Pan has other ideas.

"Boys, come on: there's no time to dawdle," he protests when we eventually succeed in lowering our heads to graze. "We must keep going. It will be dark before long."

"What's that rocky outcrop in the distance?" I ask Thorn.

"Our man calls it 'Whin Sill'," he answers, "whatever that means. He said the Wall hugs it for quite a distance westwards."

Less than a kilometre past Shield-on-the-Wall, we can cross the Wall line. Here, road, Vallum and Wall diverge. The road crosses the

Vallum and courses south-west as the Wall begins to follow Whin Sill Crags, which I soon learn are intrusive sheets of black, horizontal, basaltic rock.

"Whinstone is outstandingly hard rock," muses Pan. "It's well-nigh impossible to dig a ditch there. Consequently, Romans had little choice: they had to construct the Vallum further south, into the valley. The Vallum deviates several hundred metres from the Wall."

"What can you sense, Roamer?" challenges Thorn. "Are we back onto the Way yet?"

"The Way seems to leave the Vallum's north mound about here," I suggest tentatively. "Ahead, it appears to follow closely the Wall's southern margin."

Pan interrupts our guesswork: "Boys, we are walking along the Military Way once again. For the next few days, with luck, we should be able to follow in the footsteps of your ancestors more easily: I expect we shall discover hardly any obstacle or barrier to hinder us."

Now we are truly in the shadow of the Wall!

We follow the Way past Coesike Turret, located near a rivulet, and head towards the site of Grindon – green hill – Milecastle. Beyond, a young herd of rare, white, shorthorn calves is casually grazing. They remain aloof, unimpressed, as we trudge wearily amongst them towards Sewing Shields Farm, our destination. The farmstead, fashioned from Roman stones, was formerly Sigewine's Castle.

Where is everybody? We wait patiently as a quad bike, conveying a young farmer, chugs from the valley floor. He is driving a score of healthy, fat sheep uphill along a narrow, winding track towards us.

"Hello there!" calls the farmer, attracting Pan's attention. "Grandad's in the house, looking forward to seeing you again. Dad will be home presently."

Judy turns up promptly by car, as if on cue. She whisks Nicholas away to a lowland guesthouse, where a hot shower and a comfortable bed await. Meanwhile, Pan urgently unloads our packs. He then hastily unsaddles, brushes, waters and feeds us before retiring into the farmhouse for a cup of tea. Not long afterwards, by the time Pan has reinforced our paddock gateway with two mobile gates lashed together, he must erect his tent in the dark.

Thorn and I are alone.

"Shall we break out of here tonight?" I ask him half-heartedly.

"Escape is impossible," he decides, surveying the large, walled enclosure.

"Well, don't torment yourself," I tell him. "We've plenty of juicy vegetation to eat."

Much later, our hillside is silent.   Dim light from a solitary farmhouse situated in the distant valley signals meagre human habitation. Tonight's air temperature plunges. Thorn and I adapt easily – we are surprisingly hardy – but I wonder how Pan is coping.

Thorn:

We are on High Teppermoor, a wide-open space. Dirt blows into my eyes. I'm so thirsty that my throat aches: fresh water is scarce. However, I welcome a challenge. Indeed, who could be miserable? The sensational smell of fresh grass cuttings is wafting by with the breeze. At each stride of my walking gait, soft, luxurious moss springs and then shrinks beneath my hooves; this green, sodden, gentle blanket reminds me of home.

Only dragons will slow Fell ponies; barely two hours after exiting High Teppermoor we arrive safely at our high, hillside campsite in what appears to be, upon first glance, the middle of nowhere. I am remarkably clean, considering what rain-soaked terrain we have trudged across recently.

We've experienced no mishap today, which might mean our man is learning to anticipate and, therefore, avoid calamities, or maybe we've been lucky. Doubtless, having a human road sentry reassured Roamer.

Tonight, our man will sleep in the paddock adjoining ours. He is erecting his tent by a wall when the senior farmer approaches.

Our man greets the farmer: "Hi, Angus. I've just about finished setting up camp."

"Are you inclined to go down to the village with me for some fish and chips?" asks the farmer as our man attaches his last peg to one corner of the tent's built-in groundsheet.

At this moment, our man's telephone rings.

"Roamer's owner is on the 'phone," he replies. "She's asking whether we would like to meet her and Nicholas for fish and chips! They will be waiting in the public house at Haydon Bridge."

"Do you fancy a drink there?" inquires the farmer politely.

"Sounds like a favourable plan," agrees our man. "I won't need to cook tonight."

They climb into the farmer's four-wheel drive and are gone instantly, roaring into the valley, engulfed by darkness. It's time to explore with Roamer on a paradisaical, starry sky evening!

21st October – Housesteads Fort and Bradley Farm

Roamer:
Alan rolls into Sewing Shields early; we aren't quite ready, but he films us anyway. I don't mind: I quite enjoy watching him watching us.

"Alan, shall you manage to carry all of your gear to Housesteads?" inquires Pan just before we leave. "This will be a strenuous section: the ground is undulating and steep in places, with lots of rocks."

"I'll soon tell you," responds Alan bluntly. "At least I'll be even fitter at the end!"

"I hope our man doesn't suggest that we lug it," murmurs Thorn.

Immediately west of Sewing Shields, I can identify the Military Way and dramatic Sewingshields Crags, which, Pan informs us, rise to 326 metres, 1,068 feet, above sea level. We quickly pass Sewingshields Milecastle. The ensuing turret, built 100 metres below the crags' summit, lies 150 metres to our right and 25 metres above us. From this vantage point on the Way, I spy a large, placid, crescent-shaped lake, Broomlee Lough, in a westwards clearing. Northwards, a row of majestic Whin Sill outcrops catches my eye.

We are travelling across essentially firm ground. Cows punctuate the hillside. They aren't annoying us, and we don't antagonise them – an excellent arrangement.

The next turret marks the crossing place of a venerable drove route for Scottish cattle through Busy Gap, a break in the basaltic ridge of hills. We progress speedily from here, without interruption, to King's Wicket, where Pan must decide. To squeeze through a kissing gateway ahead, he must remove our packs. Instead, we could cross the Wall at a wicket gate on our right. Option one will allow us to take the Military Way towards what was a small Roman road that led to King's Hill Milecastle. The latter option leads to Housesteads via the Wall's northern side. Here, greater danger lurks, danger that might have thwarted barbarians attempting to breach the Wall from the north 18 centuries ago.

"I checked this section a year ago," remarks Pan ruefully. "From here, I skirted about 100 metres south of the Wall. That is my preferred, safer option now; it uses the Military Way south of Kennel Crags Turret, across King's Hill and Clew Hill, the hill with a ravine."

Today, however, he hasn't the time, energy or inclination to remove our packs.

"Let's take the northern route instead," he announces after contemplating briefly but deeply.

Now I'm worried, but only slightly. What does he mean by "greater danger"?

Pan must separate Thorn from me to squeeze through the gateway. A lone, male walker with a ferreting dog assists by holding my lead rope. Really, I don't need looking after. Curious canines don't trouble me either.

"Would you care to accompany us to Housesteads?" suggests Pan to the dog owner.

He willingly accepts Pan's offer. We are, momentarily, a team of six as we hug the northern, rocky, scrub-free slope of Kennel Crags, part of the natural Whin Sill barrier, past a turret on our left.

"We must be careful over this rock-strewn ground," Pan warns Alan, who, as usual, has the challenging task of negotiating tricky terrain whilst laden with a heavy camera and tripod. "It's a mighty quartz and dolerite intrusion."

Pan isn't kidding: with nearly every step we must avoid sharp, protruding – some might call them extruding – rocks; amongst these rocks lurk severely marshy patches. Our route is exacting. Although I am extremely happy to hug the Wall, even I become uneasy sometimes. Naturally, a Fell pony's strong legs and hard hooves will cope. Nonetheless, this kilometre is proving to be painfully slow going.

"Across these crags, Hadrian built his Wall to deter invaders," comments Pan. "Over the next two days of trekking, sheer cliffs rise maximally to 345 metres, about 1,132 feet, above sea level."

"I shall be happier when we reach the fort," I tell Thorn, slightly disconcerted. "Shall we be able to recross the Wall there, to the gentler, southern slope? I hope so."

"Roamer, stop worrying," advises Thorn. "We'll be okay."

I'm not worrying; I am simply being cautious. My inbuilt survival instinct and superior intelligence take control. Besides, my job's toughest: Thorn forces me to tread, more or less, where he has gone, which gives me relatively little warning of what's ahead.

We vigilantly pick our way to the pass, sweeping by a Roman well, aiming for the south-eastern corner of Housesteads – the farmstead where remains of a Roman fort exist.

"Romans named the fort Vercovicium," remarks Pan, "perhaps acknowledging a hilly place."

Plainly, this fort's high on a hill. At the crag's edge, a breathtaking panoramic view unfolds southwards to the South Tyne valley. Here is a magical remoteness made for galloping free!

"Fort remains abound, including all gates – north, south, east and west," continues Pan. "Archaeologists believe the fort covered an area of 186 by 112 metres, slightly more than 5 acres."

"Our man reckons 1000 soldiers lived here," interjects Thorn, "but I'd rather hear about horses and ponies."

"And Friesian cavalry, derived from north-western corners of the Netherlands and Germany, resided at this fort," adds Pan almost telepathically. "They probably would have brought their own black riding horses here. I expect future scientific research, comparing present day Fell pony and Friesian horse genetic make-up, what scientists refer to as their genomes, will disclose to what extent these two breeds are related. Undeniably, though, modern Friesians bear a rather limited resemblance to Roman cavalry horses."

"What do you say to that?" I ask Thorn. "Friesians lived here!"

"Well, perchance we are walking in Friesian cavalry footsteps," he concedes, "but even though modern Friesians might be our relatives through common, distant pasts, I suspect we are distinctive in many ways."

Our most recent companion, the dog owner, has his own schedule to consider.

"Good luck with your quest," he tells Pan before heading downhill towards the Visitor's Centre. His inquisitive dog scampers energetically ahead, relentlessly exploring virtually every hole and larval crevice.

We are at steeply dropping Knag Burn. Pan has learned that Knag Burn gateway, lying in the valley, is one of expectedly few gaps through the Wall not located at a fort or milecastle.

"Last year, I reconnoitred a route alongside this stream," he tells Alan, "but which could prove tricky for pack ponies."

Crossing the Wall line, we descend to the protection of a fort wall and buttress. Our high vantage point, on a knoll overlooking the Visitor Centre's large car park and old Cultivation Terraces where Romans farmed, offers inadequate shelter from the prevailing wind. Today, the wind's not cold; in fact, its fierce bluster is seasonally pleasant. Here, Thorn and I may graze not entirely juiceless grasses, but why are we waiting?

"This is where we are supposed to be meeting Simon, who works for Natural England," announces Pan. "We are bang on time. Where is he?"

"What is Natural England?" asks Thorn, perplexed.

"According to Pan," I respond, "it's a group of experts who advise Government on how to protect natural and semi-natural environments. That includes protecting an immeasurable variety of wild species, what the experts entitle 'biodiversity'."

"Well, now I understand completely," retorts Thorn sardonically.

"I expect it will become clearer by the time we've finished our expedition," I tell him reassuringly.

"I hope so," he remarks. "Otherwise, how will our man's filmed travelogue make any sense?"

"Could we move back from the edge," requests Alan as he relocates his camera in a sheltered hollow 30 metres away from Thorn and me. "My microphone will not pick up voices sharply enough: the wind's too powerful."

At that moment, climbing around the corner of an outcrop towards us, a stranger springs into view. Pan welcomes him.

"Hello, Simon. Glad you could pinpoint us."

"I wondered what or who Pan was looking at with his monocular a minute ago," I whisper to Thorn.

"It's quite an uphill trek from the car park," notes the young man.

Three tourists, visiting the fort, look on, possibly astonished to see ponies this high up by Hadrian's Wall.

Pan endeavours to convince people we meet that few equines, if any, especially pack ponies, have walked or trotted the Wall's entire length, from east to west, for perhaps 1,600 years. Is he correct? Who can say? Let's not forget: we are here because the National Trust granted us permission; Pan must continually negotiate equine admittance over private land.

"We have a right to be here," reasons Thorn. "Our kind did help Romans build the Wall and Way."

He has a point: the Wall's part of our heritage. We belong here. Bill and Pan chose us to retrace our ancestors' footsteps. I shall remember this moment, at this fort, always.

"Right, we are filming," Alan informs everybody.

Thorn:

"What is the job of the human who works for Natural England?" I wonder just after he arrives at Housesteads Fort.

"Not sure," replies Roamer quizzically, "but I think he's a Cumbrian land manager. He's talking about Fell ponies."

We stand utterly still and silent, at least initially, listening to a conversation that, I fear, might take until nightfall. Our man fires a string of questions.

"Equines not dissimilar to Fell ponies have existed in England's far north since before Romans reached our shores," believes our man. "Therefore, shouldn't wildlife managers choose Fell ponies to sustain northern habitats?"

"Yes, where we are looking to introduce pony grazing," acknowledges the land manager. "But usually, it's simply a matter of which livestock is on hand to manage the site."

"Hey, what is Simon implying?" whispers Roamer.

"There aren't enough of us in the right place at the right time," I explain.

"Does that mean other ponies could steal jobs that Fell ponies should be doing?"

"Yes," I tell him. "And, without employment, our kind could become extinct."

"Hey, Thorn, why are they talking about Exmoor ponies?" he adds, following a long pause.

"Our man's apprehensive," I reply. "It seems that quite a lot of Exmoor ponies but hardly any Fell ponies are working as official conservation grazers in Cumbria. In recent years, Exmoor ponies have also been grazing in Northumberland."

Northumberland, we learn, is the territory of people living north of the River Humber – the "dark river" or "good-well water".

"Why won't humans do something about our quandary?" demands Roamer, startled by this latest fact. "We Fell ponies could assist humans and other animals, and we could live free at the same time. What's better than grazing about?"

"I've just realised!" I tell Roamer. "That's why we're on this expedition: we must broadcast our breed's urgent plea for support."

"What are they talking about now?" asks Roamer a few minutes later, again fully awake after a brief snooze.

"They're discussing whether Fells are part of Britain's agriculture," I reply.

"Well, we must be," concludes Roamer. "We are grazing substantial upland and lowland areas where sheep or cattle roam. We live in harmony with agricultural animals and wildlife."

"Our man insists that the Fell pony breed is 'part of biological diversity'," I tell Roamer. "He maintains that National Government should ensure that farmers benefit from looking after us. He also says Government policy sometimes restricts ponies' free grazing on commons."

"Simon is promising Pan that Natural England will try to help graziers to preserve pony herds," quips Roamer. "It's about time somebody helped them."

"What do you know about it?" I ask.

"Not much, but Simon talks sense."

I carry on listening, despite Roamer's continual interruptions.

"Fell ponies have been undervalued in the past in terms of their contribution to habitats and ecosystems," argues the land manager. "For example, ponies are ideal for grazing gorse and other scrub, where they improve the likelihood of butterflies surviving."

"We can do that easily," interjects Roamer, "and a lot else besides."

"We are talking about conserving genetics," adds the manager. "No one wants to see the demise of the Fell pony. We need to encourage its use further south."

"It's simple," says Roamer. "Farmers, breeders and Natural England should work in synchrony to safeguard our breed's future before it is too late."

"Isn't it too late?" I speculate, vexed.

"Of course not," Roamer reassures me. "Pan hasn't given up. Neither should we, but there isn't much time left to sort out our predicament."

"There must be proper, scientific promotion," insists the manager.

"Is this what we're doing – promotion?" I ask Roamer.

"Precisely, which is why we must succeed," he replies.

"Right," I say, slightly overawed.

Our meeting is over. The man from Natural England, who has held tightly onto Roamer's lead rope throughout the conversation, hands it to our man. Waving goodbye, he then heads purposefully downhill to the Visitors' Centre. Meanwhile, Cameraman packs up his recording gear.

Footage bagged, light-hearted, we continue navigating around this grand fort towards its west gate. Our descent follows an elegant, wide, grassy track sweeping majestically towards Housesteads Museum.

"The museum is a replica of a Roman civilian building found in a nearby settlement," remarks our man.

Field gates line up westwards along the Military Way, making navigation easier. Soon we are leaving tourist chatter behind. Away from well-trodden thoroughfares, the hillside's deserted.

Steering below the museum through a National Trust gateway, we quickly head uphill again, past impressive, renovated, stone remains of Housesteads Milecastle's north gate.

"Here, in Roman times," says our man, "a 10-foot-wide road across a long field linked the south gate to a field gate marking the Way."

Passing the remains of a unique Roman limekiln, we are roughly 100 yards south of the Wall on a temperate, relaxing afternoon, a deceitful reminder of faraway, faded summer. From Housesteads Crags to Cuddy's Crags – Saint Cuthbert's rocks – we hug the Way more or less with the contour for the next three-quarters of a mile.

"Look behind you, Thorn!" whoops Roamer, some time later. "We can see Housesteads and Sewing Shields to the east, where we were. Don't those places seem far away now? Our present position represents quite a walking achievement for pack ponies, ancient or modern, I'd say."

"Whin Sill Crags undoubtedly were a forbidding natural rock barrier to invaders from the north," remarks our man.

"Yes," nods Cameraman, smiling politely, perhaps even appreciatively, for a history lesson a knowledgeable Cumbrian man doesn't require.

We trek on to Hotbank Crags, 327 metres, 1,073 feet, above sea level according to our man. From our position above and about 400 paces north-east of Milking Gap, he identifies the location of Hotbank Milecastle, a short-axis milecastle opposite Hotbank Farm.

"An excavated stone inscription, found at Hotbank, bears the builder's name, the Second Augustan Legion," declares our man. "The inscription also mentions Emperor Hadrian and Aulus Platorius Nepos, Britannia's governor at that time."

"What are these milecastles we keep hearing about?" I ask Roamer.

"An archaeologist told Pan they were small enclosures," he says. "They housed soldiers who protected gateways through the Wall every Roman mile – every 1,479 metres or 1,618 yards – or so: the precise distance between milecastles depended upon the terrain."

"Long numbers are frequently meaningless to my brain," I admit. "How do you memorise them?"

"My dam showed me how. One day, I'll explain," he promises.

From Hotbank Milecastle, zigzagging snakelike past benign native cattle, we descend into the valley and hence towards Bradley Farm, tonight's campsite. The laneway to Bradley – a farm located in a broad clearing – is incredibly muddy, but who cares? I'll handle most eventualities at this stage.

It's evening, time for well-earned food rations. What a huge, gorgeous enclosure to relish. We shall have a serious romp tonight!

"I suggest you check their field for possible escape points," advises Bradley's farmer.

"Good idea, Julian," replies our man.

Cameraman drives off, aiming for wherever he lives.

Our man purposefully walks the enclosure's perimeter fence, observing, thinking and assessing as he goes. It is impenetrable, he concludes, so he lets us loose.

As he is locking our gate, a small, red car pulls up.

"Who's that, Roamer?" I inquire.

"Hai-ai-ai! It's Mark, my Lincoln keeper."

"This is a pleasant surprise," concedes our man, waving enthusiastically to the young, fair-haired man who is disembarking.

"Just called in to see how Roamer is coping," announces the stranger. "I'm visiting my parents."

"It's a long way to drive, from Lincoln, purely to say hello to you," I tell Roamer frankly.

It's not that I'm jealous, mind. No, I'm pleased for Roamer: occasionally, he gets homesick.

"His parents live not far away," replies Roamer tersely. "He just said so. Besides, he possibly misses me. He cares about me."

"Roamer's outstanding," our man informs the visitor. "In fact, he is doing astonishingly well."

"Oi, don't forget me!" I say to myself. "I'm doing as well, perhaps even better."

"Would you care to hike at least part of the leg to Cawfields with us tomorrow?" asks our man.

"Oh, I'd be delighted," replies the other man.

"I'll look forward to your company. We leave at about 10.30 a.m."

The stranger turns his ignition key and, as I begin to graze, speeds away.

Moments later, the farmer's wife appears.

"You can sleep indoors tonight if you wish," she suggests.

"Thank you, Leslie. What a commendable idea," responds our man, who I suspect welcomes temporary respite. "Sorting out emails will be much more straightforward. I don't suppose you have an internet connection I could use?"

"Our son can set that up for you easily," she replies. "Would you like to eat with us at Twice Brewed in the valley?"

An hour later, the only humans within nearly a mile climb into a vehicle. Roamer and I are alone with our thoughts, a rich grazing feast – which won't hurt for one night – and the Wall's solitude.

Steep hills, bogs and a successful escape

22nd October – Cawfields

Roamer:

PAN warns his camera operator during preparations this early morning: "It's slightly less than nine kilometres over difficult up-and-down terrain at or near the Wall's highest point."

"I'll film you loading up," proposes Alan, ignoring Pan's disquiet.

"We have bogs and a couple of tricky climbs ahead. After yesterday, how are you feeling?" presses Pan.

"Tired," confesses Alan.

An exacting day lies ahead for certain, but is anybody bothered how I feel? In truth, I'm completely relaxed. Thorn, however, is desperate to begin walking: waiting about has made him perceptibly restless.

Mark shows up punctually. This is a sizeable crowd.

From Bradley, we set off uphill to regain the Way. Our one easy access point is via a series of gates, which our guest opens and closes efficiently. Heading through sheep pens, we are swiftly at Milking Gap, the pass lying approximately south-west of Hotbank, a clump of trees on the hill where we descended yesterday evening. Westwards beyond this gap in the Whin Sill, halfway up the next ridge, Milking Gap Turret once existed.

"Between each pair of milecastles, Romans built two turrets roughly 540 yards apart," chirps Thorn, eager to impress me with his recently acquired historical knowledge.

At this moment, I catch sight of Crag Lough, a silver lake nestling peacefully below us north of the Wall. This lake's impressive north-facing basalt crag, one of Northumberland's largest, provides enterprising humans with over 100 dark, shiny climbing routes. Quickly, however, the lake is out of sight as we march onwards along the Way, following the southern edge of Highshield Crags, a precipitous place hiding ancient shepherds' huts.

From a position about 40 metres south of the turret at the summit of Highshield Crags, we are heading steeply downwards to Sycamore Gap. A solitary tree between two tall crests in the Whin Sill marks its location. As we descend, Thorn's saddle slips for the fourth time, assuming I counted correctly. I wish our leader would sort out this chaos: I hate downhill stop-start jerkiness.

Pan adjusts the saddle. Seconds later, as we continue, he trips over a grassy tussock and then tumbles forwards. Resigned to the consequence of gravity, he rolls effortlessly downhill, head over heels for about three paces. Thorn and I stop instantly. We hover over him, unblinking, statuesque, frozen, eyeing him nonchalantly.

"Are you okay?" shouts Alan.

"Fine," responds Pan, though this unanticipated incident has shaken him slightly. "I lost my footing. I should have been more careful."

He sits there, looking up at us, for several seconds. We are unimpressed: it's not our fault! Still, I'm thankful he's not injured; I'm going nowhere without him on such unfamiliar ground.

"Stop staring so contemptuously," he says presently, looking Thorn straight in the eye.

Thorn might be wondering whether he can escape while Pan is on the ground, though I doubt it. Nevertheless, Pan's taking no chance: he's not letting go of Thorn's precious lead rope, even for a second.

The Way courses about 50 metres south of Castle Nick, a fortress milecastle built in the hillside slightly west of Sycamore Gap. Now we must climb again as we tackle the slope of Peel Crags, the "tower rocks". From the resultant, elevated position due south of Peel Crags Turret, we successfully complete our next descent into Peel Pass.

Our experience of the Military Way, particularly over the last kilometre or so, convinces Pan that Romans didn't design it for carts: "The testing climb west, out of the gap from below Castle Nick, not forgetting the earlier, tricky descent towards Sycamore Gap, could have been accomplished in Roman times only by pack animals."

"Our man is probably correct," remarks Thorn.

Thorn's judgements of practicalities are frequently faultless, but never mind logistics: I'm getting hungry. In fact, I'm too hungry to wait any longer. I pause, attempting to eat, but when I finally manage to snatch a few mouthfuls of coarse grass, Pan chides me gently. Apparently, we must keep going until we arrive there, wherever "there" is, but that won't stop me from snacking if an opportunity arises.

At Peel Pass, we briefly head north-west, up a bank and across the Wall. Skirting around Steelrigg Turret – located on a ridge with a steep path – we turn west into an ancient wooded area. Soon we begin an exacting, 450-metre traverse of the rock-strewn Whin Sill, navigating to a position roughly 150 metres north of the Wall. Now we turn abruptly south. Fleetingly, our route has disoriented me: we appear to be circling the Wall!

Right away, we are climbing steadily through field gateways to the Wall and a milecastle high above Winshields. Here, a free-living pony might have come upon a shepherd's hut, a "hutte" of turf and timber, in medieval times. I can imbibe exhilarating, inspiring views of both escarpment and valley. The latter landscape sits majestically, a deep green, water-soaked flush with occasional dabs of gold and red: clumps of deciduous trees are shedding their leaves.

"Do you realise?" I ask Thorn in a slightly superior tone of voice. "Our ancestors were likely here, high up on the Wall."

"Who told you?" he challenges.

"Well, I overheard Pan relate that somebody had found part of a Roman horse harness nearby," I riposte.

"How interesting," he concedes, following a prolonged, thoughtful pause. "Besides us, I suppose few other modern pack ponies would have set foot here. This spot is wonderful, and I'm growing accustomed to carrying my load."

"It's all right for you," I protest. "I'm carrying the same weight you carry and half as much again!"

"Are you moaning?" he jibes.

"I'm merely pointing out," I reply.

I quickly change the subject, observing, "This is a view worth cherishing."

At Winshield Crags, we have reached the Wall's highest spot, which, according to Pan, is 345 metres higher than any salty ocean.

"Yes," agrees Thorn. "I'll be sad when we climb down. Which reminds me: I can't figure out why sheer drops on Cumbrian fells send some humans dizzy."

Much later, having descended, we reach tonight's resting place, Cawfields, an open expanse where jackdaws nested long ago. We are amidst a wild place north of both Wall and Whin Sill. Southwards lie steep crags. More importantly at this moment, it is pellet time; we must eat the healthiest food to keep us powerful and vigorous.

After dinner, unshackled and contented, I canter gaily about our grassy paddock until darkness descends. Before long, it's nap time – or is it?

As you may have noticed, Thorn enjoys smashing gates and fences. Since our adventure began, he has acted rebelliously and even recklessly from time to time, kicking them down. Tonight is another such occasion. I fail to comprehend fully why he loves doing this, but he is unable to control himself. All right, I admit it: I am sometimes guilty too, though not as guilty as Thorn. He is such an artful teacher of tricks, and he unashamedly laughs loudly each time he escapes.

Tomorrow, without doubt, he will try to blame everything on me. Of course, he won't get away with it: Pan will guess the truth.

Thorn:

Climbing down a steep, rocky incline with a backpack is not an elementary proposition. That said, our technique is simple: we zigzag across the hillside.

Today, we have to negotiate three difficult descents to passes.

"We must ensure they don't injure themselves," our man advises Roamer's Lincoln keeper. "If a pack slips on a downhill slope, a dangerous situation could develop. Are you managing with your heavy camera, Alan?"

Cameraman doesn't answer: he's fully occupied watching where he's placing his feet as we descend cautiously from Peel Crags to a slim, wandering road threading its way through a gap in the Whin Sill.

Our direction is uphill, downhill and then uphill again, always towards Winshields Milecastle. We are currently situated about 50 yards below and south of this milecastle, treading an easily identified section of the Way. A Roman path once led north from the Way to the milecastle's south gate. These days, no path is recognisable: on our final approach, even we ponies fail to discern it with surety.

Our final climb to the summit of Winshield Crags, the highest point we shall attain today or any other day, has a gradient of 1 in 10 supposedly. Roamer and I bound up. Listen, as we surge effortlessly and all but noiselessly: Fells have evolved to glide over rugged terrain. We are power personified.

At the summit is what our man describes as a "triangulation pillar" and a "fixed surveying station", but I've no idea what these words mean.

Winshields Turret, originally located beyond the summit, no longer exists: Roman auxiliaries may have dismantled it. We rejoin the Military Way further west and then, at the next gap, descend to the shallow valley of Lodhams Slack and the Vallum ditch. Now we climb towards Melkridge Turret, also dismantled, at the summit of the next ridge. From this ridge, which milking cows traditionally have grazed, we overlook Melkridge Common, a wonderfully wide expanse of rich grass north of the Wall. I glimpse an alluring border landscape, awe-inspiring even for a Fell pony who has experienced some of Cumbria's wildest places.

"A generous pocket of land to the north is owned by a traditional,

Northumberland, Fell pony breeder," our man informs his two human companions.

"That could be a suitable place for a Fell pony to live and roam," I say.

"No humans would disturb us," agrees Roamer.

Terrain virtually devoid of human habitation stretches northwards below us. A cool northerly breeze fills my nostrils. I detect Scotland's incompletely tamed, autumnal beauty – a potent concoction of dying brackens, mosses and heathers. What did our Roman ancestors think, patrolling or labouring along this Wall, the first time they beheld what lay beyond this high, windswept outpost of civilisation? Encamped at the then unknown territory's extremity, did they ever spy even a solitary fire from this vantage point? Unquestionably, captive pack ponies standing here would have yearned to live unbridled.

From Melkridge Milecastle, we are heading steeply downhill towards Caw Gap, an opening at the place of the jackdaws. Roamer and I stop dead. Under no circumstance will we attempt to climb down severely precipitous rocks and ledges: such an endeavour would be foolhardy, even for us.

"This descent is dangerously steep for pack ponies," recollects our man belatedly.

I'm relieved that he has realised his error in time. What shall we do now? We seem to be stuck, with no escape route.

"We need to be a little further south, exactly tracing the Military Way," he insists.

We must backtrack to where we deviated from the Way. Our man, aided by his Lincoln guest, begins to search for the safest way down.

"During the reconnaissance, I located the correct route," explains our man. "It lies about 100 metres south of the National Trail footpath, behind one of these crags. It takes us gently to Caw Gap."

We backtrack even further.

"There should be an accessible route in that direction," recalls our man impulsively, pointing to a gap between two hillocks.

The narrow pass to which he refers gives an impression of cascading over a cliff edge.

"I'll go and check," volunteers his companion.

Meanwhile, clutching his camera and tripod, Cameraman is climbing laboriously down steps etched into the magma dolerite, searching for a revealing vantage point.

Within minutes, the Lincoln man is back.

"Yes, I presume that's it," he announces, triumphant.

We meander hesitantly downwards, southwards, behind a large, rocky mound. Presently we veer south-west, descending gradually into a rock-strewn ravine.

"There's a single possibility through here," our man warns his companion. "This patch is aptly called the Bogle Hole: it is prohibitively boggy. I assessed it last year. We could easily injure a pony, especially because of recent heavy rain. I'll go first with Thorn. Would you bring Roamer across afterwards?"

"Sure," says the other enthusiastically. "I'll have a go."

Roamer must trust the Lincoln man, I conclude; otherwise, our man wouldn't trust Roamer's keeper either. Well, I suppose the stranger did watch over Roamer on Lincoln Common for several months. Nevertheless, Roamer is not foolish: he'll observe first and then he'll decide to follow me if, I mean when, I am successful. Our man needn't fuss: I'll make it, no problem.

Our man's first attempt to determine safe passage through this black marsh is futile: upon checking the bog's depth, he notes that his walking pole is on the brink of disappearing, Excalibur-like, for ever. On the second attempt, we turn back as soon as my front hooves sink into spongy ground. I don't intend wading through that. Wait! He spots our alternative option, a tight opening between two large rocks. There's a hitch: this gap hides a four-yard-wide patch of marsh; we can't avoid it. Our man checks it with his pole. The bog is less than a foot deep in places, but not much less.

"Come on, Thorn," he commands. "Let's go for it."

Without hesitating, marsh up to my calves, I stride out boldly. Roamer and the Lincoln man are close behind. Naturally, Roamer negotiates the hazard more precisely, more delicately.

Safely through, linking harness reinstated, we tread carefully downhill through a boulder-strewn landscape to a narrow, meandering road at Caw Gap. Meanwhile, where's Cameraman? Earlier, he was filming me from a precarious, craggy ridge. I scan the hillside anxiously, at length spotting him high above us, a black ant. He is clambering warily down a steep, rocky slope, cumbersome photographic gear slung not so casually over his left shoulder, nimbly picking out the National Trail path towards the gap. I daren't watch in case he falls.

Once across the gap road, we are climbing on firmer ground, briefly west, towards Caw Gap Turret.

"We must gain entry to this field on the left," reports our man some 50 yards further on, "but the gate's padlocked."

"No problem," utters the Lincoln man as he deftly lifts the wooden gate from its hinges to let us through, replacing it without fuss mere seconds afterwards.

"I see you've practised this," observes our man dryly.

Another obstacle looms. I nip nimbly through a slender gap in a wall, a gap designed only for sheep. However, Roamer is stranded, defeated by his pack's width.

"Stand!" orders our man, giving Roamer no opportunity to consider attempting an impossible feat.

"Okay, Mark, I'll remove boxes from Roamer's left pack," he announces, when my friend is perfectly still.

Actually, Roamer isn't perturbed: he invariably does what our man tells him. Minus two white boxes, he squeezes through safely, expertly. Straight away, both men begin reloading him. Meanwhile, Cameraman is struggling to film this exercise whilst holding onto me. His footage should be riveting.

Travelling south-west, we descend without further incident to the Military Way. This sweeps majestically yet gently westwards approximately 150 yards below Cawfield Crags and south of two impressively sized Bronze Age stones. We quietly rest as our man examines the still intact foundations of Cawfields Milecastle.

"Here, the Way crosses the Vallum's north mound," explains our man. "Evidence shows that Romans built the road later than they built the Wall and Vallum."

He might as well be talking to himself: nobody except me seems to be listening.

Westwards, I spot a disused quarry full of water. Circumnavigating its eastern edge, we manage to squeeze through another tight gateway by a wall at Hole Gap. Before sunset, not soon enough for me, we are turning away from the Wall and heading north-east towards our campsite, swiftly reaching this evening's anticipated destination, Cawfields Farm.

Our man's two human travelling companions have already left Cawfields, ferried to their cars at Bradley, when, by and by, a young woman drives up. She chats with him as he brushes us, seeking a story for a book she is writing. Our man isn't particularly interested in sharing our story: there's much to do before nightfall. She drives off a few minutes later.

Today has been exceptionally adventurous. Roamer and I are pleased to be grazing in a large paddock on an unlit night at Cawfields. Our man is camping in a mature, sheltered, mixed woodland coppice 80 yards from the gateway to our field. I hear him but cannot observe him putting up his tent: dense undergrowth lies between us; thick bushes, nettles and lanky, sinewy grasses generally devoid of useful chlorophyll surround his site.

Our man's last fully functioning torch, which he earlier dropped onto a concrete path while storing our saddles in a barn, no longer shines. Likely, its bulb is broken. His remaining torch produces an unreliable beam: a strange, intermittent, Morse-like eeriness punctuates the darkness. We leave him to it.

"Hey, let's go exploring," I suggest to Roamer some time after our man has retired.

"What a first-rate idea," he blurts out excitedly. "Did you notice? Pan has left a practically full bag of feed in the pen next to our paddock. Tonight, exceptionally, he has neglected to store it in a barn or shed."

You might have guessed already: Roamer can be tempted to escape if there's a real possibility of grabbing scrumptious food!

"Fancy extra pellets?" I ask.

"I'm constantly hungry for pellets," he replies, "even though Pan feeds us well. Alas, the pen has a sturdy, modern, metal gate: we can't kick that down."

"True," I reply. "But couldn't we lift the latch up with our heads? It's not closed properly anyway."

We easily push open the swinging steel gate with our muscular necks. Under cover of darkness, I rip open the flimsy, tempting bag with my right front hoof. Quietly – we mustn't let our man hear what we're up to – we munch our way through about three-quarters of a bag of feed. That's five days' supply! It doesn't matter that we accidentally spill a dozen mouthfuls onto the concrete floor. Stealthily, with full, close-to-bursting stomachs, we sneak back to our paddock.

An hour later, I'm suffering from incompletely digested pellets. I must burn off some of this energy buzzing about inside me, or I'll be ill. My heart is set on prolonged, uninterrupted exercise.

Behind our relatively small paddock, a much grander enclosure exists. Earlier this evening, we noticed from afar, across the fence, two unfamiliar equines grazing there. An adjoining gate links their field to ours; I would love to become acquainted. North-westwards, behind their pasture, stretches a wide, beckoning expanse of open, seemingly unfenced hillside.

"Let's escape into their field," I dare Roamer. "It's massive, and I fancy a canter. We could easily break down that old, fragile, wooden gate. We might even strike out for open countryside."

Roamer leans on the gate, which further encourages me. I kick out with my hind feet. It caves in instantly. The looped rope that earlier tied the gate to a rickety fence post now hangs loose. I nudge the fractured gate further, creating a narrow gap between gate and post hardly wide enough for us to squeeze through. We are free! If anybody complains, Roamer smashed it: I didn't help him.

Our man is oblivious to our clever breakout. Now we're having fun running about with a distinguished, thoroughbred mare and a tiny, outlandish Shetland gelding. There's just one drawback: that Shetland is ill-tempered. Possibly, he chases us repeatedly because he's jealous. "Who wouldn't be?" I hear you say, but ponies usually aren't jealous. More likely, he's attempting to protect his friend, a misguided notion since we don't intend to harm anybody. We do enjoy talking and listening to her, however.

Later on, when our man ambles over to assess how we are coping, as he does habitually, he realises we have escaped. He charges about the paddock frantically with his erratically performing torch, unable to figure out where we are on an almost moonless, virtually waned night. Next, from a distance, he scrutinises the entire perimeter fence yet fails to notice the battered wooden gate. Managing to pull from a bog his temporarily lost right boot, he gives up looking. Convinced we have broken out onto hilly escarpment – Roamer also pushed the road gate open, which might have confused him – our man telephones his logistics assistant. I listen: in this otherwise silent expanse, voices travel a great distance.

"The ponies have escaped," he tells her. "I've no idea where they've gone. . . . Both gates were open. We may have no expedition tomorrow. . . . It's impossible to search for them until morning. The farmer's not answering his doorbell, and there's no one else about who could offer to help search. . . . You say, 'Don't worry,' but they could be miles away, onto unfenced hillside, by tomorrow! In which case, I'll never catch them without help, and lots of it. . . . Yes, you're right. I can't do anything until first light."

"We are less than 80 yards from his tent," I snigger gleefully. "If only he knew!"

"Pan shouldn't get upset," whispers Roamer. "Surely he realises we'll not stray too far?"

In desperation, our man calls out our names three times, but we ignore him. Instead, we creep away to explore. We have fooled him!

From his tent, our man conceivably can hear the faint, intermittent thunder of hooves. We canter about with abandon for an hour or so. Thereafter, we decide to rest: it's getting terribly late.

Roamer and I remain silent. I suspect our man assumes we have roamed a vast distance from Cawfields Farm. Doubtless, he will have a sleepless night worrying where we are, but I'm not too concerned. I expect we'll be up to our withers in grief tomorrow morning.

23rd October – Walltown Crags, Great Chesters Roman Fort and Thirlwall Castle

Roamer:
Pan peers out of his tent at first light. He notices the broken gate immediately and then spots the Shetland pony, who is bothering Thorn again.

"So there you two are!" he cries, his voice unable to disguise sheer delight. "You can stay there until I've finished my breakfast."

"I bet he's relieved we haven't wandered far," whispers Thorn as Pan scrambles back into his tent.

The truth is we wouldn't leave him: we rely on him as much as he relies on us nowadays. Nothing will separate us for long.

Shortly after dawn, the busy Cawfields farmer rouses Pan.

"Your ponies are out!" he calls, oblivious to exactly what happened last night.

"Thank you, Nicholas," shouts Pan from inside his tent, doubtlessly enjoying the unintended irony.

The Shetland resents our presence, I decide. He repeatedly and persistently chases us away from his thoroughbred pal, who is having fun chatting with Thorn. We sprint about the enclosure to safety, avoiding each attack. We could keep this game up evermore, except that Pan might worry: such wasteful frolics could cause us to overheat or, much worse, injure ourselves.

Pan, who probably is unable to relax, hurriedly finishes eating. Before dismantling his shelter, he resolves to separate us from Nicholas's two equines. This job isn't particularly easy. He drags the battered gate wide open and, with delicate, painstaking manoeuvring, successfully herds all four of us into the grassy paddock, somehow sealing the gateway behind us.

The Shetland is now chasing us relentlessly, wildly, about our paddock. Hurry up, Pan, I'm thinking. I want this nuisance off my back. Pan sprints across the paddock and throws open the stout, metal gate to the yard enclosure. Thorn and I seize our opportunity. We dart into the yard at once, eager to avoid further confrontations. Luckily, Pan lunges forward, obstructing the gateway, preventing the Shetland from following. He ushers that annoying beast and his pal back into their designated hillside home and secures the shattered gate. Peace reigns.

"Ye-ee-ee-eh!" mutters Thorn, relieved that the chasing is over.

"I've been thinking," I tell Thorn eventually. "Perhaps we shouldn't blame the Shetland. "After all, we did invade his territory."

"Look at the torment you've caused me!" grumbles Pan, presumably conscious that our escapade has eroded precious travelling time. "There's no food for you two this morning."

Thorn isn't hungry anyway; I'm not hungry either. I am, however, slightly remorseful for making Pan unnecessarily anxious. He seems tired: it takes him over an hour and a half, I guess, to strike camp and pack our saddlebags.

Much later than Pan wished to leave, we are ready to rock and roll. Lee-Anne, Nicholas's wife, who is a veterinary, is about to drive off with their toddler child. Earlier, Pan had exhorted her to check us over. He approaches her now.

"They've stolen and eaten three-quarters of a bag of feed. That's not good, is it? I hope they won't be ill"

"They look all right to me," she responds, eyeing us briefly. "They haven't got colic. Where are you heading today?"

"Thirlmere Castle," replies Pan. "We should have left by now."

"Right, I'll leave you to it."

Pan needn't panic, that's what I recommend: we worked off most of the excess food cantering about last night. Mind you, I'm eager to stride west on a strikingly pure, sunny morning. I've bags of energy.

Leaving Cawfields, we set out for Burnhead, navigating around the northern shore of a disused quarry we came upon yesterday. From Burnhead, after crossing a small stone bridge over a stream, we head approximately north, away from the Wall, along a minor road towards Burnhead Moss. Less than 300 paces later, past the head of a spring and close to the northern boundary of a temporary Roman camp, lazy, mud-drenched cattle at a filthy gateway bar our approach to a drier field and the Military Way. Pan is tired; he's in no mood to mess about. We scuttle straight through the mire. The herd scatters before us. I'm no longer frightened of cows.

At once, we are shadowing the National Trail line, travelling at a brisk pace south-west towards east-facing Great Chesters Fort, a camp, asserts Pan, that Romans called Aesica.

"Perhaps this place refers to the Celtic god Esus?" he remarks.

The Military Way enters Great Chesters at its main, east gate. We try to avoid waterlogged ground whilst hugging the Wall from here.

Pan marvels at another engineering feat: "Fellows, did you know? Romans constructed an aqueduct to channel water from the north-east, via the northern edge of Caw Burn, to the fort."

"Is he talking to us again?" queries Thorn, who is feeling sluggish after overeating.

I ignore my friend. I am imagining there would have been plenty to drink in this watery landscape.

As I am contemplating what clever engineers Romans were, two walkers, travelling in the opposite direction, motor along the National Trail within 20 metres of our route. They are using specially designed walking poles similar to ski poles, a procedure which Pan calls "Nordic walking".

"Hello!" shouts Pan.

There's no response. He calls again. They don't appear to notice us. Twenty paces apart, heads downwards tilted, walking poles flailing, they are in a terrific hurry. Within five minutes of non-stop, ferocious activity, they have slipped beyond our horizon. Thorn is impressed: he describes it as "walking with attitude".

"Can anybody observe countryside properly, walking in such a single-minded, fitness-oriented manner?" I ask him.

"Why shouldn't walkers be concerned with fitness, a noble pursuit, rather than with countryside?" he replies, smiling at their antics. "Our man surely would appreciate that goal immensely."

Perhaps Thorn is right. However, humans who rush about, without ever pausing, might fail to savour – to see, hear, smell or touch, never mind taste – a unique, primitive landscape that unintentionally has hidden at least 1001 stories for future generations to uncover. Having said that, I bet even super-fit Nordic walkers rest occasionally to consider their surroundings.

At Great Chesters, Pan must decide which of two reconnoitred routes to follow. Should he choose the straight, westerly, upland route to Walltown? This option hugs the Wall line via Cockmount Hill Turret – where wild birds still may roost – and Allolee East Turret, near a former elder glade; a well-defined terrace marks the Way. Alternatively, should we take the easier, meandering, lowland route, 300 metres further south along the Vallum?

Just as Pan is considering, the camera operator telephones.

"Okay, Alan. I'll meet you at Walltown Crags in 1½ hours," confirms Pan.

I sense we are late for a filming rendezvous, the ground is boggy and Pan continues to appear fatigued.

"All right, boys," he announces, after deliberating. "Regretfully, I've decided we must take the Vallum route. There, we'll have to contend with only a lot of interested cattle and a few unlocked gates. We can follow the high terrace route on our return leg, when time won't be against us. It's something to look forward to."

Glancing upwards, I suppose there are difficult obstacles to overcome if we travel along the ridge as Pan had intended. A lowland track, still close to the Military Way, is possibly easier. Before we can proceed further, however, there's a consequential matter of two enormous thoroughbred horses at Great Chesters.

"They might be worth meeting," surmises Thorn impishly.

"Hey, they've spotted us," I babble excitedly.

"Na-ah!" yells Thorn when Pan drags us to a premature halt.

As Pan is wondering how we might enter and exit the horse

enclosure without mishap, the thoroughbreds' owners – a husband and wife – show up on cue, a remarkable coincidence.

"Give me a minute or two and I'll move the horses," offers the helpful woman, an intervention representing good luck for Pan but miserable luck for Thorn and me.

Four hundred metres to the north, on Cockmount Hill, the exacting Military Way course is easily observable. Our chosen Vallum trek, on the other hand, is leisurely, peaceful, with only occasional muddy sections to disturb our tranquillity. Lazily grazing cattle aren't interested in us: they are gentle, native beasts.

We arrive at Walltown's hill-and-road junction on time, thanks to the detour.

"Where's Alan?" wonders Pan. "He's not answering his 'phone."

We wait. I'm content: there's tasty grass about. However, perhaps a quarter of an hour later, our master is becoming impatient.

"Come on, boys. Let's go," he orders. "We daren't wait any longer."

With that, we are climbing slowly towards the hill track above Walltown, onto the Way. As we reach the track, a vehicle pulls up at the road gate 150 metres below. Alan alights, accompanied by a National Trail warden, a man who helps look after Hadrian's Wall Path. Though Thorn and I are fidgety and keen to keep moving, we wait again as they zigzag towards us loaded with Alan's equipment.

"Sorry I'm late," says Alan. "I was doubtful where you were. Happily, the warden offered me a lift from Walltown Crags Car Park."

"You would be much better off taking the road to the crags," suggests the warden.

"Thanks for your advice, but this is my planned route, along the Military Way," explains Pan.

"It's not far, about a kilometre, to the car park."

Pan holds his ground.

"We'll go this way, but thank you again."

Alan expresses his sincere gratitude to the warden, who heads downhill to his parked four-wheel drive.

"No doubt, the warden was trying to be extremely helpful by

suggesting we take the road," Pan tells Alan, "but we must at least attempt to follow our negotiated route whenever feasible, which traces, as closely as possible, the Way."

Alan agrees.

"Are National Trail wardens worried that we might walk too close to the Wall?" I ask Thorn.

"I don't believe so, though I may be mistaken," he admits, almost reassuringly. "Don't forget: according to our man, Hadrian's Wall is a World Heritage Site; I suppose one of their legitimate occupations is to guard and protect this monument's archaeology, particularly the Wall and Vallum."

"Perhaps some wardens are unaware that we and Pan are taking great care to avoid causing even the slightest damage," I reason.

"Over 2½ years ago," recalls Pan as we set off again, "I sent expedition plans to a representative of Hadrian's Wall Heritage. Unfortunately, we didn't discuss the possible link between native ponies and Hadrian's Wall."

"Was there any need?" wonders Thorn. "Surely, all humans who help to protect the monument will be aware of the relevant history?"

"Exactly!" I declare. "Without the assistance of our ancestors, this monument, including the Wall and earthworks, might not exist: building it would have been extremely difficult, if not impossible. How was stone transported from quarries, for example?"

"Hadrian's Wall Heritage is presently funded by One North East, North West Development Agency, Natural England and English Heritage," continues Pan. "It is about to become a charity, renamed Hadrian's Wall Trust, whose role is to manage this fortification, including the National Trail. Its remit is not only to ensure appropriate protection for present and future generations but also to enhance site access."

"Uninformed humans might assume, wrongly, that two pack ponies will cause erosion," I suggest to Thorn. "Actually, we're doing no harm. Surely everybody realises we are walking, not running? What's more, we aren't wearing shoes."

"Of course, ridden horses, and even pack ponies with shoes,

might damage this monument," he replies.

"Nobody should liken us to humans, either," I tell him indignantly. "Do we traipse on or over the Wall like yahoos? No! Do we leave litter? No. Do we habitually race through muddy places, rendering them muddier, ruining topsoil? We purposely avoid doing that. Do we rush about from place to place as fleetingly as our strong, agile legs will carry us and as if our lives depend upon arriving in the minimum time imaginable? No. Do we advance cautiously with understanding? Yes. Are we here for a higher purpose – to save our kind from extinction? Yes."

"You do go on a bit," asserts my friend, "though I'm inclined to agree."

We follow the Way, sweeping with the contour below Walltown Crags towards a Roman Army fort where a modern museum exists. I continue to reflect upon the range of human attitudes towards ponies on the Military Way.

"Am I suffering from mild paranoia?" I ask Thorn tentatively when we pause to allow Alan to capture craggy footage.

"I'm not certain what p-p-paranoia is, but I'd say it's simply a matter of human ignorance," whispers Thorn. "Let's not forget. We are houyhnhnms, ponies with the purest, noblest intentions and dispositions: we are incapable of acting or thinking like humans."

"I suppose we shouldn't care," I answer uncertainly, wondering what he means. "We are walking the Wall. Nobody shall impede us on our quest at this stage. That's what matters."

Thorn persists: "Do too few humans wish to understand a great deal about countryside?"

"Pan might be inclined towards that view," I declare.

As we leave the fort and continue walking, it occurs to me that my pack is heavier than usual. Am I carrying a lot of fresh supplies? My hooves hurt; I'd rather not drag myself a step further. Nevertheless, henceforth we halt only while Pan checks his compass bearing, almost immediately setting off again, through a gateway into a sloping field. We continue into a second field and then another. Eventually, we must cross a stream. All of a sudden, impressive remains of a twelfth-century castle rise proudly before us. Yes, it's rest time!

Thorn:

We've been travelling for over a week and a half and have been averaging, I reckon, about five miles a day. When the terrain or weather is more demanding, or when our man has arranged to meet people en route, we may be lucky to cover four miles a day. Don't get a false impression, though: this is no simple stroll. So far, no day has been trouble-free.

Since I am determined to write an honest diary, I confess: calamities are not Roamer's fault alone. Normally, my manners are immaculate. However, I do behave out of turn now and then. I have broken or helped to break two fences and two gates altogether, and not merely to obtain superior grazing! Do you blame me, though? I prefer wide, unfenced spaces on hillsides. Even so, I never roam far from camp.

Today, we leave Cawfields later in the morning than our leader planned, a consequence, I suspect, of our night-time caper. Our man isn't particularly happy: he slept so poorly last night; he says it was our fault. As you know, Roamer and I had a marvellous time racing about, burning off excess energy acquired through over-indulgence. Then, annoyingly, that silly Shetland pony accused Roamer and me of trespassing; he kept chasing us until our man separated us from him.

On a mellow, relatively unexciting afternoon, our man decides to rest outside a Roman Army museum. We stand at the site of Carvoran Fort. Unusually, it lies south of the Vallum and Wall.

"Romans named this fort Magna – the rock," ponders our man.

"Where is the fort?" asks Roamer.

"How should I know?" I answer. "Time and nature have buried it, most likely. And our man said locals stole much of the stone from the east, south and west walls to build houses centuries ago, long after Roman soldiers had departed Britain."

"I heard Alan and Pan talking," says Roamer. "From Segedunum, east to west, Romans built at least 16 Wall forts; archaeologists have identified several already. According to Mike, an archaeologist who Pan says works for English Heritage, one difficulty for humans is deciding whether to count Arbeia, at South Shields, Newcastle, as a Wall fort. Though Arbeia is not located alongside the Wall, it is definitely part of the Roman defensive system. Extra forts string along the Cumbrian coast. Apparently, Romans patrolled throughout Cumbria."

While we are resting, a kind, young woman, employed in the museum, offers cups of needed coffee to our man and Cameraman.

"Hey! I'm thirsty too," pouts Roamer. "Where's mine?"

"Boys, you'll get a drink soon," our man reassures. "There's a stream ahead."

Is he a mind reader? I'm beginning to believe so.

"I'm weary, thanks to last night's fun and games," confides our man as he sits on a wooden bench outside the museum's entrance, sipping his coffee and clutching Thorn's lead rope. "How are you?"

"I'll keep going as long as necessary," replies Cameraman.

Now what's happening? Two tourists, visiting the museum, are conversing with our man as Cameraman shoots more film. Please let's go, I'm thinking. Roamer and I are desperate for water.

Shortly, we leave the museum – owned by an archaeological charity called Vindolanda Trust – via its rear, hillside gate. We meander downhill, across the Vallum, roughly 200 yards south of the Wall. Because several parallel, gateless walls cross the Wall line, our single feasible avenue is via three non-aligned fence gateways. We zigzag on an approximate north-west heading, aiming to regain the Military Way before a steep descent to Holmhead, the hill's end.

"Somehow, I have managed to lose a new walking pole," announces our man forthrightly to Cameraman as we continue to zigzag. "I've no clue where," he adds, annoyed by his own incompetence.

The pole dislodged from my pack about 400 yards ago. I heard it fall as we descended a bumpy slope. He'll be lucky to retrieve it: our route since departing the museum wasn't distinctively marked.

"I must pay for a replacement," he moans, "and there's no time to backtrack."

Will he never learn? That's three expensive poles lost because he didn't guard them adequately. Over rough, up-and-down terrain, the forces of my gait combined with gravity will easily shake free all objects not tied securely to the saddle.

Approaching Holmhead, I am still contemplating lost pole craziness when I spot a stream, Tipalt Burn, which, I gather, arises from a one-time woodland plateau roughly 2½ miles north-east of here.

"Water!" I cry excitedly to Roamer. "This could be interesting."

We must ford this burn, which is less than three feet deep at its centre: an old, too narrow pedestrian bridge spanning the stream won't accommodate pack ponies. Leaving Roamer briefly with Cameraman, our man paddles across with only me in tow, pausing to allow me to have a cooling drink. Nonetheless, he appreciates that I cannot resist playing with water, so he tarries for mere seconds. Today, he's putting up with no nonsense, resolutely marching me to the far bank, water beyond his knees. Afterwards, he returns to collect Roamer. My pal halts halfway across, drinking slowly, deliberately slurping this cool, fresh beverage. He must be genuinely thirsty.

"Come on," commands our man when Roamer is loitering midstream, still slurping, a minute later.

As they continue to wade across, our man accidentally stumbles over unseen rocks, lunging sideways. He wrestles with a momentary loss of balance, determined to avoid plunging head first into the stream at its deepest spot. I expect he bargained for soaked boots, not a drenching.

Those boots must weigh heavily with cold, slopping water. Four unshod legs are definitely advantageous when crossing boulder-littered rivulets. Cameraman, needless to say, is lucky: he can use the footbridge.

Late afternoon finds us ensconced north of the Wall within Thirlwall Castle's grounds, our man's next appointed campsite.

Although our pleasant paddock has succulent, appetising grass, its size is limited.

"Look!" I clue in Roamer. "There's a small gap between gate and post. We could sneak away later to explore."

"Never mind 'later'," he replies. "Now's our best chance to escape, while our man is inside a barn locating our new supplies."

Roamer and I are busily planning this latest exploit when two young farmers appear carrying a huge metal gate and thick, coiled rope.

"What are Michael and Ian doing?" wonders Roamer, slightly alarmed by their unforeseen intrusion.

"How do you know their names?" I ask him.

"They introduced themselves to Pan earlier."

You will have noticed: I usually can't be bothered with names. I'm useless at remembering them, unlike Roamer.

I watch the farmers intently. What's going on?

"Oh, nay, nay, nay!" I shriek.

Expertly, efficiently, they bridge that gap. They have locked us in.

"What shall we do?" I wail, exasperated.

"You guys are not escaping tonight," vows our man, inspecting their handiwork when he returns.

"Oh, well," replies Roamer impassively.

Our man sets up his semi-geodesic green shelter in soft, mown grass beside considerable remains of the castle's north wall.

"I can keep an eye on you two from here," he gibes.

"And we can observe him, too," retorts Roamer. "When I'm able to track his whereabouts, I'm never apprehensive."

Our man's boots, never mind all five pairs of socks he possesses, are sodden. The air isn't sufficiently sun warmed, so how shall he complete his necessary drying task overnight?

"Michael, do you have any newspaper I can stuff into my boots?" he asks the farmer. "I need to dry them out by tomorrow morning. Unfortunately, I've no reserve pair. Thankfully, I have spare insoles."

"But no spare boots," teases Roamer. "You would expect any self-respecting traveller to have recovered his lost boot by now, wouldn't you, Thorn?"

The farmer reappears shortly afterwards with several newspapers.

By the time our man has unpacked everything, stowed our saddles in a barn and brushed us, it is well past our normal suppertime. I am weak through lack of nourishment, especially since he deprived us of breakfast. Ah, here come our nosebags, finally!

It's time to relax on a heavenly evening: our situation is mild, dry and peaceful. We have left several villages behind; Roamer calculates we are possibly past the halfway point of our mammoth expedition, though he's guessing. One conclusion is inescapable: there's no turning back.

Crossing the Irthing

24th October – A golf club and Chapel House

Roamer:

ALAN unloads his filming equipment on a dry, sunny morning, what you might describe as autumn's perfect rambling weather. Pan, meanwhile, is talking to somebody via his mobile 'phone.

"You've found my missing boot? . . . Terrific! . . . Please could you post it to Walby Farm Park? I'll pick it up when I camp there. . . . Thank you."

Pan, frowning, switches off his 'phone. Inexplicably, he is simultaneously pleased and dismayed.

"What's the problem?" inquires Alan.

"My mislaid boot has finally turned up at Row Hope Riding Centre. They've recently discovered where their dog hid it while I was saddling up a week ago."

"That's good news," suggests Alan.

"Yes and no," retorts Pan in an agitated tone. "I posted the other boot to my Leicestershire base three days ago! Shall I ever manage to reunite right and left boots? If and when the weather deteriorates, I might welcome their protection."

Alan is vaguely amused, but Pan isn't. Our leader can't forge ahead until his non-leather footwear dries out. Fortunately, the boots' breathable, artificial linings dry speedily, even in October.

Today, we intended to visit the primary school at Greenhead, a green watershed between Tipalt Burn and the River Irthing, but Pan reminded Alan yesterday: "Pupils have a half-term break this week, so there's no point. Who knows? Perhaps we shall be able to film there on our return leg."

No filming means an easier day for Thorn and me. Who's complaining? On the other hand, I'm disappointed because we'll meet no children.

Heading west from Thirlwall Castle, located, of course, at a gap in the Wall, we halt abruptly: a train crossing confronts us. Its swing gates are passable only if Pan removes our packs. Had he forgotten about this obstacle?

"I've no intention of unloading less than five minutes after leaving camp," he insists, studying his survey map. "Let's detour 200 metres north, along the cycle route beside the railway line, to Longbyre. Then we can double back via a path adjacent to the line's western margin. Can you manage it?"

"That's okay," replies Alan, who, because of his heavy load, would benefit most from not walking a centimetre further than necessary. "It makes no difference to me. I'll keep going for hours, even days when necessary."

From the outskirts of Longbyre, formerly the location of just a long shed, the main road allows us to regain Pan's originally intended route. He adjusts our harnesses in anticipation. We climb steadily up a short, extremely steep, gorse-packed hill over a narrow, twisting, hardly used trail onto Haltwhistle Golf Course. On top of the hill, by the ninth hole, I gaze east-south-east towards Tipalt Burn. Five kilometres away as the sparrowhawk flies, in the valley, at the junction of streams by a hill, sprawls the small town named Haltwhistle. What an excellent vantage point this is.

"So we've got permission to cross the course?" asks Alan.

"Yes, on condition that we follow its eastern margin, the Vallum," confirms Pan. "We mustn't encroach onto any putting greens, naturally. Interestingly, both Hadrian's Wall Path and another long distance walking route, the Pennine Way, cross this course."

Alan is filming again as we descend to the clubhouse and hence onto a private access road. A golfer, unloading a bag of clubs from his car, is interested in what we are doing. Upon noticing Alan's camera, he inquires whether Pan would care to interview him. Just now, however, interviews aren't part of our plan. Alan and Pan chat with him only briefly about the expedition: clearly, they are in no dawdling mood.

"I imagine it's not every day the golfer sees two Fell ponies teeing off," quips Thorn as we continue walking. "I don't suppose it's exactly par for this course."

Beyond the club's driving practise nets, more or less 100 metres further west along the access road, is Wall End Farm.

"Wall End isn't marked on my Ordnance Survey map," recalls Pan. "I discussed its absence in 2010 with a man named Ridley, the Wall End farmer. I've notified Ordnance Survey. Experience tells me that mapping mistakes are extremely rare, but this must be one."

We advance gently along an excessively muddy cattle track, the Stanegate, a Roman road south of the Wall. Then, without warning, at a left bend, we veer sharply from its course. Smartly, we cut across three wet, grassy fields of lazily grazing beef cows, on a route south of Chapel House Milecastle, towards Chapel House Farm, today's early destination. The two humans are stealing a long rest. I reckon they've earned it, although Thorn and I willingly would have walked further.

Thorn:

We have been waiting at Chapel House for about 20 minutes on a warm, sunbathed afternoon: there's nobody about. It is boring standing here, so I'm relieved when, at length, our man decides to begin unloading my pack.

Suddenly, an unrecognisable voice calls out.

"Hello there! I was working in a field when I saw you arrive."

"Hi, Jamie," our man shouts back.

"I like the look of Thorn," comments the young, fair-haired farmer approvingly. "He's my kind of pony."

"What about me?" whispers Roamer. "I'm as handsome as you any day."

"Your ponies can graze either with the sheep or in that large, empty field over there on the Wall line," offers the farmer, pointing. "Or they could stay inside."

"Outside is preferable," suggests our man. "The Wall line field will be perfect."

Undeniably, as you already know, we Fell ponies hate being indoors: we enjoy breathing fresh air and browsing unusual forage. Besides, cantering across a field is exquisite fun.

"How's the weather for you at the moment, Jamie, compared with last summer?" wonders our man.

"This is a good day," answers the farmer. "Mind you, it is windy; it's always windy here. I'll make a cup of tea for you and Alan while you finish unpacking."

"Jamie, what livestock do you farm?" inquires our man when the tea is ready.

"Three years ago, we moved to a hill herd of pedigree Galloway cows."

"Could Fell ponies do useful grazing work on farms in this area?" asks our man.

"If we received some Government payment to protect the genetics of the Fell pony, I would consider setting up my own herd," enthuses the farmer unexpectedly.

"What joyful news," interrupts Roamer. "This human wants to protect Fell ponies and give us grazing jobs."

I'm in a belligerent mood, so disagree: "Why do Fell ponies need a job? Why can't we be? Why won't they leave us alone?"

"Well, our brothers, sisters and cousins may not survive here in the north without work," says my friend. "Pony keep is expensive, according to Pan."

"We're not expensive," I assert. "Give me rough grazing on a wide-open hillside or common. How expensive can that be? And I'll be as happy as a small tortoiseshell butterfly dancing on a forest track in June."

I'm trying to talk with Roamer and listen to the human conversation at the same time, which is confusing even for an exceptionally intelligent Fell pony.

"How many Fell ponies exist in this area?" wonders our man.

"Very few," admits the farmer. "In years gone by, there were herds of 20 or 30 ponies within a 10-mile radius of here. The father of a friend of mine, who farms up the road, kept in the region of 30 Fell ponies but has only 2 or 3 now."

"We could easily pay for our keep," believes Roamer.

"How?" I ask. "We've no money!"

"Who needs money? We could support the work of land guardians wherever they require hardy, acclimatised ponies to help graze land in a special way."

"What do you mean?" I demand, confused.

"We could aid rare and endangered biodiversity to survive."

"Oh, I see," I tell Roamer, though I remain slightly fuddled.

Bluntly speaking, I'm not alone in my ignorance: Fell ponies rarely discover what is happening to their relatives. It has been so throughout our tumultuous history.

"We'll discuss it when we're alone," promises Roamer, who senses my unease.

Cameraman busily fiddles with his camera and tripod, a routine occurrence prior to interviews. It's all about distance, lighting and backdrop, I gather.

"Start talking, Jamie, whenever you are ready," he eventually calls.

The farmer is discussing the future of our relatives.

"Why doesn't Pan let us loose first," mutters Roamer. "I'm restless."

"There's no chance of that happening," I tell him. "Anyway, this conversation sounds interesting."

"If we could use Fell ponies to graze in a special way they would probably be a lot less hassle than cattle are," reflects the farmer. "And they would do exactly the same, if not a better, job."

"He's not wrong," insists Roamer. "We don't give our owners strife."

"Does it matter if a herd of hefted Fell ponies disappears for ever from a hillside?" inquires our man.

"What's 'hefted'?" whispers Roamer.

"Listen," I say. "We'll surely find out."

"Our hill sheep are hefted," reveals the farmer. "Hefting means they are attached to a particular area of land which is their home. They are born on the hill. They live on the hill. Just as you and I come home to where we live, sheep sense where home is; so do hill Fell ponies; you don't need fences to keep them in one place."

"That's true, Thorn," remarks Roamer. "I recognise my home. I'm homesick right now!"

"Your hefted sheep comprehend what to eat and where to acquire food in all seasons?" supposes our man. "And they've learned those skills over hundreds or thousands of years?"

"Absolutely" continues the farmer. "If you take a flock of sheep from its natural home, I don't understand how other sheep, with no knowledge of that area, will learn to live on the hill. Once you take a flock away from its hill, it's nearly impossible to reinstate hefting, to bring a new flock back to a particular area – unless you put fences up."

"Reinstatement could cost a great deal of time and money?" imagines our man.

"Yes," agrees the farmer, "but I am uncertain of the effect of taking Fell ponies away from their hefted areas. Could you re-establish a herd years later?"

"Aye! Can any human answer this question?" laments Roamer.

"I assume not," I confess. "I don't suppose anybody has bothered to investigate. Don't forget, though: we ponies are quick learners. So who knows?"

"Well," rejoins our man, "you might conceivably be in trouble once no mare exists that knows or remembers anything about a particular hill or common."

"If the grazing becomes unmanageable, or if we lose endangered wild species because Fell ponies aren't available to maintain habitats in good shape, it will be a disastrous outcome," warns the farmer.

"Humans shouldn't remove Fell ponies from their traditional

homes, from the habitats they protect," concludes Roamer.

Eventually, after considerable further discussion about our breed's future, the interview is over.

"Would you like to sleep inside the farmhouse tonight?" asks the farmer.

Unquestionably, our man cannot resist this invitation, bearing in mind his sleepless, somewhat muddy adventure two nights ago. Roamer will miss him tonight.

I am becoming impatient. Our man realises this, so he smartly releases us into our designated enclosure of succulent, not overly rich, grass.

"He-ee-ee-ee-!" shouts Roamer. "Free at last!"

On this sunny, if now late, afternoon, we can relax surrounded by fields of friendly cattle and sheep, but something's bothering me.

"When the farmer suggested that we might do an even better job than sheep, what did he mean?" I ask Roamer.

"That's complicated," he replies. "We are clever at preventing dramatic landscape change caused by undergrazing. We are also capable of grazing several habitat types in exact ways conservation scientists and land managers desire."

"I suppose that's true," I admit. "We do help maintain pleasant living conditions for many native wild species. We are helping to save natural beauty in its wondrous variety."

"Don't forget," adds Roamer. "We are able to keep invasive plants such as thistle, bramble and gorse at bay, plants which, of course, are needed by some birds and invertebrates but which may grow too prolifically. And, according to Pan, we also help prevent the homes of rarer native plants and animals, for example, curlews, honey bees and several butterfly species, from disappearing."

"In short," I conclude, happier because I understand, "we native ponies are essential to bolster the protection of upland and lowland wildlife that has existed in Britain for thousands of years."

"Precisely!" utters Roamer. "Now, please can we play?"

25th October – Gilsland, Willowford, Birdoswald and High House

Roamer:

"Is it time to be loaded up and carry on strolling?" I ask Thorn, yawning.

"Yes, we must get going," affirms Thorn cheerfully. "Here comes Pan with our morning pellets. I would prefer not having to eat out of a leather feeding bag, though."

"I don't mind nosebags," I tell him. "At least I can't spill or waste any; I even lick the bag out! However, why must we begin walking so early every day? I wouldn't mind a longer rest."

"You know why. Each new dawn brings less daylight than previously. And winter weather could creep upon us at any time."

Pan checks our fitness twice daily. He judges I am in perfect condition this morning. Truly, no part of me is sore, not even my girth, and my limbs don't ache. However, I'm disgruntled because today my pack will be heavier than usual: Pan has added extra supplies. He is lucky: he carries nothing much on his back.

I won't deny it: very occasionally, I do become frustrated and pine for home. Nevertheless, I always enjoy discovering new fields containing mouth-watering grasses and herbs, especially at night-time. Even better, when I feel homesick, Pan may offer me a special treat. Can you guess what my favourite is? It is roundish, sweet and crunchy. Afterwards, I cheer up and am able to carry on trekking.

On time, predictably, Alan's car trundles smoothly into the yard at Chapel House. Minutes later, he is carrying a camera, bag and tripod as we recommence our Way-following.

Towards The Gap, a cosy hamlet at the watershed of the Tyne and Irthing rivers, we are on higher ground than that of Hadrian's Wall.

"A detour is necessary from here," explains Pan. "Barbed-wire fences block travel directly along the Vallum between The Gap and Crooks, a winding valley."

We must climb in a south-westerly direction, across lush fields containing beef cows, to a narrow hilltop road south of the Wall, where a tiny windmill, turning at blistering speed, is generating farm electricity.

Leaving Lawn Top, a glade at the top of the hill, we take the quiet, north-westerly road towards Crooks. There, where this road bends sharply, we momentarily regain the Military Way. Crossing the Way – a stile bars our further, immediate passage along Pan's preferred route – we are at once into peaceful Gilsland, generations ago the estate of a man called Gille.

En route towards Gilsland School, we pause approximately 100 metres, 70 paces, east of a splendidly intact, visible milecastle at Poltross Burn, a tributary of the Irthing. A narrow walker's bridge spans the burn's wooded gorge at the Cumbria-Northumberland boundary. Pan already suspects that we can't cross the Vallum here.

"There's no way you'll get your ponies over that bridge to the milecastle," reports Alan after he has reassessed the situation at closer range. "The walkway isn't wide enough."

"You've corroborated what my reconnaissance indicated last December," replies Pan disconsolately. "Even if we could cross the bridge, a notably slim swing gate creates an almost impossible barrier further on, beyond a railway line. It's a pity because, interestingly, archaeologists have unearthed Roman horse equipment at the milecastle."

"That means our ancestors may have lived here," I declare.

"It would have been cramped living," suspects Thorn, who can barely see the milecastle's extremity from where we are standing.

"From the bridge, essentially the whole Wall and both turrets, Willowford East and West, are intact for 1½ kilometres," reckons Pan. "After crossing the burn, the Military Way follows the Vallum's north berm north-westwards for well over 500 metres. Soldiers must have had a backbreaking job constructing Hadrian's Wall here."

We have been standing at the entrance to a pedestrian tunnel which offers access northwards beneath the previously mentioned railway line. There's no choice: we trundle noisily through the echoing tunnel, our exit avenue to the main road. Westwards, roughly 200 metres along this road, stands locked and deserted Gilsland School: half-term isn't quite over.

"That's a shame," I lament again. "I've been looking forward to meeting more children for days."

Thorn doesn't answer: he's fully engaged, alert, guardedly watching cruising cars as we cross the road at Willowford Farm's entrance. We are back on the Way.

"Is this the place?" inquires Alan.

"Yes, through those gates beside the Wall," confirms Pan.

What's happening? At this moment, a young woman approaches. She strokes my head three times. She seems kind.

"Ah-ha-ha!" I sigh.

Pan recognises her: "Hi, Ruth. It's good to see you. Are you ready for the interview?"

"Here we go again," remarks Thorn dismissively.

"Never mind," I pipe up. "At least we can grab a rest. Non-stop plodding along the road from Lawn Top was quite arduous."

"At shows, I have met people from all over the country with the most beautifully turned-out Fell ponies," proclaims Ruth. "They obtained their ponies from the Cumbrian fells."

"Roamer, do you fancy attending a show?" chimes Thorn quietly.

"No, honestly," I reply.

"Me neither," says Thorn. "I would prefer to be roaming the uncluttered hill where I was born. Besides, shows are mostly for humans, not equines."

"I suppose we would meet other ponies," I remind him.

"That's true. Mind you, I suspect my owner wouldn't enter me anyway. Stallions, not geldings, usually attend shows, though I don't appreciate why."

Ruth is explaining: "Fell ponies that come from herds in Cumbria do jobs all over the country fantastically well. They are a brilliant, versatile pony."

"What jobs is she talking about?" asks Thorn.

"Riding, driving and jumping," I suppose. "My owner, Judy,

mentioned several other jobs too," I recall. "In any event, our relatives seldom assist wildlife at present: Simon told us so. And I bet there aren't dozens of pack ponies like us."

"The Fell pony is rare," continues Ruth. "It's on the Rare Breeds Survival Trust Watchlist. It receives lots of benefits from the Watchlist in terms of promotion."

Thorn is unsure which list Ruth is describing. Previously unencountered technical terms often baffle us, as you might imagine.

"I've not heard it mentioned before, either," I admit. "Ruth says it's a really useful bit of paper; it's a special list of pony and other native mammal breeds that could become extinct should humans not protect them properly. Ruth told Pan earlier that there were fewer than 1,500 Fell females left in Britain who could have youngsters."

"That still sounds like a fair number of mares," presumes Thorn. "Am I misguided?"

"Remember, it's the maximum throughout the country," I reply seriously. "How many of those mares live and roam freely outside, unfettered?"

"True," says Thorn. "Our man estimates that only about 12 of 22 remaining herds graze extensively throughout all or most of the year nowadays. And some of those herds contain rather a small number of ponies."

Ruth stresses that her Trust wouldn't be happy if any extensively grazing herds disappeared. She is adamant: breeders require practical help.

"Are we producing unwanted animals?" she wonders. "Breeders should obtain work for young hill ponies. They could be used to graze wildlife areas until they are fully grown, after which time breeders could sell them more easily for more money."

"She has a point," concedes Thorn. "Your owner reached a similar conclusion. And our man keeps emphasising that hardly any of our kind presently participate in wildlife conservation projects."

"It's frustrating when I hear people in Cumbria getting annoyed about the use of Exmoor ponies to graze habitats," argues Ruth. "What we need is one Fell pony breeder to stick his neck out and say,

'This year I'm not going to send every foal to the October sale. I'll send some to a person who needs his land grazed to help wildlife and see how it goes.' I have offered conservation grazing opportunities for Fells, but no one has taken me up on it."

Conservation living would suit Thorn and me. We dream of grazing across hills, tasting a myriad of wild foods, no man or beast disturbing us.

"To varying degrees, modern-day herds may be related to those grazing the northern fells at the time of the Roman invasion," suggests Pan. "Over many generations extensively grazing herds have memorised seasonal edible plant species. Are there differences today between these ponies and completely domesticated Fell ponies?"

"There are bound to be differences between hefted and other Fell ponies," agrees Ruth.

We hill ponies are indisputably distinct. Would lowland cousins be able to cope with our winters? Could they live high up? Would they know where to acquire wild food in winter? Could they search out natural hollows and vegetation that provide shelter from storms? I say no, not most of them.

"Are they still nattering?" bleats Thorn, a short while later, rousing abruptly from a brief doze. He can sleep standing up at any time of day.

"Yes," I confirm. "Now they are talking about a fatal genetic disease that some Fell foals might inherit. Scientists verified its existence several years ago. If a colt foal receives a dose of a defective gene from both his dam and sire, he can't fight off common illnesses."

"Which illnesses?" asks Thorn, stretching, interested.

"Any illnesses, even a common cold," I tell him. "Scientists reckon the foal definitely will die within 16 weeks of birth. It's the same for filly foals."

"We haven't got anything wrong with us, have we?" he drools, concerned.

"No, Thorn. Otherwise, we'd be dead," I point out.

Still half asleep, he nods as he registers this obvious truth: "Right. That makes sense. I'm glad we're alive, Roamer."

"I've had a thought," I say. "Is this the same genetic problem that Stuart, the veterinary scientist, talked about?"

"Yes, you could be right," he replies.

"When a foal receives a dose from only one parent, he or she remains well and lives a normal, healthy life," I remind him. "Even so, breeding mares or stallions with a single dose could bestow that single dose onto their own foals."

"Oh, I vaguely remember," says Thorn. We haven't received even a single dose.

"We are clear: we've had no dose," I confirm. "A pony with a single dose of this defect in his genes is a carrier. This rule applies equally to stallions and mares."

Pan seeks Ruth's opinion on questions that Stuart has answered.

"Should breeders test all ponies that might carry the faulty gene? Should breeders be told the name of every carrier?"

"It is up to the Fell Pony Society to decide," replies Ruth.

Thorn, who now has woken up fully, is thinking hard.

"Roamer, I forget. What are they doing about it?"

"Scientists have designed a genetic test," I tell him, "which they carry out in a laboratory, to identify which ponies are carriers."

"Does that mean ponies must go to the laboratory to be tested?"

"No, silly!" I bark. "Don't you recall what Stuart said? They remove a few hairs from your mane and test those."

"Oh, I wondered why I had an insignificant bald patch," moans Thorn.

"You don't have: it's in your imagination," I retort, exasperated.

At this point, I'm convinced part of his brain hasn't escaped from dreamland.

Thorn:

This mild, sun-drenched, mid-autumn day, we arrive at Willowford Farm, an aptly named ford, via a straight farm track hugging the Wall for about 700 yards. On the way, we sight two turrets – Willowford East and Willowford West. The Wall, which is largely intact here, cascades majestically against the contour, down a steep slope, to a meadow flood plain of the meandering River Irthing.

We twist and turn through meadow gateways and towards a modern footbridge that nestles another 270 paces, I suppose, along the river's eastern bank.

"In Roman times, a Military Way bridge stood intact nearby," announces our man. "Its eastern buttress is now about 70 metres from the river. Therefore, the river's course must have changed gradually over centuries. Remains indicate the line of the Way."

Our man must unload both packs at an otherwise impassable swing gate by the footbridge. Once through the gateway, he speedily replaces them. Nevertheless, he seems frustrated.

"I planned to ford the river at its shallowest point," he briefs Cameraman, "upstream past a wooded area, to avoid this swing gate. Sadly, my plan has been thwarted: we would need to cut through a barbed-wire fence to access the river. Naturally, Willowford Farm owners would prefer me not to do that."

Cameraman is sympathetic. Roamer and I, however, don't care that much: we have become accustomed to holdups.

"Roamer, what's your judgement?" I ask pointedly.

"What?" yawns Roamer, relaxed and seemingly oblivious to our situation.

"Well, he might need to cut the wire," I remark. "How else shall we get across? Then again, the river's deep and fast-flowing past this bridge: perhaps it's too dangerous, though I'd love to splash about."

"I'm for an easy life," frets Roamer. "It does look near impossible to cross here."

Hey, where's our man leading me? He's expecting me to walk over the bridge. I'm not keen: I've never encountered a construction like it before; in between the steps are huge gaps of air; I see fast flowing water below.

"Oi-oi-oi," I whinny to Roamer. "What's he doing now?"

In fact, he's lifting up my right foreleg. Let it alone, I'm thinking initially. Then I comprehend. He wants me to place my right hoof onto the first step. Here I go, putting my trust in him. I venture onto the bridge. There's nothing to it really.

"Well done, Thorn!" praises our man.

"He's a fast learner," observes Cameraman.

"It will be safer to move the ponies across one at a time," explains our man to Cameraman, who is struggling to film me whilst minding Roamer. "The bridge is slippery in places."

Once I have traversed the bridge, our man ties my lead rope to a wooden gatepost. Then he recrosses to collect Roamer. My companion skips over effortlessly.

"All right, so you found it easy," I tease Roamer gently. "That's because you watched me. I dared go first!"

Across the meandering Irthing, we reach uninhabited Underheugh Farm, a low, projecting glade at a river bend. Immediately, we begin to climb a steep track up a grassy bank towards Birdoswald Fort.

At the top of the bank is Harrow's Scar Milecastle, an altar on a rocky cliff, which Romans dedicated to Silvanus, the spirit of the woods. Roamer remembers that the Turf Wall began here and ended at Bowness-on-Solway, our westernmost destination. When Romans rebuilt the demolished Turf Wall using stone, between our present location and Wall Bowers Milecastle they realigned it northwards; up to 10 layers of Wall stones are still visible.

A gentle stroll westwards brings us quickly to the fort's remains.

"Romans called this fort Banna – the horn or peak built on a promontory," notes our man.

That was a tough climb to Birdoswald, high above the River Irthing, I am thinking. Luckily, our man is aware of everybody's exertions.

"Come on, Alan. I need a drink," he gasps as he marches us into the fort's courtyard, where a coffee shop is open.

No tourists are about. We pause to rest. A sociable young woman who serves in the shop comes to admire us, but nobody's offering Roamer or me any food.

"The Turf Wall and ditch went through here," believes our man. "Archaeologists have concluded that Romans made the fort of turf and timber at first, but they subsequently rebuilt it in stone. Evidence of a Blacksmith's workshop was found in the north tower."

"Which proves Roman ponies must have been here," deduces Roamer. "Can you imagine that, Thorn?"

"We are not supposed to set foot inside the grounds of Birdoswald Fort," remarks our man.

"Why not?" queries Cameraman, puzzled by this statement.

"English Heritage manages the fort and surrounding fields. It wouldn't grant us access to the Vallum here. Consequently, we must travel by road for at least half a mile. In fact, I couldn't obtain admittance to property under its stewardship anywhere along the Wall."

"Is there a reason?" wonders Cameraman.

"Possibly, its decision-makers are perturbed that we would create an undesirable precedent," replies our man.

"What's a precedent?" asks Roamer.

"I'm not sure," I admit. "After our man undertakes this journey, I guess others might attempt to copy him: they might fancy negotiating the Military Way with horses or ponies. Perhaps English Heritage would prefer not to encourage equine activity on this monument."

"Why might that be true?" inquires Roamer naively.

"Our man says that English Heritage's job is to protect the historic environment," I tell him. "I suppose policy-makers may be concerned that horses might damage the monument irrevocably."

"Well," insists Roamer, "if other pack ponies, especially Fells, aspire to venture with extreme care in our footsteps, who could deny them, assuming, of course, that landowners give consent?"

I agree. What harm will occasional, unshod ponies do, if their keepers walk respectfully over only dry, hard ground along the Military Way? On the other hand, humans too often fail to follow monumental rules, even rules they have created.

"Mind you," adds Roamer casually, "a pony would need to be fearless and insane to contemplate such an undertaking, especially after hearing our stories."

Coffee time is over. We are again outside the fort, relaxed, about to begin our road slog, unaware of lurking trouble. As our man attempts to lead me forward, I realise that I have somehow managed to entangle my bridle headpiece with a slim gatepost. I cannot move my head easily.

"Ai-ai-ai!" I shriek, attempting to let him know, but it is too late.

I turn my head quickly in response to our leader's initial movement, tugging fiercely at the headpiece, pulling free but inadvertently ripping the leather. He examines the damage.

"I suppose repairs have been added unexpectedly to tonight's agenda," he tells Cameraman ruefully as we set off.

He's worrying unnecessarily: it was a minor accident, a negligible tear. He must exercise greater care in choosing where I should stand.

Getting back to the archaeology, our man obviously has consulted survey summaries and the latest maps to identify, approximately at least, where Romans placed every milecastle and turret.

"Beyond the Stone Wall's next turret rests High House Milecastle," he asserts, "which Romans built in wood on the Turf Wall but which, uniquely, they never replaced with stone. Between Harrow's Scar and there, the Vallum has no north mound, possibly because of limited space south of the Wall due to the Irthing. Instead, builders moved Vallum ditch dug-out entirely onto the south mound."

At High House Milecastle, we leave the road through a field gateway before heading approximately south, across the line of an invisible Stone Wall, towards the Vallum. About two hundred yards from the gate, we head west again. Now, it appears, we are following the original Turf Wall line.

"When Romans later demolished the Turf Wall in this vicinity, replacing it with stone, they apparently threw short sections of the turf rampart into the Wall ditch," remarks our man, who is trying, unsuccessfully I suspect, to spot surviving remains of the Turf Wall.

Hugging the Military Way, we saunter by gentle, drowsy cows belonging to High House Farm, today's moderately high destination at less than 500 feet above sea level. High House's farmer, a woman named Hilda I believe, though I can't be certain, is expecting us.

"Hello," she calls to our man. "You've made it. Good! I heard through the local grapevine that you were in this vicinity. Would the ponies enjoy some hay?"

Yes, please, we would. We'll dispose of whatever you can spare.

I gobble up my hay and then notice that Cameraman mysteriously has vanished from view. He resurfaces some considerable time later, after sampling the farmer's suppertime feast.

"I couldn't eat any more," he tells our man. "That was simply great!"

"Would you prefer to sleep inside the house?" the farmer asks our man as Cameraman departs. "It's going to be extremely cold tonight."

He gratefully accepts her invitation, adding, "First, though, I'll release the ponies and stow my gear."

"Hey, Roamer!" I chirp excitedly. "He's letting us loose in a vast hillside field. It's huge compared with our usual overnight camps."

"Shall we trot off and explore?" suggests my friend instantly.

Much later, perhaps two hours after we begin grazing, on a starless, moonless evening, no earthly light is visible from our vantage point. Suddenly, muffled voices startle me. Two shadowy figures, guided by a narrow torch beam, eventually draw closer. I recognise the farmer and our man. They lurch by, pushing a wheelbarrow with difficulty, upon which they have placed a precariously balanced square, wooden board. Inevitably, the board slides off sideways. They pause to rebalance it. They've come to repair temporarily a perimeter fence that cordons us from the road.

"I'd be bothered they might get out," confides the farmer.

"So would I," declares our man. "They are experts at escaping from fields, but this will hold them."

They heave and strain, successfully sealing the damaged roadside fence in no time. Our man thanks his relieved companion as they push the empty barrow homewards.

Moments afterwards, we are alone again, among the peaceful solitude and blackness of High House. I dare say we wouldn't have attempted to escape: there's plenty of space and tasty grazing here. Nothing else shall disturb us tonight.

Baskets, barding and a quarry: the re-enactment

26ᵗʰ October – Combe Crag and Quarry Side

Roamer:

THIS exquisite, sunny morning, we are grazing about 300 paces from the farmhouse and are in no particular hurry to leave. Consequently, Pan takes considerable time to collect us and lead us to Hilda's yard.

"Get along, boys," he encourages. "I anticipate an exciting day ahead. Wait and see."

After our usual breakfast, Pan hastily harnesses us up. Alan, eager as ever, breezes in early, before we are ready, giving him time for a relaxing cup of tea with Hilda.

"I'll walk with you along the Vallum, to my boundary with Lanerton Farm," offers Hilda.

"I would appreciate that," replies Pan, possibly mindful of his need to navigate precisely on a busy day.

Choosing an optimal roadside vantage point, Alan films us as we continue to trace approximately the original Turf Wall line between road and Vallum, metres from the course of the Military Way, towards where Appletree Turret existed. At the next road gate, Hilda shakes Pan's hand – she looks forward to seeing him again, during the return journey – and then trudges smartly off to feed her hungry cattle. What a considerate woman she is.

We continue effortlessly, initially heading south via a track leading to Lanerton, the homestead in a glade. Soon, however, we leave this track, turn west towards Wall Bowers Milecastle – where the Stone Wall once more follows the Turf Wall line – and eventually regain the minor road. Here, Pan glances at his map.

"Boys, are you ready? Let's move," he urges. "We've road work ahead, alongside the Wall, and we're behind schedule."

"Behind schedule for what?" I quiz Thorn. "Humans are often in a hurry for no reason in particular."

"Beats me," he insists, sighing impatiently, "but all at once we're hoofing it at a fierce pace. Keep up."

"We've no alternative to the road," Pan informs Alan. "Nearby landowners have refused to give us access to the Vallum."

At this moment, sheep hiding behind a bush spook Thorn. I am ill prepared for his consequent, unannounced sidestep. He pulls too strongly on our connecting strap, ripping it even further.

"Luckily, a new connecting harness is waiting for us at Quarry Side Campsite," comments our leader matter-of-factly as he carries out an emergency repair. "Roger, one of my Leicestershire saddlers, posted it there two days ago."

We pause briefly at Combe Crag Wood.

"For the re-enactment," reasons Pan, "we shall retrace our steps, with wicker baskets, to this spot. First, though, we must hurry to Quarry Side, where our baskets are stored."

"What's a re-enactment?" wonders Thorn. "What does our man expect of us now? I suppose we'll be the last to find out, as usual."

Swiftly, purposefully, we stride past the remains of a turret near Meg's Well, which refers to somebody named Meg Merrilies. Ignoring the turn-off to Gunshole, originally Gunni's hill, we hurry beyond the turret at Leahill – the hill of a woodland clearing – and then hasten from Bankhead Milecastle to Banks East Turret.

En route, Pan reveals that he failed to obtain permission to access land from Combe Crag Wood to Bankshead Farm via Wallholme Farm. Wallholme lies roughly 650 metres south of the Wall, adjacent to the River Irthing.

"I considered detouring from Gunshole," he tells Alan, "but

negotiating access along this section of the monument has proven to be unusually difficult."

Presently, walking at our fastest non-stop pace, we approach Quarry Side, three kilometres west-south-west of Combe Crag, the valley rock. Quarry Side's owner, an ex-farmer named David, greets us affectionately.

"You've made it, as you predicted!" he congratulates Pan. "Your ponies can stay in our new campsite field tonight."

David admires us close up.

"They look tremendous," he tells Pan.

We are tremendous; Thorn and I never doubt it.

Effortlessly Pan detaches our packs, but he doesn't remove our saddles. What's he up to?

"May I have the baskets?" requests Pan.

"Yes, certainly," says David enthusiastically. "They're safely stored in the garage. They arrived by post 24 hours ago."

Pan unpacks four straw-coloured, bucket-sized wicker baskets from two sealed, cuboid, brown cardboard boxes. He also retrieves two natural-fibre ropes and something resembling a strange-looking horse coat.

Thorn turns around: his acute sense of curiosity is obvious.

"Have you any idea what those baskets are for, Thorn?" I ask.

"No, but I bet it's something to do with us," he decides.

I am never jealous, of course, but I look on, baffled, as Thorn becomes the centre of attention. Pan places the coat, or perhaps it's a cloak, over Thorn's back and head. He guides my pal's sensitive ears gently through two holes at the head end's cusp. Thorn doesn't react: he's sleepy-eyed. The cloak fits admirably over his saddle, but I can't resist smirking. He does look silly wearing this unfashionable coat – you might assume he is modelling it – made of brown sackcloth with red, sown trim and, atop the saddle, a central rectangle of grey, waterproof fabric.

"Stop laughing," demands Thorn, upon sensing my reaction.

"Sorry, but I can't help it," I quip. "You look incredibly strange! Are you particularly cold?"

Meanwhile, David is listening as Pan describes existing archaeological evidence surrounding Thorn's garment: "Thorn is 13¼ hands tall. On average, Roman pack ponies were, I believe, about an inch, 2½ centimetres, shorter; Roman leather workers would have made coats for slightly smaller, less stocky, thinner-legged ponies than Thorn. We reconstructed the horse cover as accurately as possible using precise dimensions taken from archaeological drawings. A Leicestershire master saddler, Tony, made it. Archaeologists refer to this cover as 'barding'."

"Where was the original found?" asks David.

"Leather evidence has been discovered on the Stanegate – at Carlisle and Vindolanda – and at additional Wall locations. Roman saddlers possibly stitched together nine goatskins to create the original cover. We chose sacking instead, which is much cheaper than leather, as this was our first reconstruction attempt. The cover's central section, which fits over the saddle, is made from thick, cotton-based fabric."

"Interesting," says David, who seems engrossed.

"What's the Stanegate?" asks Thorn, beginning to pay attention.

"Pan says it's a Roman stone road that crosses Britain at its narrowest point, from the River Tyne to the Solway Firth," I tell him. "Romans built it about half a century before Hadrian built his Wall, in order to link their forts at Corbridge, to the east, and Carlisle, which is ahead of us, westwards. Before we reached Chapel House Farm, Pan mentioned that Romans built Vindolanda – their 'white expanse' or 'shining lawn' – about midway along the road's length, perhaps upon snow-covered ground, perhaps upon farmland. Oh, I have just remembered something else. Carlisle was a Roman fortified town called Luguvalium, the place of Luguvalos, the stronghold of Lugus, a Celtic god."

Thorn frequently succumbs to boredom easily, as everybody knows. However, even he has concluded that archaeology is, on occasion, spellbinding.

Pan continues to describe the cover: "There is no universal agreement on whether Romans made this barding for a cavalry horse, a packhorse or a mule. Although I might be easily misled, I believe they may have constructed it for a pack animal, possibly a pony. Four slits in the centre of the barding appear to fit over four horns that a Roman saddle maker would have attached to a saddle. Archaeologists describe these slits as 'ansata shaped'. Four attachment rings on top of Thorn's packsaddle represent the horns, as you can see. Notice that the ansatae fit over the rings. I based the size and shape of the rings partly upon the size and shape of previously discovered small, leather pockets. Romans attached a pocket over each slit in the original barding, but I haven't reconstructed the pockets."

David, who is still intrigued, examines the barding.

"These four ansatae form a rectangle," explains Pan, pointing. "On each side of Thorn's saddle, the distance between front and rear ansatae, and therefore between front and rear rings, is exactly 32 centimetres. At the saddle's front and rear, the distance between left and right ansatae, and therefore between left and right rings, is 29 centimetres. Until this moment, the reconstructed barding and saddle haven't been matched."

"Your saddle must have taken some making," presumes David. "Is it an accurate copy of what the Romans used?"

"Possibly, but I'm doubtful," responds Pan. "Construction was largely guesswork: interpreted evidence is presently scant and inconclusive. I suppose the saddle is as accurate as possible, based upon meagre shreds of archaeological evidence I could gather, 'dig up' if you like from archives, including a frieze from Pompeii in Italy, preserved by the AD 79 Vesuvius eruption. First, we reconstructed the saddle pommel from a tempered iron pommel discovered in 1938 during an excavation of Stane Street, a Roman road built before AD 70 between Londinium and Noviomagus, now called Chichester. Although archaeologists have catalogued the pommel officially as a Roman artefact, I am uncertain whether it is contemporary with the building of the Wall and, indeed, whether it is an authentic Roman pommel. We measured its dimensions precisely. Reconstruction, a duplication using steel, required several mathematical calculations; sometimes, we needed to employ trial and error to recreate the original shape exactly. Then we made, also from steel, plausible saddle rings – an equivalent of what archaeologists refer to as 'horns' – and the most probable cantle. Ring construction took into consideration what might be two horn attachment holes in the original iron pommel; significantly, perhaps, those holes are 29 centimetres apart. I also examined the shapes and sizes of Roman contemporary iron artefacts, particularly metal rings. A skilled metallurgist, John, at Uppingham in Leicestershire, forged each piece from my drawings. We spent three weeks getting everything right."

"That's a lot of figuring out," I tell Thorn quietly. "You should feel privileged to wear it."

"Afterwards, Tony reconstructed the saddle frame using beech wood," continues Pan. "He fashioned the saddle's steel rivets by hand, according to specifications provided by hand-made iron rivets attached to the Stane Street pommel. We aimed to duplicate the sizes and positions of rivet and attachment holes indicated on the iron pommel. We then used these dimensions as a template for the cantle. Then master saddler Chris at Southport, a leading British expert on making Roman cavalry saddles, added the leather, padding and harness buckles to the frame. Another Leicestershire expert saddler, Kelly at Melton Mowbray, made the harness by copying faithfully my British Army packsaddle's straps and fittings: I couldn't ascertain, within the available time frame, what Roman packsaddle harnesses looked like, and I dared not risk instability."

"So, it was a team effort?" concludes David.

"Yes, it was, definitely. And don't forget Roger, a saddler who lives near Countesthorpe in Leicestershire. He cleverly reconstructed my Roman saddlebags based upon etchings on Trajan's column in Rome. They fit the saddle remarkably well. And this barding isn't a bad fit either, I'd say, bearing in mind that Roman ponies were smaller."

"No straps on the barding?" observes David.

"No, there weren't any, according to leather evidence at Vindolanda and Carlisle," confirms Pan. "Oh, look. Thorn has shaken it off his ears: they are so sensitive; it was irritating him.

Unfortunately, we have made the ear openings without pockets; Roman barding had a wide pocket, a glove, for each ear, with stitched slits at the glove's base, which allowed the openings to expand easily to fit the pony's ears. Our openings don't have slits. Therefore, I suspect, they may be marginally too narrow for Thorn. Come on, Thorn: you're not following the plan."

Pan gently rearranges the barding. Thorn again shakes his head vigorously, again releasing the barding's grip on his ears. Hypersensitive Thorn still dislikes anything or anybody, even Pan, touching his ears; Pan knows this. Besides, my pal was attempting to have another nap.

"Now, this is the point," continues Pan eagerly. "I would like to propose tentatively, perhaps contrary to expert opinion, that the original barding may have been a heat blanket. Evidence suggests it possessed a cloth or linen liner once upon a time. When Roman builders of the Wall – not forgetting milecastles, turrets, forts, bridges and roads – broke off from their labours in the middle of a cold day to eat and rest, possibly they wouldn't have unsaddled their pack animals. They might have placed barding over the saddle to prevent the pony's body from cooling too rapidly, thereby minimising any risk of illness. A blanket over the saddle allows better air circulation: recent Australian research has shown that the most effective type of heat blanket does not sit directly onto the pony's skin."

"It is quite a good fit," confirms David. "He's at home with it, isn't he?"

Thorn yawns contentedly. His barding is so warm he's dozing off.

"If Romans did manufacture this barding as a heat blanket, it was probably required only in winter," theorises Pan. "For this reason, the archaeological evidence may have been preserved in relatively good condition. Who knows?"

"That would make sense," says David.

"Thorn, are you happy with it?" chortles Pan. "You're not concerned, are you? Come here."

Pan strokes Thorn's nose.

"Hai-ai-ai!" gasps Thorn, lifting his head, surprised. "What's going on?"

"Oh, I'm sorry Thorn!" says Pan. "I didn't realise you were nearly asleep."

Pan gently removes the barding, stores it away and then silently studies the wicker baskets and a pocket reference book.

"Of course I was asleep," confesses Thorn to me the moment we are alone. "His blanket's marvellously cosy. I was having a fascinating dream. I was travelling with a wild herd. You were there."

At length, Pan judges that he has attached two baskets correctly to each of our saddles using his specially made, natural fibre ropes. Supposedly, he has employed a diamond hitch knot, as his Army Manual of Horsemanship, Equitation and Animal Transport describes. In fact, the baskets aren't secure, as he shall discover.

"This 1937 edition of the manual is rare," he tells David, "but it's evident, from Trajan's Column, that Romans used the same diamond hitch nearly 2000 years ago to attach loads to mules on the march."

David's neighbour, Dan, who lives opposite Quarry Side, arrives and introduces himself. He has studied his local quarry's history.

"Our baskets are similar in size to today's builders' buckets," explains Pan. "Expert basket weavers constructed them as closely as possible to those etched on Trajan's Column in Rome. A solitary distinction is that a Roman basket did not have a grip hole beneath its top lip. Instead, it had a slightly deeper rim, which road builders could grip strongly: stone-filled baskets were heavy. The single grip hole in each of our baskets allows easy handling."

Dan is admiring the Roman packsaddle.

"What amazes me is this," he reflects. "Assuming the Romans got this far in saddle design, why couldn't they think up the idea of stirrups?"

"That's an intriguing question," admits Pan, "if we are talking about Roman cavalry horses rather than pack ponies. We shouldn't forget, of course, that this present design is an experimental proposal: it represents one hypothesis."

"Are your halters and bridles authentic?" asks Dan.

"No, no," confirms Pan. "I would need to carry out extra

archaeological research. Besides, bridle bits that I'm using are among the best, state-of-art, non-leverage training bits: they are much gentler on ponies' mouths. This is especially true because, in almost all situations, including training, I attach my lead rope to the bridle's chinstrap ring, not to the O-rings. Roman bits are severe and seem to me to be cruel. Indeed, even most modern snaffle bits hurt ridden and driven horses: they affect the maxillary, inferior alveolar, infraorbital and lingual nerves. Ideally, I would prefer to use bridles without bits, but I've opted for slightly increased control in case of unforeseen traffic emergencies."

Why must I wear a bit? I'm walking behind, so it shouldn't be essential. Admittedly, it never hurts because any pressure comes from Thorn, but periodically it annoys me. All right, I accept that, just because Pan hasn't needed to guide Thorn or me out of trouble, it doesn't mean he'll never need to. I'm just saying he could have designed the bridles better – without bits.

Pan questions Dan about a nearby causeway.

"It runs south from Coombe Crag Farm," certifies Dan. "The Romans quarried both sides of the causeway. There is a narrow strip, 20 to 30 feet wide, that runs down to the River Irthing. However, I understand much of the quarrying was done from the south side of that river because of sheer, rocky cliffs."

"I'm familiar with the location," acknowledges Pan.

"It's obvious that pieces of stone for the Wall were broken from these cliffs either by fire or by bits of water-swollen wood," explains Dan. "Resulting blocks of stone would have been carried to the crossing point before being carried up the steep incline, via the causeway, to the actual site of the Wall."

Alan, who often judges time by the sun's position, reckons we're further behind schedule. Perhaps he and Pan should not have paused for tea and irresistible cakes prepared by Elizabeth, David's wife, who runs a guesthouse. We arrived at Quarry Side over an hour ago. Now, amidst an energetic flurry that even Thorn didn't anticipate, Pan is marching us briskly back towards Gunshole and Combe Crag Wood. Alan, accompanied by Dan, shadows us closely in his car, riding his clutch in a stop-start, stop-start action.

"Are we going home?" I ask Thorn, disoriented by Pan's 180-degree direction change.

He doesn't answer. Thorn is uneasy about his right-hand-side basket, which is hanging loose. We stop. Pan tries to fix it. Approximately 170 paces later, we pause again: Thorn's other basket is loose. Thorn isn't particularly bothered any longer. Pan, on the other hand, is becoming increasingly exasperated: he dislikes messing about.

Reaching a turnoff to the right, we head steeply downhill to Gunshole. This baffles me. What's going on? At Gunshole, Pan begins loading our baskets with pieces of stone lying in untidy piles. I still fail to comprehend fully his intention.

"The Gunshole owner has given us permission to borrow these," confirms Pan. "They formed part of either the original Wall or a milecastle. Local landowners pilfered Wall stone centuries ago, in the wake of the Roman Army retreat, to build their farm dwellings."

"Some locals plainly didn't respect Roman craftsmanship," I remark.

"Well, I suppose we must be grateful so much of Hadrian's Wall remains standing," retorts Thorn. "Throughout the history of our equine ancestors, humans have built up walls to divide peoples and then, later on, torn them down: our man says so."

Pan reattaches the baskets. He didn't tie perfect diamond hitches at Quarry Side, so he consults his manual once more. Not soon enough for Alan's liking, we are ready to begin the climb to the road. Loaded to half capacity with Wall stones, I am unperturbed: my abnormal pack weighs a trifle.

"We need to get a move on," warns Alan. "It will be too dark to film in another hour."

I sense Pan's sudden urgency. He encourages us to get going. He isn't panicking, not quite, but he'll not postpone the quarry visit until tomorrow: we'll be a whole day behind schedule.

He pleads with Alan: "We must film this re-enactment today at all costs. Planning took weeks; we mustn't fail."

Thorn and I are doing our utmost. We move slickly and smoothly whenever Pan demands it, the embodiment of a finely tuned, keenly coordinated unit as elegant as any Roman chariot duo.

At Combe Crag Wood, Pan unloads the Wall stones. He places them in a neat, conspicuous pile for later retrieval. Straight away, we begin our second descent, a cautious negotiation of a winding, wooded, leaf-littered track less than four pack widths wide in many places, occasionally less than two. We curve steeply downwards, amongst almost leafless birch and pine, towards the River Irthing and a known Roman quarry.

"Hey, Thorn," I observe, "did our Roman ancestors have to contend with hundreds of trees?"

"Probably not, Roamer; our man's theory is that trees weren't as abundant about 19 centuries ago. Roman ponies probably would have had an easier task downhill in this respect."

At a tight bend in the river, we stand precariously on a hill knoll, looking out across the valley to a sheer cliff face where Romans would have quarried stone.

"What a steep escarpment," proclaims Pan. "Perhaps masons left this winding, narrow walkway undisturbed, unquarried, so that ponies, rather than men, could carry stone easily uphill to the Wall."

Our present, leafy causeway suits Thorn and me: sure-footed, we would never have an accident. Disturbingly, nonetheless, Pan hasn't noticed that Thorn's headband has slipped over his left ear. Continual jolting's to blame. Pan is overeager, intent on keeping going whatever the cost, but if he doesn't rectify Thorn's hindrance soon, there might be a serious incident.

Beside the river bed, Pan commences placing stones into our baskets. Either the river's persistent force or Roman endeavour – or perhaps, sometimes, their combined effect – has shaped each stone.

"I hope he is not going to load us excessively," I tell Thorn. "I was beginning to enjoy myself without a pack."

"It's okay, Roamer," my friend reassures me. "Your basket's barely more than half full. You often dream of carrying such a load."

"That's it!" I reply. "I'm feeling sleepy. We should be in a field by now, dreaming."

Tarrying for only seconds, Pan allows us to enjoy this river's song far too briefly. Then he turns Thorn around to begin our steep ascent to the Wall. As we climb, Alan's camera awakens silently – but not in time to record Thorn's mistake; he overshoots an acute-angled bend before shimmying down the slope a couple of metres in double-quick tempo, taking Pan and me with him.

"Oi-oi-oi, watch out!" I yell. "Quit playing about, Thorn. Warn me next time, will you?"

"Sorry Roamer.   Insufficient   turning   room," he   replies impassively.

As I said, my friend likes to joke.

"That was a near miss!" utters Pan, who manages, against my expectation, to remain upright: Thorn threw him completely off balance; forget what I was saying about accidents.

It's dusk when we return to Quarry Side. As darkness engulfs us, we are grazing David's peacefully situated, fresh-tasting meadow, which doubles as a summer campsite for National Trail followers. No campers or tents are present to interrupt our enjoyment of non-chlorinated water and succulent grasses.

My feet usually don't ache, but this evening they are particularly tired. Slogging thrice over the same stretch of metalled road, partly because a few landowners were unable to assist us, was niggling. Thankfully, it seems that most humans living by the Wall can help us. Otherwise, we might fail to attain our ultimate destination and goal.

Thorn:

This has been an event-packed day. Our mini-adventure in Combe Crag's gorge is over. We have climbed to the road atop a ridge. Buried Wall lies beneath our hooves.

"Filming will become impossible in 10 minutes," announces Cameraman. "In fact, even now it's murky."

"Let's record without delay," counters our man.

All eyes are on a knowledgeable local man with a beard, who has accompanied us to and from the Irthing this afternoon.

"Did Romans certainly use this causeway to move quarried stone?" asks our man.

"This definitely is a way up," replies the man, a scribe who seems to understand this place's history. "An additional way up is via Lanerton, which is half a mile that way." He points east, adding, "And Gunshole is half a mile in the opposite direction. They would have found ways of climbing up about every half mile."

"You saw Thorn and Roamer carrying stone uphill from Gunshole and from the river at Combe Crag Quarry," remarks our man. "What are your thoughts on how they carried it?"

"It was impressive!" agrees the scribe.

"Bone evidence implies that the average height of ponies working near the Wall was possibly 13 hands or marginally over," believes our man. "That's about Roamer's height and 2 centimetres shorter than Thorn. Would it have been feasible to load such ponies using this sort of basket?"

"I suppose they would have had to carry 50 kilograms each," suggests the scribe.

"That sounds reasonable," agrees our man. "Ponies somewhat larger than Thorn and Roamer possibly could carry up to about 75 or even 80 kilograms, 176 pounds, including their saddles and harnesses."

"In that case, they probably could carry up to four standard Wall stones."

"Yes," accepts our man, "depending upon the weight of the stones, but I wouldn't recommend such a heavy load, particularly on a regular basis."

"He-he-he-he!" I cry. "Four sounds ridiculously heavy to me."

"Well, I imagine we could do it if we had to," counters Roamer in a serious tone, "but I'm carrying over 60 kilograms already, which is heavy enough."

"I'm slightly taller and heavier than you," I argue. "Therefore, I should be slightly stronger."

"Not necessarily," rebukes Roamer. "It's to do with the thickness of our leg bones; what Pan calls 'metacarpals'. Anyway, I'm not anxious to find out. Are you?"

He has a point.

"Can anyone describe exactly how Romans carried stones to the Wall?" speculates our man.

"No," replies the scribe. "One suggestion is that they strapped quarried pieces onto pack boards with leather."

"That sounds feasible," acknowledges our man. "I suppose, once they had hauled stones to the Wall, masons could have broken them up into smaller pieces?"

"No. Always, stones were quarried to the correct dimensions on site: without question, that was to save carrying."

"What about stone chips used on roads?"

"Naturally, stones would break. They would have filled the roads with chips in the baskets or found small stones from the fields."

"Would ponies have brought stones up to the Wall?" wonders our man.

"In all probability," surmises the scribe, "although oxen commonly were utilised for pulling. Ponies can carry, but they don't have as much pulling power. Oxen, being slower moving, are able to exert a much greater pull. On flat, level ground at least, the Romans probably moved stones on sledges drawn by oxen, whereas carrying up a steep incline had to be accomplished either manually or with ponies such as yours. There must have been a sizeable number of ponies going up and down."

"Fells possess plenty of pulling power," protests Roamer. "We can handle carts and carriages; you and I, acting jointly, could pull a laden sledge easily; we are capable of moving a considerable mass of stone."

"True," I agree, "but we should accept what the local expert is saying: oxen are more powerful on the flat. Also, don't forget: we are talking about Roman pack ponies, not Fell ponies."

"So, in your opinion, both oxen and ponies were utilised?" concludes our man.

"Yes: oxen on the level with sledges, and ponies to lift stones up steep hills," replies the scribe. "The point is that horses needed oats to keep them going while they were doing strenuous work, and there were probably few cereals grown up here at that time. Most likely, grain was reserved for the cavalry horses."

"Is where we are right now considered to be a steep incline?" wonders our man.

"Yes, it is. This is beyond oxen and sledges, I would say."

"Are you aware of any steeper inclines out of quarries?"

"Not off hand," replies the scribe, "though there are noticeably steep bits at Birdoswald and at Gilsland."

"If we were building this Wall today, could Fell ponies do the job properly?" speculates our man.

"That's a silly question," blurts Roamer. "Pan already has proof. In the Lake District National Park, a few of our cousins carry stone, along with other materials, up to high passes; Park officers use the stone to protect and repair eroded footpaths. Didn't he tell somebody so?"

"Yes, Roamer," I whisper. "You're right."

"They could carry up the steeper slopes," answers the scribe, "but oxen would be the chosen animal on level ground because it's easier to load a ground level sledge than a basket."

"Let me get this straight," rationalises Roamer, who has been listening carefully to the entire conversation. "Historians still haven't decided precisely how Romans did it?"

"Possibly not," I concede. "Maybe they haven't looked at every clue yet."

"Well," says Roamer, "Pan is aware that archaeologists have discovered horse, ass, mule and ox bones at Vindolanda. Secondly, available evidence implies our ancestors participated in constructing the Wall, roads and other stone buildings."

"And don't forget: wicker baskets were probably employed at some stage," I reply, pleased that I have remembered this fact.

"Well, I'm glad we've sorted everything out," admits Roamer, sighing audibly. "Perhaps, one day, when humans unearth and correctly interpret sufficient proof, there will be no doubts. You can't uncover the truth about anything without deep, relentless digging."

Solo:

I am impatient to be with Thorn and Roamer. Shouldn't they have completed their adventure by now?

Oh, forgive me: I didn't recount the conclusion of my dream. You might remember: I was desperate to gain a human friend.

In my search, I came face to face with a forest as black as a starless night. It was unloved. I stared at it, wondering whether I should dare to enter. I lingered at its edge. Finally, I made my decision: I ambled through its black heart.

I kept hearing the same scratching noise I had heard in the stable. Hours elapsed. Long after midnight, the noise stopped; not a single sound punctuated an uneasy silence. I became too tired to lumber on, so I slept in a tiny clearing.

A low, growling noise woke me up. I pricked up my ears and jumped to my full height. Side to side, up and down, I searched for the source of this new disturbance. Leaves rustled in a nearby bush. Something was lurking in the forest shadows. Suddenly, out from behind a tree leapt a grey wolf.

"Gggrrrrrrr!" he snarled as he clawed the ground beneath him. Slather drooled from his mouth. His teeth sparkled in the feeble moonlight. Slowly he crept forward, closer and closer. I stared at him, bewildered.

Without warning, he pounced with claws sharper than a holly bush. Bang! He hit the ground behind me. Somehow, I had evaded his grasp. I bucked and kicked, hoping he would run away, but he didn't. He slowly wobbled to his feet and then growled louder.

My eyes were wide. I stared at him again, waiting for him to move. Then, exhausted and in desperation, I reared. He whimpered before scurrying back into the forest. I slept.

Sunrise eventually came. Splendid, filtered light pierced narrow openings between towering trees. I carried on with my quest.

At last, I reached the forest's end. To my surprise, I saw a village crowded with people. I gazed at them, uncertain whether they would notice me and whether my journey was over.

Excitement coursed through me. I galloped into the village and stood silently. After a while, I caught the eye of a man who was selling winter firewood. He slowly walked towards me, pushing against a chattering crowd. We stood face to face.

He asked, "Do you want to live with me at my stables?"

I thought and then answered, "Na-ah!" and galloped off.

During my difficult, dangerous journey, I had perceived that it was mostly fun galloping over the snow, and that, after all, I would much rather be wilder than in a stable.

That's how my dream ended.

I have this message but no means of delivering it. Where are you, Thorn and Roamer? Please come back soon, wherever you are. Life isn't fun without our wonderful jaunts together.

Waterlogged ground, frightened cows and a blown-away tent

27th October – Lanercost Priory and Howgill

Roamer:

PAN collects us from our campsite enclosure early this morning. We've revitalised ourselves, but I don't believe he slept very well last evening despite being indoors.

He winces as he lifts two large, grey, rectangular bags, partly laden with fresh supplies, onto my saddle. I realise he's in slight pain: perhaps he damaged back ligaments pulling Thorn's slipped pack straight when my friend bolted more than a week ago. I have an impression Pan's injury isn't improving quickly enough, due to continual, daily lifting and carrying. I hope he soon recovers: Thorn and I need him to be 100 per cent fit.

"David, would you mind storing my baskets and ropes until I need them again?" begs Pan. "A courier will ferry them back to Leicestershire after the expedition ends."

"That's no problem," replies our extremely helpful host. "We'll look after them."

"Talking of couriers," adds Pan, "Roamer is carrying, from coast to coast, two letters franked by a national mail company. The aim's to inform people that Fell ponies used to help deliver mailed letters and parcels throughout Cumberland and Westmorland."

Aha! There's a surprise. I might be officially the only modern-day, British postal pony. It's true: my ancestors delivered post to isolated Lake District locations until about three pony generations ago. The world needs reminding continually of how crucial we were, and still are, to human endeavour.

"Today, just now, we face a slightly less pleasant journey than I expected," continues Pan, "due to unplanned road work. Discouragingly, a farmer has not authorised passage across his land, although my originally proposed route followed a well-marked farm track."

"What was the reason?" asks David, perplexed.

"I'm unsure," replies Pan. "My expedition assistant reported the farmer's decision yesterday; I couldn't persuade him to change his mind. From Banks we have no access to two key fields: we can't proceed off-road beside the Wall to Lanercost Priory via Hare Hill Turret, which means re-routing. It's disappointing."

David is sympathetic and reassuring: "Don't distress yourself. You've tried your best."

At least Pan has a contingency plan.

"One possible alternative route takes us," he explains, "for about 1½ kilometres, further south of the Wall and Military Way than we have ventured so far."

Pan bids farewell to Elizabeth and David, thanking them for their kind-hearted support. A short, road-bound stroll later, we are heading south, passing Lanercost Primary School as we descend gently towards the River Irthing.

"Why aren't we pausing to meet children here?" I ask Thorn.

"Our man told Elizabeth yesterday that, unfortunately, this school's schedule is too hectic to accommodate us," he replies.

"That's a terrible shame!" I wail.

"The school is closed today, anyway," points out Thorn. "It's still half-term here. So why torment yourself?"

"It would have been enthralling to visit the school," I reply. "You know how much I love meeting children."

On another rain-free morning, Pan is implementing his contingency plan. We arrive at Lanercost Priory, a church in a clearing. Located handily before the priory's entrance is a wooden gate leading to a field south of the priory complex and alongside the Irthing, a possible overnight spot.

"Philip, who owns this field, and Stephen, the man who farms it and who also owns Miller Hill Farm, have given us liberty to camp here," ponders Pan, gazing towards the serenely flowing river. "Miller Hill possibly was the site of a pele tower four centuries ago."

Is he thinking out loud again, or is he talking to us?

"We could stay at Lanercost tonight, but the weather may deteriorate," he reasons. "Instead, we should push on to Howgill Farm, our next possible campsite. I suppose we could camp here on our return leg. What's it to be, boys?"

"Pushing on is all right by us," mutters Thorn disdainfully. "The day's young, and our man undoubtedly detects that we're keen to keep moving. So why ask?"

We pause outside the priory's main door. Pan possibly is appreciating this place of worship's grand, imposing presence. Such lovingly maintained and manicured lawns and grounds would have enticed many recluse sojourners in a bygone age.

Presumably, we have permission to enter Lanercost Tea Room's car park via the priory's side-gate. Two tea room staff, Victoria and Deborah, recognise Pan from last year's reconnaissance. Deborah brings him a cup of tea and offers him coffee cake; he never refuses cake. Of course, both women are delighted to meet Thorn and me and are keen to find out about us

Barely a quarter of an hour later, refreshed, Pan decides to head north on a track to Heytongate, steering us towards the Wall. Leaving this track at a field gate north-east of Abbey Gills Wood, woodland located in a ravine, we begin treading north-west through tall, seeded grasses, past a solitary, old, majestic, autumn-cloaked oak tree. Soon we are back onto Pan's planned route between Wall and Vallum.

The Wall line stretches westwards across open, cattle-free fields, past the site of Randylands – borderlands – Milecastle, which Romans made of turf and timber initially. Pan pauses to deliberate whether this milecastle was, indeed, the furthest west structure Hadrian rebuilt in stone.

At Burtholme Beck – the stream of a dry enclosure partly surrounded by water – there's a major snag. Bridge entry and exit gateways are wide enough for ponies with packs only if Pan removes the swing gates. This operation will prove to be trickier than he envisaged, if not impossible, he concludes: apparently, somebody has fastened the gates exceedingly tightly to their hinges since his reconnaissance.

"It's unacceptably risky," believes Pan, to abandon Thorn and me at the brook, albeit temporarily, while he single-handedly attempts to unhinge those gates. "Instead," he insists, "we must wait patiently for a National Trail walker to arrive at the scene: she or he might be able to help remove them."

Pan appears to have neglected something, I am thinking. He would have to lead us separately across the bridge, which is even riskier in my opinion: Thorn and I would be about 50 metres apart.

We wait, and wait ... and wait. No hiker turns up.

"All right, boys: I've decided we can't afford to loiter any longer," announces Pan, business-like and determined. "We'll make a short detour."

Detouring means following a peripheral path around the western and southern edges of Abbey Gills Wood before heading west by road to Burtholme. Ultimately, the road swings north towards the Vallum.

Slightly less than three kilometres since we began backtracking from Burtholme Beck, we are on course again, though only a paltry half kilometre further on from the original footbridge. Between Wall and Vallum, across terribly muddy fields where wallowing, inactive, indifferent cows graze, we spy Howgill Farm, the farm in a hollow ravine, which Roman builders constructed across the Vallum.

Pan chats briefly with Alan, Howgill's farmer.

"I knew your father, Harry," says Pan. "We met by chance one sunny afternoon about a year ago when I was reconnoitring a gully. He was on his quad bike and gave me useful advice. I am extremely sorry to hear of his fatal accident, caused by a charging cow."

"You see," I tell Thorn. "Some cattle are exceedingly dangerous in particular situations."

"They can be unpredictable," he agrees. "What a tragedy that must have been for his family."

Alan offers us a choice of campsites: "If you prefer, you're welcome to camp in the field just before Low Wall. You can store your gear in a shelter there. Go up the farm track. Then head left through the gates."

Pan pitches his tent in an open-sided barn located 200 metres south of the Wall. Doubtless, he is thankful: this building will provide partial protection from heavy showers he anticipates will occur frequently throughout tonight. His dome-shaped sanctuary stands defiantly within a small oasis of dry grass.

Thorn:

This afternoon has vanished, spent detouring. Reaching Howgill Farm, we trace the Vallum for roughly another 170 paces to Low Wall. Our man notes that, according to his map, we are less than 213 feet above sea level. He sets up camp here, about 225 yards south-west of Low Wall Milecastle, which humans named three centuries ago.

Shortly after our man releases us to roam, I glance about but fail to spot him anywhere.

"Where has he gone?" I ask Roamer, baffled. "His tent door is open."

"I assume he's looking for fresh drinking water," replies Roamer.

"There's plenty in a nearby trough over there," I say, nodding in the water butt's direction.

"It's for him, not us. He set off towards two dwellings in the distance, beyond the open-walled barn."

Roamer guessed right. Our man eventually returns carrying a brimming collapsible bucket.

Some time later, we are grazing near his tent when a telephone ring tone shatters the twilight silence, startling me.

"Good evening, Julian," he begins. "I am sorry you're unable to travel to the Wall. . . . If you prefer, we could record your comments by telephone instead. . . . Okay, I'll set up my voice recorder and call you back."

Several minutes of further silence elapse before I hear voices again.

Our man has begun a telephone interview.   His 'phone's loudspeaker is on.

"You are a member of the Farm Animal Genetic Resources Committee. What is your committee's purpose?"

"We advise the U.K. Government on protecting and conserving farm animals, including equines, as genetic resources," replies the unrecognisable voice, which I presume belongs to the human called Julian. "Additionally, we advise on using farm animals in ways that do not harm the environment, long-term."

Our man is justifiably concerned.

"The Fell pony is a native equine breed at risk of becoming extinct in its natural environment," he begins. "Few freely grazing females are left. Should we monitor this breed more closely?"

"Yes, indeed," endorses the stranger, who is evidently an expert on farm animal genetic resources.   "We must ensure regular monitoring of the status of native breeds such as the Fell pony."

"Breeders often refer to extensively grazing Fell ponies within the agricultural system as 'semi-feral'," says our man.

"We don't recognise the term 'semi-feral' as a way of identifying a separate sub-population within the breed," insists the adviser.

"I suppose a better description is 'acclimatised' and 'hefted'?"

"Yes. They are valuable because of what they contribute to sound environmental land management."

"What does our man mean by a-, acc-, accli-, whatever that word is?" I ask Roamer. "Long scientific words confuse me. Why doesn't he use simple language that we can understand?"

"I guess he's saying a sub-population of Fell ponies lives outside all year round," ventures Roamer after a protracted pause and considerable thought. "These herds are seasoned: they have adapted over innumerable pony generations to live in various wilder – natural or semi-natural – places."

"Oh, I see, sort of," I tell him. "Is he referring to ponies who will survive under diverse geographical conditions and can eat various types of natural vegetation at different times of the year?"

"Yes, I believe so. You and I are acclimatised," declares Roamer with assurance. "And, when we were younger, we lived in hefted herds."

"It might be informative and worthwhile to determine, through research, any differences between hefted and non-hefted populations," suggests our man.

The adviser concurs.

"Part of Government's new strategy discusses how native breeds of farm animals help to manage habitats," says our man. "Does this include the Fell pony?"

"Yes," certifies the other voice. "The Fell pony is definitely a farmed, domesticated animal. 'Farmed' doesn't necessarily mean you must eat products from the animal."

"Farmers and other breeders look after extensively grazing herds," reasons Roamer, "but I wouldn't label those herds 'domesticated'. Would you, Thorn?"

I shake my head in agreement.

"Though you and I might act wildly on occasion, thanks to our special training we are tame enough," adds Roamer. "We are fit to live in a human environment. Still, you wouldn't say free-living herds are tame: some don't see humans for weeks, even months, at a time."

"I get your point, Roamer," I reply, nodding. "They live mostly on farmland, but nobody has domesticated them. Mind you, to be truly wild, herds should be living in untamed landscapes: landscapes completely uncultivated by well-meaning human conservationists; landscapes left to nature; landscapes with a natural sense of place."

"Pan says that hardly any such areas can be found in Britain," reveals Roamer. "He reckons high parts of the Carneddau plateau, a mountain range of cairns in North Wales – once a foreign land, where virtually wild ponies still roam – just about qualify. He also mentioned a couple of Scottish islands."

"I wouldn't mind being left to my own devices," I reply, "with no human interference, living on one mountain, my mountain, throughout my life. I could cope, given enough space to roam."

"Trouble is," counters Roamer, "though you could probably find quite a few hillsides in Cumbria and Northumberland large enough for a herd to roam, what happens when the herd gets too big? What happens when we end up fighting for food and space?"

"Younger ponies would be forced to seek out new areas to populate," I suggest.

"Suppose humans fenced us in, with no means of spreading out?" speculates Roamer.

"Well," I reply, "I guess it would be a case of survival of the fittest. Either that or humans would have to split up the herd: they would have to remove, possibly even kill, some ponies."

"If they removed ponies, the herd wouldn't retain its natural balance," contends Roamer. "I would rather live and die where I was born, even if it meant I was too weak to feed myself."

"You're forgetting something," I point out.

"Am I?" he retorts, glancing at me quizzically.

"What would happen if a wild pony became too ill or old to cope, and no owner or vet' was there to treat the pony?" I ask.

"That's part of living wild, part of what humans call 'wilding'," he concludes. "One thing's certain: my family would never abandon me."

"True, if you say so, but most humans wouldn't want to see us suffer," I reply. "They would insist on either making us better or putting us out of our misery. Could humans handle natural death? I doubt it. In my 6½ years, I have met few who live in absolute harmony with nature. Most are estranged from a natural way of living, never mind dying."

"I would rather fend for myself to the end," proclaims Roamer candidly.

"If I was so ill that I couldn't take proper care of myself, I would rather be shot," I tell him, "even though I detest guns."

"Anyway," he reasons, "we'll probably never have any opportunity to live completely without owners: land's too precious in this country. Which human will give it up for the likes of us?"

"We can dare to hope," I tell him.

While Roamer and I have been revisiting wild thoughts, we have lost track of what the humans were saying. Their present conversation is no clearer to me than the rain-saturated sky! Nevertheless, I keep listening.

"What's the Fell pony's official status?" asks our man. "Can the breed really be thought of as agricultural biodiversity?"

"The pony is a part of agricultural biodiversity," confirms the adviser, "and agricultural biodiversity has been recognised internationally for many years as part of overall biodiversity. In addition, England's new Biodiversity Strategy recognises, I believe for the first time, the concept of agricultural genetic diversity, or agricultural biodiversity, being part of overall biodiversity in England."

Apparently, "biodiversity" no longer refers only to wild plants and animals, but I'm no expert, as you might guess. Perhaps you, the reader, can fathom it.

"Is this fellow saying native cattle, sheep and pony breeds are biodiversity?" I ask Roamer.

"Aye, lad," he purrs.

"At last," I whinny gleefully. "At least some humans accept the fact that we are biodiversity! I suspect that relatively few have thought about us in this manner before."

"If we are biodiversity, our owner-breeders must protect us from becoming extinct," points out Roamer. "And somebody should pay them to protect us."

The telephone conversation is continuing.

"What about recent recommendations of the European Parliament?" inquires our man.

"They emphasise the importance of the Fell pony as agricultural biodiversity and a genetic resource," answers the unseen adviser.

"Presumably, recognising the pony as biological diversity will give it enhanced status nationally and internationally?"

"Yes," agrees the adviser. "I would say it needs to be accepted as a core part of United Kingdom and world biodiversity."

"Hear that?" chirps Roamer enthusiastically.

"Yes," I reply, "but to be accepted, our man or somebody else must first persuade every British policy-making human and organisation to recognise that we are officially biological diversity and to act upon that recognition, which might be no easy task."

"Haven't Government policy-makers overlooked the true value of extensively-grazing ponies?" presses our man. "There's little incentive, little reward, for using Fell ponies in mixed grazing, yet they can help to keep natural and semi-natural habitats in good environmental condition."

"The value of Fell ponies hasn't been completely overlooked," states the adviser. "In the English Government's Higher Level Stewardship scheme they are on the list of 'native breeds at risk' that are eligible for financial support. However, this scheme's major concern includes wild biodiversity, landscape and access: genetic conservation of native breeds at risk is a secondary aim."

Our man asks, "How could Government change the scheme in order to provide financial assistance for farmer-breeders who are striving to conserve the breed's genetic diversity?"

"We need financial incentives for those utilising Fell ponies in agri-environment schemes within the correct ecosystems, in suitable numbers and in ways that don't damage the environment," proposes the adviser. "It would be beneficial, additionally, if these initiatives were available in every part of the United Kingdom, in order to 'spread' the geographical concentration of native breeds that are at risk."

"Without farmer-breeders, there would be a sudden loss of the majority of remaining hill herds," argues our man. "Will Government policy support breeders better in future?"

"I hope breeders will receive more recognition than they may have received in the past," replies the expert. "Conservationists are beginning to recognise the Fell pony as part of the agricultural and overall biodiversity of this country. That's a big breakthrough. The tide is running in the right direction: there are opportunities for comprehensive support within the next Common Agricultural Policy reforms and the new Rural Development Regulations."

"Without action, will recognition from conservationists and Government lawmakers amount to much?" deliberates Roamer. "I doubt so."

"Could supplementary financial support be provided to farmer-breeders," suggests our man, "in recognition of the breed's potential contribution to maintaining and enhancing biological diversity through its grazing behaviour?"

"Existing support should be improved," admits the adviser. "Incentives to graze with mixtures of appropriate livestock grazing species should be available. We also need financial encouragement for breeders of acclimatised, hefted, closed herds that are suited to their locality. And Government could assist with the training of new breeders and with off-site infrastructure, for instance, through Rural Development Programmes."

"What's a closed herd?" I ask Roamer, confused once more by clever words.

"No idea," he replies.

"Closed herds potentially reduce the risk of disease transmission and improve biosecurity," concludes our man. "Can we assume that herd managers would introduce no outside breeding stallions or mares into truly closed herds?"

"There's your answer!" declares Roamer.

"Even in closed herds," points out the adviser, "stallions will have to be introduced from time to time in order to avoid inbreeding within the same family lines: stallions should not breed with their own progeny, grand progeny, and so on."

"True," acknowledges our man, "though the introduction of sufficient disease-free stallions at the herd's formation stage, followed by careful herd management, could avoid inbreeding for many years. Of course, in a truly wild situation, by encouraging their offspring to leave the herd, horses avoid inbreeding."

" 'Almost closed herds' is a human solution to a human-made problem," concludes Roamer, "but I suppose we'll have to accept this idea if it helps to maintain our breed's genetics and protect our future health and survival."

"If you reckon so," I tell him, "that's good enough for me, though I'd rather live free any day!"

"Is climate change likely to have a role in persuading the British Government to protect remaining Fell pony breed lines?" inquires our man.

"It should have, and I hope it will have. Climate change will require breed lines to adapt over time. The proper way of doing this is to guarantee we conserve them in their natural state, in their traditional homes, their locations of origin: that is, in situ."

"Why should we conserve breed lines in their original – northern England – habitats?" asks our man.

"We must protect the breed's maximum genetic diversity," stresses the adviser. "We can't be certain what genetic resources we might need in future."

"Is our predicament mainly about human needs?" I ask Roamer.

"Aye, often, my friend," he replies, "but that's not our biggest problem. Many humans see themselves at the epicentre of world ecosystems. Really, they are at the edge; a spoke in the wheel; a link in a reparable chain. If there were no humans, the wheel wouldn't collapse and the chain would mend itself slowly, magically, perhaps becoming even stronger. This is my considered opinion."

"You're losing me," I reply, "but you are probably right."

"Fortunately for us," continues Roamer, "as we are discovering en route, humans like Julian also exist; experts who will help us and all agricultural biodiversity; humans who demonstrate what Pan calls 'biophilia'."

"There you go again," I tell Roamer. "Don't bother explaining what bio-, whatever you said, means: I won't remember."

"In 2011, British Fell pony breeders registered only 123 newly born semi-wild foals," alleges our man. "These foals live within extensively grazing herds mainly on upland commons. Several herds have suffered Government-imposed grazing restrictions recently, which may be preventing those herds from becoming or remaining acclimatised in some semi-natural, sometimes harsh, environments; no longer may we legitimately classify them as 'fairly wild' or even 'marginally wild'. How should we protect remaining herds in their original homes?"

"The most urgent thing is to assess what genetic diversity still exists within the living population," insists the adviser, "and especially within any ex-situ resource."

"What does 'ex situ' mean?" I ask Roamer.

I am completely befuddled. I expect anybody reading this will be, too!

"That's easy," replies Roamer calmly. "Pan mentioned earlier that it refers to any part of the Fell pony population that humans have removed from a threatened natural habitat – from surroundings where we have developed our distinctive genetic and learned characteristics – and placed in a new, wild or managed, environment. Apparently, it also refers to humans collecting our eggs, fertilised or not, and our sperm and storing them at a low temperature in a laboratory gene bank for possible future use decades later."

"Sounds complicated and worrying," I tell my friend. "It occurs to me that already most of our kind may be living in ex-situ conditions, outside of our natural, or even semi-natural, homes."

"Aye, Thorn," he retorts. "Soon will there be any in-situ equine herds, never mind Fell herds, left in Britain?"

"How might the Fell Pony Society halt the loss of herds in their native, traditional habitats?" wonders our man.

"The Fell pony's future depends on the Society," asserts the adviser. "The Society is the breed's primary guardian and steward. It could encourage authorities to carry out a genetic diversity survey. It could ensure the breed's plight is constantly brought to the attentions of relevant persons."

"Extensively grazing herds have learned to graze in a special way," stresses our man. "Can we afford to lose them?"

"Learned characteristics are essential for native pony breeds involved in environmentally helpful grazing," confirms the adviser.

"Actions of humans may be eroding these characteristics," laments our man, "yet we have conducted virtually no scientific research on their importance in native ponies."

"Such research would be useful."

"Presently," notes our man, "American scientists are comparing the genetic characteristics, the genomes, of 36 native equine breeds worldwide, including the Fell pony. The study is examining equine breed diversity.   If this research shows that the Fell pony has relatively high within-breed diversity, how might this affect the pony's status?"

"If research shows that the Fell pony has unique genetic characteristics," replies the adviser, "this will give the breed even greater importance than it already has."

I have listened attentively for an age to this spasmodically optimistic conversation. My brain hurts. It's time to explore our new surroundings.

"Have you seen what I've seen?" I ask Roamer excitedly.

He has. Six trekking ponies are grazing in a field on the opposite side of the fence beside the Wall. I suspect humans ride them regularly. This evening, we graze by the fence rather than near our man's tent, hoping to chat with them.

In between infrequent, heavy squalls, the sky is utterly empty, unmarked and glass-like. Late tonight, the air temperature drops further than we have experienced previously since leaving Tynemouth. Roamer and I remain comfortably warm: our new coats are growing faster.

28th October – Newtown

Roamer:

When Pan looks for us after first light, we are chatting with our new equine acquaintances. We are in no mood to hurry.

An opportunistic National Trail hiker appears. He passes along a narrow, grassy, fenced laneway between our field and that of our friendly neighbours, head down, walking poles flailing, travelling purposefully west. His appearance signals the imminent beginning of our latest unpredictable episode of Wall adventure.

Pan prepares us for today's exertions with immense difficulty due to our field's exceptionally boggy ground. No spot is dry, yet he refuses to tack us up in the barn: its gateway entrance is waterlogged, and long, stringy grass would render hazardous any tricky manoeuvre.

On a fresh, rain-free morning, we gingerly pick our line across mire to our campsite's single feasible exit point south of the Vallum. The resolute landowner has secured this gate with two double strands of fiercely intertwined barbed wire. To disentangle these, escape the field and then replace them without injury is a precarious, exacting chore without the aid of pliers. Inevitably, Pan cuts his thumb deeply and must patch up the wound.

Last November, Pan sought permission for the next stage of his planned route, off-road between Wall and Vallum from Low Wall; he was unsuccessful. Instead, via a connecting track, we soon attain a narrow road alongside the Wall. Following this to Dovecote, a Vallum cottage where doves originally nested, we hence reach Dovecote Bridge. At the bridge, Pan detours to the river bank to gaze at inviting, clear, clean, gently flowing King Water.

"Boys, there's no easy crossing here," he announces. "This stream's shallow enough, but leading you out at the far side would prove too difficult: the far bank is extremely steep and has thick undergrowth."

"What's he anxious about?" I ask my friend.

"Maybe he hoped to ford the stream close to where Romans originally forded it," surmises Thorn.

"Oh, well," I conclude, "Pan has decided: we're pressing on without crossing. The water is enticing, though."

Over the bridge, we are momentarily off-road, steering through cattle fields across Beeches Farm, advancing uphill with the Wall line to deserted Walton Village, which was once a single farm by the Wall. Hurrying through the empty village, we quickly veer off-road again, taking a straight, tranquil track for half a kilometre alongside a hedge parallel to and south of where the Wall stood. I am savouring a peaceful, pleasantly warm afternoon. The hedgerow, a suntrap, isn't yet devoid of mottled green leaves clinging to late autumn life against all odds.

We are progressing steadily. The track leads to Sandysike Farm, a few houses by a small, sandy stream. At Sandysike, Pan waves to two farmers engrossed in private conference. They wave back.

"How are you Richard?" he calls.

Richard and the other man, who I presume to be his son, approach us.

"We didn't think you would attempt it this late in the year," remarks Richard. "Margaret, come and meet these ponies. They look great!"

Margaret, the farmer's wife, is preoccupied: she politely declines.

"Richard, you promised me a cup of tea, if I ever got here!" jibes Pan.

"Yes, of course. We can organise that," he replies graciously.

His son slips away, returning minutes later with a steaming cuppa. Pan accounts for our delay. They chat about our saddles. Then it's time to go. With luck, we expect to revisit on the return leg.

"Cut across our field of cows to avoid the road," suggests Richard, pointing. "It's quicker."

Without hesitating, Pan takes Richard's advice: there's no time to dawdle. Our presence both amuses and bemuses cattle that seem otherwise devoid of life.

Our direction is initially north-west, across the ditch north of the Wall, to Swainsteads, Sveinn's place centuries ago. Afterwards, we take the westwards track towards Cam Beck, a crooked tributary of the Irthing. Here, the footbridge would take us in the wrong direction. Instead, we cross safely at a ford as the beck meanders southwards. The ford, which is 20 metres wide and racing, is merely 25 or so centimetres deep. From the far bank, travelling uphill north of the Wall, we gain a picturesque track that initially twists alongside the beck before veering south-west towards Cambeckhill.

Reaching The Beck Farm, we turn into a slender, grassy byway where nothing wider than a lightweight tractor could fit. I stroll happily, changing my pace to suit Pan's requirement, oblivious to unanticipated dangers lurking ahead. Thankfully, perhaps 1½ hours later and despite several mishaps, we reach tonight's pre-arranged campsite. We are dishevelled but safe; Thorn, doubtless, will enlighten you.

Thorn:

Time ticks on. I sense our man's urgency, but route finding to Newtown, a comparatively modern village, isn't straightforward. Turning away from Swainsteads footbridge, we easily ford Cam Beck at a shallow crossing over boulders raised up by centuries of deposits. From the river's far bank, our chosen track now heads roughly south, meeting the Wall ditch and Wall approximately 300 yards later. We trace the ditch to Cambeckhill. Distinctively situated Castlesteads Fort, which Romans called Camboglanna, meaning "the bank at the bend", is isolated between Wall and Vallum. However, from our present position we cannot observe its remains. Our man recounts how Romans constructed the fort on a high bluff 330 yards west-south-west of here, overlooking a bend in the Cambeck valley.

"The first erected fort was made of turf, the second of stone," reckons our man. "Tungrian horses lived there. They probably came from Gaul and belonged to tribal peoples called the Germani."

By Cambeckhill Milecastle, dragons prevent access to the Vallum. We must detour from the Wall's south-west line by heading, instead, west-south-west to The Beck Farm, situated by a stream. Here we take an old, narrow, waterlogged lonning enclosed by dense hedges and leading to Roughlane House. The going is slow: in places, we are fetlock-deep in squelchy, liquid mud. We press forward until a recently fallen, mature beech, a storm casualty, blocks our path. Our man measures the clearance. We ponies barely scrape beneath an almost horizontal limb – and he can duck! This really is a rough lane.

After successfully overcoming our latest obstacle, Roamer almost immediately entangles his pack in barbed wire littering the path. Our man may assume Roamer is panicking: he isn't; he believes in self-preservation, as does every Fell pony. Would you willingly drag behind you a sharp, spring-coiled, life-threatening, steel rope that could rip into your loins at any moment? Our leader should have spotted this danger before Roamer accelerated away.

"Pht-pht!" utters Roamer, swiftly shaking off the wire.

Our man calms him: "Don't fret. You're out of danger, and the pack's hardly damaged."

In fact, Roamer isn't out of danger, and neither am I. Seconds later, at the next bend, two fully-grown, trapped and frightened cows confront us head on. Where did they come from? What shall we do? Despite our patience, they refuse to pass. Instead, they turn and flee in the direction we are heading. Inadvertently, we herd them quietly before us for some minutes, always keeping our distance, reminding me that our drover ancestors had arduous jobs over a century ago.

As we approach the lane's end and our exit gate, we face a new predicament: unintentionally, we have trapped the beasts. To escape, they must charge through a gap not wide enough to avoid hitting Roamer and me. If they panic and stampede, they could easily injure either or both of us and damage our packs – and they might unwittingly pin our man to a thorny hedge.

We back off and then stand stock-still as our man considers options. Fortunately, he notices an insignificant iron gate on our right, roughly two paces from the cattle. Somehow, slowly, cautiously, he unfastens it. Next, he nudges it open without alarming them further. Silently, he ushers us inside. Those beasts seize their opportunity to escape, bolting along the lonning and around a corner, caped in mud.

"I must inform the cattle owner that two of his animals are loose," promises our man as we exit this incident-strewn laneway onto a minor road.

At the road's bend, as pre-planned, we veer left through a gateway and then follow a field hedge, past a herd of lazy beef cows, towards Newtown. Unscathed, amazingly, we are standing alongside the main road at Newtown's western edge.

"That's my idea of an adventurous day," confesses Roamer as I inspect tonight's campsite at Newtown Farm on the Vallum.

"My husband is in the barn, around the corner," explains the farmer's wife, who clearly has anticipated our arrival. "I have your supplies: the postman delivered several parcels recently. Would you care for a shower? Perhaps, also, you might like to join Malcolm and me for dinner later?"

"Thank you. What splendid suggestions, Susan," admits our man, who is particularly grateful, I suspect, for not having to cook this evening.

We track down the farmer, who is industriously packing potatoes into boxes.

"Hello! Everything all right?" he asks as he continues hand picking from a conveyor belt.

"Yes, fine, thank you, Malcolm," answers our man, "except that your neighbour's cows are loose in the lane. Could you let him know?"

"We're fine now," declares Roamer, "but I wouldn't suggest we've encountered no misfortune today."

"Our man is an expert at understating difficulties," I sympathise, nodding.

"Camp in the field behind our house if you wish," recommends the farmer. "There's good grazing, and it's sheltered."

"Perfect," responds our leader. "Is there somewhere I could charge my computer? Otherwise, I might try using my solar charger, though I've not yet perfected a laptop charging method."

The farmer shows our man a power point inside his cowshed.

"My wife will sort out your supplies," he adds. "See you at suppertime."

He leaves. A farmer's life is, I guess, unbelievably busy, especially during rapidly shortening days.

Mysteriously, the sky repeatedly pretends to circle the sun until a huge lump of rain arrives, a torrential shower, attacking the farm and us. Stranger still, no rainbow manifests itself. Drops shine on my dripping nose.

Much later, no lights are visible. We are grazing near the tent:

Roamer likes to keep his favourite human within sight. About midnight our man leaves the warmth of his sleeping bag to reprimand us gently.

"Boys, you are munching too loudly, keeping me awake! Please graze somewhere else. Off you go."

"Come on," I whisper. "Let's give him some peace. We'll return at daybreak."

We saunter away. Minutes afterwards, all I can hear is the grinding of Roamer's teeth and the intermittent, distant, shrill pitter-patter of uninvited raindrops pelting our man's tent from an otherwise silent, strangely transparent night sky.

29ᵗʰ *October – Bleatarn*

Roamer:

Sunrise reveals a startling, turbulent firmament of gold and orange laced with streaks of purple. Malcolm warns Pan at breakfast time that the weather forecast predicts downpours between Newtown and today's destination, Bleatarn, the dark tarn. Pan hastily prepares us, mindful of this prediction and his own observations. As he saddles me, a ferociously cold cloudburst begins. It persists for over 1½ hours.

Pan, who isn't fond of trekking into what he envisions may be a deluge, warns us: "Guys, we won't pack your raincoats today. Almost certainly you'll be wearing them."

We don't require artificial coats. Thorn detests them. Although they are waterproof, light, comfortable, trendy and black, we much prefer to walk unhampered, free of additional encumbrances.

"Sorry, Thorn," adds Pan in anticipation. "I realise you hate wearing a raincoat, but I must protect the saddles and gear."

"Why? Aren't they protected by the waterproof packs?" moans Thorn under his breath. "And leather saddles are waterproof anyway. He shouldn't fetter us."

"I suppose we must trust his judgement," I reply.

Pan unwraps an oblong-shaped parcel that a sponsor has posted here, revealing his desperately needed new rucksack. A second, roundish parcel – another welcome donation – contains gloves and winter socks sent by his assistant. He smiles broadly, especially pleased to discover a strip of sticking plasters and cream to protect and revitalise sore, wounded hands: uncounted minuscule cuts, caused by repeatedly handling rough, wet gear, no doubt inflict agonising if fleeting pain when he packs and unpacks us.

"Why doesn't he wear those gloves to load and unload?" observes Thorn forthrightly.

Pan, of course, is oblivious to Thorn's sound practical advice.

"That's a sensible idea," I conclude, as our leader, wincing almost imperceptibly, places our latest food supplies, fresh pellets, into my left saddlebag.

Pan's preparations are barely complete when I recognise Alan's silhouette through lingering fog. It's time to march on.

Amazingly, precisely as we leave camp, the rain ceases; the sunshine is winning, at least temporarily. Pan, pack those raincoats away.

On a storm-predicted day, we head towards the village's western edge, the site of Newtown Milecastle. There we turn south-west across pasture fields, true to the Wall line. Dozy, mud-lashed native cattle are inquisitive but pose no threat. The ground's firm: our route chooses the highest lie. South of White Flat, we are following a path, a field boundary these days, alongside the Wall.

"From here we must navigate around two stiles," Pan informs Alan almost straight away, "which means crossing the Wall and then, about 200 metres later, doubling back along the other side of the fence ahead."

Pan's early optimism, fanned by our initial rapid progress, is short-lived. Past the turn-off to Cumrenton, a valley farmstead lying roughly 300 paces west of our present position, a shower commences. Worse, beyond where a bridle path leading to Laversdale, formerly Leofhere's valley, crosses the Wall, a wicket gate is impassable.

"I'd forgotten about this dragon," sighs Pan. "There's nothing else for it: both packs must come off."

"I'll film you while you're working," taunts Alan mischievously.

Wait! This is Pan's lucky day. Cumrenton's farmer, whose name also happens to be Alan, and who somehow has either spotted or anticipated our dilemma, magically appears.

"I knew you were heading this way today," he begins. "Can I lend a hand?"

As Pan unpacks, the farmer ferries our gear, bit by bit, through the gateway.

"Your timely help certainly makes life easier," acknowledges Pan.

"What a lot of fuss about nothing," chuckles Thorn disparagingly, upon observing what he considers to be quite amusing antics. "Our man would have been wiser to manufacture slimmer packs at the expedition's outset."

"You're missing the point," I reply. "Your pack, at least, is supposed to be an authentic reproduction. What's more, we're carrying a wealth of essential gear."

Pan smartly reloads us. He thanks Alan. We set off again, relaxed and happy, along a peaceful, straight, tree-lined lonning. At Chapel Field, the Wall and Vallum diverge slightly. From here to Old Wall Farm, passing Old Wall Milecastle, we are adhering precisely to the Military Way line. Clearly, somebody built this farmhouse partially by robbing the Wall and milecastle of stones.

Our progress is excellent as we head west-south-west past the high bank site of High Strand Milecastle. Without ado, about 300 paces before this afternoon's destination, Bleatarn Farm, to avoid a fence and another stile ahead, we enter a gateway leading to the Wall's northern side and then navigate a route beside the ditch. The Wall runs north of the farm buildings, where we double back, strolling casually into the main yard well before dusk.

Thorn:

Bleatarn Farm's yard is eerily quiet – cattle are sheltering inside barns – as our man begins to unpack.

A stranger, probably the senior farmer, arrives in his tractor.

"Good afternoon," he calls. "My son, Andrew, will be about later. He'll advise you where you can camp. Meanwhile, would you like to store your gear in the barn and feed your ponies there?"

"Thanks, David," replies our man. "That's a good idea."

"My cattle won't bother your ponies," reassures the farmer. "Are they happy with cows?"

Is he joking? Cows can't fluster us these days! Black and whites eye us inquisitively but warily from adjoining stalls as Thorn and I cheerfully tuck into our rations.

Cameraman has discontinued filming.

"I don't suppose there's any chance of a lift to Newtown?" he inquires.

"Sure," responds the farmer. "I'll be happy to take you."

"See you at Walby Farm Park," promises Cameraman as he heads home.

Unceremoniously, our man unloads our packs and unsaddles us, storing every item of tack meticulously in the watertight barn: he expects further heavy rainfall tonight. As he finalises our grooming, a younger farmer appears.

"How are you Andrew?" asks our man. "I've already spoken to your father."

Obviously, these two have met before.

"There's a corner field that may suit your ponies, just before the lane leading to the tarn," suggests the farmer. "You passed by it as you arrived. Will it do?"

"Unquestionably," endorses our man. "They flourish on rough grazing."

"Would you prefer to camp with your ponies?" he asks. "Alternatively, we have a proper campsite across the road, but we'll need to charge you, unfortunately. No one's there tonight: you'll have the place to yourself."

"Your campsite sounds perfect," declares our man, "whatever the cost."

"I'm not surprised there's nobody else about," reasons Roamer. "Which human in his right mind would be camping tonight? This weather isn't for faint-hearted tent enthusiasts."

"He'll be okay on a proper campsite," I convince him. "Besides, we'll get some privacy."

"There are hot showers," continues the farmer, "and I'll leave the office open, in case you want to charge your 'phone or call anybody."

"Spot on," enthuses our man. "I'll be able to update my computerised diary and check tomorrow's logistics in comfort."

"His computer is that heavy, black, metal box I'm carrying," I tell Roamer.

"Are you being serious?" challenges Roamer. "It hardly weighs anything. I'd readily carry it if we could change packs."

"Hardly weighs anything!" I retort indignantly. "I wouldn't be surprised if it's heavier than any other portable brand. Humans designed it for police and army use, so it's bound to be almost waterproof and virtually indestructible."

"Oh, I didn't know," admits Roamer.

As twilight approaches, we are safely settled. Now our man must painstakingly ferry his camping gear approximately 100 yards from the barn to his campsite. He will certainly struggle to erect his igloo-shaped, two-man tent: it's not that simple, even in calm weather, and today the wind is gusting badly. Roamer and I have watched this ritual many times. First, our man threads three flexible, multi-sectioned, glass fibre poles through thin fabric tunnels attached to the tent's exterior walls. The poles cross at the tent's apex. Next, he elevates the structure into place before securing the ends of each pole to the sewn-in groundsheet through tiny steel eyelets, a procedure requiring concerted strength.

According to our man's later account of events, he has barely put up his mobile home when a sudden, fiercer-than-usual gust causes it to become airborne. He observes it bounce over the campsite's five-foot-high, dry stone, wall. It then fleetingly soars skyward, gravity and a sudden lull in the wind causing it to land upside down in the lane, across the path of a shepherded flock of startled sheep. Luckily, the tent remains undamaged. Our man retrieves it. As for ruffled, loudly bleating jumpers, they calm down by the time they reach their safe enclosure: smaller brains cannot cope with excessive distraction.

Quickly, the wind becomes angrier. Apparently, his tent pegs won't stay in the ground: He is concerned: the roundhouse could end up halfway to the Wall or, even worse, in the tarn! He envisages a sleepless night.

"Time for drastic action," he concludes, procuring our two tethering stakes and his mallet from Roamer's saddlebag.

He hammers the 14-inch spikes, doubtless at acute angles, into the ground and then attaches the tent's front and rear guy ropes.

"Multipurpose" is part of his motto. Afterwards, he reckons, he could "sleep through a hurricane".

Right now, of course, Roamer and I are oblivious to our man's tent caper. We are relaxing.

Later this evening, a cooler wind is gusting with increased frequency and ferocity. It starts to rain. Continual torrential showers persist throughout the night. For his sake, I hope our man was clever enough to cook dinner during a dry spell. Roamer and I remain as undaunted as ever: we are sheltering behind a high hedge.

Families, donkeys, busy roads and another school

30th October – Walby Farm Park

Roamer:

L AST night the rain lashed down, and it is continuing intermittently this early morning. I don't mind rain as long as it doesn't last for days on end in winter. I can cope with almost any weather: teeming rain, scorching sunshine, tempestuous winds, arctic air and even brutal blizzards.

Fortunately, the sky is clear, the day invigorating, when Pan comes looking for us. He's late. He whistles from, I suppose, 70 paces away. Thorn ceases grazing. Recognising this characteristic, shrill tone, he trots over to Pan obligingly, as hungry for pellets as ever. I, however, am not anxious to leave: I am content gobbling grass in my secluded corner.

"Why have you made me tramp the field's length for you?" wails Pan as our eyes meet.

Don't interpret my attitude wrongly: I simply feel lazy today. Usually, I love my daily rambles, and I have great affection for my new, temporary guardian; I trust that we shall stay together, sharing further happy adventures, when this expedition ends. In fact, I daren't contemplate what might become of Pan or what might happen to Thorn, Solo and me when that moment arrives.

While we munch pellets, Pan telephones Alan.

"Because the clocks have gone back to Greenwich Mean Time,"

says Pan, "it will get dark more than an hour earlier tonight. . . . From now on, to avoid being stranded at sunset, I'm planning to begin each day's trek much earlier than previously."

Apparently, British Summer Time ended at two o'clock this morning. Thorn and I didn't notice. Why should we care? Such an artificial perception of time is amusing; I can't help chuckling. My natural clock seems far less confusing.

Pan hurriedly packs up a soaked tent. Nevertheless, it takes over three hours to strike camp and then tack and load us.

At about eleven o'clock according to Pan, though it seems more like midday to me, we finally commence today's journey, travelling along a clearly defined, grassy causeway marking the base of the Wall and the line of the Military Way. A gravel road originally, the Way is all of 6⅔ metres wide here, I'd guess; that's 22 feet to the uninitiated.

"In this vicinity, the Vallum has two marginal and two other parallel mounds," observes Pan as we pause to admire ribbon-like Bleatarn glimmering in tepid sunshine. "Romans didn't dig a ditch: its steep, marshy sides might have collapsed. Instead, cleverly, they fashioned an 'above-ground' ditch by building two extra mounds!"

We approach White Moss, a supposedly wide, dry expanse.

"What's that noise?" I ask Thorn, startled. "I hear a vehicle, but there's no nearby road."

We turn to see David hailing Pan from his quad bike, which is approaching swiftly. A young, dark-haired woman, visiting the farm, has hitched a ride.

"Andrew told me of your expedition, so I decided to see the ponies for myself," she explains. "They are awesome!"

Pan nods and then addresses David: "How fortuitous: as you arrived, I realised I'd left my walking pole in your barn."

"Not to worry," replies David good-humouredly. "I'll fetch it."

Off he chugs over ridge-and-furrow-like ground, his bike disappearing quickly from sight. Meanwhile, the woman chats with Pan about our expedition aims as she strokes Thorn first, me second. I am, for an instant, mesmerised: the perfume she wears is more delicate than honeysuckle, not unlike a combination of rosebay willowherb and bell heather, the latter of which, by the way, we ponies refuse to eat: it is poisonous; one of my elders has observed its harmful effects on sheep and cattle. In fact, we don't usually pick wildflowers. Where was I? Oh, yes, I remember: even the faintest out-of-place fragrance will overpower the subtle odours of an over-ripe autumn landscape.

"That scent's pleasant," accepts Thorn, "but it's not as sweet-smelling as us! We Fell ponies exude an extremely agreeable aroma."

A short while later, pole retrieved, we continue west. Thorn is ever eager to move: he dislikes hanging about. From Wallhead, a place at the Wall east of where Wallhead Milecastle existed, we travel swiftly along a deserted country lane. It marks the Way towards Walby, another place by the Wall. Southwards, a multitude of wire fences render the Vallum inaccessible.

Seven hundred metres beyond Walby, I guess, the road bends sharply, not quite 90 degrees, north-east. Leaving this road here, we follow the Way across fields. About 250 metres later, where Wall and road almost meet and where Walby East Milecastle stood, we head south-west across the Vallum. Pan reckons archaeological scholars dispute the Way's exact position here. Skirting cleverly around field hedges, we gain entry to the rear of Walby Farm Park, today's destination.

"This is too short a trek," jeers Thorn. "We're just getting going."

I'm happy, though: we've time to relax, to cherish friendlier, balmy weather.

"Let's enjoy the rest," I tell him. "Pan says tomorrow will be much harder."

Thorn:

Just a gentle stroll from Bleatarn is a lively, bustling, 30-acre farm park. This gem, our man has discovered, sparkles at the heart of a 400-acre farm lying astride the Wall within the Solway basin. After passing fields of rapidly growing winter crops of wheat, barley and maize, we wander through a grassy enclosure of young goats to the park's Visitor Centre.

It's Sunday afternoon, a busy time. Dozens of families with young children mill about, inside and outside, playing, having fun. They can meet all kinds of farm animals. I notice goats, sheep, cattle, pigs and hens, for example. Each breed has its own paddock or pen.

"I'd hate to be penned up day after day," remarks Roamer.

I am about to respond, when two young, striking equines with shiny, light brown coats – donkeys I assume – catch my eye. They are standing quietly, alone, in a tranquil enclosure away from human crowds and other animals. I have never seen such stretched ears.

"I'd love to chat with those donkeys," I confess. "They are incomparable to us, yet similar in numerous respects."

"Me too, but Pan might have alternative plans," replies my friend. "Somebody has announced our arrival over a loud speaker system. I'm eager to meet people."

The farm park's friendly proprietor salutes our arrival personally: "They're handsome-looking ponies. Would you care to do an outside presentation? Today's the last Sunday of the school holiday, so lots of families are here."

"Of course, Neil," answers our man, who clearly has anticipated this proposal. "I'm looking forward to it. People may ask whatever questions they can conjure up. Thorn and Roamer will relish it."

"There's a snag," I tell Roamer. "I suspect our man wanted to film families meeting us. Unfortunately, Cameraman and his assistant are resting today: we're on our own."

Roamer nods.

"Oh well, it's inevitable," he contends all-knowingly. "Disappearing opportunities will abound simply because, before our expedition began, Pan decided upon limited filming with a skeleton crew. Besides, Alan deserves a break."

"After you have finished," confirms the park owner, "I'll show you where to unpack and store your gear. Would you prefer tea or coffee?"

"Coffee's fine, thanks," replies our man.

"Hmm, we could do with some water!" I venture. "That's water, not coffee, if you don't mind."

Nobody's listening to me.

"Holly and Isabel are my daughters," continues the owner. "You met them last year on your reconnaissance. They are keen to hear about your ponies. I'll leave them with you."

Our man asks how old the children are.

"I'm Holly and I'm nine," declares the eldest. "Isabel is seven, and we have another sister, Olivia, who's four."

"Isabel is a fraction older than you, Thorn," observes Roamer. "And Olivia is the same age as me. What inspiring ages!"

Both children, smiling broadly, begin to stroke Roamer confidently. He invariably hogs attention, especially from children. He's such a softie really.

"He-ee-ee-ee-ee!" I whinny. "Don't forget me."

Good: they notice me. They may stroke me too.

Our man has attached our lead ropes to an immovable paddock gate some 30 paces from those curious donkeys. Immediately, a group of six inquisitive children, accompanied by parents, gather around to meet us.

Visitors conjure up expected and a few unusual questions. My favourites are "For how many days have the ponies been walking the Wall?" and "Where are you heading?" and "Are they quite friendly?" and "How could I buy my own Fell pony?" and, of course, "Can you ride them?"

Our man describes to families how Romans might have used ponies in building the Wall and why northern Fell ponies aren't plentiful these days. Afterwards, he seems tired, Roamer is practically asleep and I'm hungry.

The park owner returns.

"When you're ready, come over to the restaurant for a meal," he suggests. "Our chef is superb. He'll prepare you a special vegetable curry."

"Thank you, Neil. That's very kind of him," replies our man. "I must admit, I do crave some high-energy sustenance right now, but first I'll sort out Thorn and Roamer."

Seemingly, our man enjoys occasional mild curries, but he insists that spicy food, whatever that tastes like, wouldn't suit our palates or stomachs. Give us crunchy pellets any day, naturally. That said, just once I wouldn't mind trying something spicier.

The owner's two eldest children are passionately interested in equine matters. They volunteer to help unload, brush and feed us in a quiet, dry barn close to their family farmhouse, roughly 150 paces from the park.

As Roamer and I finish supper, bubbly Isabel persuades our man to watch her negotiate the park's giant indoor slide with style and ingenious tricks. Our man dare not relax yet, however. First, he must routinely assess the suitability of our evening quarters.

A pleasant surprise awaits us: tonight's secluded paddock is adjacent to that of those two personable donkeys. Only a low, wooden fence separates us from them. Nothing is stopping us: we can introduce ourselves properly.

Seconds after our man releases us, my head is over the fence and I am chatting away. We shall become well acquainted with these donkeys. They are gentle animals and will be faultless night-time companions. Nobody will suspect what games – mischief, you might say – we're up to far from human eyes on this lovely, new-moon evening.

31st October – Tarraby, Stanwix School and Linstock Castle

Roamer:

Chatting with our donkey friends was entertaining last night. I hardly slept.

At daybreak, I am wide awake, grazing. Thorn asks me whether I am ever envious because he is leading. I tell him that I, a true noble beast, could never be jealous of any pony, never mind a friend. I'm unsure whether he believes me, but how do I convince him?

"Pan's coming," I tell Thorn. "Let's forget it."

Our constant human companion greets us with his customary, "Hi there, boys! Did you have a good night?" Leading us into the farmyard, he adds, "Prepare yourselves for a steady workout."

Pan disappears from view, leaving Thorn and I standing alone. Where is my breakfast? I'm going nowhere without breakfast.

Several minutes later, Thorn is wondering about his breakfast too. He takes a deep breath and, with a loud sigh, vibrates his vocal cords and nostrils.

"Pfft," he snorts politely.

We are hungrier than ever when Pan reappears, declaring, "Sorry to keep you waiting, boys."

Obviously anticipating a long, testing day, he leaves us again in order to retrieve our gear from a nearby barn.

"Roamer, are you sure that you aren't just a little jealous?" jests Thorn before he begins to gobble his high-fibre pellets.

"Please, Thorn, this isn't a joke, I plead, irritated. "A long time ago, I resented being at the back, but I was never jealous of you."

"Okay, you win," he says in a muffled tone after swallowing hard. "I am genuinely sorry I upset you. In future, I won't mention leading. Are we still best friends?"

"Always, whatever happens," I reassure him. "Apology accepted."

Pan returns with our saddles and bridles as I finish eating.

"You'll be meeting schoolchildren this afternoon," he says.

I can't wait. Thorn appears indifferent, but he can't wait either.

Before going to school, Holly and Isabel, neatly dressed in their uniforms, want to assist Pan's daily preparations. Their spotless, gleaming white socks are unlikely to remain clean near us. Olivia, whom we haven't met, trails in their wake to say hello. All three girls smile infectiously, encouraging my optimism whatever challenges lie ahead today.

Pan enjoys a late breakfast cooked by the resident chef, but we are ready to depart just as Alan is parking his car. Thorn leads, of course. He sets a snappy pace through Walby cattle yard, past Walby Hall and onto a private farm road. We are following the Way's line in the direction of Brunstock, possibly once the site of a racecourse after burning cleared the land over 7½ centuries ago.

Three hundred metres later, beyond a line of electricity pylons, Pan stops to consult his map and to discuss our route with Alan.

"We can't continue much further in this direction," he warns. "Ahead the track is blocked by thick, dangerous scrub. I checked it out last November."

"So, which way now?" demands Alan, eager to keep going.

"If we turn right and head north-west beside the hedge, across this pasture," rationalises Pan, "we'll meet a long, hardly trodden track heading south-west towards Brunstock Park. From there, we've only a short detour north of the Vallum."

Minutes later, Pan is examining the track. Dense, lethally sharp hawthorn trees, overgrown bushes of various species, young saplings and dying, gangly, woody shrubs block the first 50 paces ahead.

"Hacking through there will be impossible," insists Alan.

Pan, who has encountered tropical jungles that are more easily penetrable, eventually concedes: "Last December I spent several hours checking this route; it was navigable with difficulty, but only without ponies. I understood that the farmer had cleared it recently, a mistaken notion, obviously. We're obliged to backtrack."

This setback, it seems to me, may be the consequence of confusion caused by our leader's inadequate communication.

Back onto the private road, Pan entrusts us to Alan: he's off in search of a western link-up with Brunstock Castle. He is uneasy about leaving us, even with Alan, even for minutes or meagre seconds, but we won't cause the camera operator any trouble in a tense situation.

Pan returns directly. He's disconsolate.

"There's no possible way through," he tells Alan, "forcing us to head cross-country to the main road, missing out Walby West Milecastle. We must hurry: arriving late at school isn't an option."

No, Pan, don't arrive late, or else you'll not bag footage; neither will they offer you a cup of tea. He drinks a lot of tea.

Due to our dithering, twisting and weaving, time is against us on a grey morning. We turn briefly south-east, hugging the edge of a ploughed field towards the right-angled bend of Birky Lane, site of the farmstead of the Britons, and thus are onto grass verge adorning the main road to Brunstock Castle.

"I wanted to avoid this dangerous road," laments Pan.

Why be alarmed? Because Alan is behind me, walking drag, our passage is impeccable. Besides, I'm forever on guard, looking, listening. Panoramic eyes and road-trained ears are our best defence. Iron monsters shall not overcome us.

From a roundabout at Old Grove, we are bang on course, traversing the southern corner of Brunstock Park to meet a minor road at the Wall's corner. Shortly, we turn south towards the main road's grass verge.

"There's no choice: we must cross the motorway at the bridge near Drawdykes Castle," pronounces Pan. "This compounds our difficulty."

Alan, a Carlisle man, fully appreciates Pan's geographical conundrum.

"How will they handle motorway traffic?" asks Alan.

"We'll soon discover how effective their training was," reasons Pan. "Fortunately, there's a wide path alongside the bridge road."

Why be concerned unnecessarily? Thorn and I have no fear nowadays.

Alert but without flinching or wavering, we deal casually with speeding vehicles approaching from four directions. Once over the bridge, we are approximately 100 metres south-east of the Wall line, within shouting distance of Drawdykes Milecastle.

Drawdykes is the site of a medieval, probably fourteenth-century, castle whose walls – yes, you've guessed it – consist of mostly Wall sandstone. Ditches surround it. Westwards lies the Vallum.

We head off-road across waterlogged fields, coursing along the Vallum about 220 metres south of the Wall. What's happening now? Unexpectedly, we about turn and begin backtracking across the same fields.

"The gate leading to the road is locked," grumbles Pan. "Surely I asked my assistant to advise the landowner of our intentions today?"

Our present situation easily could be a second example of failed communication on Pan's part, I am thinking. I'm sorrier for Alan, who deserves our sympathy: he must haul heavy, expensive equipment across this bog twice. He never complains.

Pan announces the obvious: we are now alarmingly late visiting Stanwix Primary School. Everybody should stay calm: that's what I think.

From Tarraby, known as Theodoric's Village greater than eight centuries ago, Pan easily identifies the field gateway that will provide access to the approximate Military Way line into Stanwix. We've another minor problem, however: somebody has padlocked this gate, and the field's owner, Anne, who also owns Clydesdale Stud, isn't at home.

"What next?" mumbles Pan under his breath.

"Tommy, a farmer who lives at Tarraby Farm, has a key," Pan tells Alan, "but that means detouring to his place. We'll arrive too late at Stanwix School."

"Now we are in serious trouble," jokes Thorn.

"What's new, then? Tell me," I retort.

At this moment, two industrious builders, constructing riding stables for Clydesdale Stud, notice our dilemma. Might they rescue the situation? Deftly, slickly, they remove the gate, replacing it just as smartly behind us!

"Please don't disappear just yet," begs Pan. "I suspect we might require your further expertise right away."

Immediately before us, over a brook at Tarraby, is a footbridge where a kissing gate now prevents any progress. Our alternative is a wider, shepherd's gateway about 10 human strides away. However, Pan dare not risk leading us across a muddy water sink to access this gateway: he estimates the sink is over half a metre deep. In truth, Thorn, who is clever at calculating depths and estimating dangers, has refused to cross already.

"I've assessed this location several times during the past two years," divulges Pan to the builders. "We might have avoided the kissing gate, but today's torrential rain has defeated us. And, unfortunately, Carlisle Council officers aren't here to remove the gate, which was the agreed, prearranged solution."

Luckily, our new-found, temporary team members grab two spanners and dismantle the gate within minutes. Meanwhile, Pan is frantically unloading us, mindful we might end up hopelessly late for our appointment.

"A lot of children will be disappointed," he tells Alan.

I'm dismayed, too: I'm counting on kids stroking me. Come on, Pan, I'm thinking. We'll make it, won't we? This is part of our destiny.

We slide, saddles attached, between temporarily gateless posts. Pan repacks us in record time.

"Thanks to those builders and the Clydesdale Stud, we might meet our deadline after all!" declares our leader enthusiastically.

"What's a Clydesdale?" asks Thorn, always eager to learn about other equine breeds.

"Clydesdales are a breed of draught horse, distinct from Fell ponies though with historical connections to us," I recall. "I've seen one. They originate from the farm horses of Clydesdale in Scotland. According to Pan, Clydesdale is the valley of the Clyde, a loud river heard from a great distance. This is my sum knowledge of Clydesdales."

We are strolling serenely, purposefully, via a footpath skirting a Wall-line hedge. To the north are fields that may mark the berm; in his scouting mission, Pan couldn't establish who owned them, despite his earnest endeavour.

"At this point, does it matter who owns what?" I ask myself as we glide past Cumbria College of Art and Design onto a dangerous, winding, car-littered road.

The road, which closely mimics the Military Way's probable course, takes us into Stanwix Village.

"Stanwix is the stony settlement, a place of stone walls, possibly referring to the nearby ruins of a waterside Roman cavalry fort, Uxelodunum," notes Pan.

"Where's our police escort?" pleads Alan pointedly.

"I've no idea whatsoever," apologises Pan despondently. "Believe me: I thought I'd planned it meticulously."

Alan needn't fret. Taking advantage of his recently acquired expertise, we negotiate traffic and roadworks impeccably.

Past the village green, almost opposite Saint Michael's Church, is a deserted playground. Afternoon playtime is over.

"Christians constructed the church on the site of Uxelodunum, which might mean 'high fort'," proclaims Pan. "In fact, there have been several churches on this site since Roman invaders left. They built Saint Michael's 170 years ago. The original fort was turf and timber; Romans then rebuilt it in stone."

"Thorn, did you hear?" I rant. "I imagine that up to 500 cavalrymen might have lived here in Hadrian's day."

"That's a lot of horses," marvels Thorn. "They must have been deprived of personal space; it would have been too cramped for my liking."

"East of the fort," states Pan, "they built a special exercise area covering about 7½ acres."

That's an impressive gymnasium.

Ernie, Alan's assistant, is patiently waiting for us outside the playground.

"They want us to go around to the rear entrance?" he announces.

"Ernie, please could you warn the headteacher that we've arrived?" asks Pan. "And do they have a bucket of fresh water for the ponies?"

Our hooves pitter-patter across cobbled ground. Pan abruptly halts us inside the tiniest courtyard imaginable. Although punctuality isn't our foremost trait, although Pan's best-laid plans regularly fail, we've made it. Scrapes and bruises may cover me, but I am dancing over the moon.

Elephantine railings tower high above my head. Possibly 70 mini-humans come charging towards me. As I lurch sideways, a young girl places a steadying hand on my neck with great care. I relax as other hands tenderly stroke my velvety fur. Now the children retreat. Seconds later, when Pan asks a question, several wave their hands in the air.

Pan removes a blue, metal box, about 10 centimetres long, 6 centimetres wide and 2 centimetres thick, from a red, waterproof bag. Attached to the box by insulated copper cable is a thin, metal stick about 15 centimetres long but less than half a centimetre in diameter. He switches on the device.

"This is a data logger," he declares, holding up the box and stick. "It runs by battery. The long probe is a sensor. What do you think the sensor measures?"

"Breathing," answers a girl.

"The box can record breathing rate, yes. Anything else the sensor might be measuring?"

"Is it a thermometer?" guesses a clued-in 10-year-old boy at the front.

"Yes, this is a temperature sensor. The sensor and a recording device, when connected, make up a digital thermometer. The box is recording and storing temperature readings."

I am mostly useless at understanding science. Still, I listen politely along with about one-third of the school. Children have gathered around in their tiny, cramped backyard. Thorn has the prime view, as you might expect.

"Perhaps your teacher could select a student for this quick experiment?" asks Pan.

A 10-year-old girl meanders through the crowd towards us.

"What is the air temperature at this moment?" Pan asks two other girls, who are standing closest to Thorn.

One of the pair studies the blue box's display.

"One degree Celsius," she announces.

"One degree?" queries Pan. "Everyone here would be nearly freezing! Try again. What does it say?"

Her friend reads out the correct temperature.

"It's 15.1, no, 15.4 degrees," she states confidently.

"Could everyone please remember 15.4?" says Pan. "Who thinks Thorn's skin temperature is going to be hotter than the air temperature today?"

About half of the children raise their hands. A few estimate it will be colder. The remainder aren't certain.

Our chosen mini-scientist is now standing beside Thorn's neck. Pan hands her the logger and attached sensor.

"Put the sensor against his skin," he tells her. "He won't hurt you. Hold it near his heart."

The girl presses the metal stick against Thorn's neck. With Pan's help, she then moves it to my friend's breast. He pins his ears back, reluctant to participate: there are so many children to cope with. Pan should have chosen me.

"What's the temperature?" asks Pan.

"It's going up," she replies.

"Let's wait for the digital read-out to stabilise," urges Pan.

We wait.

"What is it?"

"16.4 degrees," she announces.

Thorn's body, even his skin, is definitely warmer than the outside air: I could have told anybody that without a fancy instrument.

"Now let's measure the other pony's temperature," suggests Pan. "We are going to place the thermometer under his packsaddle."

Hey, he means me. The girl slides that cool metal rod beneath my saddle pad. It tickles.

"What's the temperature?" asks Pan. "Is the read-out constant?"

"It's 16.8, no, 16.7, no, 16.8."

"Well done!" he tells the young investigator. "Why is it even warmer under his saddle?"

"The saddle's stopping his body heat from escaping," answers an attentive 10-year-old boy.

Pan congratulates him. But wait a moment, I'm thinking. Everybody may be forgetting at least one important consideration: my body temperature might be slightly warmer than Thorn's anyway since I am carrying a heavier load. Having said that, what do I know about experiments?

"Now, children, it's time for your questions," announces Pan.

"Yeah!" I snort when Ernie reappears with a white, plastic bucket that is three-quarters full of fresh water.

I slurp three monstrous, cooling mouthfuls. Alan, Ernie and Pan refuse to be outdone: a golden-haired, female teacher promptly turns up with steaming cups of coffee.

Evidently, Thorn is either not thirsty or too fussy. Whichever is true, I must be labouring harder, as usual.

"He'll have this water over us, if we let him," Pan warns Ernie, wary of Thorn's past antics.

Pan snatches the bucket away too late.

"Ugh!" screams one of three girls standing closest to Thorn, realising that she and her friends have narrowly avoided an unwanted soaking.

Alan manages to film lots of children enquiring about us. As one group waves farewell, a new group arrives in the yard. Before we leave, Pan invites every child to write a brief story.

"Imagine you are an expedition pony," he implores. "Describe your thoughts and feelings as you are travelling along Hadrian's Wall."

How could humans, even mini-humans who are able to empathise with us, imagine how it feels to be Thorn or me? That might require an unimaginable imagination.

"They couldn't possibly guess what we're thinking!" maintains Thorn adamantly. "Our reasoning's incomparable with that of humans, thank goodness."

"But they seem to know a lot about us," I point out mischievously. "They've been observing us. And I bet they've watched what the camera operator calls 'internet film clips'."

"Yes," agrees Thorn, "but they would need to study us, live with us for a considerable time, to appreciate our feelings."

"That's true," I admit. "Do you believe Pan knows what we are thinking and feeling?"

"Periodically, perhaps, he empathises with us a little," acknowledges Thorn. "We, on the other hand, nearly always figure out exactly what he's thinking: we can virtually mind-read. In little-known and poorly understood ways we're much cleverer than humans, I've decided. Our man says we have 64 chromosomes;

humans boast only 46. Is that part of the reason, I wonder?"

Thorn:

This bright, sunny afternoon, I trot where traffic is intense. Though they aren't sore, my hooves are a little warm due to hard, stony roads. I still wear a Roman saddle; my friend sports the British one. I am the leader; I suspect that Roamer is slightly jealous, but I might be wrong.

Despite a testing morning, we have safely reached the eastern periphery of Carlisle with our man and the bearded man who carries a heavy, black camera. Additional, hurried road pounding brings us, at last, to Stanwix School. Our arrival is much later than we expected; the church clock shows 2.15. Still, it's early enough to chat with everybody.

Excited, smiling mini-humans stroke Roamer; he's content. In double-quick time, Cameraman and his assistant are ready to shoot.

Stanwix children have prepared more questions for our man than you could record in any diary.

"What are their names?" asks a nine-year-old boy standing patiently behind a blue railing.

"Lathomdale Roamer and Huntsmans Blackthorn," answers our man. "My reserve pony is Thornbeck Solitaire."

"Call me simply Thorn," I mutter. "Everybody refers to me as Thorn: I prefer it."

"How did you catch your ponies from the wild?" wonders a 10-year-old girl.

"These days there are no truly wild British ponies," explains our man, "possibly except for a few living on high Welsh mountains and remote Scottish islands. Out of 400 breeding Fell mares throughout Britain, give or take, only about 100 are grazing in a semi-wild state. They are semi-wild rather that wild because, although they roam freely on unenclosed commons located on the mountains, moorlands and, less frequently, marshes of northern England, traditional breeders own them. Thorn and Roamer were free-living until this expedition began, though their owner-breeders kept a watchful eye on them. They are easy to catch once they trust you."

"Exactly how do you catch them?" inquires another pupil.

"When they were semi-wild, we enticed them with food; they would come to you only after you shook a nosebag containing a mouthful of special pony pellets. We haltered them while they were feeding. Thorn led me a merry dance on the expedition's second day: I couldn't catch him. Now, each morning, they usually come straight to me, especially if I whistle: they've realised they will be fed!"

"How long does it take to train them?" asks a nine-year-old girl.

"Each received roughly 20 hours of training from scratch. Soon afterwards, they toddled through busy Tyneside traffic without hesitation."

"Are they calm or quite jumpy?" she wants to know.

"Initially, they were uncontrollable, but they have been unbelievably calm since we trained them purposely on tracks less than 20 metres away from a motorway."

"Are they spooked or distracted easily?" inquires another nine-year-old.

"Occasionally, cows slightly distract them. However, incredibly, they really focus when they're on roads. Whenever I ask them to stand at a junction, they stand, not moving a muscle and unmovable. When I ask them to walk on, they walk on. I can lead from either side; they won't flinch. On roads, to protect them, I always position myself to their right, between them and traffic."

He has forgotten to mention that I keep two watchful eyes on approaching traffic, and Roamer keeps both ears pinned and primed.

"Do they stay together?" asks a boy.

"Yes, continuously," observes our man. "And even when they are grazing freely, what one decides to do, the other usually copies."

That's true. We stick closely together, just like two sides of the same page in my diary, though we are also individuals.

"What's the difference between these and other native breed ponies?" asks another boy.

"All British native pony breeds have desirable common features," says our man. "Free-living individuals are extremely hardy and are able to survive and thrive outside throughout the year. The Fell pony has several special physical characteristics, not simply its size and colours. Presently, in America, scientists are comparing its genetic characteristics with those of 35 other equine breeds worldwide. This study should help to identify some differences."

Our man continues to explain: "Small horses existed in Britain in prehistoric times. The Fell pony's earliest ancestors were probably smaller than today's breed. We do know that humans have used pack ponies in Britain to carry goods for nearly a thousand years. And, of course, less than a century ago the Fell pony was often England's pack pony of choice, both in the mines and to transport goods."

One fact is beyond doubt: we are northern England's unique native pony breed.

"Are their hooves heavy?" inquires an eight-year-old girl standing by me.

"No," replies our man. "Native ponies retain hard, light, resilient, blue-horn hooves similar in composition to those of the prehistoric horse. Besides, Thorn and Roamer aren't wearing steel shoes. You don't need to shoe Fell pack ponies – unless, of course, they walk on roads all day, every day."

I'm glad I don't wear shoes: that would mean extra weight to carry.

"What's their healthy diet?" wonders a boy who asked an earlier question.

"They never eat sweets!" insists our man. "On the Cumbrian hills, they will eat a variety of vegetation, including grasses, rushes, leaves and even tree branches. During this expedition, I have been feeding them a specially prepared, high-fibre, high-protein diet without too much fat."

"But we also relish the odd carrot or apple, don't we?" interrupts Roamer.

"That's true," I agree, "which reminds me: I'm hungry."

"Do they ever feel the cold?" asks a young girl.

"No," says our man. "Because they are hardy, they cope easily with snow and ice. At this time of year, before extremely cold weather arrives, they begin to grow thick winter coats. To counter an exceptionally strong, cold wind, they will search out a wall or hillock to shelter behind and will stand with their backs to the wind."

You wouldn't catch Roamer or me inside by choice, regardless of the weather. Our winter coats have half grown already.

"Is their hair soft?" asks an even younger girl.

"Their body hair is silky soft," explains our man, "but that of their manes, tails and fetlocks – we call fetlock hair 'the feather' – is fairly coarse. Come and stroke Thorn."

"Do horses hibernate sometimes?" wonders a clever nine-year-old boy.

"That's a fascinating question. No, they don't. Wild ponies and horses are able to obtain enough wild food in winter to survive in reasonably good condition until spring. Fully acclimatised native ponies live outside all winter. Even if snow falls onto their backs, their blood circulation system keeps them warm: blood moves away from the skin, conserving heat. Rather than melting, the snow remains on their backs, and they can shake it off. I anticipate that wild and some semi-wild Fell ponies will be able to live outside throughout the year regardless of long-term climate changes."

Three children stroke my nose and neck; I could get used to such attention. One inquires how he should measure our heights; the mathematics here – hands, inches and centimetres – can confuse me at times. A girl volunteers to measure our body temperatures using the data logger.

"What types of saddle are they?" asks an 11-year-old boy, gesturing.

"Thorn's saddle is a modern-day attempt to replicate a Roman packsaddle," answers our man. "Three archaeologists, four saddlers, a carpenter, a farrier and a metallurgist helped me construct it. We brought together meagre archaeological evidence from Britain and elsewhere in Europe. Evidence came from discoveries made at Vindolanda – an archaeological site close to the Wall, from artefacts preserved in museums at Carlisle and Guildford, from Italian sculptures and paintings and from previous Roman saddlery research. For example, Thorn's pack is an approximate copy of packs depicted on a monument in Rome. It's also worth considering why we are using a Fell pony to test the saddle and pack. Although we can't be sure, Fell ponies might be among the closest living British relatives of ponies that wore Roman packsaddles in Britain, or that helped build the Wall, good reasons to prevent the breed from fading away."

"No, we must never fade away," interrupts Roamer.

"Roamer's saddle is a Military packsaddle identical to that used by the British Army in both world wars," continues our man. "It has an adjustable tree, which allows the saddle arches to sit in sympathy with the shape of any pony's back."

I suspect Roamer's saddle is slightly more comfortable than mine is, but I'm not complaining.

A small boy, standing half hidden behind everybody else, is concerned about our health: "How do they carry all that stuff each day?"

That's my point precisely!

"They are bred to be stocky, strong and powerful for their height," explains our man. "They have firm, muscular necks and shoulders, shortish backs, strong, well-shaped quarters, stout, shortish legs and hard feet. Look how wide their leg bones are. The wider the leg bone – the greater the cross-sectional area – the greater the weight an animal can carry. Plus, they are very fit: they average about five miles a day with their loads but could walk much further."

This is, without doubt, the wrong time of day for children to fathom mathematics or science. Nonetheless, they and their teachers are manifestly interested. Roamer and I, of course, could recite our man's banter off by heart: we've heard it before.

"How much weight can the Fell pony carry before it collapses?" bluntly inquires a nine-year-old boy.

"I hope I don't collapse, ever," mumbles Roamer. "And Pan mustn't forget: I'm still quite young."

"You should never load a pony close to its limit," insists our man. "A fit, well fed, fully grown, above-average height Fell pony will carry a load, including the saddle, of about 65 kilograms easily if the load is properly balanced. Up to the end of World War II at least, British Army pack animals – these were often either larger, Highland ponies of up to 14½ hands or large mules – carried between 73 and 109 kilograms – from 160 to 240 pounds – including the saddle, and they travelled between 15 and 20 miles, 32 kilometres, a day, sometimes for days on end. The precise maximum allowable load depended upon the type of Army equipment carried."

Using equines to help fight any human war is inhuman, I am thinking. How terrified warhorses would have been. We ponies have never been, and could never be, inhouyhnhnm.

"In the latter part of the eighteenth century," continues our man, "Scottish Galloway ponies, relatives of today's Dales and Fell pony breeds, regularly transported iron and lead ore from England's mines in the north-west to factories in the north-east. Recognised for their strength and endurance, they reportedly carried a hundredweight, 112 pounds, on each side of a wooden saddle, the maximum pack load including the saddle being 240 pounds. In the nineteenth century, the strongest and fittest Dales and Fell 'Galloways' did similar jobs. We aren't certain how much Roman pack ponies, which were probably slightly smaller than Thorn and Roamer, might have carried. Then, and at several other times in our history, some people may have abused their pack animals by forcing them to carry too much or by not feeding them properly. Who knows?"

"One hundred and nine kilograms seems too heavy for any equine!" grumbles Roamer. "Sixty-one kilograms is quite enough for me, as I keep saying."

"But you aren't as tall as those other ponies would have been," I point out. "And we aren't being abused, are we?"

"The largest, modern-day Fell ponies possibly could carry your father, depending upon his weight and that of the saddle," adds our man. "But remember, a ridden pony is subject to considerable, often unreasonable, stresses by an unbalanced rider, so the maximum safe load for a ridden Fell pony may be quite a bit lower than that for a carefully packed pony."

"Cool. I'll ask my dad to buy one," responds the boy earnestly.

One eight-year-old girl informs everybody, "I go horse riding. I don't ride a wild one, but –"

She pauses and points to Roamer.

"Do you ride a Fell pony?" asks our man.

"Yes," she replies, nodding. She smiles and then inquires, "Are they used to having people ride on them?"

"Fell ponies aren't difficult to ride," confides our man. "However, these two have never been ridden." Pointing to me, he adds, "Thorn would accept you on his back, providing you could ride. They display gentle temperaments."

"Pan has probably forgotten," asserts Roamer. "I've had students very briefly on my back a couple of times. I'm easy-going, but would you allow children on your back, Thorn?"

"I'm unsure," I concede. "Possibly, but no human could ride or should attempt to ride any free-living pony without first gaining the pony's trust. The human and the pony would then need to educate each other carefully."

One boy wonders, "What will you do when the expedition's over?"

"I, along with other people, will be trying to persuade Government that semi-wild Fell ponies are an important part of British biodiversity that must be protected," replies our man. "For example, they help create suitable nesting sites for birdlife and butterflies. And they don't normally damage wildflowers in flower. Suppose free-living ponies cease to exist. Which other large mammals will be able to graze our wild mountainous places and valleys properly throughout the year? England's landscape will change: it may become unrecognisable, with too much scrub. If we are successful, breeders of free-living Fell ponies may receive more Government help. Alternatively, Fell ponies could virtually die out in this area within a decade, which would be sad. This was the common pony here 70 years ago. These days, it is rare. It is your native pony."

"What's the plan to save native Fell ponies?" asks an astute 10-year-old.

"That's a key question! First, we must save the herds – about 200 mares plus several stallions – grazing in a semi-wild state. Assuming all wildlife managers accept that Fell ponies are biodiversity, we might be able to protect them, and breeders may receive rewards. Second, farmers could be encouraged to breed ponies in semi-wild places of northern England where the breed once lived. Third, we might persuade those who protect the land – conservationists – to use Fell ponies to graze other semi-wild areas. Don't forget, ponies may have lived here, in the north, for at least 2000 years."

"Ye-ee-ee-eh," murmurs Roamer.

I also decide that this is a feasible plan, but can it succeed? Who will help to save free-living herds in future?

Suddenly, Cameraman's filming light becomes inadequate: high backyard walls partially hide a gradually retiring sun. This school day's end looms. Patient parents are queuing up behind Roamer to collect their children; he's feeling mildly claustrophobic.

A few children can't resist stroking us as they head home.

"Go for it! And don't forget Roamer," I tell one, but I'm uncertain whether she understands me.

Within a few minutes, only two children linger, still waiting for their parents.

"Time to be gone," announces our man as our camera crew pack up their filming gear.

We retrace our steps through Stanwix along rush-hour village roads. I now understand what "high fort" refers to as we turn south down a steep bank towards Rickerby Park and the calmly gushing forth Eden River. Cameraman again trails behind Roamer; he becomes a temporary police sentry, arresting traffic while we scuttle across a major highway to the relative safety of Rickerby Park's most northerly entrance. Easily through a gateway alongside a cattle grid, we are following the peaceful, uncluttered road to Linstock Village.

"See you tomorrow, here, at this car park," shouts Cameraman as he waves goodbye to our man before turning around and marching briskly uphill towards his waiting assistant and vehicle.

"Come on you two," orders our man. "That sun's sinking fast; we have a fair distance to go."

We stride out, heading roughly north-east from Rickerby Park's car park, in what seems to me to be the wrong direction. We pause only fleetingly on a grassy verge alongside the road to Rickerby, a small hamlet where, I suspect, a well-known man called Richard formerly lived. Our man is checking his map.

"Why are we backtracking?" I ask Roamer quietly.

"Possibly we're heading to the nearest available campsite," guesses Roamer, thinking of survival as he frequently does.

"You may be right," I say. "Our man did mutter something about not wishing to pitch his tent in the dark. In that case, couldn't we utilise the cycle path on our left, which is signposted as 'Hadrian's Wall Path'?"

"We could," replies Roamer, "but it's extremely narrow: we may meet cyclists in a hurry, whereas this road's unobstructed and quiet. I prefer the open road."

Less than two miles further on, a lively march has taken us through Rickerby Village and back towards the motorway. Crossing another motorway bridge, south of the bridge we crossed into Tarraby, we arrive at Linstock, an outlying hamlet where humans grew flax in bygone years.

"Take a right fork at the upcoming junction," advises a local woman. "Then keep straight on. Your destination is on your left."

One final spurt of brisk trudging brings tonight's home, Linstock Castle, into view. It is late.

"Boys, we're just in time," says our man as the sun hangs almost entirely below a rapidly cooling, late autumn horizon.

The farm's owner – our man calls him Alistair – warmly greets us.

"We will be going home shortly," advises the owner. "Help yourself to our office and kitchen facilities. You can store all your gear in the room opening to our cattle yard: tacking up will be easier tomorrow. Here are the keys. I believe you know Alistair well. He'll show you where to let the ponies graze."

"I'm confused," says Roamer. "Two people called Alistair?"

"I am too," I reply. "I presume the second is our man's friend or acquaintance."

"I see, sort of," says Roamer. "We keep meeting humans with the same names: two Ernies, two people called Nicholas, and now two Alistairs, not forgetting three Davids. It's hard to keep track."

"Don't ask me," I tell him. "I hardly ever attempt to remember human names: I'm relying on you."

At this moment, coincidentally, a stranger appears. I guess he is the second Alistair.

"The ponies seem to be in good shape," he tells our man.

Apparently, the stranger breeds Fell ponies. He and our man chat only briefly: the breeder has finished his farm work and must head home. Within minutes, the place is deserted.

Our man is discernibly relieved: we've made it to camp before nightfall and before a dark grey, rain-laden sky awakes. He untacks, brushes, checks and feeds us silently and slickly, afterwards leading us to a huge field.

Off we trot, quickly settling down to nibble grass, a hectic day firmly behind us. Roamer and I are content.

"Plenty of flavoursome grazing here," he drools.

The cloud-ridden, brooding sky is turning black. Roughly 100 yards from where we are grazing, the office's peerless porch light punctuates moonless gloom. On the opposite side of the farm track, intermittent bursts of a flashing light relay untranslatable, unintended Morse-like code to us: our man is climbing over a stile, his tent under one arm, to access his designated camping field, an awkward manoeuvre without reliable light. Will he ever again possess a properly functioning torch?

A deluge begins which continues unabated until dawn. It shall not dampen our spirits: we are on a charge.

Obstacles along the Eden

1st November – Rickerby Park Memorial Bridge and Knockupworth

Roamer:

DURING the night, a powerful downpour bombarded Pan's tent. I expect he worried needlessly about Thorn and me: we enjoyed a cool, refreshing, tingling shower; later on, we sheltered by a hedge.

At sunrise, the air is dry, clean and sharp.

From my observation, I conclude that Pan's acquaintance, Alistair, takes charge of dairy cattle at Linstock Castle: he is up early, milking in the gloom. By and by, he pauses from his strenuous exertions to chat with Pan.

"Good morning," he begins as Pan is brushing us. "Now I've finished milking, shall I take a look at their feet?"

What a fabulous idea! Yesterday, Thorn was complaining his hooves were irritating him slightly.

"Yes please, Alistair. That would reassure me," replies Pan. "They haven't been trimmed for about three weeks."

"I'm first," I tell Thorn.

You may consider me vain. Who cares? I'm partial to pedicures.

Alistair would have performed this task often with members of his small Fell herd, which, according to Pan, grazes near here. He slides his hand down the back of my left foreleg, causing me to lift it up immediately. Holding my hoof in his right hand, he examines it and then cleans it from the heel towards the toe using a hoof pick, managing to avoid my sensitive frog, my inner hoof, which he cleans easily with his hand. Next, the quietly spoken cattleman expertly trims the hoof walls with nippers.

"I need a rasp to smooth and level the bottom of the hoof," he admits.

"Hang on," responds Pan. "A blacksmith gave me this rasp when he last checked the ponies' feet"

"That's kind of him: they aren't cheap," acknowledges Alistair.

Pan hands Alistair a 30-centimetre-long, 3-centimetre-wide, metal file. Effortlessly, Alistair rasps my hoof, keeping each wall the same length, each stroke beginning at the heel and ending at the toe to prevent uneven areas in the hoof wall. Next, he trims the dead, flaky part of my sole with a curved trimming knife, aiming to keep the load-bearing pressure on my hoof wall and off my sensitive inner hoof. This requires care: he must ensure that my frog will contact the ground at each step. Finally, he rounds the edges of my hoof wall. Unbelievably, by my counting, this whole job takes him scarcely four minutes. He repeats the procedure on each of my other hooves. The result is rather pleasing; I'm raring to step out.

It's Thorn's turn. Alistair cleverly begins to trim his right rear hoof, but Thorn isn't keen to take his weight on three feet. He attempts, unsuccessfully, to thrust his hoof down prematurely.

"Come on," urges Alistair reassuringly, leaning into Thorn.

"Steady, boy," adds Pan, who is gripping my pal's halter and head collar firmly but gently.

I'm impressed: a month ago, Thorn wouldn't let Pan, or anybody, touch his feet.

"Stop being awkward, Thorn," I warble at him.

"Na-ah!" he wails. "You know I hate humans messing about with my feet."

"Who's worrying about nothing now?" I tease.

"Roamer and Thorn are in tremendous shape," concludes Alistair, roughly 20 minutes later. "Roamer's feet are perhaps in marginally better condition."

"So my feet are superior," I joke, teasing Thorn.

"Hardly, and only because you mess about on grass verges, trying to avoid roads," he retaliates as he dances about, mimicking my roadside behaviour.

Pan thanks Alistair and asks about his herd. Then, more swiftly than usual, he saddles and loads us, mindful of today's anticipated time-consuming haul through Carlisle. We encounter numerous gates every day; today, we must overcome 15; some might be dragons that bar progress. Fortunately, so far this morning, we seem to be on schedule.

Leaving Linstock Castle, Thorn is smarting over my comment about his hooves. He sets a blistering road pace for over two kilometres, initially south-west alongside a cycleway, the Hadrian's Wall Path route. We recross last evening's motorway bridge and carry on to our pre-arranged rendezvous point, a tiny car park in a corner of luscious, hushed Rickerby Park. In bright sunshine, we tread over soft, damp earth and grass.

"I recognise that car," declares Thorn.

Alan and Ernie, reliable as ever, are waiting.

"What a night, wasn't it, Ernie?" laments Pan. "It literally teemed down almost relentlessly at Linstock: six or seven prolonged, heavy showers hit us in succession."

"Oh, it was certainly chucking it down," concurs Ernie, seemingly unruffled by nature's vagaries.

"Last night's rain means it's going to be extremely boggy between here and the coast," continues Pan. "Pounding on my tent and incessant activity at a nearby, motorway, truck terminus equalled a noisy bedtime. The ponies didn't seem to mind, but I'm worse for it today."

"Well, I was up till about two o'clock in the morning," retorts Ernie matter-of-factly.

"He evidently sleeps like a newborn baby," quips Pan, casually pointing to Alan. "I bet he never hears bad weather."

"I have a clear conscience," insists Alan dryly.

"I'm heading south to Memorial Bridge," proclaims Pan as the two cinematographers grab a quick cup of home-made coffee. "That's where we're meeting Andrew, who's going to talk to us about Fell ponies living on Cumbrian commons."

"Is this another Andrew?" I ask Thorn.

"No idea," he replies. "It might be."

"Ready to go," shouts Alan enthusiastically, ending one of the shortest rests I can remember.

Alan and Ernie walk behind me, filming, concentrating now. We hug the glassy, rapidly flowing Eden's northern shore, meandering with this river, as planned, towards a suspension bridge.

"We're exactly on time, for a change!" announces Pan, not quite believing his good fortune.

Time, a fabricated, human commodity, is of less significance to equines. However, trekking requires daylight, a valuable asset that dissipates sooner with each passing autumn day.

We reach the bridge after a few minutes. Our brief, casual acquaintance with the riverbank is temporarily over.

"A council officer should be here to unlock the barrier," explains Pan to Alan and Ernie.

As Pan is considering options, a young, smiling man, the Carlisle Council Countryside Officer it transpires, approaches us and greets Pan cheerfully.

"Hi, I'm Jonathan," he says. "I apologise that we couldn't help you at the Tarraby swing gate yesterday. One of our team, designated to look after you, was ill."

"I'm sorry to hear that he was unwell, and please don't worry: two local workmen cleverly removed and replaced the gate as fast as I could count to 50!"

"Recently, we have redesigned the bridge barriers here, upgrading them to assist cyclists," reveals Jonathan. "The gap should be wide enough to take your ponies through fully laden without unlocking any barrier."

Pan thanks Jonathan for his assistance. The Countryside Officer's assessment is correct: Thorn and I slip effortlessly through the barrier gap onto the bridge. We advance casually. The rhythmic banging of hooves on wooden boards, consequent upon such an undertaking, no longer afflicts Thorn: he has conquered his fear of bridges over troubling waters. We even halt midstream, tarrying a while to admire the river snaking calmly towards city turbulence.

Andrew, whom Thorn and I have never met, and who is a founder of the Federation of Cumbria Commoners, is waiting for us exactly on cue at the far bank.

"I'll set up my camera over there," decides Alan, pointing to a quiet, grassy hollow among trees on the southern shore.

"What's today's date?" wonders Pan, mindful of recording accurate narrative as Alan begins to film.

"Have you noticed?" remarks Thorn, chuckling.

"Noticed what?" I ask, clueless.

"Our man rarely recalls what day of the month it is."

"It's the first of November, All Saints Day," replies Alan unemotionally.

"What's the basic role of the Cumbria Commoners Association?" inquires Pan, eager to learn about the commons.

"Well, it's to give commoners a voice," explains Andrew.

"How many grazed commons are we talking about, vast and tiny, in Cumbria?"

"Altogether there are 300 covering about 300,000 acres," replies Andrew. "Commoners have sheep grazing rights on about 90 per cent of those 300 commons, cattle grazing rights on about 80 per cent, and horse and pony grazing rights on about 40 per cent."

"Do we know on which commons ponies graze at present? Has there been any census?"

"No," says Andrew, "and you have hit on a major point. It's necessary to gather evidence."

"Do the vast majority of farmers graze only sheep or cattle on commons?"

"Yes," confirms Andrew. "Sheep dominate all commons, but cattle play a key role on some. Ponies are having a difficult time. Over the last 60 to 70 years, the number of pony grazing rights used by graziers has dropped significantly. Ponies have had important economic jobs historically, but this role has declined. You need to identify other reasons for keeping them, which perhaps are their genetic characteristics and their contribution to biodiversity."

"Would it be fair to assume that most sheep and cattle graziers don't appreciate the historical importance of Fell ponies?" suggests Pan.

"Unquestionably," agrees Andrew, "they are apt to put a breed that doesn't fit economically on one side. If we were talking about a rare plant, for example, a disappearing orchid, all sorts of people would campaign for it. However, as it's a farm animal, somehow it doesn't enter the equation."

Thorn nudges me.

"Roamer!" he whispers.

"What is it?" I chide softly.

"A police officer is talking with teenagers under the bridge."

"Oh, aye," I mouth. "Never mind. I'm trying to listen to Andrew."

"The Fell pony is the native pony of Cumbria and Northumberland," reminisces Pan, who is desperate to learn about grazing rights. "Its distant ancestors were native to this area for hundreds, possibly thousands, of years. For about a century, since humans formed the Fell Pony Society, hill breeders have striven to retain the pony's original characteristics. Does your Federation of Cumbria Commoners consider ponies to be part of our English agricultural system?"

"The Fell's history and culture are rooted in agriculture," confirms Andrew, "but the European Union hasn't regarded the pony as an agricultural animal: the Union doesn't recognise it for support purposes, which puts it at risk. In recent times, farmers have preferred quad bikes over ponies. After the 1965 Registration Act, it could well be that farmers didn't register quite a number of pony rights. Rights that farmers did register cannot be extinguished, although whether they are used or not depends upon where they exist and who owns them."

"Recently," notes Pan, "the European Parliament proposed that 'native breeds at risk' should be classified as biological diversity. Native ponies within agricultural systems, including those grazing commons with sheep or cattle, qualify for such a designation. Is the

Federation in favour of having commons ponies gazetted as biological diversity, in line with this recommendation?"

"Yes, indeed," confirms Andrew. "The Fell pony has a rightful place on commons where traditional pony rights have existed. It is part of northern culture. It goes back to the genesis of agriculture. It is also part of the diversity of commons. Some people don't consider biodiversity should include farm animals. We must break that idea."

"Will the European recommendation favour the breed, in your opinion?"

"It should do," reasons Andrew, "but we are going to have to fight for recognition for our livestock. High-nature-value farming is based on semi-natural vegetation, which demands the right mix of stock to maintain that vegetation in optimal condition."

"Do you remember?" I quiz Thorn quietly. "Julian discussed this matter by 'phone."

"Yes," he replies. "It's a crucial point."

"Do we know exactly who has pony rights on any common today?" asks Pan.

"Rights would have been recorded in the Commons Registers filled in between 1968 and 1972. Whoever owned rights in 1972 may not be alive now, or rights may have been transferred to somebody else."

"How does a new farmer with pony grazing rights take up those rights again?"

"If he has rights, he is free to use them," maintains Andrew.

"What about graziers who might wish to transfer their grazing rights from sheep to ponies, or vice versa?" wonders Pan.

"Registers sometimes allow you to graze sheep and cattle on the basis that four sheep equals one cow, or a certain number of sheep equals one pony. We call this 'equivalence'."

"Sounds complicated," I tell Thorn.

"Shouldn't farmers be able to use their grazing rights to graze ponies rather than sheep, if they prefer?" queries Pan.

"Before the Registration Act, no farmer quantified his rights," explains Andrew. "People were not asked to provide proper evidence for the registration of their rights. You would have unlimited grazing rights for the number of livestock that your farm could support from its own resources in winter."

"So there was flexibility? People had choices?"

"Yes," responds Andrew.

"What is the sheep-to-pony ratio for Cumbrian commons?"

"It's usually about six sheep to one horse or four sheep to one pony," answers Andrew. "It varies from common to common, however; on some commons, one sheep equals one pony."

"And sheep vary in size, naturally."

"Yes, it is imprecise," argues Andrew. "I wish to see it made more precise across Cumbria and Northumberland."

"How do humans work out their ratios?" whispers Thorn.

"I've no idea," I reply.

"I guess," he says, "they take into account how much each breed eats. Do you think a Fell pony eats four times as much as one sheep?"

"Who can be sure?" I tell him. "It may depend upon the sheep breed."

"Suppose a farmer has grazing rights for 300 sheep," surmises Pan, "and she or he wants to use, let's say, rights for 36 of those sheep to graze six ponies instead. Can the farmer do this?"

"That's a tricky question," warns Andrew. "In principle, an individual cannot convert sheep rights into pony rights. But if all the graziers and the owner of the soil – the Lord of the Manor normally – were to agree, and that's how it was done in the past, through custom, the ratio of sheep to ponies could be changed irrespective of what was written in the register."

Pan presses home a point: "Because semi-wild ponies aren't being bred for food in this country, that doesn't mean they are not a crucial part of the agricultural system. We know they can contribute to optimum grazing and habitat conditions. However, graziers who wish to graze Fell ponies have little chance of being able to secure a foothold on many commons."

"Without being disrespectful to specific organisations, there is a lot of poor science about," admits Andrew. "Agri-environment schemes impose stocking rates based on no strong experimental evidence or observation. We need robust empirical evidence. This is equally true for cattle and sheep."

"Roamer, have Cumbrian Fell ponies lost some of their common grazing rights for ever?" asks Thorn.

"Perhaps not," I reply, "but we need a plan to reclaim them."

"So you would be in favour of mixed grazing – sheep, cattle and ponies?" inquires Pan.

"Yes, but we need unambiguous scientific evidence as to what does well where. For example, on Dartmoor commons, native ponies are believed to be important winter grazers."

"Hefted Fell ponies, which have adapted their grazing behaviour for several centuries, are now endangered in their natural habitats," suggests Pan. "Will the loss of hefted herds have any negative effect?"

"Yes. Fell ponies are relevant only if they are in a habitat to which they relate, from which they have emerged and to which they contribute."

"How might commons councils benefit the Fell pony?" asks Pan.

"Commoners must be able to take decisions themselves; traditionally, in the manorial court, commoners sat with their peers and undertook the business of the day. Manorial courts ceased to exist for various reasons. Now, under the 2006 Act, new commons councils will allow commoners to create their own bylaws that everybody must follow."

"Once in a while, Fell pony breeders complain they are lone voices," says Pan. "For example, if a pony breeder is on a common grazed by 10 sheep farmers, the breeder's voice tends to be drowned out. This is especially true if other graziers do not appreciate the importance of lost pony grazing rights."

"Although pony breeders are a minority group, if they articulate their case, the Federation will listen to what they are saying," promises Andrew. "Bringing voices together is the critical first step."

"By the time this happens, we might have no hefted hill herds left in Cumbria," worries Pan. "Nearly all remaining herds are under threat for various reasons. Particularly, several major breeders are likely to retire soon: there may be no younger breeders to take over."

"Government's Single Payment scheme doesn't recognise ponies," insists Andrew. "There must be recognition of the contribution agricultural animals make to biodiversity on common land. We must encourage and help pony breeders who have links with commons to come together. Let's make a difference."

"Roamer, will that policeman wish to say 'hello' to us?" inquires Thorn, distracted again.

"I doubt it," I murmur forcefully. "I imagine he has a busy daily schedule, and he wouldn't interrupt our filming."

"Oh, I was just wondering."

I ignore him. Sometimes, Thorn's over-exuberance takes over: he can't control it.

"Could pony grazing rights that are not being used on any common be loaned to, or leased by, someone who intends to create a herd?" suggests Pan.

"If I own a common right," replies Andrew, "and if fields go with that common right, I cannot sell it as an asset on the open market, though I can lease it to someone for a two-year period or less. Leases are renewable."

"And the Federation could advise farmers and the Fell Pony Society concerning the benefits of leasing?"

"Yes. And commons councils will have a role."

"It is sad that too few local people recognise this pony as Cumbria's and Northumberland's native pony," worries Pan.

"I have asked people what breed of sheep became extinct in Cumbria in the 1950s. They don't know. It was the Crag sheep. We lost the Cumberland pig as well. Organisations are excited, understandably, about an endangered butterfly or orchid, yet the loss of agricultural animals doesn't seem to strike home in the same way."

"Should breeders of Fell ponies within the agricultural system receive Government economic help as part of any future proposed agri-environment scheme?" wonders Pan.

"We will support that principle with whatever evidence is available," promises Andrew.

Thorn:

Roamer and I have been waiting too patiently at this suspension bridge. I am grateful, therefore, when our man's lengthy though interesting chat with the Commoners' Federation fellow is over. This knowledgeable visitor bids our man farewell and is out of sight in no time. Meanwhile, Cameraman's assistant strides back over the bridge, presumably on a mission to retrieve his vehicle at the park's boundary.

During the conversation, I noticed a policeman some distance away.

"How puzzling," I tell Roamer. "He hasn't left yet."

"We've more important things to worry about," responds Roamer, "such as getting to tonight's campsite safely."

Departing the scene, we advance westwards along the Eden's southern bank this early afternoon. Briefly, from Memorial Bridge, we make use of a national cycle network route that courses with the river.

"Alan, if you have the time, I would appreciate your help about two kilometres ahead," begs our man as we adopt an easy rhythm along the path. "We shall meet two motorcycle barriers: these represent severe obstacles for pack ponies. We must descend a steep slope to avoid them."

"Unfortunately," explains Cameraman, "Ernie and I have another, urgent assignment elsewhere. I'm confident you'll be all right."

We pause at the next track junction, perhaps 100 paces further on. Cameraman's assistant is waiting, having driven his vehicle to a prearranged rendezvous point. He and Cameraman hastily pack away. An ignition key turns. An engine purrs. They speed off. We three are alone.

For the remainder of today, we must mirror the meanders of the River Eden to Knockupworth – a farm known as Hubert's Hillock possibly seven centuries ago. Travelling in harmony with the river's prehistoric, not quite ox-bowed course will offer our man geographical and archaeological enlightenment. At least, he hopes so. Doubtless, from various vantage points he will be able to appreciate more clearly some difficulties Roman Wall builders and their stone-conveying animals faced.

Skirting along the perimeter of The Swifts, a golf course, our route eventually branches right, up a dozen or so steps and through a tunnel under a major arterial road bridge linking settlements north of the Eden with Carlisle's city centre. Gently, leisurely, we circumnavigate around Carlisle Castle's northern boundary walls at Bitts Park, situated at the head of the valley. Over Sheepmount – sheep trophy – Bridge, which spans the cold River Caldew near its confluence with the Eden, we are standing alongside the Wall's course, having kept its location within sight throughout this detour.

Squeezing first past metal car barriers, afterwards through a tight gateway, our direction is across a car park and then alongside an athletics track. Our route briefly melds with the designated National Trail; we are about to leave Carlisle behind.

At the next bridge, which carries a railway, looms the first dreaded bike barrier. Our man studied this obstacle last year. He realises that, even if he removes our packs, the slim gap between two circular metal bars will be impassable. An alternative, which he has anticipated, is to climb steeply to the bank's crest and then descend to the river from the bridge's opposite side. He checks our packs before adjusting breast collars and breechings, ready for a tricky operation.

Roamer and I have energy enough: we clamber easily to the bank top. Now, however, we face a severely steep descent of roughly 25 wooden, railway-sleeper steps – my counting isn't particularly accurate – to regain the river footpath. Protruding n-shaped nails, possibly a score, pepper every step. Presumably, they provide assured grip for human footwear. Ironically, they spell danger for our feet: we aren't wearing shoes. Our situation is potentially perilous.

"Okay boys, let's take this steadily," insists our man. "We mustn't have an accident: I cannot risk either of you becoming lame."

He unhooks our connecting harness and tethers Roamer to a beech tree winding down for winter.

"Roamer, stay here," he commands firmly, fixing his gaze on Roamer's eyes. "I'll be gone for less than three minutes. Be a good boy, Roamer. Come on, Thorn. Steady!"

We zigzag down the slope, aiming to avoid the steps, but this isn't always possible. Roamer looks on, alarmed that we might leave him.

We are now over 40 yards away from my pal; he can't see us. Our man calms him.

"Good boy, Roamer!" he shouts.

"I wasn't keen on being alone, but I was forced to trust Pan," divulges Roamer afterwards. "I trusted he wouldn't desert me."

As expeditiously as is safely possible, we descend to the path. Our man ties my lead rope to a tree and orders me to stay. He then scampers up the steps to Roamer. Now it's my turn to wonder. Thankfully, seconds later, Roamer and our man reappear around a corner halfway down the slope.

Our man is calmer, more relaxed and almost casual as he adjusts our harnesses.

"Well done, Thorn and Roamer!" he praises. "Let's keep going."

Why did he worry? I wasn't about to break free and gallop off without Roamer, my closest friend in the entire world.

Straight ahead, parts of three thick, oval, metal rings, each about 2 feet high and 2½ feet in diameter, are protruding from the ground at a narrow access point marking the beginning of pretty Engine Lonning Nature Reserve. Negotiation will be tricky, perhaps impossible. Instead, our man decides to avoid this human-contrived deterrent to motorcyclists by taking a right-hand fork, a track that sympathetically hugs the riverbank. Steeply below us, the Eden sweeps between tree thickets not yet denuded of rapidly withering ash and beech leaves.

"Were you aware, boys?" enthuses our man. "For a century, until it closed down in the 1960s, this area was a lively railway passenger and freight terminal."

We weren't aware, as usual, and it's just as well that nobody's about: an eavesdropper would infer that he was talking to himself; that he was slightly insane.

"There were several engine sheds here," he adds as an afterthought whilst inspecting his map. "Hence the name Engine

Lonning is apt."

Beyond a small bridge lies a wooden stile, our latest dragon. What happens now? Our man has a plan. We backtrack 100 yards before turning uphill towards a small, unobtrusive, padlocked gate at a field corner. He takes out his mobile 'phone.

"Hi, Jimmy. . . . How are you? . . . We are at your boundary fence. . . . Are you able to unlock the gate? . . . That's superb! . . . See you shortly."

Replacing his 'phone securely in its holster, he smiles.

"Right, we'll wait," he announces.

It turns out that this fellow called Jimmy owns Knockupworth Farm, today's destination. His farmhouse stands more than 1,000 yards away. He and our man worked out a feasible route across his land last December, I later learn.

The farmer, who finds us within minutes, greets our man.

"I'm glad you've made it, especially as it's so late in the year," he applauds. "Ahead the ground is very wet. Be careful."

We are onto grazing ground devoid of trees, offering us an open vista to the Eden. Nevertheless, this old flood plain is deceptively rain-sodden. With the farmer's expert assistance, we detour initially away from the flowing highway, prudently negotiating waterlogged patches.

"Beyond here, my field is too boggy for ponies," cautions the farmer after 300 yards of slow progress. "I advise you to head downhill to the river. Then follow the river until you reach an electricity pylon, where you must work your way uphill towards a private gate in the far corner of the hedge. I'll meet you there."

The farmer continues alone across his waterlogged field.

At our present location, beyond the milecastle at Boomby Gill, a ravine with an unexplained name, our man observes on his map that Wall and Vallum diverge. Romans built their Wall along the riverbank as far as Grinsdale to the north, but the Vallum turns north-west towards Kirkandrews. We are able to enjoy a dry line, hugging the Wall's original position before navigating uphill with the Vallum. About 20 minutes after detouring towards the river, we are meandering gingerly across deep mud towards the designated gate, where Knockupworth's farmer patiently waits.

"Just off the road, you'll find a small field where your ponies can stay," suggests the farmer. "There are no livestock and it's secure. Unfortunately, the grazing is rough."

"The rougher the better," replies our man. "That's exactly what they require."

"You could store your gear in the shed there, to keep it dry," proposes the farmer. "If you want to camp away from the ponies, there's another tiny enclosure opposite their field. Would you care to have supper with us?"

"Thank you, yes," replies our man. "That sounds excellent! First, I should ascertain whether both ponies are all right and then I'll pitch my tent. Is there water nearby?"

"I'll fetch you some."

The farmer drives off, returning after several minutes with two buckets and two heavy, plastic, screw-top containers of fresh water.

"Let's have some fun," I implore Roamer.

"What do you mean?" he demands, bemused.

"Watch," I tell him.

Our man fills a bucket. He places it on the ground under my nose. I take a couple of quick gulps. I'm not very thirsty, and I'm not that keen on the taste of tap water anyway. I nudge the bucket forcefully with my nose, spilling it completely. It's a clever prank.

"Oi, Thorn, pack it in!" orders our man, visibly annoyed. "You're up to your old tricks. Don't expect water straight after you've been fed: I don't want you ill with colic."

I take no notice. I'm determined to spill Roamer's bucket too, but our leader's too clever: he smartly removes it and then me from the vicinity. Oh, well, never mind.

"That's not funny," scolds Roamer. "I am thirsty, but there's nothing to drink now."

Luckily for Roamer, our man returns his bucketful promptly. His whinnying ceases.

Free of our head collars a short time later, it's time to settle down to the serious job of eating thistles. They're crunchy and quite juicy. You should try them. Ye-ee-eh, I'm serious!

While I am busily browsing, our man discovers surprisingly hard ground: tent pegs will not penetrate limestone beneath a markedly thin covering of grass and mud. He must tie one main guy rope to a tree, the other to a fence. Otherwise, a severe storm might blow his roundhouse away, even with him inside it.

The farmer's back.

"Supper's ready when you are," he declares. "It's Shepherd's Pie. Is that okay?"

"Oh, I'm sorry, Jimmy," replies our man, closing his field gate securely. "I completely forgot to mention: I'm usually a vegetarian."

In view of this sudden revelation, I suspect that the pie might contain part of a sheep or, maybe, bits of a cow.

"But please don't worry," he adds quickly. "I'll still enjoy eating it."

"We've got plenty of vegetables," ventures Jimmy sympathetically.

"In fact," admits our man, "for that matter I'm hungry enough to eat half a cow or even half a horse!"

"Is somebody thinking of eating one of us?" quizzes Roamer, aroused from a half-awake state by this announcement.

"Our man is joking, Roamer," I reply. "It's a nonsense human saying: it doesn't mean that he literally wants to eat a horse. Besides, who will carry his packs, if not us? Quit worrying. Relax."

"That's true," murmurs Roamer. "Mind you, he could employ Solo to take my place. I'm sorry, Thorn. I don't know what I'm saying: I was falling asleep until I heard the words 'eat half a horse'."

"Don't be silly, Roamer," I tell him. "You and I are his favourite pack ponies. He has often said so."

"Of course we are. Ignore me. I was dozing off, imagining what Solo was doing. I miss him."

"He'll be sleeping, eating and playing, if he has any sense," I reassure Roamer.

Occasionally, my friend needs reassuring. I suspect we all do.

It begins raining heavily, but don't alarm yourself: rain doesn't prevent us from snoozing! We'd rather have bad weather tonight than tomorrow morning. Rain walking with a packsaddle and a waterproof overcoat is decidedly uncomfortable. However, with luck, the skies will have emptied by sunrise.

Solo:

I had another odd dream last night. Can you guess what happened? I was participating in the Wall expedition with Thorn and Roamer. The weather was uninspiring: it poured down or was strikingly windy every day.

I wore a large, Roman Army saddle and carried a pack that weighed a monumental amount. At least, it seemed too heavy for an exceptionally young pony on such an arduous trek. The leather breasting and breeching irritated me, making me sore, wearing me out. I had a second serious concern: was the saddle damaging my back?

I was unhappy. What's more, the packhorseman slept in a weatherproof tent, but we ponies had no choice: we remained outside. The wind screamed; the rain teemed down; I yearned to fit into that shelter; I could hardly bear it.

"Roamer, I can't carry my load another pace!" I cried when we eventually made it to our destination. "Our journey has been exhausting. I could sleep for ever."

Three days later, we returned to our base and could recover. We raced happily together.

"He-ee-ee-ee! Look at me galloping!" I called. "Beat you both! Oh, no, it's raining again."

I prematurely awoke from my dream. It really was raining. I was alone once more.

Inquisitive cattle, kissing gates and a strange fence

2ⁿᵈ *November – Grinsdale, Kirkandrews and Beaumont Hall*

Roamer:

IT is over three weeks since we left Newcastle. Thorn and I still tread the Military Way beside Hadrian's Wall. Before heading for Burgh-by-Sands School tomorrow, we will camp overnight in the grounds of Beaumont Parish Hall in the village of Kirkandrews-on-Eden.

Cool, drenching cloudbursts cease before daybreak. Pan packs up a soaked tent, which creates added weight for Thorn to carry. Never mind: he'll handle it easily. Ever shortening days force us to strike camp earlier from now on. Pan must guarantee us sufficient natural light to reach planned destinations, especially whenever he has arranged to meet knowledgeable experts for chats.

"Perfect timing," calls Pan as Jimmy's four-by-four trundles to a halt at his campsite. "I've just finished loading up the ponies."

Jimmy escorts us across his land. We face a kilometre of unsurprisingly wet, boggy terrain both before and beyond a bypass, newly constructed because an ever-increasing car-owning population demanded a new route around Carlisle City. Jimmy discusses with Pan one consequence of this bypass, which bisects his land: he can't move cows about so easily these days.

Last December, Pan's reconnoitre failed to determine any path for equines through a minefield of partly completed modern construction. He and Jimmy reluctantly had accepted that the practical solution might be to take the country road from Knockupworth to Grinsdale, a village in Grimr's valley. Grimr was a Norseman, in case you were wondering. This road would have taken Pan away from the Vallum. Now, however, an underpass has changed everything: it allows pedestrian passage beneath the bypass. Fortuitously for us, humans completed construction of this tunnel two months ago.

"Yesterday evening, bypass lights reminded me of Wembley Stadium on match night," remarks Pan. "Torches were redundant."

"Now I understand," I whinny to Thorn. "Those lights explain why last night resembled summer daytime and why I became confused."

"Wembley Stadium?" ponders Thorn.

"How do you cope with glaring lights?" inquires Pan solemnly. "Can you sleep?"

"Special curtains improve the situation," confesses Jimmy, "but the bypass is disrupting: this place was peaceful before. I'd rather have my farm in one piece."

"What about undesirable consequences of artificial night light on wildlife?" frets Thorn. "I imagine light pollution must disorient some mammals, birds, insects and even trees; it must badly affect their sleeping patterns or harm them in other ways."

From the underpass, our route is gently uphill towards the Vallum and approximate line of the Way. Attaining the highest ground of Jimmy's farm, we glide, nevertheless, across a severely waterlogged field to a farm gate, steering arrow-like for Kirkandrews. Less than 20 minutes later, I suppose, we reach a gateway leading to an uncluttered lonning, our eventual exit point onto the road into Grinsdale.

"I'll leave you here," announces Jimmy.

"Thanks for all your support," acknowledges Pan. "See you later hopefully, on our return leg."

Jimmy about faces and begins to trudge home, retracing water-filled boot prints.

Pan has chosen to enter Grinsdale Village and then follow the Wall line. This route overlooks riverside flats before converging with the Vallum briefly at Kirkandrews. Selection, instead, of the minor road to Kirkandrews, on a course south of the Vallum, would have represented a lesser challenge, but that's not how Pan thinks.

"I prefer a negotiated access rather than blind road work," he told Jimmy yesterday. "The return, eastbound journey is another matter, however: poor weather may limit or eliminate options."

I'm much happier: we are on firmer, drier, open ground. From Park Farm in Grinsdale, we hug hedges on a high line to Sourmilk Bridge, where foaming water flowed in earlier times. Today, the bridge spans a tiny stream. Was the next, now missing, milecastle located here?

Two unnavigable stiles, one at each end of the bridge, force us to swing left through a field gateway and then backtrack underneath humming electricity pylons. Our course is initially to the right of a hedgerow, afterwards through a large field of excessively inquisitive cattle, briskly across the Vallum towards a minor road.

Earlier today, Park Farm's owner warned Pan: "Be careful. Watch out for the cows."

Pan hurriedly seizes a cycle horn from his rucksack, ready to frighten off any aggressive individuals. At this point, he realises he has accidentally left his only surviving metal walking pole at Knockupworth: it would have been a potential deterrent. The beasts stalk us en masse, gradually gaining speed as we approach our exit gate. Pan is definitely the most rattled.

From the road, we turn sharp right, through a smallholding gateway.

"He-ee-ee, Thorn," I whinny. "Look! Two thoroughbred horses are grazing in this field."

We attract their spirited attention straight away. However, upon belatedly realising those thoroughbreds are aroused, Pan isn't impressed. I guess he's thinking they could become uncontrollable, injuring us or initiating a stampede. He decides that discretion necessitates a hasty retreat via the nearest field gate.

"How disappointing," moans Thorn. "Our man's premature exit has thwarted our intended frolics."

Pan's unanticipated manoeuvre forces us briefly onto a roadside grass verge. Ninety metres later, on a temporary beeline back towards Sourmilk Bridge, we cut across a sheep pasture, which we quickly exit via a gateway onto an enclosed, muddy lonning. This allows Pan to lead us through a further gateway into the grounds of a smallholding. Are we in a maze? I'm dizzy.

Now we are travelling south of and parallel to the Wall, arrowing towards Kirkandrews. Halfway across the next field, we stop dead.

"Hai-ai-ai! What's wrong?" I ask Thorn.

"It's obvious," he chirps. "There's no way through. We are undone."

Thorn's observation is no overstatement: the landowner has stretched a temporary electric fence between gateposts at the far gateway.

"Boys, forgive me, but we must retrace our steps to the road," announces Pan loudly, undeterred by this additional setback. "This fence is not supposed to be here. I assumed, obviously wrongly, that I had made every relevant landowner aware of where we were travelling today."

Pan, don't stress yourself, I'm thinking. We Fell ponies are flexible and usually patient.

At Kirkandrews, where Vallum and Wall diverge, trickier dragons seek to hinder us. Pan must remove our saddlebags at a newly constructed, otherwise impassable, kissing gate. Menacing ground surrounds the gate. A path of half-metre square, roughly hewn, stone slabs cleverly punctuates foot-deep bog. National Trail maintenance staff likely laid these for the benefit of walkers and the monument. There's insufficient room to turn around. Pan searches for his 'phone.

"Hi, Colin," he begins. "We are less than 200 metres from the hall. . . . This new kissing gate, whose existence I was unaware of, is hindering me. . . . I am unloading the ponies at the slabs. . . . Okay, I'll wait here."

Pan has unloaded us, moved us through the gateway and is about to repack, when an immaculately dressed man appears, seemingly from nowhere. The stranger is Colin, who, I ascertain later, is Beaumont Parish Council's treasurer and a National Trail warden; during the last six months, he has negotiated this section of our route with locals on behalf of Pan.

Thorn and I are perched insecurely. If we step off this stone path, we could sink up to our hocks: there's deep, squishy marsh all around. We stand perfectly still. Colin begins transporting our loads through the gateway. Perhaps Pan should warn him to be exceptionally careful. Oh, no, it's too late! The warden loses his balance; he lands front first in the mire. Drenched in brown liquid, he elegantly extricates himself.

"I'm sorry you've received a mud-bath for your trouble," utters Pan as he effortlessly tightens Thorn's surcingle around a reloaded pack. "Are you all right?" he adds, genuinely distressed by Colin's plight.

"I'm fine," contends Colin cheerfully. "It's nothing a quick shower won't sort out."

Thorn is having a quiet chuckle.

"What's so funny?" I ask.

"They are," he replies. "We're supposed to be the muddied ones. We don't mind mud, but look at us. Apart from our hooves we are far, far cleaner."

"This part of the trail has been rerouted recently," Colin informs Pan. "Will the ponies be able to cross soft ground ahead to reach the track just above us? It's a sharp climb."

"That shouldn't cause a problem," replies Pan reassuringly.

Stretching for 20 metres in front of us is a sodden, soggy quagmire. Beyond this bog is a severely waterlogged, sharply inclined bank. Thorn and I aren't a bit bothered. Without hesitating, we powerfully but carefully surge forwards and upwards, easily gaining a narrow path that traverses higher, drier ground. We remain virtually mudless.

"We can't access the hall's grounds via its rear gate," reveals Colin apologetically when we pause on a narrow ledge. "It has been repaired recently and is impassable with horses. Consequently, we must exit the riverside through a friend's private gateway."

Before long, still on the ledge, we are standing by Colin's designated gateway, which isn't quite wide enough for ponies with packs. Neither can we move forwards: immediately ahead is a wire fence and wooden stile. Backtracking is impossible, too.

"I'll need to unload Thorn and Roamer again," confirms Pan, resigned to this inevitable consequence.

"I'll borrow a wheelbarrow to move your gear," offers Colin, who is as cheerful and helpful as ever. Off he goes, searching.

Minus our packs, Pan leads us briskly through private gardens, along the road 50 metres and hence through large entrance gates into the grounds of our planned destination, Beaumont Hall. He and Colin now must ferry every piece of equipment, by hand or wheelbarrow, through the hall's riverside gateway, a task requiring multiple journeys. Meanwhile, Thorn and I can relax.

"All right," admits Pan, sighing. "Perhaps we should have strolled the last 400 metres by road, which would have saved nearly two hours – but it wouldn't have been so interesting."

"Is he talking to us?" I ask Thorn, perplexed.

"No, himself again, definitely," reckons Thorn. "Human foresight, it appears, is prescribed, precious but scarce on expeditions; hindsight is abundant but worthless. Native ponies share natural foresight. Foresight, not hindsight, means survival to us."

"Well, Pan should see the funny side," I conclude, "even though it was the most time-consuming 400 metres of the trek so far."

"You must admit, Roamer: he is entertaining. Does he ever do anything the easy way?"

"That's not his way," I reply. "And don't forget: when they built their Wall, Romans would have had no easy, cop-out options."

So far, we've completed over 140 kilometres. Tomorrow, we will meet scores of children and their teachers in Burgh. I'm excited. I fall asleep easily, eagerly anticipating engrossing encounters with engaging mini-humans.

Thorn:

What a perplexing day! Our man must repeatedly unload and then reload our packs. We start, stop, start again, twist and turn. I'm convinced we head in countless conceivable directions – north, south, east, west and numerous bearings in-between. We venture forwards, consequently needing to backtrack. Does our man have any idea where he is going?

A Fell pony's innate sense of direction is legendary. We customarily choose the easiest and quickest route, but always the safest, between two points. Humans frequently dither because they cannot read natural signs. We rarely rest our heads on straw: they commonly fill their heads with it.

"Trust in Pan," advises Roamer whenever he suspects I am beginning to lose faith.

Roamer is usually right. Nevertheless, humans occasionally panic in situations where Fell ponies remain calm. Let's face it. Few humans understand that we are noble beasts. Even fewer undertake to learn from us.

After two further hours of tiring tramping, I am weary and exceedingly hungry. We are in the proximity of where Romans erected Braelees Milecastle, which, according to our man, is a name that could mean "clearing on a steep slope". Thankfully, nearby is tonight's livery, a lush, peaceful paddock surrounding Beaumont Hall. My superior hearing detects the faint, gentle chatter of the Eden flowing effortlessly, endlessly about 500 feet below us.

Kirkandrews – where Saint Andrew's Church stands – is not simply tonight's safe haven: because we are running out of food, equine and human, it is a welcome, fortuitous supply point. Roamer has concluded so, and he generally assesses our supply situation accurately: he has a mystifying ability to sense even slightly reduced pack weight.

Our man exits the hall's main entrance, carrying over his shoulder an unopened bag of pony pellets. I am salivating instantly. Let me at them now! I'm ravenous. When he cuts open the bag with his pocket knife, the flavour mist invades my nostrils. I tug at the rail

246

where our man has tied me with a poorly executed trekking knot, managing to break free. As he is measuring feed into Roamer's nosebag I casually, furtively, sidle up to my friend.

"Pack it in!" demands our man, grabbing my dangling halter.

He marches me back to my rail, securing me expertly this time. I am flustered. Come on. Hurry up! That almost imperceptible aroma, the wafting of toasted oats, wheat and straw, is overpowering.

A short time later, while Roamer and I are devouring those fresh pellets, a car pulls up outside the hall. A youngish man – a National Trail warden I presume from his apparel – steps out. He walks purposefully over to the human Roamer describes as the treasurer, who is advising our man where to store our tack and saddlebags overnight.

I stop eating to listen. The stranger briefly discusses with the treasurer an upcoming business meeting of National Trail wardens and then departs.

Having carried our saddles to the hall, our man thanks the treasurer warmly for supporting our expedition and its goals. He then removes Roamer's nosebag.

"Boys," he quips, "one day, when this mission is over, let's hope that everybody will see the bigger picture."

"Pan is confusing me," grumbles Roamer. "What's he on about?"

I finish consuming my ration of munchies as if it's my last meal on earth.

Roamer is persistent.

"What does he mean by 'bigger picture'?" he asks, as soon as I can speak

"I'm not sure," I admit. "Don't worry: our man's aim is simple. What matters is that we are here, carrying out his intentions. Nobody can deny our achievement. With luck, we shall be a part of history, the first and conceivably only modern-day, twenty-first-century pack animals to travel the Wall's length, end to end. Enough humans will wish to understand how and why we did it. Isn't that the point?"

"That's it!" agrees Roamer. "To realise 'why' is to see the bigger picture."

Darkness is descending as our man releases us. Finally, we are free to explore.

"What's going on over there?" murmurs Roamer.

I'm dumbfounded. At our enclosure's eastern extremity is a narrow gap between the perimeter fence and a hedge. From there, a grassy avenue leads amongst beech trees towards a steep slope, which plunges sharply to the Eden. Across this gap, our man is busily pressing six white, plastic posts with pointed tips into the ground. The treasurer is assisting him.

"Let's trot over and find out," I suggest.

"Thanks for looking after it, Colin," remarks our man as we observe the scene. "They exhibit a worrying knack of wandering, given half a chance; if they reach the river, we'll never retrieve them."

"Glad to help," replies the treasurer. "They won't stray, once it's in place, will they?"

"That's a good question. They haven't met an electric fence before."

"Have they not?"

"Perhaps they'll accept it right away," concludes our man unconvincingly. "We've been lucky up to now: most overnight fields and paddocks have been escape proof. However, on reflection, I should have used this fence at three other campsites, including the Errington Arms near Corbridge."

The two men build their electric barrier into a roughly rectangular shape across the gap.

"Unfortunately, we can't erect it perfectly tonight," admits our man. "It's too dark now, but this should hold them."

"After tomorrow, I'll continue to store the fence in our hall if you like," offers the treasurer.

"Good idea," replies our man. "It will be handily placed in case I need to arrange to ferry it elsewhere in an emergency situation."

Later, when nobody is about, we creep over to examine the humans' handiwork.

"They've not done a particularly first-rate job," I suggest. "We could easily knock over that flimsy gadget."

"I'm not gambling," counters Roamer. "It might be electrified, though I'm uncertain how that could bother us. And have you noticed? Pan has also bridged the gap with our tethering chains, perhaps to dissuade us from going near his fence."

"Oh, okay," I sigh, relying on Roamer's judgement. "I'm with you."

You might have concluded already that I love to seek amusing adventures and frivolous evening entertainment, but I'm resigned: we'll not break out tonight. Although those nearby woods may be enticing, a Fell pony rarely contemplates hazardous activity without justifiable reason.

"Why bother breaking out?" continues Roamer. "We've lots of space and juicy grazing here."

He's right. Anyway, something else has caught my eye. In the centre of our paddock is a wooden mountain. It takes Roamer and me several minutes to amble around it, exploring the variety of smells from freshly pruned sycamore, ash and beech. Humans have piled dozens and dozens of tree branches far higher than our ears.

Roamer is baffled: "What's it for?"

I protest I've no idea, but then I remember: "I did hear our man talking to the treasurer about bonfire night, when lots of children will be coming here."

"I dislike fire," ventures Roamer. "No, I hate fire and smoke."

"Me too," I reply, sympathising, although I'm not sure what he is referring to: I've never seen fire except that shooting from our man's butane stove, which purrs continuously when he is cooking.

In fact, our man is boiling water right now. A steel pot is perched precariously on a circle of light about eight inches above the ground; the never-ending mini-gale of burning gas forms a perfect ring of blue flame. This mini-stove is busy outside the door of our man's tent, which he has pitched adjacent to the hall's sidewall. My fell experience tells me that such a tent arrangement offers him and his stove rudimentary protection from severe weather.

We keep our distance. Fire might seem harmless enough, but we instinctively avoid it. A primordial, nagging voice, deep within my brain, says, "Be cautious!"

Roamer, who is even warier of fire than I am, is adamant: "We had better be long gone before they light their bonfire."

As we are talking, the treasurer returns with a flask of coffee for our man.

"My wife made this for you and has sent you something to eat. It's a shame you couldn't have had tea with us."

"Please thank Marion," replies our man, upon discovering cake and biscuits. "Would you convey my apologies to her for not being able to come to your house: I was determined to stow all equipment safely inside the hall and pitch my tent before dark. That aside, you have a committee meeting commencing in about 25 minutes: I don't want to disturb you."

"Yes, it's to discuss the November fifth bonfire party," explains the treasurer. "I've made every member aware that there are two Fell ponies here. They have all promised to close the gates on arrival."

"Thanks, Colin. I appreciate it," says our man. "I'm taking no risks: during your meeting, I guarantee Roamer and Thorn won't play their old tricks."

What is our man planning?

Time passes peacefully until, much later, Roamer and I hear two voices. Our man is alone, inside his tent. He is either chatting on his telephone or listening to a conversation recorded previously on his voice tracer; I'm unsure which.

Our man is speaking: "Thank you for calling back, David. What's your specific job with Natural England?"

"Isn't Simon, who we met at Housesteads Fort, a representative of Natural England?" Roamer reminds me.

I nod twice: "Yes, he is if you say so."

"I'm involved in agri-environment schemes," replies an unrecognisable voice. "I am particularly interested in the grazing management of upland grass habitats."

"Another David!" chirps Roamer. "How many have we met?"

"I've given up counting," I reply. "What's an agri-environment scheme?"

"Let me think," says Roamer. "Isn't it a method of protecting

250

from destruction habitats containing wild animals and plants in places where farmers grow crops or graze sheep or cattle?"

"Tell me," inquires our man. "Why has Natural England restricted cattle, sheep and equine grazing in the north of England recently?"

"Uncontrolled increases in stock numbers on commons over the second half of the twentieth century," expounds the grazing manager, "meant that registered rights of farmers to graze land exceeded the land's environmental carrying capacity. This has led to heathland being destroyed."

"Roamer, what is 'environmental carrying capacity'?" I ask. "Such complicated phrases mean little to me."

"Am I an encyclopaedia?" he jibes good-humouredly.

"Well, you seem to be the expert on farming matters," I retort. "You do listen avidly to human conversations."

"You win. I suppose, though I'm guessing, it's the maximum number of sheep or cattle that can survive indefinitely within a given area of heathland, or within any other habitat for that matter. Too many grazing animals will mean insufficient food, water and shelter for them all; they will destroy the environment, including the homes of wildlife living there. One of my cousins has seen it happen."

"Since the late 1980s," reveals the land manager, "new regulations have insisted that farmers should not overgraze land. Special Government schemes restrict stock numbers to allow heathland to recover and flourish. These schemes restore habitats, help species survive, and match the amount of grazing to the vegetation present. This is sustainable grazing."

"Should ponies be part of sustainable grazing?" speculates our man.

"Yes. We are trying to encourage mixed grazing using cattle and ponies, not grazing with sheep alone."

Our man persists: "Does Natural England recognise the importance of Fell ponies that graze within the agricultural system?"

"We are looking for animals with suitable characteristics, such as hardiness, to graze natural habitats. Hill herds would and should feature in some of the schemes we set up with hill farmers."

"Why do grazing restrictions have a far worse effect on Fell ponies than on several native sheep and cattle breeds within the agricultural system?" wonders our man.

"Ponies have suffered from not being agricultural livestock in the way sheep and cattle are. Sheep and cattle are a greater part of farming economics. We could encourage farmers to use Fell ponies as well as cattle."

"We are valuable," interrupts Roamer, sighing audibly. "Why can't humans see what's blindingly obvious?"

"One of Government's primary responsibilities is to ensure that the greatest variety of agricultural animals and plants is saved from extinction," argues our man. "I guess this commitment applies to the Fell pony?"

"Yes," confirms the manager. "I don't see why Fell ponies couldn't be considered to be farm animals: they've had a working role on farms and farmed landscapes. Besides, they are recognised as a threatened native breed and are valuable culturally."

"Ye-ee-ee-eh, I agree!" squeals Roamer. "That's what Julian and Andrew were on about."

Our man elaborates: "An aim of this expedition is to persuade all Government and private land managers to recognise the Fell pony as a farm animal genetic resource and as biological diversity."

"The idea of agricultural diversity is mentioned in Government policy," notes the manager.

"We haven't yet identified scientifically many of the Fell pony's genetic characteristics that we must preserve," believes our man. "Presently, it can graze a wide range of habitats successfully: it can help create suitable living conditions for a variety of vertebrates, invertebrates and wildflowers. However, possibly unscientific or injudicious breeding might be causing, or could cause, the gradual erosion, even irrevocable loss, of some crucial traits. Therefore, should we protect the pony's genetic make-up better?"

"Though I don't fully understand," confides Roamer, "after meeting so many experts on our trek, I have concluded that our kind could benefit wildlife hugely."

"Some scientists believe that saving and protecting genetic characteristics of farm animals such as the Fell pony should be a main aim of agri-environment schemes," confirms the manager. "Perhaps a future aim should be to make extra payments to breeders whose acclimatised herds are part of grazing schemes."

"Hey, is that a good idea?" I ask Roamer.

"Ye-ee-ee-eh," squeals Roamer again. "In case you had forgotten, Julian made a roughly similar proposal. Who knows? We Fell ponies may possess several important, if not unique, genetic grazing characteristics."

"Oh, I see, sort of," I respond unenthusiastically. "Human conversations are less than straightforward unless you understand technical words."

"Frequently, Government overlooks pony breeders when agri-environment scheme payments are set up," observes our man.

"If farmers and others use grazing animals to protect habitats and wildlife in the manner Natural England recommends, they do receive financial help," explains the manager. "However, we base our payments on the land area grazed. Therefore, we usually don't pay our Supplement where several different animal groups are grazing together on a common: it's difficult to decide whether any particular group of animals is having a direct benefit, which disadvantages ponies that run on common land."

"How could you record observations that would advise Government about the grazing benefits of Fell ponies?" inquires our man.

"Detailed monitoring research is expensive. Perhaps we could monitor the ponies of specific breeders who already participate in agri-environment schemes. It helps the case for Fell ponies, as conservation grazers, to have that information."

"Truth is," mutters Roamer softly, "as we have found out during our travels, few Fell ponies are involved in grazing schemes."

"In future, could this Supplement be paid to pony breeders?" asks our man.

"Yes," agrees the manager. "Fell ponies have an important role to play in providing the highest habitat quality. Additionally, there may be situations where, part of the time, ponies at large on the fell could graze non-common land where there is a conservation grazing need. Where ponies can produce habitat benefits off of common land, breeders are entitled to receive a basic payment to look after those habitats and, on top of that, a payment for 'at risk' native breeds."

"That's a bold idea," declares Roamer, "though I wonder whether I truly understand the significance of this conversation."

"Should the Fell Pony Society be aware of available financial incentives?" queries our man. "Should it be looking for opportunities to employ ponies in grazing schemes?"

"Yes, absolutely," agrees the manager.

Our man's onto another subject: "Will climate change affect the roles of native ponies within Britain's agricultural system?"

"We must create landscapes adaptable to climate change," insists the manager. "There are roles for particular types of grazing animal within particular habitats. We must match the animal with the type of grazing."

"Shouldn't we understand better the learned grazing behaviour of Fell ponies and how to preserve their hefting characteristics?" wonders our man.

"Ponies have particular areas and vegetation types they prefer to graze at different seasons, different times of the season and even different times of the day. Improving our understanding of that would help us set better grazing conditions. Unfortunately, it's not easy to acquire Government money for grazing behaviour research."

At least I know what hefting is: Jamie told us.

"So it's crucial that breeders talk to Government?" queries our man.

"We have, in recent times, received some criticism from hill farmers for not taking their views on board," acknowledges the expert. "We want hill farmers to have more input into how our present scheme is set up and its objectives."

"Wherever possible, shouldn't ponies used for conservation

originate from the local area where grazing is required?"

"Cultural links with the breed should be maintained," accepts the manager. "Fell ponies are part of the community and part of the landscape for this area."

"Yes, he's right of course," says Roamer, "but cultural links sometimes don't stop land guardians from using breeds that don't belong here."

"Hill breeders face economic problems," points out our man. "What should we do to stop the hill pony disappearing?"

"Promotion of the breed as a successful conservation grazing animal is necessary," reckons the manager. "Furthermore, you may be able to persuade people who are involved in conservation within Cumbria and Northumberland to appreciate the Fell pony as a distinctive part of those landscapes they conserve."

"That's what you and I are doing, isn't it, Thorn?" concludes Roamer. "We're promoting the breed."

"It comes down to how important National Government considers protection of this breed to be," adds the Natural England representative. "First, we should identify how many Fell ponies remain on commons, where they are exactly, times during the year they are outside and which areas they are grazing."

"Hill breeders intend to record where their ponies presently graze," verifies our man. "Their total roaming area has reduced considerably during the last 25 years."

I'm pleased: at least one Government expert appreciates the need to help safeguard acclimatised, hefted ponies in their natural habitats, and other experts might agree.

At this moment, Roamer becomes aware that the first car is arriving for the council meeting. I am distracted too: we are both interested in our paddock gate.

"Hey, Roamer, we might be able to escape," I reason.

"Nay, forget it," he tells me. "Look! Our man has heard the car. He's out of his tent already and is opening the gates: I think he intends to stand guard."

"Oh well, I'm content here anyway," I decide.

"I hope Pan isn't tired tomorrow morning," remarks Roamer.

The meeting ends a couple of hours after it began. Our man secures the front gates when every car has departed and then, switching on his torch, he confirms our whereabouts before retiring to the hall. Maybe he intends to prepare supplies, or perchance he wishes to avail himself of the hall's kitchen facilities.

It's time I slept.

"Good night," I whisper to Roamer, who is dozing already; he is swaying gently.

Fierce rain pelts down intermittently this cool, stormy night. I snuggle closer to my dear friend.

A ford, more mini-humans and knee-deep mud

3rd November – Burgh-by-Sands School, Dykesfield and Drumburgh Castle

Roamer:

B Y daybreak, torrential rain has ceased. Weak rays struggle to pierce a grey sky.

"Come on," yawns Thorn. "Fancy some exercise? Let's stretch our legs."

We canter uncontrollably, clockwise, around the prepared heap of damp, sawn-off branches, tearing up huge divots of grass and soil from the sodden lawn.

"He-ee-ee-ee-ee!" I cry, realising we have gone full circle. "Go again!"

Off we charge wildly once more.

We have hardly completed a double circuit when Pan, hearing the heavy thud, thud, thud of hooves, emerges from his tent, wondering what's going on.

"Calm down you two!" he orders.

Reluctantly, we halt, linger for several seconds to reflect upon our footwork and then casually saunter away. We aren't anxious to cause trouble.

Pan, frowning, walks slowly towards the woodpile to inspect the scene. Hoof-shaped holes, up to 15 centimetres deep, pepper rain-drenched ground surrounding the wide, makeshift construction. He will need to apologise to Colin: anybody could easily twist an ankle in the dark during the forthcoming bonfire party, which Pan won't ignore. I'd fill those divots with soil.

Breakfast, a peaceful, relaxing affair, is quickly over. It's tack-up time again. Where will we end up today?

"I recognise the man in that vehicle," declares Thorn as Pan systematically balances my saddlebags in readiness for our visit to Burgh-by-Sands, formerly a fortified place near the estuary.

Jimmy alights. He and his wife have brought Pan's metal walking pole and our first-aid kit, left by mistake at Knockupworth yesterday. Pan thanks him. In a trice, Jimmy's four-wheel drive is pulling away.

Alan is back. By eleven o'clock, but not British Summertime, we are on the move. About 1½ hours later, but I'm guessing, Burgh-by-Sands School is in sight.

"This will be fun," I say to myself.

As we enter the main gateway to an extensive playground bordering empty playing fields, dozens of children appear at classroom windows. They gaze at us, the most beautiful ponies ever. Mind, sudden stardom may prove overawing occasionally, even for equines.

Pan secures my lead rope to a wooden fence post. Unblemished, pungent-smelling, autumn hedge-grass tempts me; I nibble a swathe; it tastes exquisitely juicy; I carry on eating.

Before long, a distant buzz distracts me. I recognise the unmistakable clamour of exuberant children rushing outside to welcome us. They remind me of humble-bees on the trail of exotic colours. I love kids, of course, but it's slightly scary whenever humans run towards me. Ah-ha, I can breathe more easily: they are standing quietly, waiting for Pan to begin.

Pan hardly has enough time to introduce us to everybody before lunchtime commences. A female teacher offers us carrots. What a superb treat! Normally, we eat little in the middle of the day; today we munch and munch. Meanwhile, Pan and Alan enjoy a well-earned cuppa, but there's another surprise: soon they are tucking into hot meals, delivered outside to order.

More children than we can count are in the playground. They take turns to stroke my head and neck.

"Ah-ha-ha," I murmur. "This is undeniably relaxing."

I am savouring their caresses, when a distant, high-pitched bell destroys my tranquillity. Without warning, all the children retreat into the school building, and a young woman named Sonia, the headteacher, appears. I don't understand what's happening. Alan is filming. Pan begins firing questions

"We currently have 61 children on roll," explains Sonia.

"How many come from farming backgrounds?" wonders Pan.

"Two, at the moment," replies Sonia. "That's not as many as we used to have."

"What's the advantage of bringing ponies into school?"

"Given our surroundings, I think it's crucial for children to be learning about the outside environment," she insists. "You don't see Fell ponies roaming much anymore. I don't think children realise how big they are and what kind of weight they can carry."

"Many of the children wanted to touch Roamer," enthuses Pan. "They could feel how hot his skin and breath were."

"You cannot beat first-hand experience for children's imagination," agrees Sonia.

"I imagine some of your children have never seen a live horse or pony," suggests Pan.

"No, that's right. Learning from first-hand experience enhances what you can do in a classroom. Some of our children own horses and their families actually breed horses. It would be interesting to get their impressions on the differences between the horses they are used to and Fell ponies."

This morning's exertions have made me sleepy, so I decide to take a nap when Alan stops filming. Minutes later, as I am snoozing, mini-humans return with teachers to their playground, rousing me. They line up expectantly. I'm completely relaxed when, before I can say "Na-ah" Pan places his weird metal device onto my skin near my heart. It is cold and tickles. Two girls announce my body temperature; I already know what it is.

Children quiz Pan intensely.

A 10-year-old boy raises his hand.

"What's the biggest bone in a Fell pony?" he asks.

"The thigh bone," says Pan. "The upper bone of the pony's hind leg is similar to your femur, the bone between your knee and hip. Have you noticed how thick Roamer's femur is? This and his strong back are reasons why he manages to carry heavy loads safely."

"How big are their ears?" wonders a smiling nine-year-old girl with a ponytail.

"Good question," admits Pan. "They are about 10 centimetres long, that's 4 inches, from base to tip. A master saddler helped me make a special horse cloak using archaeological evidence found near Hadrian's Wall and linked to the Roman presence there. Archaeologists call this cloak 'barding': it may have been a heat blanket, used to keep a working pony warm in winter. It fits over the pony's head and body, including its ears. Possibly, the ears of modern-day Fell ponies are a little fatter and longer compared with those of Roman ponies. We tried to ensure that the cloak would fit Thorn and Roamer by fashioning the ear holes slightly wider than the evidence suggests."

"You are lucky," I whisper to Thorn. "You know all about the barding, but I've never tried it on."

"I still won't tolerate anything touching my ears," he mumbles, mildly agitated. "I hated wearing that cloak on my head: it was so annoying."

"Some Roman ponies stationed at Hadrian's Wall were possibly about 220 centimetres long from ears to tail," continues Pan. "We conclude this from the barding evidence found underground. Thorn and Roamer measure roughly 235 centimetres; that's 6 inches longer."

In reality, Pan has deduced, many of our dimensions closely resemble those of our Roman ancestors.

"How long is Roamer's tail?" somebody wants to know.

"Fell pony tails vary," answers Pan. "Roamer's is about 100 centimetres from the base."

He's guessing: I don't remember him measuring me.

"Do you ever cut the tail?" inquires an eight-year-old.

"The long tails of free-living Fell ponies usually remain uncut," explains Pan, "unless they might freeze onto deep snow. They aren't simply for swatting flies. Where ponies live on exposed hillsides throughout the year, their tails, manes and winter coats keep them warm: in winter, semi-wild ponies resemble woolly mammoths."

"Nobody's cutting my tail, thank you!" I protest to Thorn. "It helps me balance."

"Or mine," he replies. "I'm no show horse. Give me wide-open spaces rather than the ring any time."

"Even the tails of most Fell show ponies are left to grow long," I point out.

"I didn't know," admits Thorn. "But, after all, that's how it was meant to be."

"How heavy is the pack?" asks a boy of nine with a rare interest in logistics.

We know the answer to that!

"Roamer is carrying about 61 kilograms," says Pan, "including the saddle and harness. Thorn is carrying up to 50 kilograms. They each could carry 65 kilograms easily, assuming, of course, that the load is properly balanced."

Hey, I am thinking, why am I still carrying more? No wonder he's less tired than I am at day's end.

"Well, I guess statistics don't lie," I taunt Thorn jokingly. "I must be the stronger pony."

"I thought we'd agreed we wouldn't bring up such a nonsensical argument," he protests quietly. "Besides, I have the job of leading, which is far more difficult than following."

"Try striding properly behind you, Thorn," I retaliate. "That's not easy, either."

"Where did Roamer and Thorn come from?" queries a younger boy.

"There are a dozen or more breeders of truly semi-wild Fell ponies in Britain," declares Pan. "Their herds are mainly in Cumbria, although some run freely in Northumberland, Lancashire, Durham and over the Scottish border. Thorn was born in Sedbergh, Cumbria, on a flat-topped hill. Roamer comes from Skelmersdale in West Lancashire, long ago the valley of a man called Skjaldmarr, who hailed from the district of the Roman fort on the River Lune, the pure river. Recently, Roamer has been living on Lincoln Common, a place where, about 1,800 years ago, retired Roman legionaries settled down. Solo was born just over the Scottish border, at Gretna, the great hill."

That reminds me: what a boring trip it was from Lincoln; I thought it would never end.

"How long have you had your ponies?" wonders a 10-year-old girl.

"We spent over a year selecting the best three ponies for the job," says Pan. "I began training them in late June."

"Are they broken in?" asks another girl, who has been waiting patiently, hand aloft.

"Yes, but I'm not keen on the words 'broken in'. In olden days, some misinformed people said you had to break a pony's will. That's definitely not the way to train a pony. You must win the pony's confidence. If you succeed, whatever difficult situation you find yourself in with your pony –"

"He will trust you," interrupts the girl.

"Exactly!" confirms Pan. "Both ponies will allow me to guide them in tricky situations."

"Do you trust him unconditionally, Thorn?" I ask.

" 'Unconditionally' is a big word," he maintains. "I trust him most of the time, but I'm less trustworthy than you are. Don't forget, I was free-living for much longer."

"Fells are possibly the easiest ponies in the world to train," continues Pan. "Thorn was not handled for six years. Yet, after only 20 hours of training, he and Roamer performed faultlessly as a team through Newcastle's busy city streets. That's pretty good, isn't it?"

"Yes," she agrees, nodding thoughtfully.

"You did behave well," I praise Thorn.

"That's because I'm sharp, sensible and wise," he retorts

impassively.

"Are we allowed to ride them?" earnestly inquires a girl aged about eight.

"I haven't trained Roamer for riding," admits Pan, "but if you said to me, 'Would he let me sit on his back?' my answer would be, 'Yes, he probably would.' If they received a little extra training, you could easily ride either pony. Fell ponies are usually enjoyable rides."

Hang on! I'd let Pan ride me, but I trust no stranger. Thorn, too, is adamant: he wouldn't tolerate novice riders.

A boy of 10, standing quietly, is intrigued: "How quickly can you get along the whole Roman Wall?"

"Some very fast walkers, in the summertime and without ponies, can manage it in 4 or 5 days, but it's more interesting if you plan a longer journey," replies Pan. "It will have taken us 24 days by the time Thorn, Roamer and I reach the west coast."

It feels much longer to me. I expect journeying without us might have been far easier and perhaps quicker for Pan – though certainly not as much fun.

"How long is Hadrian's Wall?" inquires a senior girl.

"Altogether, 117 kilometres or 73 British miles," answers Pan. "It composes a stone wall, 72 kilometres long, in the east, and a turf rampart, 45 kilometres long, in the west."

I'm glad Pan hasn't confused her: Romans would have argued that the Wall was 80 miles long.

"However," he adds, "we are trying to retrace the Military Way, the single-file horse route that Romans invented. Our planned route is about 177 kilometres, or 110 miles, from coast to coast."

Believe me: that's far enough in one stint for inexperienced ponies straight from the hills.

"How far have you come?" ponders a boy of nine.

Pan informs the children that we've covered about 90 miles, that's 145 kilometres, to their school.

"At the end of each day, when they have finished walking, do you leave them tied up?" frets the boy's friend.

"No," insists Pan. "I aim to let them graze reasonably freely.

Yesterday, they were cantering about the hall grounds at Kirkandrews-on-Eden, leaving deep divots. In case you go to the firework display and bonfire party there on the fifth, watch out for potholes. I wouldn't want anyone to sprain an ankle."

Thorn looks at me knowingly and then whispers, "Imagine what would happen if he, or anybody, tied us up at night?"

There would be no fence standing next morning, and we would be long gone, I am thinking.

"How many Fell ponies are there in the world?" pipes up a small boy hidden from my view.

"I haven't counted precisely," admits Pan. "Fell ponies live in Holland, France, America and elsewhere. Worldwide, there could be up to 650 living, breeding females. This year, about 380 registered Fell foals were born throughout Britain: that's not a lot, and most are not free-living. Fell ponies, especially extensively grazing, semi-wild ponies, are notably rare in Northumberland and the Scottish Borders, and they are becoming rarer in Cumbria. We must save free-ranging herds that still exist."

"We need to do something radical," whispers Thorn.

Somebody inquires, "What is the object around the pony's tail?"

An older boy correctly identifies it as a crupper. Pan explains that it helps keep the saddle in place, but that Roman packsaddles probably didn't have cruppers. A girl describes what a girth is. I'm convinced: these two children ride ponies regularly.

Our leader gives the children a quick lesson on naming other parts of Thorn's harness: breeching, breasting and surcingle. Everybody is chanting.

"We don't know exactly how the breeching, which passed around the pony's or mule's buttocks, was attached to a Roman packsaddle," he admits. "It stopped the loaded saddle slipping forwards on steep descents. The breast strap prevented it from slipping backwards during climbs."

Another nine-year-old politely asks how tall Fell ponies might be, and two seven-year-old girls are wondering how heavy they are. Suddenly, Alan declares he has run out of digital recording tape, an unprecedented situation!

Two action-packed hours have elapsed since we entered Burgh-by-Sands School. Undeniably, it's time to leave. Pan hurriedly prepares us. I'm sad to say goodbye to these children, yet happy to be continuing our adventure.

From Burgh, this bright, sunny afternoon, we are hiking west along a grassy, tree-lined lonning. Then, abruptly, Pan turns north-east towards the Wall line. We cross a mucky field. On a narrow, waterlogged, tractor lane, Thorn and I are sinking into mud up to our fetlock joints. Though he isn't complaining, Alan is struggling valiantly to keep his footing whilst shouldering a heavy camera.

"This is a waste of time," judges Pan after approximately 20 minutes of slogging.

We backtrack, identify a preferred lonning Pan missed originally and are speedily onto drier ground. Our problems aren't quite over, however. En route to Drumburgh Castle, a fourteenth-century, fortified farmhouse built initially from Wall masonry and located less than 150 paces east of today's destination, I nearly fall into an unseen, disused mining dug-out.

Disaster averted, Thorn and I manage to avoid further incidents. Our day's trekking safely achieved, it's time to roll in a field of long grasses.

Thorn:

At dawn, as I awaken, another downpour persists. Water drips from my eyelashes onto my nose. I wait. The rain stops. Let's play! For fun, we canter around the bonfire twice. Roamer even considers breaking into a gallop. Oops, our man's annoyed!

We set off on our quest again. A hint of early winter fills the air. I am prancing purposefully with Roamer, our man and Cameraman along the left edge of the main road leading to Beaumont, a beautiful hill. There, north of the village church, we take a grassy, open track atop the Wall ditch, past the position of Wormanby Milecastle. We are north of Wormanby Farm, which humans might have recognised as Winmer's place or Wilmer's place in a bygone time.

Easily negotiating a gate adorned with barbed wire, we ford Powburgh Beck, a stream in a hollow close to a once fortified place. Roamer and I skim smartly through the water, which doesn't touch us above our fetlocks. It's barely harder than tiptoeing over a squishy, muddy puddle. My feet are decidedly cooler afterwards.

Turning promptly from a lonning onto the village road leading west towards Burgh, we have returned to the Military Way, which lies about 65 yards south of the Wall. At Burgh's eastern margin stands Saint Michael's Church, built over 800 years ago.

"Englishmen erected the church at the south-eastern corner of where a Roman fort, Aballava, previously stood," believes our man. "I wonder: did an apple orchard bloom here once upon a time?"

Apparently, church builders used – rather, I should say robbed – some of the fort's stones. Logically, they might have considered their actions to be enterprising and labour saving. I suppose the Wall meant nothing to humans living centuries after Romans departed the island.

"Archaeologists have concluded that the Wall ditch passed under the fort here," announces our man as we hurry on. "Sadly, we haven't enough time to explore this idea."

Past Burgh Church, about 300 yards along the quiet turn-off road in the direction of Thurstonfield – a village that was originally open countryside belonging to a man called Torsteinn – slumbers Burgh School. Wake everybody up: soon we'll be there.

Wait! Unaccountably, my saddle is slipping sideways. Now my left-hand pack is virtually under my belly. I have forfeited control, forcing me to halt instantly.

"Hai-ai-ai-ai!" I call.

Fortunately, our man recognises what's happening just in time: I easily could have injured myself. He heaves and pulls, skilfully adjusting the girth and breasting.

"Phe-he, that was a tricky moment," I tell Roamer.

Eager Burgh children are waiting patiently to greet us as we approach them. I look at a little girl; she is beaming, delighted to meet me personally. An older boy tickles my nose; I couldn't be happier.

"Fell ponies are fun," sings a seven-year-old girl.

Mini-humans admire us because, you might say, we are majestic creatures.

We spend two happy, entertaining hours with these children. Inevitably, however, our man is anxious to set off west, towards the rounded, bow-shaped headland of Bowness. I suppose we might revisit Burgh people, one day. Who knows?

Our course to Bowness-on-Solway is via the hamlets of Dykesfield – a ditch field – and Drumburgh – a fortified ridge that bucks may have frequented in earlier days. Our man expects to arrive at Bowness Primary School tomorrow afternoon. No doubt, as usual, children there will be captivating. After we reach the Solway Peninsula, I've no clue where we'll go, but I have decided: whatever happens next, I'll live a wonderful life.

The Vallum runs through fields from Burgh's western end to Dykesfield. We stand at the edge of the salt marshes, a foreboding place where the incoming tide, rushing with feeble warning up the Solway Estuary, could easily cut us off. Deep potholes, creeks, dangerous currents, quicksand and a continually changing topography could trap the unwary and unacquainted. The local shepherd, a man called Robert I understand, has memorised where diminutive sheep bridges, half hidden by a shifting estuary, exist. Months ago, he offered to show our man a navigable way across the marshes. Regrettably, however, despite careful preparations, our man already has decided to reserve this option for future, summer, fair weather trekking.

From Burgh, we briefly divert north of the Wall along a lonning, turning west-south-west at a track junction 400 yards later, thus avoiding sheep pens and those lethal marshes. Deep, filthy mud, churned up by farm vehicles, is slowing human progress considerably, although Roamer and I aren't too bothered. Abruptly, 160 paces further on, we turn south, back towards the main road leading to Dykesfield.

"This situation is far from ideal," acknowledges our man to

Cameraman when we regain the road. "My reconnaissance last year confirmed our next off-road option: north of the Wall, some 320 metres ahead, a lonning leads northwards, past a sewage treatment plant. From there, we can veer south-west across Dykesfield Farm to recross the Wall 350 metres south-east of Dykesfield Milecastle. John, the Dykesfield farmer, okayed it. However, poor ground conditions and limited daylight are forcing me to rethink even this route."

Cameraman, who is labouring gamely in diabolical conditions, is having second thoughts too.

"This waterlogged track makes walking extremely difficult," he observes.

They further discuss their predicament.

"We could lose more valuable time and may not reach my intended campsite today," admits our man. "In view of these present circumstances, a quicker and perhaps easier option is to follow the quiet village road south of the Vallum to Dykesfield."

Cameraman isn't arguing: he is carrying heavier gear than usual.

Selecting the road to Dykesfield, we soon retrieve lost time. I learn that archaeologists have found no evidence that the Wall ever existed at Dykesfield. Did it cross the marsh? Did the marsh engulf the Wall or erode it away?

Leaving this hamlet, our man unceremoniously follows the higher ground of the Vallum, the sea defence dyke, to Drumburgh. We descend to the single-track road, elevated on a raised bed above Burgh Marsh, only in order to circumnavigate around fences at cattle grids. Resting at formerly fortified Boustead Hill, I gaze north-eastwards. Cattle graze contentedly on deceptively benign, pale green, salt marshes.

Nobody's certain where Easton Milecastle existed: it has disappeared with the mires of time. Undoubtedly, we are following the Wall line beyond a turn-off road to Easton, the eastern farm, maintaining a heading west-north-west on a straight course bordering the site of Drumburgh Milecastle.

Tucked away from salt marsh, at a safe onshore location just beyond a small, medieval castle, sits Drumburgh Grange. Formerly an abbey's outlying farm, this is tonight's grazing spot and our man's campsite. Father-and-son farmers – Roamer tells me their names are Alan and John – greet us heartily.

"Pitch your tent anywhere you like," advises the older farmer. "The ponies can graze in the field closest to our house. Will the sheep upset them?"

"Not a bit, Alan," replies our man.

"Are you afraid of sheep, Roamer?" I tease.

"You're a real joker," he replies disdainfully.

We polish off an exceptionally generous, well-deserved feed, needed following a tiring, energetic day. Soon afterwards, our man releases us into a vast field sloping gently towards the estuary. The farmer's wife – I think her name is Sarah – has invited our man to supper. He leaves us grazing along the Wall line. Before midnight, the air temperature drops considerably below its previous autumn low.

Solo:

I long to visit Thorn and Roamer, but by now they could be beyond the most distant hills I can spy; they could be beyond reach.

Recently, one windy night, I dreamt of climbing a mountain. In my dream, my keeper did 200 hours of training with me. He never said it was going to be easy. I grew muscles.

Weeks passed. I was no longer pony-sized: I was a fully-grown horse. I was ready. I was beside my keeper, helping to sort out our equipment for the expedition. Soon we would be climbing. This time, I had luggage.

We began our journey. Ahead was a service station. We considered purchasing all kinds of life-sustaining food. Shortly afterwards, we left the streets behind. The ground was as muddy as a pigsty. My rear hooves repeatedly became stuck.

Eventually, we stood in awe at the bottom of an enormous, blue, snow-clad peak. We climbed slowly, painstakingly, to the middle of the mountain. Oxygen was becoming thinner as we scrambled higher.

I was desperately thirsty. We came to a resplendent, cascading, crashing waterfall. I retrieved from my backpack a couple of carrots and three apples. They were delectable; what a marvellous feast I had.

Darkness descended. I was exceptionally tired. We camped out. My keeper erected a gigantic, white tent for me to sleep in.

Morning came. I ate revitalising breakfast my keeper had prepared.

We made it to the top of the mountain after a heroic struggle. High up, I could almost touch the sky; the coldest air imaginable encircled us.

On the return trip, I chased a rainbow and finally caught every colour, even violet.

"He-ee-ee-ee-ee!" I sang out repeatedly.

I woke up from my dream at, I guess, three o'clock in the morning. Other, nearby Fell ponies were soundly asleep. I realised that I was at home, a great distance from any mountains, far away from Thorn and Roamer. Come home safely, you two.

The last school: Wall's end

4ᵗʰ November – Bowness-on-Solway School and North Plain

Roamer:

THORN and I gobble breakfast frantically this sunny morning. There's no time to waste, it seems. Pan has barely completed packing his tent – he pitched it under an open barn – before Alan arrives, camera primed, ready for action. Then I realise why Pan is rushing.

"We must reach Bowness School by 2.30 this afternoon," he tells Alan as he continues to load Thorn's saddle urgently. "Today is Friday: this is our last chance to meet the children before we head east on Sunday."

"Where would you prefer to interview the Fell Pony Society breeders?" inquires Alan, mindful of today's first job.

"About 200 metres along the road towards Bowness will be perfect," replies Pan, "at a bend where a track leads down to Drumburgh Marsh."

This is shaping up to be our busiest day ever: we have Fell pony breeders and schoolchildren to talk to, never mind a demanding trek to North Plain.

"No bother," encourages Thorn. "We could accomplish it asleep!"

Half an hour later, as Pan, aided by Alan, is securing Thorn's pack with its surcingle, a woman and two men turn up unannounced. Obviously, they must be the breeders.

"How did you track us down?" asks Pan, surprised by their

sudden appearance.

"Somebody at the farm informed us you were here," answers Tom, a young man with glasses and black, wavy hair.

Almost immediately, we are moving. A brisk walk later, we reach a turn-off that I presume leads to the marsh.

Alan begins filming. I learn that Tom and the other man, his father, Walter, own and manage the herd on Hades Hill, an unploughed hill.

"Our current mares and fillies are slightly larger than we have bred previously," reveals Tom. "Their heights now average between 13 and 13½ hands, though we still have one smaller line of ponies."

"From our perspective, 12½ to 13 hands is the right height," adds Walter. "Ponies running on the open fell must be able to shelter behind a wall in terribly bad weather."

"Usually, though, I don't bother to shelter," whispers Thorn.

"Are Fell ponies generally taller, on average, than 30 years ago?" wonders Pan.

"Yes," argues Walter. "Many are pushing up towards 14 hands now. People desire taller ponies to show and jump. But ponies of 12½ to 13 hands were easier to load for packing purposes."

"Is a Fell pony a little pony that can survive on top of the Howgill Fells through the hardest winter?" ponders Tom. "Or might it have been bred in Wiltshire or in Dorset or in Devon? In these cases, it might have a piece of paper which says its bloodline is that of a Fell pony, even though it might not survive on the open fell."

"I know of ponies who live on the Howgills, a group of Cumbrian hills," declares Thorn, "but I've never heard of Wiltshire, Dorset or Devon."

"Those shires are much, much further south," I tell him later on, when we are alone. "Wiltshire is centred on a farmstead near a stream, Dorset is the territory of the people around Dorn, and Devon is the territory of some other district. Don't bother asking me how I know: it's a long story."

"We bought a stallion from down south a couple of years ago," confides Alison, the youngest breeder. "In his first winter, he ended up with stress laminitis. We had to keep him inside. He couldn't cope with the cold. Our ponies go quite high up. Not every bloodline possesses the characteristics required to live out on the Howgills."

"She's definitely talking about the hills with narrow valleys," confirms Thorn.

Well, I am hill bred. So is Thorn. We can cope, definitely.

"Alison," begins Pan, "tell us about your breed line –"

"My uncontrollable beast!" cries Alison, ignoring Pan's request.

She means me. She's holding my lead rein. I fancy snuggling up to her, but she keeps pushing me away whenever I move a pace towards her.

"Get the ponies out of the way altogether," orders Alan in desperation from behind his camera. "Then, maybe, we can do this interview undisturbed."

"Come here, Roamer," implores Pan.

"Hey, what's he doing?" I protest to Thorn. "I'm not hurting anybody. I am merely inquisitive, interested in the conversation. This isn't fair!"

"It's your own fault," replies Thorn.

Pan ties my lead rope to a fence post alongside a hedge. Nay, this is bad. I was enjoying Alison's attention. Now I can't talk to her. I can't graze, either. Bother!

"Ha, ha," laughs Alison, evidently amused by my antics.

She tries again to describe her herd.

"We have the Lownthwaite stud. My mother took it over from my grandad, who took it over from his dad. It has been in the family for generations. Our ponies run out on the northern Pennines. We have fell grazing rights."

I imagine galloping free, mountain summit breezes ruffling my mane, right now! What a seductive thought. However, I suppose I must be patient for Pan's sake.

"A few years ago," continues Alison, "Natural England fenced off much of the fell, and the beck in particular, for wildlife, which means our ponies cannot move onto the far side of the fell. The only way they could cross over, is by climbing up the fell and around the fence line's top corner; they won't do that since they can't obtain any water."

"So are they grazing extensively now, or are they tied down to a restricted area?" inquires Pan.

"It's not a small area, but they don't tend to go as far up the fell as they used to. This means there is not as much grass for them to eat: in summer, they have already consumed the grass they normally would eat in winter months. We must feed them out on the fell earlier. And, because they don't go away from the inbye as much, they haven't learned where to locate seasonal grazing."

"One day in the future," I warn Thorn, "possibly not too far off, no pony within Alison's herd will be able to identify correctly what to eat or where to browse in winter."

"I can always recognise and acquire wild food easily, whatever the season," he insists, ignoring the plight of our cousins.

"Yes," I nod, "but why? It's because you have lived on the hill all your life."

"We have maybe a dozen Fell herds running in their natural habitat," worries Tom, "and most of their breeders are part of an ageing population; some breeders are over 70 years old. Only breeders with younger family members will carry on breeding. In about 10 years there will be a decisive change, with even fewer herds running on the open fell."

"It might be impossible to save our natural homes," I tell Thorn.

"But we must try," he resolves, exuding positivity.

"Fifty years ago, numerous mares grazed extensively on specific fells," explains Walter. "During the 1968 commons registration, lots of people registered rights for ponies to graze on the open fell, on common land, but few exercised their rights. These days, many farmers who have rights to graze ponies don't take them up."

"And quite a lot of farms owned at least one Fell pony?" supposes Pan.

"Well, going back even further, before you saw wheels on the fells, many jobs were done with pack ponies," replies Walter. "For example, on each side of the packsaddle they would have a box with a hinged bottom. They would fill these two boxes – called dung pots – with horse or cow manure and then walk to the site where they wanted the manure scattered. Taking the weight of the nearside box, they would reach over and pull out the pin that held the bottom of the other box, and all the dung would fall to the ground. They would walk on four paces and then release the nearside box bottom. Typically, a hill farm would have had a stable for two ponies, though farmers didn't keep their ponies in stables much."

Hill ponies would have preferred to wander about outside in their spare time, indisputably.

"Fell ponies once moved supplies about a lot," notes Tom.

His father agrees: "If you go back to the days before the turnpikes, they moved all manner of agricultural and mineral products on pack ponies, including coal, charcoal and salt. You could fill two pages with examples of produce ponies carried. More recently, people have begun to enlist Fell ponies to carry luggage on hiking holidays."

I knew it! They can't do without us, even today. We evermore carry for humans.

"Are any of your Fell ponies involved in conservation grazing?" inquires Pan.

"A couple of years ago, a lady from Kendal bought two of my Fells," recounts Alison. "They are three years old now, and to this day they are conservation grazers."

"Have you any idea where Kendal is?" I ask Thorn.

"A cousin did tell me," he whispers. "It's in southern Lakeland, I think. Long ago, ponies knew it as the village with a church in the valley of the sacred stream. These days, it's a large market town."

"In summer, we graze part of a wetland with ponies," declares Tom. "This creates a contrasting habitat to the kind sheep or cattle will leave. Different plant species grow, which ecologists like."

"Didn't Jamie say something similar to that?" I ask Thorn.

"Yes, I believe he did," replies my friend. "Everybody's talking about conservation grazing."

"Any new job we secure for the ponies will improve their

situation," continues Tom. "Nobody who's breeding Fell ponies is in it to make money. We do it for love of the ponies."

I wouldn't be surprised if your ponies loved you guys too, Tom!

"Do land guardians generally recognise the value of Fell ponies?" wonders Pan.

"I don't think so," confesses Tom. "Maybe Lake District National Park managers should highlight Fell ponies as a tourist attraction and should make people aware that they run in herds on open fells."

"Should farmers be given financial rewards if their ponies are involved officially in conserving wildlife?" asks Pan.

"Even a little bit of recognition would help," asserts Tom. "It costs a lot of time and money to register and microchip a pony, to test it for the syndrome and to look after it. There should be recompense."

"If you wish to buy a farm with fell rights, it's an awful lot of money," adds Walter.

"If somebody decided to run a herd of semi-feral ponies, he or she would need several hundred thousand pounds to buy a farm with fell rights," agrees Tom. "So it's remarkably difficult to bring new breeders in."

"Many of the fell rights to graze ponies, cattle and sheep are part of substantial estates," continues Walter. "For example, the National Trust owns a lot of farms that keep Herdwick sheep. Beatrix Potter left land to Trust people on condition they kept it stocked with these mountain sheep. It's a pity she didn't encourage Fell ponies in the same way: that could have made a difference."

"Pan reckons that Beatrix, whoever she was, supported our ancestors quite considerably in the 1930's," I tell Thorn. "Apparently, she called the Fell ponies 'our grand old local breed', and she made badly needed donations to the Fell Pony Society."

"I bet this woman didn't realise that our breed would be facing oblivion within her beloved Lake District less than a century later," surmises Thorn.

"Aye, you may be right," I reply.

"Perhaps, though, a modern-day benefactor will rescue our kind," ventures Thorn thoughtfully. "I've concluded we could do with one, pronto."

"Where farms are part of the big estates," suggests Walter, "we should be talking to estate managers about the advantages of keeping ponies. We should persuade landowners to encourage tenant farmers to keep ponies on estate land."

Walter has additional down-to-earth advice: "If a lot of people are competing to rent a farm that belongs to a large estate, why doesn't the landlord include a question such as, 'Are you intending to keep Fell ponies on this land?' It could be to the credit of those who answered, 'Yes.'"

"Some sort of credit rating?" presses Pan.

"Yes, exactly, but it doesn't have to be an Environmentally Sensitive Area," reckons Walter. "It could be an open fell. Before the foot and mouth disease outbreak, which decimated sheep stocks, there were too many sheep on the fell. They were overgrazing it, but ponies weren't overgrazing it. Ponies and sheep have unrelated likes and dislikes. You can graze up to the maximum number of allowable sheep and still put ponies on that same land without causing damage to the fell."

"Presently," emphasises Pan, "the number of extensively grazing, breeding mares continues to diminish alarmingly. I understand, after talking with Fell Pony Society office staff, that the number having a foal this year is about 123."

"If you have fewer mares, you're not going to have enough bloodlines," maintains Alison solemnly. "We've had foal syndrome already due to lack of bloodlines. Our quandary will get worse. There will be inbreeding. You will probably end up having another genetic defect."

"The number of tigers in the wild is decreasing," points out Walter, "and people are fearful about the possibility of inbreeding."

"What's a tiger?" I ask Thorn.

"No idea, Roamer," he murmurs sleepily.

"Tigers are so sparse that they don't necessarily meet up with another bloodline," continues Walter. "Big cats, in general, are decreasing partly because their habitat is disappearing. This is the case with Fell ponies: they often aren't allowed onto their habitat."

So tigers are big cats, I gather. I've never seen any cats, large or small, on the hills. They must live elsewhere.

"Another thing holding back Fell pony breeders is bureaucracy," says Walter. "Europeans tend to eat horsemeat whereas practically nobody in this country does. I'm unaware of a horsemeat shop left in this country. There were some when the war ended; when meat was scarce."

"Huh-huh-huh," mumbles Thorn, twitching frantically. "What's going on? I was nodding off until somebody mentioned eating horses."

"Calm down," I reply. "They eat horsemeat on mainland Europe but not usually here in Britain. That aside, I thought you didn't worry about being eaten?"

"Oh, what a relief," he admits. "To be honest, I am worried, but only slightly. Mind, I wouldn't be surprised to discover that one or two British butchers are selling horsemeat and maybe even selling our kind: some misguided humans probably think it's a good idea. Why are we discussing horsemeat, anyway?"

"It's complicated," I tell him. "Walter was explaining that breeders must obtain a passport for every Fell pony and that computer micro-chipping of foals is now compulsory for identification purposes. In Walter's opinion, such requirements are an unnecessary expense for breeders."

"What humans refer to as 'Health and Safety' is the supposed reason for having passports, so I understand," says Thorn. "They help protect humans and equines from diseases. They also help to prevent anybody from stealing us."

"In fact," I venture, "though I'm no expert, I'm now convinced the passport law exists simply to protect humans, mostly abroad, who might want to eat horsemeat."

"Are you implying that, if nobody ate equines, we wouldn't need passports?"

"Precisely!" I reply. "Which reminds me: I have been carrying our passports throughout the expedition, though I fail to see why. We're not leaving the country, are we?"

"Nay, lad, I hope not," confesses Thorn, who is now wide awake. "Otherwise, we might easily find ourselves on a foreign table, or even inadvertently on a British table! Don't you realise? Our passports must accompany us wherever we go: it's the law. You had better not lose them."

"There's not much freedom promised for a Fell pony in twenty-first century England," I conclude. "Is there?"

"No," he says. "Mind you, we're the lucky ones. Humans or tigers, if any tigers exist in this country, aren't about to eat us –"

I interrupt him: "Listen, Thorn. They're talking about Exmoor ponies now."

"Three Exmoor ponies are grazing at Drumburgh Moss Nature Reserve, just over a kilometre south-west of here," remarks Pan. "Exmoors enjoy a much higher profile than Fells."

"Fell ponies have been here for centuries, yet most people aren't aware of semi-wild herds running in this area," bemoans Alison. "If the Fell Pony Society increased the ponies' profile it would benefit everybody."

"What about ponies that carry the syndrome?" continues Pan.

"If you know the carriers, you can be certain of breeding either carriers or clear ponies," answers Tom. "You can guarantee you won't have a foal that dies."

"That's what the veterinary scientist said," remembers Thorn.

"If people buy only clear ponies, straight away that will reduce the number of bloodlines," cautions Tom. "We will lose some of the gene pool because some people will not breed with a pony that is a carrier."

"But if you knew where all carriers were, couldn't you check that breeders were using them to breed?" suggests Pan.

"Well, I dislike compulsory testing or compulsory control," counters Walter. "Farmers who are breeders might say, 'I'm not going to be bothered with the paperwork.' We may put any mare to a stallion that is not a carrier. Then, although foals produced may be carriers themselves, that will be our sole problem. Mind you, there will always be breeders who are prepared to risk it and not go through with any test."

"I don't believe the Fell Pony Society will be able to control it," adds Alison. "And there's a cost implication."

This scientific matter is taxing: my young brain struggles to fathom it. We must trust breeders to do the right thing.

"Suppose Government policy makers accept that the Fell pony is part of English biodiversity?" speculates Pan.

"That would amount to recognition that Fell ponies should be, and deserve to be, out there, on the fells," says Tom, "where they have grazed with sheep and cattle for centuries."

"Aha. Nobody should prevent us accessing the fells," asserts Thorn quietly. "It's our evolutionary right to graze Cumbrian and Northumbrian hills."

"It would be ideal for the landscape, birds and other small animals," adds Alison. "We should let the ponies do what they have been doing for many hundreds of years. Then we breeders could carry on. It's sad to see people giving up. We must involve one or two new hill breeders. Breeders are a little social network: you would miss those people if they weren't there."

She is right. I'd miss my friends if I couldn't see them regularly. I miss Solo and my pals on Lincoln Common right now.

"The Fell Pony Society needs to look into issues seriously," warns Tom. "We also need a full-time fund-raiser. We must talk with the Lake District National Park and with the National Trust. To reverse the trend, we must identify one or two places where people could set up herds."

"We've done enough talking this morning," chirps Thorn. "When can we begin trekking?"

No doubt, tonight Thorn will urge me to discuss technical bits of the breeders' conversation. At this moment, however, I am also restless, and my legs ache: I don't recommend standing immobile, heavily laden, for well over an hour.

"We are late," notices Pan, finally seeming to sense Thorn's and my agitation. "We had better get going."

Pan consults his map.

"The track I intended to take, across fields, may be waterlogged," he informs Alan, "but we have a bigger problem: reportedly, we won't be able to get beyond a cattle grid near Brackenrigg."

"Why not?" inquires Alan politely.

"A local farmer kindly offered to place a large wooden board across the grid, which would have given us access from the track to the road: there's no other possible exit point. Last night, unfortunately, I heard by 'phone that he isn't available today to position the board. We could end up stranded, which would mean back-tracking. Instead, to ensure that we reach the school on time, I think we'll need to take a non-stop shortcut using the coast road north of the Wall."

Leaving those breeders to relax or to further contemplate their dilemma, we set off in haste by road, a great shame: I much prefer soft, cooling grass to hard, unforgiving stone beneath my hooves; fields, it seems to me, ooze remnants of past, happy forests.

Our long tails swishing gently, easily, from side to side, Thorn and I forge ahead along the road. Nevertheless, somehow, Thorn can't avoid paddling through several piles of mud. Inevitably, his hooves become remarkably filthy. Reaching Port Carlisle, I have an irresistible urge to beg a favour of Pan: I am dying to ask him to buy polish for Thorn's hooves. I look out for an equine shop. Unfortunately, I fail to spot one. In any case, I reason, would Pan ever guess what I wanted? Besides, he wouldn't be remotely interested in our mischief making: he would never tolerate polished hooves.

"Hurry up, you two," he cajoles. "We must get back on schedule. And please refrain from splashing mud over me."

Pan's face fails to disguise his anxiety when the narrow, snaking coastal road very occasionally becomes overcrowded. Luckily, hardly a car or truck bothers us as we approach Bowness.

Travelling westwards beyond the village, we finally sight our anticipated destination. A smiling female teacher, who has spotted our arrival, unlocks a wide, iron gate leading to a safe playground.

Children spill outside, onto their playground. They are calm, enthusiastic and unafraid of us. I have eagerly awaited this part.

As usual, the children ask many, many interesting questions, and two 10-year-olds ascertain Thorn's skin temperature using Pan's data logger. Thorn and I are familiar with every aspect of this logging procedure by now. You might say we are Pan's official assistants.

Just as we leave Bowness School and head further west, two impetuous boys, perhaps 10 and 8 years old, decide to join us. They rush up alongside us, initially startling me. The younger boy is running, the older one cycling.

The sky darkens. Colder air swirls around us. My backpack is bothering me.

"Na-ah!" I shout loudly.

We trot on faster, eating up the coast road. Pan seems to be searching for a safe, warm, friendly place to sleep. I'd give up tonight's rations to rest this instant, but resting's impossible: I must carry on.

Thorn:

On a bright morning, our meeting with three pony breeders takes place near the site of Drumburgh's Roman fort, which Romans likely named Coggabata or Congavata, or possibly even Congabata.

"Congabata might mean 'fort on the small hill'," suggests our man, checking his map. "Or it might mean 'dish-like': the road follows a dish-shaped knoll."

The fort overlooked the Firth of Solway, the estuary where the ford of the pillar is located. The pillar, notes our man, likely refers to a large, ice-carried, granite boulder, the Lochmaben Stone, resting roughly 1000 feet above high water at the estuary's Scottish end. We are not destined to observe it, but he says it exists.

Our man's admittedly interesting discussion with the breeders continues unabated well beyond his planned time allowance. Consequently, we must forge ahead hastily, without respite. Roamer and I don't mind: we are impatient to trek, and we are anxious to meet more children. We must spell out, once again, what they could do to help save our kind. Furthermore, children are habitually kind to us.

The Wall resurfaces nearby, close to a drumlin-elevated milecastle, where our man briefs Cameraman: "From here, my planned route traces the Wall line across fields to Glasson, continues along the Vallum south of Kirkland Milecastle and then heads roughly west along Brackenrigg Farm's track. Hence, we shall reach the road beyond Bowness Hall. After that, it's just over half a mile into Bowness Village."

"Right, I'm ready. Shall we go?" urges Cameraman earnestly, an eye fixed on less-than-optimal afternoon light intensity.

"There's one complication," persists our man.

He explains to Cameraman that, as we are behind schedule, we can't afford delays from navigation obstacles, or we'll fail to reach Bowness Primary School before it closes for the weekend.

Reluctantly, after considerable deliberation, the humans decide to abandon their carefully planned Vallum route via Brackenrigg, a bracken ridge. Instead, we take the dangerous coastal road, which our man valiantly had sought to avoid by negotiation with local landowners.

"We shall, with luck, attempt our pre-planned route on the return trip," affirms our man, consoling himself. "Nevertheless, this is a sad decision: obtaining local permissions for this final leg of our outward journey wasn't straightforward."

"That's enough talking," I scream silently. "Let's move, now!"

"As I've said before," reassures Cameraman, "you may be excused for altering well-laid plans in order to meet school and interview deadlines. Sometimes in life, we are forced to compromise."

I agree with Cameraman: ponies have made the best of terrible situations for millennia. I suspect our man has understood also, during his last two decades on earth, that any successful expedition exacts concessions: from time to time, he must trade personal dreams for the grander goal, the less selfish prize,

Swiftly, purposefully, we are heading north-west on the final stretch to Bowness, past the supposed location of Raven Bank

Milecastle, slightly elevated land previously frequented by ravens. Fortunately, this road is peaceful. Cameraman walks drag again; he's becoming an expert at it.

"We are nearly there," announces our man nonchalantly as we arrive at a sign declaring "Coast".

We have reached the sea, almost. From this point, there's no Roman ditch. Cumulus clouds hover on the estuary's seaward horizon, seeming to touch this salty expanse on a darkening day.

There's little time to pause at Kirkland Milecastle. Eden's channel flanks us northwards; Wall and Vallum lie only about 100 yards to the south. We are, true to our man's aim, close to the line of the Way again, though much of its course nearby is obscure. Ahead, in the more southerly road hedge, is what remains of Kirkland Turret.

"From Port Carlisle, the Wall follows a line up to 275 metres south of the coastal road," our man informs Cameraman. "Romans rebuilt the Turf Wall in stone here approximately 1,850 years ago."

Apparently, the Vallum continues north of Acremire Lane to Bowness. This ancient, narrow track runs parallel to and adjacent to the Wall. Our man suspects the lane might have been where the Military Way was located, although locals reckon the Way was behind but even closer to the Wall, which is logical.

"Perhaps locals know best," suggests Roamer.

Beyond Port Carlisle – a fishing village whose original name was Fisher's Cross, where a canal once carried goods to Carlisle – the narrow road bends sharply, leaving the drivers of oncoming cars unsighted. Although Roamer and I trust our man completely in traffic, we must be especially vigilant here: our situation is exceptionally vulnerable. Presently, the road straightens. We spy Bowness-on-Solway School, which stands about 250 yards west of Bowness Village centre. Are we in time?

Situated between the village and the school is a fort whose remains are barely visible. We amble through its estimated middle.

"As you might expect, Romans constructed this fort originally from turf and timber, later from stone," notes our man. "Its name, Maia, means 'larger', but I'm unsure why. It was 128 by 188 metres in area, not quite 6 acres, and marked the Wall's western terminal."

Who cares about forts at this moment? As our man imparts further archaeological information, mostly meaningless to Fell ponies, I am suddenly aware that Roamer and I have travelled the entire length of Hadrian's Wall! Even better, wherever possible we have tried to follow an ancient, Roman, horse route, the Military Way. We have triumphed as pack ponies.

"Argh-argh!" shouts Roamer, which loosely means, "We have arrived!"

"Hai-ai-ai-ai-ai!" I whinny, delighted. "Do you realise, Roamer? We have travelled across the country, from sea to sea."

A watery estuary and salt-drenched breeze remind me of Tynemouth, where we began weeks ago. Our challenge across England's width has been less relentless than I expected. Of course, our adventure's still far from over. Anything could happen.

As I am contemplating our success, we reach the school. A lone female teacher unlocks a playground gate. Yeah! Children and teachers haven't gone home yet. They are waiting to greet us.

Today is becoming exhausting. First, we met the breeders; now we are visiting Bowness School. Roamer doesn't care: he treasures school days because he loves children. Well, truthfully, we both do. It's simply that he rants on for days afterwards about our visits. He'll often ask, "Wasn't that an intriguing question?" and he'll keep reminding me what a particular boy or girl said about us.

I suppose I have become accustomed to children. I usually stand next to our man, listening. It's amusing and uplifting to hear their honest, optimistic, enthusiastic voices. Roamer, mesmerised by their stroking, may become so relaxed that he takes a nap halfway through an encounter. Later on, usually at night, he pesters me to fill in what he missed. It's as well my memory is first-rate – apart from names, that is.

In the playground, energetic mini-humans fire cleverly thought-out, well-prepared questions. Ten- and eleven-year-olds are first.

"How many ponies were there in the beginning?" asks a girl.

That's a tricky question.

"No one knows exactly," says our man. "Wild ponies existed over 35,000 years ago. At one time, more than 100,000 wild ponies may have inhabited the world. Today, only isolated scatterings remain – predominantly in China, Mongolia, Russia and Ukraine, and also in Australia, Brazil, Canada, Holland, Sweden, South Africa and the United States – partly because humans hunted them for food and clothing, partly because they were forced off of their wild grazing sites."

"I hope we don't end our days as food!" wails Roamer.

"So you said the other day," I reply. "I've decided: you and I are unequivocally unfit for human consumption. We must both quit worrying about being eaten."

Our man continues. Well, there's no shutting him up. He is describing our past connections with humans.

"Since before Roman times, people have used – and at times abused – the Fell pony's ancestors. Britons were probably using ponies 2,500 years before Romans built their Wall. For a thousand years, ponies have ploughed fields, shepherded animals, moved feed and implements about the farm and ferried produce to market. Over the last 300 years, we have welcomed them for riding, packing, jumping and driving."

Clearly, humans could not have coped without us, which makes me proud, though not boastful. We houyhnhnms are unassuming, unlike fully-grown yahoos, who sometimes brag about their achievements before they've achieved anything. Why, however, do so many humans choose to forget or ignore our notable accomplishments? Recognition wouldn't hurt.

A boy asks about our Roman ancestors.

"Archaeologists have dug up bones within the Wall's vicinity," explains our man, "which indicate that Fell ponies are similar, in size at least, to one type of Roman pony. This Roman type was, I believe, slightly shorter than the Fell and had thinner legs. Ponies have changed: they have adapted over time to changing environmental conditions. Horse breeders have assisted that change, though not necessarily always for the better."

286

Now it's the turn of nine-year-olds.

"How fast can a Fell pony run?" asks a girl.

"That depends partly upon the rider's required speed but mainly upon the sizes of pony and rider," argues our man. "Ponies are able to gallop without riders at speeds of up to 45 miles an hour; that's about 20 metres a second. On wide-open hills, free-living ponies will walk and trot speedily for hours, and they will canter smoothly, but they rarely gallop flat out unless they sense an emergency."

If it is necessary, we can gallop as fast as Ospreys skimming on summer breezes. We fly without wings. Put it another way: when Roamer and I galloped away from our man in tandem over two weeks ago, harnessed together and fully loaded, even the world's fastest human sprinter could not have overtaken us.

"How tall are the biggest Fell ponies?" ask two boys simultaneously.

"The tallest are 14 hands; that's 56 inches or 1 metre 42 centimetres," stresses our man. "If a pony is taller it may still be a purebred Fell pony, but it cannot be registered as such. Whenever any pony, whichever breed, grows to be at least 14½ hands tall, that's 58 inches or 147.3 centimetres, it's called a horse."

That's okay: Roamer and I definitely aren't the tallest Fell ponies.

Eight-year-olds take over, posing questions similar to those asked by children at earlier schools, questions even I could answer now, such as "How long's the Roman Wall?" and "How strong are the ponies?" and "Why did Romans choose horses to carry the bricks?"

"Donkeys likely wouldn't have survived easily in the British climate," reasons our man. "Hence, there were relatively few mules in Britain, although mule bones have been identified at Vindolanda, near the Wall. Some Roman ponies were about 12½ hands tall, roughly the same size as today's smallest Fell ponies. Romans required animals that could carry stones up a steep hill from a quarry, particularly where the distance between quarry and building site was too far for builders to transport stones manually. They possibly used a combination of their own horses and British wild ponies."

Trip after trip, day after day, was fatiguing for the ponies, I bet.

"How many stones could the ponies carry at once?" inquires a 10-year-old girl who hasn't had an opportunity to speak.

"Typical facing stones may have weighed roughly 29 kilograms each, perhaps less," says our man. "If ponies moved two stones at a time, this represented a total load of 58 kilograms plus the saddle, which strong, fit pack animals could have handled easily. However, they might have carried over 100 kilograms on occasions. Romans might have asked them to carry three or even four facing stones, two on each side of the saddle to balance the load, which is a total load in excess of 116 kilograms. We can't be certain how much they carried, but such an excessively heavy load could have seriously injured a pony."

"We already know that humans have often abused our ancestors in centuries gone by," Roamer reminds me. "I'm sad when I think about what may have happened to some ponies, and mules for that matter, during the Wall's construction."

"Wouldn't pack animals have been very precious along the Wall?" I ask him. "I would imagine they were scarce. Therefore, Romans almost certainly would have looked after them."

"I pray that you are right," whispers Roamer. "Let's hope that all humans learn to respect pack ponies in future."

"In a recent experiment," explains our man, "I tied two baskets made of wicker to each packsaddle. Modern basket makers manufactured these to scale based upon ancient, sculptured etchings found on Trajan's Column in Rome. Although Roman baskets are slightly larger than modern-day, household, plastic buckets, both containers are similar in shape. We two-thirds filled Thorn's and Roamer's wicker baskets with quarry stones and then led the ponies up a 750-foot-high slope to the Wall."

So far, I've not fathomed why we did it. Was it a silly exercise?

"It must have taken Roman horses a great deal of time to carry the stones up the slopes?" an eight-year-old girl suspects.

"Quite likely, especially if the loads were heavy," agrees our man. "And it might have been quite dangerous. Our attempt at carrying small stones was precarious, wasn't it, Alan?"

"Categorically!" recalls Cameraman.

"At Combe Crag Wood, it took us about 20 minutes to climb from the valley quarry to the Wall," calculates our man. "Roman ponies or mules would have needed to keep going, up and down, all day. Some may have carried stone from Combe Crag to Birdoswald Fort, a distance of about 2½ miles – that's 4 kilometres – though oxen likely were used too."

My stone-carrying trip was easy: I carried a light load. Mind you, even though I am sure-footed, I almost slipped from a ledge.

It's the turn of seven-year-olds. One boy is interested in how far we can walk in a day.

"Between 15 and 20 miles, that's between 24 and 32 kilometres, along a fairly flat, safe track while carrying their reasonable, not very heavy, loads," guesstimates our man. "However, Thorn and Roamer have averaged only about 5 miles a day, which is roughly 8 kilometres, during this expedition. The terrain poses some difficulties, they must overcome obstacles and we are camping out most nights. It also takes quite a bit of time to properly harness and pack the ponies each morning, and we have limited daylight. In addition, we take time to talk with interesting people, especially children, on our way."

He has forgotten to mention that we carry packs for in excess of six hours each day.

"How do the bones get inside a pony?" inquires a very young boy.

Nobody has asked that before.

"Ponies are mammals, replies our man. "As the unborn pony is growing inside its mother, its bones form. A newborn pony already has all its bones, though they don't develop fully until it is four or five years old."

Our man points to a special part of my pal's backbone: "Spinal processes behind the withers don't develop completely in many ponies until about age five. That's one reason why I've limited Roamer's load."

Such testing questions deserve lengthy answers, demand more time than we have, I've decided. I bet every child will be heading homewards soon. Let's get a move on, I'm thinking. Our campsite is probably miles away, and I'm not lumbering in the dark.

Somebody wonders why we came to Bowness. Our leader reveals that we are trying to help save semi-wild, extensively grazing Fell pony breed lines partly because they help wildlife to survive. He appeals to the children to write stories about our visit. To anybody reading this, please assist us. If humans fail to figure out how to protect free-living herds, rapidly they will cease to exist.

"We must support men and women who own and look after such herds," warns our man. "Fells are an important part of our biodiversity and wildish places."

Everything sounds complicated, but I think I understand at last. Wise humans will comprehend too.

It's getting late, already past the children's home time, when our man pulls scientific equipment from his rucksack: it's his data logger, naturally, to which a temperature sensor is connected.

"Please could I have two volunteers to measure Thorn's body temperature?" he asks.

Two 10-year-old girls willingly step forward, nominated by the headteacher, whose name, Roamer tells me, is Christopher. Our man instructs the girls; they take it in turns to read out the air temperature and then my body temperature close to my heart. Normally, Roamer prefers to do most of the experimental stuff. Today, I quite fancy some attention! My body's a lot warmer than the air, the girls discover. Nothing's new there: I am definitely alive.

"Children, you can write your stories about Thorn and Roamer," proposes the headteacher enthusiastically."

We have run out of time. The mini-humans file into their classrooms to don coats. Alan packs up his gear and scurries home, exhausted by a tough day's filming, not to mention an arduous trek. Even I am becoming thirsty due to our exertions.

"All right, boys. Let's go," orders our man sharply. "From our present location, some experts contend, the Wall continued another 1½ kilometres further west. More or less, we still must cover twice that distance."

This latest news startles Roamer: "Do you realise, Thorn? After all, we may not have travelled the Wall's entire length yet."

On our right stretches Campfield Marsh. Beyond, the River Eden glides serenely in its channel, ever nearer journey's end. Scanning across the estuary, amidst creeping gloom, I barely discern the river's northern shoreline, a slither of Scotland, land of the Gaels.

Before dusk, we hurry along the coastal road to our man's prearranged camping spot. Unexpectedly, 150 or so paces from Bowness School, two young boys, brothers I think but I can't be certain, are alongside us. They have decided to join our brisk march. One's on foot. The other's cycling.

"Won't your mother be wondering where you are?" asks our man, half a mile further on. "Shouldn't you go home now?"

"It's all right," declares the runner confidently.

The cyclist shouts, "I'll show you where Norman lives," and he disappears around a bend, pedalling furiously.

Who is Norman? More importantly, how is such a young mini-human – Roamer thinks he's about eight – able to keep up with us on foot? He must be fit: we are moving at a hectic, energy-sapping, non-stop pace.

"We must check in before nightfall," insists our man.

I sense his urgency. Thump, thump, thump beats my heart as we trot along. Is it about to explode? Heavy, aching legs pound on unforgiving concrete. I'm thirstier than ever. Nearly two miles further on, we plod wearily, more steadily. My heart is jumping, jumping, jumping, about to scream. Can I keep up? Can the runner keep up?

Past Scargravel Point – an estuarine notch where coarse sand and stones accumulate – is situated this afternoon's final destination, North Plain. Here, the colourful, painted sign of a kingfisher marks a wetland reserve managed by the Royal Society for the Protection of Birds. A subtle, balanced combination of wet grassland, saltmarsh, peat bogs and farmed land provides a safe haven for an extraordinary array of wild creatures. This is the season of teals, pintails and hen harriers on Campfield Marsh Nature Reserve.

The final, 1¾ miles, coastal road trek from Bowness School was tough, even gruelling, but this time we have definitely made it: we have travelled coast to coast. Now, standing at the expedition's most westerly point, Roamer and I are ecstatic. Our man, however, is less happy: it is 4:15 according to his black survival watch, natural light is fading fast and a cattle grid bars our admittance to the bird sanctuary's track. To the grid's left, a pedestrian entrance between two low walls is wide enough for us to squeeze through, but only without our saddlebags.

As our man is contemplating whether to unload our packs where we are standing, the cyclist's timely appearance at the track's entrance is reassuring.

"I've told Norman you're here," he reports dutifully.

Our man thanks the boy, who, without uttering another word, heads home along the coastal road, always pedalling furiously. I watch him briefly, mesmerised by his impressive human-powered speed. The runner, who did manage to keep up, turned back earlier; his mother is likely to be worried.

We wait. Mere minutes elapse before a tall, bearded stranger purposefully approaches. He sports a checked, woollen jacket and a ranger's cap.

"Hi, Norman," begins our man.

"I'm glad you've managed to get this far without misfortune," declares the stranger, who is evidently this nature reserve's overseer. "Welcome."

"I'm happy to be here," acknowledges our man. "Unfortunately, I must unpack the ponies right away: your public gateway's too tight a fit."

"If you lead them across the grassy area, I'll show you how to access the site via another entrance," recommends the overseer, pointing to a rough, waterlogged patch of ground adjacent to a walled field.

We take two paces forward.

"It's dangerously deep bog," observes our man instantly, pulling me sideways sharply. "The ponies could sink under the weight of

292

their packs."

I already have decided: I am venturing no further across this quagmire under any circumstance. Fell ponies usually sense danger well before humans have any inkling.

"Okay, unload here," concedes the overseer. "I'll bring the four-wheel drive to transport your gear to the paddock."

Our man agrees: "That plan sounds perfect, Norman."

Scarcely 15 minutes elapse, I guess, before our man has loaded the saddles, harnesses and packs into the back of a truck. Promptly, the overseer drives the truck south along a track towards an open-sided barn. Meanwhile, we eagerly follow our man along the same track, a new-found swagger in our previously shortening steps.

When we arrive at the barn, approximately 100 human strides later, our next supply batch is waiting. I count two rectangular cardboard boxes: presumably, one is food and survival essentials for our man, the other a sizeable bag of pellets for us! Beside the barn, beneath a plastic-roofed, lean-to shelter, stands the site's tiny office, a modest, permanently parked caravan. Less than 50 yards away is the gate to a substantial wetland area.

"Would you prefer them to graze close to your campsite or in the more extensive wetland area you passed along the road earlier?" asks the overseer.

"Although the latter would satisfy their adventurous inclinations, I wouldn't be able to round them up easily," admits our man. "If I remember correctly from my reconnaissance, that area's vast and extremely wet in places. I'd rather they stayed here in your spacious enclosure next to the barn."

He's right. In that wetland, we'd be as happy as fledgling swallows flitting for midges over a July wheat field before sunset.

"Here's the key to my office," explains the bearded man. "Would you care to sleep in there? It might be easier. There's a cooking stove, too. Help yourself. Behind the caravan, you should be able to locate a stopcock that turns on fresh water. We shut it off to prevent pipes freezing up. You might hear one or two unusual bird species tonight. If any local is inquisitive tomorrow, just mention my name. I must go: I'm late for an appointment. Catch you later."

Our man thanks the overseer for his generosity, ensures we are well fed and then releases us onto a wonderfully wide, wet pasture.

"Off you go, boys," he announces cheerfully. "There's no packing tomorrow, so enjoy a lovely rest."

Roamer and I are alone again, at the edge of our known world. Waterfowl nest about us. A vast sky canopies a black night that, at every compass bearing, remains uncluttered by the slightest artificial light.

Later this evening, as we are grazing by the pasture gate, I overhear our man, who is telephoning Cameraman.

"Alan, when you come to film tomorrow, please would you bring fresh water? . . . It's too dark for me to locate the stopcock. I'm wondering whether it really exists! I have only a paltry half pint in my flask plus a third-filled kettle. . . . I feel dehydrated. . . . Oh, please could you also bring me a couple of chocolate bars? . . . No, I am resisting Norman's kind offer of his caravan to sleep in. Later on, its larger air space will be much cooler than that of my tent. . . . His electric fan heater doesn't appear to be working. I'll definitely be warmer inside the tent. . . . Yes, it's going to be a cold night on the peninsula. ... Okay. See you tomorrow."

Intensely sharp, late-night air pierces far-flung corners of our immense field, hanging on our breath. A thick blanket of drenching, freezing fog rolls in from the Solway Firth's deep creek with the incoming tide. We don't mind frosts and we've plenty of water: the field is awash in places. More worryingly, how will our man cope?

"I've been thinking," says Roamer as we survey the emptiness.

"About what?" I ask warily.

Roamer does a lot of thinking, as you might have realised. This could mean trouble.

"About why there's little space for Fell ponies in a person-centred world," he replies. "It occurs to me that there are just too many humans in England."

"I'm not with you," I reply even more warily.

"Well, a smaller human population would need fewer sheep and cattle on commons."

"What has the human population to do with anything?" I ask, slightly irritated by this apparently nonsensical statement.

"Fewer people would want to eat sheep and cows, so there would be more room for us on our hills."

"Okay, I accept your argument, sort of," I say, grudgingly. "But you could look at it another way."

"What other way is there?"

"Millions of British sheep earn the right to roam for one reason: humans devour them for food," I point out. "I detest the idea as much as you do, probably more, but if they ate a few of us, as in France, then our race definitely would be protected."

"No way!" cries Roamer. "I thought we had agreed: eating horse or pony meat is uncivilised. I have a much better solution: all humans should become vegetarians, or at least they should eat much less meat. Then they wouldn't need to keep oodles of sheep; more ponies could graze in truly natural environments; we could win back our rightful share of the land."

"There's little chance of that happening," I chide. "Be practical."

"You're possibly right," admits Roamer. "My considered opinion is that the human population must quickly stop growing. Otherwise, there will be no space whatsoever for the likes of us unless we live as people live, cooped up in tiny shelters. It's all right for humans who have forgotten the exhilaration of running free, but many of our free-living relatives wouldn't easily survive the ordeal."

"Luckily, our man never ties us up at night," I say. "We wouldn't tolerate it. We'd break out, whatever the cost. Off we would go at a canter."

"Talking of canters, how about one right now?" suggests Roamer.

He dashes towards a faraway hedge. I'm behind him for a change, taken by surprise.

Two male barn owls, out hunting before midnight, shriek over the pasture. I still see no light. We are free to wander widely, albeit in a low place.

Freezing fog, fireworks, birds but no water

5th November – Campfield Marsh Nature Reserve

Roamer:

WELL beyond midnight, Pan unzips his icy tent door to confront a deafeningly silent scene on a below freezing Solway Peninsula. He is on the prowl, sharply aware of an air temperature lower than at any time since we began our trek, a chill factor increased by drenching estuary dew. Indeed, what reading would his temperature sensor register now? Frost has turned the wilting, sodden grass white.

Is our favourite human having difficulty sleeping? Is his sleeping bag adequate? He told his assistant, by telephone yesterday evening, that it is ideal for early to middle autumn conditions, but this unexpected cold snap more closely resembles early winter. He said a bag's tog rating measures its insulating property. I've no idea what he meant, but I gather that his bag is optimally comfortable at air temperatures of plus two degrees Celsius. As he returns to the comparative warmth of his shelter, I suspect he may be experiencing an uncomfortable night. We don't mind cold weather: winter fur helps to protect us. Before this month expires, our shaggy, black, impenetrable coats will be fully grown. We can manage, but can he?

At daybreak, the sun is still asleep. Thick, drenching fog, gathered in by the early morning tide, hides Pan's tent. Thorn and I are resting, sampling unusual-tasting foods in a rich, marshy landscape. When the fog clears, we shall explore this genuinely wild, or at least nearly wild, place.

I pause from my grazing to listen when Pan briefly telephones representatives of two local newspapers to inform them of our arrival at the Wall's western extremity. I suppose he is being diligent. However, for whatever reason, his telephone calls are half-hearted. On-duty editors are unlikely to take him seriously. Of course, it's Saturday: perhaps he is aware that many news-reporting establishments retain only skeleton staff at weekends; that the chances of a reporter visiting this remote peninsula today are negligible.

I'm puzzled: uncharacteristically, our leader didn't plan any publicity beforehand. So far, he has secured near zero media interest in this expedition. Why doesn't he seem to care whether the world is informed? I'm baffled why, right now, he's content for us to remain unnoticed, anonymous. Is that what he intended? Perhaps his post-expedition video diary will do the trick. I presume he prefers to report our story accurately, using Alan's footage, only when we succeed in completing our mission. Yet it occurs to me we have succeeded in one respect: we have travelled the Wall's length. Let's hope a finalised documentary will reveal all at some future date, though I'm sceptical.

Much later this placid morning, in a surreal moment, Alan's car cruises by our camp. It is heading south-east towards a distant corner of the nature reserve. Pan, who was cleaning tack in the barn, rushes towards the lonning, waving frantically in a vain attempt to attract Alan's attention; already, his carriage is speeding away. Ultimately, I expect, the camera operator will realise his error.

As Pan returns to the barn, he whistles to us across near frozen moss. Thorn and I trot to the gate, expecting pellets. In fact, we are disappointed. Pan, who is now busy sorting out his food supplies for the next three days, mostly dehydrated and tinned, ignores us. What does he want?

Pan's roundhouse is sparkling: frozen dew clings to its roof and walls. Under the lean-to, a few metres away, are saddles, bridles, harnesses, saddlebags and saddle pads, all ready for cleaning if cleaning is necessary. He has laid out separately every item of equipment, which he intends to check and repack.

"We've carried all that gear?" I ask Thorn, in disbelief.

"There's a lot," he agrees. "Does our man really need it all?"

"Some we've seen already," I reply. "For example, he uses a monocular and his Global Positioning System for route-planning. I don't recognise every item, though. There's a remarkable deal of additional equine equipment: a horse first aid kit; a reserve harness; two spare, leather lead reins, one shorter; pony brushes; a leather head collar; breast girth sleeves; and ankle protectors."

"Don't forget his camping and survival bits," interrupts Thorn. "He has a collapsible spade, a pocket balance, a first aid kit and a collapsible, lightweight air bed. Bad weather clothes are also essential: his fleece; a gillet; a waterproof jacket; black, cotton trousers; windproof trousers; and waterproof overtrousers. Oh, I haven't included other supposedly indispensable items: two T-shirts; four undergarments; sleeping trousers; six pairs of socks; a fleece hat; gloves; and gaiters. Yes, Roamer, I've learned to count. Phew!"

"Why has he brought three artificial-fibre towels?" I wonder.

"Well, they are lightweight and pack into tiny spaces," reckons Thorn, who is practically minded. "Their uses abound in wet weather."

"Look," I tell Thorn. "Pan has two spare bungee straps, possibly brought in case he damages or loses the originals. He sporadically loses crucial items. Without bungees, how would he attach his tent easily, if at all, to your saddle?"

"There's more," he replies. "I have noticed numerous assorted, jumbled items: tent and footwear waterproofers; four maps; brightly coloured waterproof bags of various sizes; saddle soap and conditioner; spray-on cleaner; a clothes-line; and a cleaning brush and cloths. It's a lot to brood over!"

"What's he holding?" I ask Thorn, noticing that Pan is fiddling with cables and wires.

"They are his solar charger connectors," guesses Thorn.

Pan's efficient solar charger, carried in my pack, today slung across his roundhouse roof, will quickly reach 100 per cent electrical storage capacity for unforeseen emergencies – when the sun sneaks out! He told Alan it recharges flat batteries from most of his gadgets: hand and head torches; a razor; two mobile 'phones; a Global Positioning System; a lightweight, dedicated word processor; a data logger; his voice recorder; saddle lights; an electric fence; and possibly his laptop computer. It's clever. He is also attempting to devise a method of charging his camera battery. Occasionally, he can't connect to mains electricity. Then, at least he has sunlight energy on tap, so to speak, if he needs it. Naturally, Fell ponies have no use for electrical energy. "Travel light" is our motto.

"You are lugging a heap of scientific equipment!" notes Thorn, astonished. "It's never-ending: two battery rechargers that run off mains electricity; lots of rechargeable batteries; temperature, sound and breathing rate sensors for our man's data logger; and what our man refers to as back-up storage and a mobile broadband interface, though I've no idea what he is talking about."

"Yes, Thorn, that's a lot of carrying," I confirm. "By the way, you didn't mention his scientific extras: camera lenses; a lens cleaning kit and soft carrying cases; internet attachments; computer memory cards and electronic connecting cables; a 'smart' pen – whatever that does – with its spare inks; and writing sheets, blank compact disks and a disk marked 'speech recognition software'! And don't forget his digital voice recorder, headphones and microphone. Oh, and there's the spare mobile 'phone. Have I missed anything?"

"Possibly," gasps Thorn, still bewildered. "Why does he need it all? What does it mean, Roamer?"

"I'm not sure," I reply. "At some time or other I've overheard Pan referring to different bits of it. He also has a compass, an emergency whistle and a multi-purpose pocket knife. Oh, look over there. I can see various documents and his copy of the British Army's 'Manual of Horsemastership'."

"But why would he carry a manual?"

"Don't you recollect?" I answer. "During our re-enactment, it told him how Romans attached their wicker baskets. And he mentioned to Cameraman that it contains a horse medical directory and advice for packing and tack care."

"We've seen his lightweight cooking and cleaning equipment countless times," continues Thorn, "but I still couldn't name it all."

"I could," I tell him. "Let's see: two sets of eating utensils; a tin opener; a flint; steel firelighters; safety matches; two collapsible stoves; butane and propane gas cylinders; and a set of three steel saucepans. His recycled plastic utensils include a plate, a bowl and a cup. And there's biodegradable body wash, wash-up liquid, shampoo, sanitiser and toilet paper. Oh, I almost forgot two folding buckets, a pocket shower that he never uses, a recycled, half-litre, carbon flask and a steel flask."

"Wow!" cries Thorn. "It's tiring just looking at everything. By the way, you didn't mention his tent, sleeping bag or several additional back-breakers. Contemplating how much we carry sends me dizzy."

As we finish taking stock, Alan appears.

"How are you feeling this fine morning?" he asks.

"Surprisingly well," replies Pan, "considering last night was the coolest of the trip. You look rested. I tried to attract your attention as you shot past."

"I realised where you were, but I couldn't turn around after I'd passed the gate: the track's too narrow. I had to keep going."

"It was violently cold here between midnight and dawn," persists Pan. "I estimated the air temperature went down to about minus four degrees. Thick fog is only now beginning to disperse."

"Further inland, the weather has been quite warm," responds Alan. "There's no fog. You've been unlucky."

"Did you bring any water?" asks Pan. "I'm desperate for a drink."

Alan produces two 1-litre bottles of fresh water and half a dozen chocolate bars, as promised. Pan grabs a bottle and takes a slow swig, then another, and another.

"You aren't short of food, are you?" inquires Alan as they share his flask of coffee.

"No. Adequate supplies were waiting here. I simply fancied some chocolate. Thank you for bringing it."

Refreshed, Pan sits by his tent, recording yesterday's diary on his black laptop computer as Alan sets up his camera.

"Let's film your gear before we film the ponies," suggests Alan. "I'll test the lighting."

"So that's why Pan whistled us," I tell Thorn.

"Come on, Roamer," responds my friend. "Obviously, we're not needed yet. Race you to that patch of scrub in the distance."

Off we charge, bouncing with energy, eager to enjoy our free day.

Thorn:

By midday, the fog has dissipated. On a transformed, astoundingly sunny, even warm afternoon, two opportunist red admiral butterflies dance in the scrub. At low tide, shelducks fly overhead towards the estuary tide-line.

I doze fleetingly, waking up to discover that Roamer is only two paces away; he has been dozing too. It is indescribably comforting to walk, graze, sleep, wake and play beside my greatest friend. Roamer and I stretch, smile at each other and then, without speaking, storm towards the bright sunshine.

Later this lazy afternoon, our man rambles slowly towards us across a wetland expanse, attempting to avoid patches of surface water. He calls us, but we are uninterested: we are relaxing. From afar, Cameraman films us grazing contentedly.

Our man approaches. He collars us. Now, Roamer on his left and me on his right, he leads us closer to the camera.

"That's excellent," praises the pleased documentary recordist. "They seem to be at home here."

We are at home! Indeed, we are delighted when our man quickly releases us: we can continue grazing undisturbed.

Cameraman departs soon afterwards, promising to return early tomorrow morning.

Our man now grabs this opportunity to re-erect his tent under the lean-to shelter. When he eventually sets off along the farm track towards Bowness nearly two miles away, carrying an empty bottle in search of drinking water, it is already dark.

According to my inbuilt clock barely any time has passed, amazingly, before he reappears, looking for us as he often does, ensuring we are safe. What's the news?

"My luck was in," relates our man. "A passing motorist, a local mother whose two children you met, gave me a lift. She ferried me from the cattle grid to her house. 'You can fill your water container there,' she offered, pointing to a yard tap."

"Is he referring to that young cyclist and his brother, the runner?" whispers Roamer.

"Possibly," I reply.

"I'm not going to die of thirst," proclaims our man, "at least not immediately! Boys, I'll see you tomorrow."

Our man has chats with us regularly these days. Well, let's face it: frequently no humans are about, so he has little choice. Does he suspect we understand him?

A short while after our man has retired, Roamer and I are beginning to settle down when I hear the distant rumble of what I suppose is thunder. That's odd, I conclude: tonight's sky is as pure as a Cumbrian mountain's midwinter beck – and the air is crisp. Then I remember: it is bonfire night. Our man reassured us earlier today; he told us not to let rocketing, multi-coloured, fizzing, flashing and shimmering lights and cracks, rising from the estuary's Scottish shore, frighten us. He recounted an event that occurred near Lochness, a lake in the Scottish Highlands, exactly 12 years ago. On that occasion his Highland pack pony, Ailsa of Croila, terrified of booms, frantically galloped back and forth, to and from his tent, for over an hour. Roamer and I also hate fire and loud bangs, as you will have realised, but we remain unperturbed. In this extreme westerly location, we are isolated, distant, well away from potentially harmful consequences of human activity.

Several hours have elapsed. Artificial sights and sounds have dissipated. Late night air sits crisply in my nostrils. Barn owls communicate intermittently as the estuary's temperature drops even more severely than last night.

Solo:

This afternoon was unusually warm. In fact, it was so warm that I fell asleep. I had the strangest dream yet.

I dreamt that I was one of many ponies slaving away non-stop one stormy night. I was carrying 25 litres of water down a street. Pausing to rest, I glimpsed, in the distance, the prettiest pony ever. I trotted towards her, managing to catch up with her within a few minutes. Her name was Lucy.

Lucy and I played together regularly after that night – cantering, jumping streams and hiding from each other. On her birthday, I gave her a present – three carrots and a blue, sequined saddle.

One evening, several weeks later, I could not find Lucy. Her new owner must have taken her somewhere, I decided. I was depressed. Who would play with me now? At that moment, incredibly, Thorn and Roamer were standing beside me, smiling.

"What is happening?" I asked, confused, but they ignored me. Instead, Thorn beckoned to me to go exploring with them. We strolled together for 100 miles, saddleless, free, without meeting anybody.

"Let us go home now," I implored Roamer. "I must find Lucy."

I awoke from my dream, aroused by the faint sound of grinding teeth. An acquaintance from my herd was grazing nearby.

A frozen tent, seaweed and more fog

6th November – Eastwards to Drumburgh

Roamer:

A second sub-zero night on the peninsula is over. When Pan hails us this misty, magical morning, we cannot see him, so we decide to stand and wait. Dense fog fills Campfield Marsh, a grassland speckled white with sugar-shaker frost that crackles beneath our hooves. Eventually, he discovers us, hiding in a far-off corner of this presently not-so-squishy plain.

"Look, over there!" urges Thorn as Pan leads us to the barn.

"At what am I supposed to be looking?" I reply.

"Look how our man's shelter sparkles and glistens!" he says, mesmerised.

He's right. Pan's tent has frozen rigid despite being under the lean-to. Thousands of tiny ice beads cling to its synthetic, waterproof fibres, seeming to emit a blue-white shine.

Alan has arrived earlier than usual. He is waiting patiently at the barn to film Norman, the capped man with a brightly coloured jacket and green Wellington boots.

Pan relates to Alan how his roundhouse door zip broke last night: "My tent was frozen at three o'clock when I got up for an obvious reason. The zip was so icy, several teeth snapped. What an unblemished, flickering sky greeted me. I estimated it was about minus six degrees at one stage; I couldn't sleep properly."

"I was warm, in bed," responds Alan wryly. "It is a gloriously warm, bright sunshine day in Carlisle. In fact, it's warm everywhere in Cumbria except on this peninsula."

The sun is visible, just, through the haze, a pale ivory disc hovering menacingly over North Plain.

"There's absolutely no heat pollution here, of course," admits Pan, "but I failed to anticipate such a challenging night. Let's hope my winter sleeping bag arrives within the next 48 hours."

I suspect we are in better condition than Pan is, following our day off. Right now, however, I'm more interested in where we are going today.

"Any idea where our next campsite will be?" I ask Thorn.

He doesn't reply: he's too busy enjoying his pellets.

About an hour passes before Pan is able to pack away his thawed but still soaked tent, perceptibly increasing Thorn's carrying load. My friend is displeased, naturally, but I can't help smiling on such rare occasions: his slight predicament does not affect me.

Pan leads us, wearing bridles but minus saddles and packs, back along the bird sanctuary's track to the cattle grid immediately before the road junction. Norman's pick-up truck trundles to a halt alongside us directly. As he and Pan unload the saddles and packed saddlebags, Norman points to an intertidal wetland area across the road.

"We could do our interview there. Is it suitable?" he asks.

"Looks good," confirms Alan.

Damp fog engulfs the marsh even at eleven o'clock, outstaying its welcome.

"To my mind, this is by far the chilliest morning of our trip," Pan tells Norman.

Norman is sympathetic: he's aware of how severe peninsula weather might become.

At this moment, Pan, who is holding Thorn's lead rope, notices that my friend is blissfully eating seaweed. He must still be hungry.

"How amazing!" asserts Pan emphatically. "I have never observed a Fell pony eating serrated wrack before. It's just another indication of how versatile they are as grazers. Minerals in the seaweed will help keep them healthy, too."

"This cast-ashore vegetation is mouth-wateringly zingy," remarks Thorn. "I crave more! Try a mouthful, Roamer."

Norman is gripping my lead rope, but I manage to taste the weed. Thorn isn't joking: it is spicy.

"Norman, what's your job on this R.S.P.B. nature reserve," begins Pan as soon as Alan has set up the microphone.

"I'm the coastal reserves manager."

"How large is the reserve, roughly?"

"This area of saltmarsh, where we are standing, is about 250 acres. It is inundated by tides twice daily, hence the seaweed. Big tides will come up and they'll cover most of the marsh, right up to higher ground. The whole reserve is about 1,000 acres. It takes in farmland, wet grassland and quite a sizeable chunk of Bowness Common, which is lowland raised mire, a peat bog."

At this point, unable to resist further, I decide to join Thorn in a spot of serious browsing.

"This weed is tantalisingly tasty," I mumble, a minute later. "I can't eat enough of it! There's lots of foraging for us here."

Thorn ignores me. His head is down; he is crunching away.

"We manage most of the ground for breeding waders," continues Norman, trying to ignore our antics. "That's our priority. We are recreating the habitats they require – wet ground where there are invertebrates for waders to feed on. Lapwing, redshank, snipe and curlew are the four main lowland wader species. They have declined drastically in Britain."

"Is he saying that few waders now survive?" I ask Thorn.

"Probably," he garbles, straight away continuing to crunch.

"But they're on the increase at North Plain," enthuses Norman. "We now have 60 to 70 pairs of breeding waders. So far, we have recorded – either heard or seen – 218 bird species on the reserve. Some are farmland birds, which are also in decline."

Pan wants to know why they are declining.

"Primarily it's because of habitat loss and changes in land

management practices," insists Norman. "They need wetland habitat, but there's little left for them. My principal job is to re-wet the area. In 1990, there was hardly any wet ground here at all: farmers had drained every agricultural area. We are trying to turn the clock back to what this place would have resembled when it was farmed far less intensively."

Pan abruptly halts the interview. Alan is unperturbed: by now, he is used to unplanned interruptions during filming.

"Norman, could you give Roamer a little more lead rope?" asks Pan politely. "Let him nibble. He might stop dancing about if he's grazing. There you go, Roamer. I think he's happy now. No, he isn't. Stand still, Roamer."

I am certainly unhappy! I wish they'd leave me alone. I've spotted a pile of wet, salty, tangy seaweed just two strides away, but I can't quite reach it.

"Hang on a second, please," advises Pan. "I'm going to tether the ponies. They've had enough seaweed, anyhow: too much iodine might be harmful."

Pan tethers us to a solitary wooden post less than three paces away, forcing us to eat grass. Mind you, it's saltier than normal. Hmm, it's delicious actually, a welcome change from pellets. Thorn and I settle down.

"Norman, which grazing animals are on the reserve?" inquires Pan.

"We need the sward at the right height," explains Norman earnestly, "and plenty of small tussocks where birds can tuck themselves away and hide to nest. Therefore, grazing animals are crucial. Although black and white cows aren't ideal, they are readily available for the drier land. It's difficult to find animals that are happy to go into wetter areas to graze. If they didn't graze, we would end up with spots too dense for breeding waders to enjoy. Waders like tussocks, open patches and a bit of rush. They also like wet, muddy areas such as this pool near where we're standing, where they take their chicks to feed. Without grazing animals, we would probably lose all of our breeding waders."

"Have you ever tried using Fell ponies?" asks Pan. "Mine have been quite happy here for the last day or so. They'll eat grass around pools."

"Of course we'll eat grass," whispers Thorn as he sidles up to me. "We could be a tremendous asset to the warden."

"We haven't tried ponies," declares Norman, "but it's something that's sparking my interest. I favour the idea of using native breeds rather than stock that evolution hasn't designed for the job. It would please me to see native breeds wandering about on the reserve. It would add interest for our visitors as well."

Pan emphasises that we are the native pony breed of local origin and that we have developed unusual, northern grazing habits.

"They will eat a wide variety of coarse and woody vegetation, including rushes," he explains.

"Rush control is probably one of our severest problems," divulges Norman.

I've caught Pan's eye. Oh, no, he's blaming me again.

"Excuse me, Norman. Roamer is taking a bite out of Thorn. I'll have to warn him off. Stop it, Roamer!"

It was just a friendly nibble. Thorn was attempting to graze my patch of grass. We were simply having fun. Besides, it's partly Pan's fault: he has tethered us too closely together.

"How many ponies might you require?" inquires Pan, the moment we are standing quietly.

"I would seek advice," contends Norman. "We mustn't let an area become too badly poached or muddy. On the other hand, we want the majority of vegetation eaten off. Some of our areas are very wet and extremely rushy, whereas others are drier. It could be a case of 'suck it and see'."

"I guess a discussion between yourselves and the Fell Pony Society might help?"

"We would welcome that," replies Norman. "We could ascertain the number required and their availability."

"You could determine what positive effects ponies might have on the salt marsh and moss areas," suggests Pan.

"Yes, we could consider a pilot project. We would need to consider their containment and ease of handling. There could be costs for fencing or for controlling them where there is field access to visitors."

"We have visited four schools along the Wall with Thorn and Roamer," Pan informs Norman. "Children were physically close to them; there has been no incident, which augurs well."

I am engrossed in this human conversation, remembering that we adore meeting children, when I become aware that Thorn is annoying me, trying to bite me back.

"Hai-ai-ai-ai!" I cry. "Get off!"

"Stop it, you two!" orders Pan again, eyeing us sternly.

Pan blames Thorn on this occasion. We resolve to behave.

Thorn is customarily a clever rascal. Nowadays, however, will I allow him to trick me? There's nay chance, I'd say. Unfortunately, he still gets me into trouble occasionally.

"Of course, extensively grazing ponies are acclimatised to live outside throughout the year," continues Pan after we have settled down once more.

"At the moment," observes Norman, "we graze with cattle alone through the summer months until the end of October. Nearly all of our cattle have gone now. It might be quite useful to be able to tackle rush growth through the winter, so it is stubbier, more tussocky, at the start of the breeding season in spring."

"If foals have been hefted properly, they will browse rushes in winter without hesitation," believes Pan. "And using young stock would ensure naturally grazing Fell mares don't become extinct."

"That's something the R.S.P.B. would be keen to support," confesses Norman.

I've eaten enough: I'm becoming impatient. Please, let us trek, I'm thinking. I put my head gently onto Pan's shoulder and nuzzle his face, purely to remind him that I'm here, waiting. Instead, he kisses my nose. He's laughing. Norman is laughing too, but it wasn't meant to be funny. Well, all right, I suppose we ponies can be amusing.

"Might the R.S.P.B. run a scientific pilot project?" suggests Pan.

"I could talk to my colleagues about that," reckons Norman.

"Could you and I live here at a future time?" I propose to Thorn. "I fancy this estuary's wide-open spaces."

"Possibly we could, Roamer, but humans may choose us to carry out other important work elsewhere. However, younger Fell ponies might like to graze these wetlands."

"It was below minus five degrees Celsius last night and the night before," continues Pan. "The freeze woke me at 3.00 a.m. this morning. I grabbed my torch to look for these two; they were happily grazing 100 metres away. They haven't grown full winter coats yet. Nevertheless, as you see, they are in excellent condition. Frosty nights don't bother them."

I nudge Pan in approval. It's true: our black winter coats will look smart and keep us cosy. We were definitely warmer than he was last evening. He should acquire a winter jacket.

Wait a second: Alan is packing up his gear! At last, we are trekking on, but where are we heading? Where will today's journey end?

Norman helps to attach full saddlebags, containing new food supplies, to our saddles. Pan thanks him.

"Sometime, not too far into the future, I'll visit again," Pan assures Norman as the two men shake hands heartily.

I have been standing still for too long. Drenched, biting air is beginning to prey upon my ears, creating a weird sensation of imaginary pins piercing my back beneath a loaded saddle. Water droplets on my hooves have frozen in sympathy with winter's first ice on a nearby duck pond.

Obviously, Pan has decided to commence our trek east, away from this isolated peninsula. As we stride briskly towards Bowness School, I hear Alan following slowly in his car. His wife, who has accompanied him today, Sunday, is driving. For perhaps the first kilometre, he films us through the passenger side window. Then, without warning, the vehicle accelerates quietly and slowly overtakes us, purring gently before disappearing into drenching mist. I can see nothing except Thorn's silhouette. The fog is thicker.

Thorn:

This morning, our man talks with the bearded bird warden who oversees the marshes. Alan records everything. During their lengthy conversation, Roamer and I are becoming hungry; we decide to sample seaweed. The recent, outgoing tide has scattered it about the marsh in irregularly dumped, spherical heaps. Eating seaweed might seem less than appealing to you, but I rate the stuff highly. It is chewy and gratifyingly salty, with a pungent, fresh smell.

As I am chewing away, Roamer tosses a tangled bunch onto me by mistake. I can't resist having fun. We playfully toss the brown wrack about, tugging at the tastiest bits with our teeth. Our man fails to notice what's happening behind him: he's occupied conversing with the bird expert.

At midday, our stomachs full of pellets mixed with grass and seaweed, we depart Campfield Marsh. Roamer wonders where we are going next; I am also intrigued. Are we returning home soon? I hope and believe not.

"Boys, it's numbingly cold at night here," mutters our man as Port Carlisle looms ahead. "We must leave this peninsula as rapidly as possible."

Which route east shall we take? We know that our man has resolved, for the second time, not to undertake his reconnoitred route via Brackenrigg; very recently, a local landowner warned him that somebody had built a new dwelling over the track, rendering it impassable with ponies. In any event, he would prefer an alternative course from Bowness, along Acremire Lane, an ancient track. Unhappily, the landowners, who are local farmers, have not granted him access: apparently, the coastal road is inaccessible from the lane's eastern extremity.

"Acremire Lane avoids the road for over two kilometres and possibly marks the Military Way line," explained our man to Cameraman earlier today. "Unfortunately, it's on private land. Its eastern terminus is fenced off. Originally, it was a Roman road, but nobody ever registered it as a highway after it fell into disuse and disrepair. I visited Bowness in 2010 and again in 2011 in a forlorn attempt to obtain permission to use the lane."

We'll never know whether there might have been any passable route via the old lane. Our man is dejected: he fancies roads even less than Roamer.

At least he has a contingency plan, which initially takes us back along the coastal road to Kirkland House, originally church land. Here, he sojourns to talk with a farmer, yet another David, who kindly helped our man to plan this section of the route. Daphne, the farmer's smiling wife, makes him a cup of steaming coffee. Oh, in case you are wondering, these names are accurate: I checked with Roamer. Yes, I had forgotten them.

"You've actually done it!" acknowledges the farmer, noticeably surprised and pleased by our sudden appearance. "It's been ages since we heard from you. We thought you'd given up this year."

"It has been a long haul, David," reveals our man, "taking almost two years to plan. What's your opinion of Thorn and Roamer?"

"They look well," comments the farmer. "I'm delighted to see them."

He gently strokes Roamer first, me second. Soothing caresses are always worth waiting for.

While our man sips his coffee, he and the farmer discuss perennial route difficulties between Bowness and Drumburgh. The farmer confirms our intended off-road Vallum route across his land to Glasson, the place by a green river.

"My son, Mike, will indicate the way," insists the kind farmer.

Our man waves goodbye. We set off anew. Ignoring his hectic schedule, the farmer's young son willingly accompanies us across a mist-drowned landscape. We meander alongside mysterious, half-hidden hedges, initially in an approximately south-west direction. Quickly, we turn south-east towards Kirkland Milecastle, continuing to explore cloaked fields of mud, grass and damp hay.

A quarter of an hour after leaving Kirkland House, his task accomplished upon entering a lonning, our guide turns homewards. Fog quickly swallows him up. Will this blanket lift, even belatedly, today?

312

We move smoothly, following the Vallum along a straight, dying laneway to Glasson. At Glasson crossroads, a public house is straight ahead. Such a sight would represent an altogether more enticing proposition for us in midsummer. This gloomy day, however, heralds winter's early onset on a temporarily bleak peninsula. Fortunately, my coat is beginning to thicken; I can sense it.

"Now, boys, what should we do?" deliberates our man. "Should we head for the road or take a faintly discernible track?"

Don't keep asking us, I'm thinking. You're in charge, supposedly: you're the navigator and route finder.

A local man, ambling by at this moment, recommends caution.

"You may not be able to access the track alongside the barn ahead due to new build," he fears.

Our man surveyed this route section last December, when icy snow accompanied thicker, freezing, bone-piercing fog.

"That might have been one of the worst times ever to check out the Wall," he mutters to himself. "It was a winter to forget."

Our man is aware that a dismantled railway track meets the line of the Wall at the road, 550 yards eastwards. Where, however, is our entry point onto the track? Although he is keen not to waste time, he searches vainly, scarcely believing that builders have blocked it off.

"Let's get a move on, boys," he decides, 10 minutes of fruitless searching later. "We're behind schedule again. Even if we manage to gain access to the track, it is likely to be unimaginably muddy. We'll follow the minor road instead."

As we set off briskly towards the coastal road, our leader hasn't noticed that his right bootlace is undone. I try, honestly, but am unable to avoid treading on it. You can guess the rest. I accidentally pin his boot and, therefore, his foot to the road. He falls headlong, sprawling onto tarmacadam.

"Oi-oi!" shouts Roamer, wondering why we have unintentionally halted. "This is no time to be messing about!"

"Our man has injured his left knee," I tell Roamer.

"Oh, no! Is it serious?"

"I hope not," I reply. "He's rubbing it furiously. It's probably just bruised."

"Please watch where you are putting your feet in future!" orders Roamer.

"It's not my fault," I counter. "Our man should examine his bootlaces regularly. Such a silly mistake could kill our expedition abruptly. The slightest accident could render it stone dead."

Arriving back at Drumburgh Grange before nightfall, our man quickly feeds us, stores his gear in a shed and then releases us to roam.

After pitching his tent as before, in the open-sided barn, he telephones his assistant in Leicestershire, an urgent tone in his voice.

"Please could you send out a winter sleeping bag and winter fleeces? The weather has deteriorated. It is especially severe during early mornings."

"I'll post out what you need as quickly as possible," she promises.

They discuss other logistics.

Later on, we are grazing on a wide, grassy plain about 250 yards from the sea channel of the River Eden. I perceive that tonight is even cooler than last evening. I imagine that slender, stringy mini-icicles will already cling to our man's tent door. Winter clothes and possibly a winter tent will not materialise fast enough if this weather persists.

7th *November – Drumburgh Nature Reserve*

Roamer:

Before daybreak, the air temperature plummets to its lowest of the entire expedition. As it has previously, freezing fog clings to the estuary.

About an hour after dawn, human time, we are at the paddock gate, ready and eager for Pan to collect us for the next leg of our walk. Besides, we are hungry. However, he doesn't appear: he is resting. He was ill during the night, we later discover.

Two hours elapse. Pan's tent remains standing, still frozen.

Alan is also late; I cannot spot him or his car anywhere. He's supposed to record Pan's interview with a Cumbria Wildlife Trust representative. He also intends to film our distant cousins, Exmoor ponies, who originate from moorland on the water. Seemingly, they are grazing at Drumburgh Moss, though I'm uncertain why.

"Where are you Alan?" inquires Pan frantically when, at length, he finds time to telephone the camera operator. "You are always punctual, so I was worried about you. . . . I'm extremely sorry to hear that your car has broken down. . . . Ernie will drive you here? That's great! . . . Shall I rearrange the interview for this afternoon? . . . Didn't feel like travelling far today in any case: I was violently sick last night. . . . It's likely some kind of viral or bacterial infection. . . . I'm unsure what caused it. Possibly, it was something I ate, but I'm guessing. . . . I'll see you here at about 1:30. . . . Thanks a lot, Alan."

As you know, Ernie is Alan's occasional assistant. On this occasion, he appears to have rescued a sticky situation.

We hang about the hillside gate all morning, slightly bewildered. Pan returns, sure enough, to check that we are behaving and to give us bad news.

"Boys, unfortunately, we're going nowhere right now," he confides disconsolately.

"Nay, nay," complains Thorn. "I was looking forward to a workout."

"But we can't leave until after Alan arrives," I say. "Besides, Pan may not be perfectly well; he might not have recovered fully."

"Well, I suppose we have abundant grazing and an entertaining landscape to investigate," accepts my pal grudgingly.

Pan disappears into the barn to sort out tack. The farm's cook, whose name I have forgotten, searches him out.

"Would you care to come into the kitchen for breakfast?" she asks considerately.

"I'm not particularly hungry, thank you," he replies wearily, "but I would very much welcome a cup or two of tea."

Our leader is possibly dehydrated and suffering from other, unidentified after-effects of whatever assailed him last night. About

315

three-quarters of an hour later, he returns from the farmhouse looking measurably perkier.

"It's almost eleven," he notes, checking his watch. "Where's my visitor?"

"What visitor is he referring to?" asks Thorn.

"I suppose it could be the Trust representative," I suggest.

At this moment, on cue, a young, dark-haired man with spectacles, who indeed works for the Cumbria Wildlife Trust, rattles the farmhouse front door. Kitted up with a fleece jacket and boots, he, at least, is prepared for action.

"David, could we possibly film the interview at two o'clock?" begs Pan. "Alan's car has broken down. He's borrowing another. I apologise for messing you about."

In consideration of my pilgrimage experience so far, and in view of Pan's present conversation, please forgive me for thinking that a huge number of British human males bear the name David. Thorn, however, disagrees: he believes in coincidences.

"It's no trouble at all," insists David. "I needed to check the nature reserve today anyway. Ring me when he arrives. I'll be in the vicinity."

"I will. That's kind of you," says Pan, grateful for another opportunity to film.

Thorn:

Today, I have plenty of reserve energy for the return trek east along the Wall. I prance about early on, ears forward, eager to begin. Then, unexpectedly, our man announces we are not leaving. I am truly disappointed. This trekking bug has consumed me. I've become fanatical: it's probably because I'm a natural explorer, a wanderer who is keen to visit new places.

Our man is engrossed checking his equipment when Cameraman finally materialises with his assistant.

"Alan, I'm so glad that you and Ernie have managed to get here," he enthuses, visibly relieved.

After telephoning an expert from the Cumbria Wildlife Trust, our man immediately begins to lead us, Roamer on his left and me on his right, down a steep lane roughly 50 paces west of Drumburgh Castle's entrance. Cameraman and his assistant are marching with us. This sudden action, late in the day, has unsettled Roamer.

"Hey, Thorn, where's he taking us, and without saddles?" he asks, bemused.

"We'll soon find out," I reply, managing to calm him down. "It won't be far: there's not much daylight left."

"We'll do the interview at Drumburgh Moss," our man informs Cameraman. "Hopefully, we can also film Exmoor ponies grazing there."

"Perhaps we'll meet those ponies," suggests Roamer.

Not many minutes later, we are 400 paces, give or take, further down the lane.

"Is this is the correct spot?" inquires Cameraman.

Our man nods.

The Wildlife Trust officer parks his four-wheel drive. Accompanied by his colleague, another male officer, he approaches us. Unbelievably, everybody's here.

"Let's do it," orders Cameraman, ever keen to hasten while bright daylight prevails.

Unfortunately, Roamer and I are brimming with energy from overeating and lazing about. Keeping still isn't our forte. With his assistant's help, Cameraman attempts to film not once, not twice, but thrice, each time failing. Yes, it's true: we're getting in their way, though not on purpose: we are simply edgy.

"Okay, okay," I tell Roamer finally. "Our fun's over. Let's stop capering about. We'll be good. Let them commence filming. When our man has asked his questions, maybe we can get back to frolicking."

"We're here, at Drumburgh Moss Nature Reserve, on a cloudless day," declares our man in the happiest voice he can muster.

"Cloudless" is correct. This weather pleases Roamer and me enormously.

"Tell me," he begins. "What does your Trust do?"

"We help conserve Cumbrian wildlife in all its forms," pronounces the Trust manager. "We administer 40 reserves throughout the county."

"That's quite a lot," suggests our man.

"Yes," agrees the manager. "There are huge ones and tiny ones. Drumburgh is one of the biggest. It's about 120 hectares."

"And what types of habitats exist within it?"

"The most important habitat is raised bog," explains the manager, "which is a specialist habitat formed out of peat. It only forms in excessively wet conditions. Associated with the peat are wet heathland, wet woodland and bits of rushy pasture. Generally, it is wetland habitat."

"What conservation work have you carried out here?"

"We've taken out a lot of scrub," replies the manager. "Recently, we've been using a mechanical flail to clear gorse scrub by smashing it up into little bits. We're re-profiling the bog edges. It's about cutting down water loss from the site."

"Why are you keen to repair this land to its original, wet state?" asks our man.

"Raised bogs are incredibly rare. There are hardly any undamaged examples left."

"Which domesticated animals graze on your sites?"

"Primarily cattle; it's to do with availability," reasons the manager. "On grassland, cattle also tend to give you better floristic diversity than sheep, and they eat virtually anything. We are using them either to maintain sites in an open condition or to control scrub, bramble or that kind of thing. We use sheep on sites occasionally. Also, we have used ponies sometimes."

"What's the advantage of using sheep?"

"Availability primarily," reiterates the manager.

Roamer, who is suddenly an expert, snorts. He doubts whether the correct solution is to use only cattle and sheep.

"We could do their job just as well, perhaps better under some circumstances," he argues. "Our voyage of learning has taught me that much."

"How many of your 40 sites employ ponies?" wonders our man.

"Just this one," answers the manager.

Roamer's ears prick up.

"Thorn," he murmurs, "I see no ponies here, apart from us."

"They might be hiding in the scrub further along, around the corner," adds the manager, seeming to hear and understand Roamer's horse talk, though, of course, no human understands Roamer except, I suppose, our man to some extent.

"Alan will film them later," suggests our man.

In fact, Cameraman and his assistant are overstretched: they dart about, popping up sporadically like pre-programmed, repetitive, cuckoo-like jacks-in-the-box, striving to conjure up better angles for this interview.

"Why are you using ponies on only one site?" asks our man.

"We have long-standing relationships with farmers who graze cattle," notes the manager. "Obviously, if the results are ecologically desirable, you tend to stick with graziers you know, providing you get on well with those people."

"For how long have you grazed ponies on this site?"

"I'm not sure exactly; probably seven or eight years," estimates the manager.

"You've had good results?"

"Yes. Ponies have helped keep scrub at bay."

"Which pony breed are you using?"

"Exmoors," answers the manager emphatically.

"Is David saying that Exmoor ponies are the star conservation grazers here?" challenges Roamer, astonished by this apparent revelation.

"Yes," I reply. "I assumed you realised why they were here."

"We've already discussed this controversy with others en route," he reminds me.

"Yes," I whisper. "Why doesn't the Wildlife Trust employ Fell ponies here?"

"Precisely, Thorn!" replies my pal. "We're the best – in Cumbria at any rate. Mind you, I'm fond of Exmoors. I'm itching to meet up with them right now. We'd have awesome fun."

"Maybe we will meet them," I say.

"Exmoor ponies are not native to this area," points out our man, taking the words out of my mouth. "Fell ponies are. Why did you choose Exmoors?"

"Exmoors chose us," discloses the manager. "We had the grazing. Someone approached us and said, 'I have Exmoor ponies. Would you like me to graze them on your site?' Since we wanted the site grazed and it's a difficult site to graze – it's wet and conditions are poor – we said, 'Yes, please.' We thought no one else would offer."

"Would you consider using Fell ponies, instead?" asks our man.

"Yes, we could use Fell ponies," agrees the manager. "They are the local native breed; they are part of the local landscape, heritage and culture. You shouldn't ignore such things."

"Precisely!" squeals Roamer again but in an even higher-pitched voice.

"Unfortunately," adds the manager, "we aren't aware of anyone who could provide Fell ponies and who actually wants the task."

"Initially, would you prefer people with Fell ponies to contact you?" wonders our man.

"In future, we might want more people to say, 'We have ponies. Would you be interested in using them?' It would be useful to know of Fell pony owners who we could approach in any particular location. It's not that we desire a particular breed: we need one that will cope with the conditions."

"It's quite simple," insists Roamer. "Land managers in this region of England should employ Fell ponies first and foremost. Any clued-in pony breeder understands why."

"Could the Fell Pony Society be more proactive by informing you of ponies that are available?" suggests our man.

"Yes," agrees the manager. "It's about us having better contacts, isn't it? It's about matching the land to the animal."

"You realise what this means?" quizzes Roamer.

"Tell me," I whisper.

"We are too late!" he murmurs. "Exmoor ponies have beaten us to it here and possibly elsewhere, and we may have a terribly hard, if not impossible, task changing human habits: frequently, humans too readily accept previously ordained ways of doing things."

"But we should try," I protest gently. "If our breed guardians are committed, we'll succeed. We could convince land managers to employ Fell ponies, but as we have learned, breeders must be willing to provide those ponies."

"Yes, Thorn, I suppose you are right: I won't give up," he promises. "We must persuade all involved humans to listen to reason. I'm with you."

"How many Exmoor ponies are grazing here?" inquires our man.

"Seven or eight at the moment," indicates the manager.

"Who oversees them?"

"Owner-breeders look after them primarily," explains the manager, "but we provide volunteer help, which means owners don't need to go on site every day, locate every animal and check that it's okay."

"If you require a breeder's ponies for, say, three months, what happens to them afterwards?"

"That's a tricky one," agrees the manager. "Very small sites are problematic for us: they are not sizeable enough to take animals for any length of time. A site like this, on the other hand, allows essentially continuous grazing. The 'off' period isn't long. Once ponies arrive, we assure the breeder that they will have a home for at least a year or two."

I turn to Roamer.

"Would you be happy grazing here?" I ask.

"Well, Thorn, I wouldn't know until I tried it," he says. "It could be fun: wide-open spaces and lots of unusual tasting vegetation. On second thoughts, I might long for mountains."

Our man points to us.

"What's your opinion, having seen them today?" he asks.

"They are pleasing to the eye," admits the manager. "And they look extremely friendly and docile."

We are friendly. Still, we consider ourselves somewhat less than docile; on occasion, you might describe us as headstrong. We especially love kicking down rickety gates, stealing food and playing tricks on each other, as readers of my diary will appreciate. Above all, a hill-born pony never forgets his or her instincts in any free-living situation. However, today both Roamer and I are half-asleep, disarmed by briefly mild weather.

"They could take care of themselves on this reserve," believes our man."

"You see ponies out on the fell, so I'm convinced they would cope with conditions here," agrees the manager. "This reserve is at a comparatively low altitude. Yes, it is extremely wet, but they would have a more productive life here than being stuck high up on a fell above Tebay or somewhere."

"Hang on," I tell Roamer. "Our cousins living high up are exceptional maintainers of upland habitats for other species, and that includes humans who walk across hills."

"True," replies Roamer, "but I guess breeders could spare at least a few of us youngsters reared on fells. We could aid, either temporarily or permanently, a variety of lowland habitats and species, and we would be promoting our grazing abilities."

Upon reflection, Roamer and the manager may be right: the more habitats we graze, the better it would be for wildlife and for us.

"Although they have trodden and grazed wet ground for the last two weeks, they have been extremely happy," points out our man.

"Undeniably, you can see that they are in perfect condition," observes the manager.

"Don't get carried away, Thorn," insists Roamer. "I'm in better condition."

He must be wearing blinkers.

Interview over, our man marches us uphill, back to our sheltered, estuary-side paddock.

"Let's find those Exmoor ponies," proposes the Trust manager.

Our man nods. Promptly, all five humans set off again for the reserve, leaving us behind.

"Nay!" shouts Roamer. "Don't lock us in here! We want to meet them too."

"Save your voice," I sigh, resigned, as a muddy four-wheel drive and Cameraman's car accelerate away. "We aren't invited."

When our man returns to the farm, it's late. In fact, it's too late to strike camp. Instead, he should use this opportunity to recover fully from last night's illness.

"If you like, I can ferry you to a nearby guesthouse in Bowness, where you will get a warm night's sleep," suggests the wife of the senior farmer.

"Thanks, Sarah," replies our man. "That's probably a good idea, but I shouldn't leave the ponies."

Don't panic, I am thinking. We'll be fine. We are going nowhere without you.

"Don't worry about Thorn and Roamer. I'll keep a careful eye on them tonight," she convinces him.

Though our man is reluctant to leave us, his instinct trusts her. It's settled. Furthermore, I am pleased to report that our winter coats are growing ever faster.

Solo:

Last night, I had another astonishing dream. In this dream, my name was Flyer, a packhorse in the service of the Britons. I carried medical and other essential supplies.

One winter afternoon, north of the partially constructed Wall, Roman invaders, infantrymen I think, challenged our packhorse train. One threw a javelin; it injured the train's leader, a woman. I carried the leader a great distance to a healer's house, where she received special treatment. I helped to save her life.

Inexplicably, I woke up at this point. My dream didn't deserve to be over. It had disoriented me. Where was I? Then I remembered.

I couldn't understand why Thorn and Roamer hadn't returned home. I haven't seen them for 27 lonely sunsets.

The final trek and then homeward bound

8ᵗʰ November – Dykesfield and Beaumont Hall

Roamer:

AT breakfast time, we are grazing three fields away from the farmhouse. Pan whistles, wanting us to meet him at the closed gate. He trudges us silently to the barn.

Harry, Alan's brother, inquires whether Pan is feeling better.

"Yes, much better than yesterday, thank you," replies Pan. "I walked briskly to Glasson this morning. There, a local resident, a parent of one of the schoolchildren we met at Bowness, courteously offered me a lift here."

Evidently, sleeping in last night's guesthouse bed has revived Pan somewhat, but that stomach infection might be an ongoing hindrance as he strains to load my pack.

We are just about on schedule. At midday, we set off towards Dykesfield. We are off-road, following the highest point of the marsh dyke, which forces Pan to duck frequently beneath low-lying branches. However, at each fence we must mimic our outward journey: we descend to the road and a cattle grid before skirting around potentially lethal bog.

Two kilometres from Drumburgh Castle, before we reach Boustead Hill, a four-wheel drive travelling in the opposite direction pulls up. Sarah alights. We pause. She chats briefly with Pan, wishes us a safe journey and then drives off. We carry on.

From Dykesfield, Pan ruminates briefly over which route to follow.

"Listen, boys," he says. "Should we head north-east across the Vallum and Wall, or should we take the road to Burgh-by-Sands?"

Why look to us for inspiration? He must decide. We're easy-going: whatever he does, we're with him. John, Dykesfield's farmer, is anticipating our arrival. Even so, perhaps the road's less risky: Pan seems physically drained.

"If I take it easier than I intended today," he reasons finally, "I should recover fully by tomorrow."

With those words, we set off at a lively pace, initially steering south of the Vallum. Into Burgh, the road crosses the Vallum and Wall and then quickly recrosses the Wall. At the village green, we confront the statue of King Edward I of England.

"So he died on Burgh Marsh, one mile north of here, on the 7th of July 1307, it is rumoured from dysentery," Pan tells himself dryly after reading the plaque.

"Is Pan wondering whether a similar fate might befall him?" I ask Thorn half-jokingly.

"Most definitely not!" he declares. "I suspect dysentery was a much more serious affliction. Besides, our man's certainly over the worst."

Leaving the site of Aballava Fort, we head west-south-west with the Vallum, along the road past Wormanby Farm, to Monkhill – monks once lived here – and hence to Kirkandrews, where Wall and Vallum courses converge. Beaumont Hall is in sight by mid-afternoon.

"Hey, Thorn, we've been here before!" I boom, recognising our surroundings.

"Yes," acknowledges Thorn. "Look, there's a huge, circular area of ashes and burnt grass in the paddock centre. Do you recollect? We cantered around a pile of wood?"

From his backpack, Pan pulls out his 'phone.

"Hi, Alan," he begins. "Please, could you get over here now to film? . . . It's imperative we record this part of the expedition. . . . I'm not taking the ponies any further, at least not immediately. . . . I need to recover completely."

"What does he mean, Thorn?" I ask.

"I can't figure out what's going on," Thorn tells me. "Let's listen."

"I've decided to halt the trek for at least a couple of days," Pan informs Alan. "The time's right. . . . We have much of the necessary footage. . . . Yes, we've achieved most of our major objectives. . . . I could return to Shap, rest briefly and continue afterwards. I haven't made a final decision yet. . . . Okay, I'll expect to see you within the next hour or so."

"I'm sorry our man isn't fully fit, but that's no reason to give up," insists Thorn.

"Well, whether Pan chooses to halt temporarily or permanently, we'll have to accept it: he knows what's best," I reply. "Has he misjudged situations previously? No. Those frosts on the peninsula over the last four nights may have sapped his strength."

"But he is an experienced cold weather camper, and the nights will be warmer inland," protests Thorn. "And he slept indoors last night. No, he looks dehydrated. I sense it's the after-effect of his stomach problem."

"Perhaps he won't risk injuring us," I say. "Consider our situation. Ground conditions are diabolical: some of the terrain may be too dangerous for us."

Pan makes another 'phone call.

"Hello, Ernie. . . . Is there any chance you might drive the horse trailer here to pick up the ponies tomorrow? . . . I'm bringing them back to Stoney Gill, at least for the time being. . . . Yes, they have performed marvellously. . . . Annoyingly, I've contracted a debilitating gut infection, which I'm unable to shake off easily."

"I told you so," quips Thorn.

Pan is still talking: "You can get here tonight? . . . Yes, that would be admirable. I'll prepare the ponies, ready for your arrival. . . . Perfect! . . . See you in a couple of hours."

"By all accounts, it seems that Ernie is transporting us home from Beaumont Hall right away," I tell Thorn.

"Hai-ai-ai-ai-ai!" moans Thorn, sulking even more at the prospect of leaving the Wall. "I don't want to leave: we're in the middle of a great adventure. Besides, we thrive in this weather. And we're superbly fit, able to tackle anything."

"Never mind," I retort. "Don't forget: he did promise to consider ferrying us back when he has recovered fully. By then, he will have acquired his midwinter sleeping bag. Anyway, I could do with a rest: I've been working hard. We'll have fun back at Shap, regardless; you could break down a gate whenever you become bored."

"Well," he concedes, "I suppose going home offers us the prospect of seeing Solo."

Pan removes our loads and begins to prepare our feed. I can tell by how deliberately and mechanically he is moving that he's not his usual, energetic self.

An unknown local resident, one of Colin's committee friends, arrives from his village home as we are chomping away. He has the hall's keys.

"Welcome. I'm Tony," announces the man warmly. "Colin has asked me to look after you. He's on holiday."

I'm having a hard time hearing the whole conversation, thanks to Thorn's munching noises; he has an enormous appetite and is a thunderously noisy eater.

Pan explains that he has opted to move us to Shap tonight. Tony is surprised and genuinely sad.

"That's a shame," he says. "We were looking forward to having Thorn and Roamer stay here again."

"We'll probably be back," suggests Pan. "Yes, one day we'll almost definitely be back."

Pan is grateful for Tony's assistance. Together, they busily pack up supplies that were stored inside the hall for this return leg.

"What about your electric fence?" inquires Tony.

"Would you please hang onto it?" asks Pan. "I anticipate needing containment elsewhere if we continue. I've arranged for a postal service to return it to base upon our official completion of the expedition."

"No nuisance at all," he says, smiling.

When the camera operator arrives, earlier than Pan expected, we are still eating.

"This is the right decision," remarks Alan as he performs his familiar, meticulous, setting-up ritual. "It has been a tough, demanding month. You could return if returning becomes necessary. Are you ready for me to shoot?"

Alan peers into the camera's viewfinder, customary fierce concentration etched across his forehead.

Pan talks to the camera, describing the last couple of days, justifying his decision to viewers – if, indeed, there ever will be viewers. He's upbeat, emphasising how Thorn and I have helped him.

"Quite right," declares Thorn, who has licked his nosebag dry. "We are his greatest allies. He couldn't have achieved anything significant without us."

"Alan, there's one immediate problem," worries Pan.

"What's that?" asks Alan.

"We are supposed to be filming the veterinary from Carlisle tomorrow: he's an expert on Foal Immunodeficiency Syndrome."

"Expert on what?" blurts out Thorn. "Here's a challenge, Roamer. Can you repeat what our man just said?"

"No," I confess, "but Pan used the same phrase in his interview with the scientist, Stuart. No doubt, the vet' will enlighten us further."

"I'll ring him," continues Pan, "requesting he meets us tomorrow at Stoney Gill on the edge of Birk Beck Common. He could assess the ponies' conditions there."

Birk Beck is the stream where birch trees grow, not far from where I first met Thorn and Solo.

"That's not a bad plan," agrees Alan, who has just completed filming us without our saddles.

Perhaps an hour later, he and Pan have finished packing and are sipping Alan's flask tea, when a shiny, pristine horsebox, pulled by a shiny, pristine four-wheel drive, rumbles into the hall's grounds.

"Hi," hails Ernie, alighting. "How are the ponies? As I hadn't heard from you for well over a week, I was wondering how you were progressing."

Barbara, who is Ernie's daughter, and John, Barbara's husband, begin to lead Thorn and me into the trailer.

"The ponies are in magnificent condition," confirms Pan. "They could carry on for ever. So could I, had I not succumbed to some sort of bug. Although I'm not feeling 100 per cent fit, I'm much better than I was yesterday."

Ernie consoles him: "You've done well to get this far, especially at this time of year. I wasn't convinced you would succeed after that first day."

"I never doubted Thorn or Roamer," explains Pan, "but having them uninjured and in such great shape at this stage is a bonus."

Thorn:

At Beaumont Hall, a watery sun is setting. Our man has untacked us, but we still wear head collars. Two men and a woman, all of whom I recognise, have just alighted from a vehicle. The driver and his wife intend to lead Roamer and me, side by side, into the same trailer that carried us to Tyneside to embark upon our epic journey a month ago.

"Na-ah!" I cry. "What's going on? I'm not entering their box on wheels: I'm in no mood. Let me loose in a field. They'll not force me up that ramp."

"Thorn, if you're not budging, neither am I," asserts Roamer uncharacteristically. "I'm going nowhere without Pan."

"You couldn't lend a hand to lead Thorn in quietly?" requests the thwarted driver. "He's being stubborn."

"Hold on," responds our man, who is chatting with the driver's father-in-law less than half a dozen human strides away.

In a flash, he is at my side, whispering in my ear, urging me: "Come on, boy. It's easy."

I'll give our man no hassle. He leads me up the ramp into the trailer's left-hand side. Now he has trapped himself. Oh, no he hasn't. He slips through a tight gap in my compartment's metal meshwork and then exits through the trailer's front door. He has tricked me.

"Na-ah-na-ah!" I whinny, meaning, "Don't leave me here!"

"Thorn, everything's all right," declares our man's soothing voice from behind me seconds later. "I'm coming with you."

The woman leads Roamer easily into the trailer: where I go, Roamer goes, always, and vice versa. Now he's beside me, I'm less apprehensive.

The driver carefully secures us, via our head collars, to a safety rail; we can't walk about.

"I'm off home," announces Cameraman. "See you tomorrow morning, nine o'clock."

Moments later, the low drone of his car engine is rapidly fading away.

We've travelled in this metal box on wheels before, so why am I so uneasy? Is it because the ground trembles when the trailer moves? More likely, I'm fearful of what lies ahead.

"Hai-ai-ai-ai!" I whinny to Roamer, perplexed and slightly unnerved by the suddenness of our departure. "Are we going home right now?"

"I think so," he calls back in a less than confident tone.

"I'm uncertain whether they'll be all right," remarks our man, troubled by how we might react to the journey.

Hearing our man's voice, I confess, reassures me; I become less agitated.

"We'll stop for a break on the motorway, to make sure the ponies are happy," promises the driver's father-in-law.

Our trailer's back door closes, the driver fires up its pulling motor, and we bounce gently out of the hall grounds.

Nearly three hours and a stressful, bumpy ride later, on the darkest night, we turn onto Stoney Gill's farm track near Shap. Familiar, safe fields, where we languished innocently before our Wall adventure began, greet us, drawing us in with welcoming arms.

"Hey, we're home!" yells Roamer, unable to disguise his delight.

"Somehow, I didn't expect to be here tonight," I reply, bewildered. "I would prefer to be grazing by the Wall at this instant."

Roamer consoles me: "Don't worry. We may soon return to the

Way."

"I was having an unparalleled time," I persist, "but I'm thankful that we are home unscathed."

"Boys, forgive me, but you'll have to stay indoors all night," declares our man quietly. "You are quite hot: travelling in the horse trailer has made you sweat. A sudden temperature difference could make you ill."

"I hate being inside," seethes Roamer. "I suppose it's for our own good," he adds after deliberating. "Bill and Pan are trying to protect us."

From under a starless sky, our man leads me into a dry, clean, straw-lined stable. Roamer is next door. Seconds later, I become nervous. Where is our man? I can't see him, but then I realise he is in the yard, talking to my owner.

"We have two remaining interviews to record," confides our man. "Tomorrow, the veterinary will be here to inspect the ponies. Could Alan film him outside, on the hill?"

"Aye, lad," replies Bill. "Where are you staying tonight?"

"I've booked a room at the public house in Shap," answers our man. "May I leave the saddles and packs here, under your lean-to, for a day or two?"

"Aye, okay. They'll be safe, lad. Come into the house for something to eat."

Prior to leaving Stoney Gill later this evening, our man reappears briefly at my stable door. Presumably, he wishes to ensure that I have settled down. Seconds after he departs, only Roamer, shuffling about in the adjoining stable, disturbs the farmyard's silence.

My life has changed again, but I am too tired to think clearly. My body, sore from the trailer's buffeting, aches.

"Good night, Roamer," I whisper. "See you tomorrow, I hope."

I nibble nervously on hay before gradually drifting into a standing, erratic half-sleep.

Veterinary check-up: a long rest

9th November – Stoney Gill, Shap

Roamer:

WE are at Thorn's place. When we tiptoed into Stoney Gill's yard last evening, I yearned for a peaceful rest: the motorway trip certainly shook me up.

Last night, Thorn and I slept comfortably, if intermittently, in Bill's stable. Bill and Ernie reckoned our disconcerting road journey had made us hot and nervous. I would rather have been outside, though: as you are aware, I can't abide anybody locking me up. Between snatches of sleep, I could hear Thorn moving about restlessly in his stable too.

Yesterday evening was unnerving for another reason: until the day before, nothing had separated Pan from us overnight; I always knew exactly where he was. Now I'm wondering what's next on his agenda for us. Having no control over my destiny is upsetting, to say the least.

Probably hours have elapsed since daybreak. At last, Pan turns up at my stable door. He's apologetic. I smile. I'm pleased to see him. He halters me, leads me into the yard and ties my lead rope to a fence. Purposefully, he returns to the stables for Thorn. Minutes later, Pan leads us out of the yard onto the hillside. Cool air, a wide, grey sky and a rolling common beckon. I feel exhilarated to be home. Nonetheless, already I'm impatient to return to the Wall.

In the distance, on a hilly horizon, Bill's Fell herd grazes contentedly, oblivious to our presence. Thorn and I are inclined to join our cousins right now, but Bill and Pan think differently.

Hey, wait! Alan has arrived and, as usual, is setting up his camera. Well, we know what this means.

A stranger, Paul, an equine veterinary, chugs up in his four-wheel drive. Pan welcomes him. He and Pan are soon in earnest discussion.

"I've come here to look at your ponies," declares Paul, "to see what state they're in at the end of their walk."

"Hear that, Roamer?" remarks Thorn, his ears pricked up. "Pan officially has terminated our load-carrying employment, at least for the present."

"Never mind," I answer. "But why would the vet' want to examine us? There's nothing wrong with us, is there? I could complete the return journey right now, no bother. I'm undoubtedly one of the fittest and healthiest ponies alive."

"I expect it's simply a common-sense precaution," suggests Thorn. "And it shows that some humans care about us."

"They have clocked up about 120 miles each along the Military Way," estimates Pan. "Would you give Roamer the once-over?"

The vet' takes control of my lead rope. He eyes Thorn, who is attempting to hide behind Pan. Now he studies me. He runs his hands over my body.

Ah-ha, that's relaxing, but I still don't understand.

"Why are you examining us?" I murmur.

Nobody's paying attention.

"Their condition is good," says Paul. "Unquestionably, they're strong enough. I haven't seen them before, but they don't appear to have lost weight over the walk."

Our weights are perfect, I'd say. High-fibre pellets kept us going. Anyhow, if opportunity arose, we raided the larder for extra helpings, as you, the reader, will testify!

"Their coats are in good condition," continues Paul. "I have examined them all over. They have no sign of wear, of rubs, from the tack. Obviously, the tack was an issue: you didn't know whether it would fit or not. There's no sign of pressure at all. They are bright and alert, happy and comfortable."

I nod three times in agreement: we are alert. Look out! Bill's hill ponies are beginning to amble casually towards us from their common. This might prove exciting.

"What about their feet, Paul?" inquires Pan. "They have packed without shoes for the entire expedition? A farrier and, later on, a Fell pony breeder trimmed their feet for me."

"Well, as I say, they are in good condition," certifies Paul. "I look at whether their hooves are split, cracked or chipped, or even worn away too much."

"We filed a couple of little chips smooth during the trip," says Pan.

"Chipping is a totally natural process," replies Paul. "That's what they'll do on the fell."

"Would you like to examine Thorn more closely?" asks Pan as he swaps lead ropes with Paul. "I'll hold onto Roamer."

"So it's my turn for a check-over," mumbles Thorn. "He'll discover nothing wrong with me."

"My biggest concern," reveals Paul, picking up Thorn's left foreleg, "is whether their feet have become sore. The way you detect soreness is to determine whether there is a pulse there or not. And there isn't with that foot."

Once upon a time, Thorn disapproved of all humans who attempted to pick up his feet, even Pan. Nowadays he's unbothered.

"Roamer was following, so he had a slightly harder job," argues Pan. "Despite his marginally lesser stride length, he had to keep up with Thorn."

Thorn will charge happily along roads, to my occasional annoyance, as you know.

"However," continues Pan, "Roamer avoided roads whenever possible, which very occasionally created a slight difficulty for Thorn."

I suppose he's right: wherever I can nip onto a grass verge, I will.

"At the beginning," recounts Pan, "I examined Roamer's feet. They were perfect. Though he'll walk on roads untroubled, Roamer merely prefers walking on grass, given the choice."

Paul is adamant: "There will not be anything wrong with his feet.

334

It's simply that his feet might have a different make-up, maybe slightly thinner soles; this means he doesn't like stones. Some ponies will walk happily barefoot on stones, and some won't."

"So that's why you led us a dance on the verges," chortles Thorn. "You insist on taking care of your feet, don't you?"

I do. Roads don't bother me, though: I simply love the feel of soft, springy grass. Besides, I prefer walking alongside my pal.

"You should look after your feet too, Thorn," I tell him.

"You're lucky," ripostes Thorn. "Don't forget. I can't walk on grass verges even if I want to: our man controls my lead rein."

"The expedition has done them no harm at all," emphasises Paul. "And, unmistakably, they have developed. They were virtually unhandled before you started, so they have 'come on' in many ways."

He's observant. We are disaster-proof.

Pan confesses, "I was unable to pick Thorn's hooves up before we left Shap. Now, because I've needed to clean his feet each morning, he doesn't mind."

"He's ready to do a job now," observes Paul.

"What's he saying, Roamer?" mouths Thorn to me. "What job? What does he imagine we've been doing?"

"These days, Thorn is fantastic," continues Pan. "He'll do anything I ask of him. The fact that he is standing perfectly still amazes me. And you couldn't have touched his ears before."

"I'm not keen on anybody handling my ears even now," Thorn reminds me, "unless, maybe, it's our man. Hey, they're at it again. Leave my ears alone!"

"Both ponies are in excellent condition," concludes Paul. "Fell ponies are the ideal breed for the job you took on. They are powerful enough and hardy enough for it. You wouldn't need to worry about them at night in bad weather. Evolution has designed their legs, back and feet to take it. And, living in this area, it would be the breed to choose."

We experienced bad weather much of the time recently; it didn't hurt us a bit.

"Right," says Pan. "I'm going to settle Thorn and Roamer

elsewhere before we talk to Paul about his experiences with Fell ponies."

"Alan, is the wind causing a sound problem," inquires Paul?

"No, it's manageable," replies Alan as calmly as ever. "I can be quite a few feet away. I can tell you have given interviews before. There's nothing worse than someone pushing a camera into your face, is there? I have often said I would rather be behind the camera than in front of it. Some people handle it and are comfortable; other people aren't. Let's hope it doesn't rain."

"I don't believe it will, although I suppose it rains most days here," surmises Paul.

"Yes, it probably does," agrees Alan. "Hang on. I want to record some footage of Bill's ponies."

Alan turns his tripod around. Six or seven mares trot over the rise towards us. Bill is hurrying them on with his quad bike, which I recognise: he used it to train us.

Using his customary trekking knot, Pan attaches our lead ropes to a wooden rail away from the vet'. Thorn and I have no choice: we must listen further to this human conversation.

"Right!" calls Alan as he continues filming. "Carry on when you are ready, Paul."

Thorn:

We are safely home after our exciting journey through an ancient, virtually lost world.

Today, we meet the vet' for a check-up, to see whether anything is wrong. He announces a clean bill of health. Our man says we are incredibly fit, healthy ponies.

"How long have you been a practising veterinary," inquires our man.

"Twenty-seven years," reveals the vet'.

"That's a lot of experience," concludes our man. "I guess you see Fell ponies mainly if they have ailments?"

"Yes. For any animal, around foaling time is the most stressful time: it's then when things are likely to go wrong."

"Later, as foals are growing up, will they normally require attention?" asks our man.

"No, especially if they are kept in their natural environment."

"A vet' has never visited me before," confides Roamer.

"I thought you were snoozing, as usual," I tease. "Since you mention it, I haven't encountered one either."

"Some Fell ponies occasionally suffer from laminitis," continues our man. "Is this to do with them not being in their natural environment?"

"Yes, almost without exception," agrees the vet'. "Laminitis is a disease of over-indulgence. In their natural environment, including this one, grazing is extensive, varied and poor value except during summer: ponies might walk 5, 6 or even 10 miles a day, so they exercise. In a small, enclosed field, there's little opportunity to exercise. They have everything in front of them: probably improved grazing; probably fertilised as well. They have what you don't want them to have, whereas ponies in their natural environment have everything you do want them to have."

"I wouldn't tolerate always living in a minute field," pouts Roamer. "I'd be restless."

"We'd find a way to escape," I answer.

"Over your 27 years as a vet', has the number of extensively grazing Fell ponies diminished considerably?" wonders our man.

"Yes," agrees the vet'. "Ponies in ideal situations are becoming scarcer. More and more are being kept in farm fields."

"Another consideration is Foal Immunodeficiency Syndrome. What is this exactly?"

"Ah! I realise what Pan's on about," interrupts Roamer. "Don't you remember? We overheard a telephone conversation, umpteen days ago, between Pan and Stuart."

"Oh yes," I answer, recollecting vaguely. "I still can't pronounce that crazy word, though. You know: im-imm – I give up!"

"Some Fell pony foals couldn't survive the first four months of life," explains the vet'. "No one could establish what was causing their deaths."

"There you are!" shouts Roamer. "I thought so."

By this stage, several Greenholme ponies, bred by my owner, are effectively on top of us.

"Perhaps you should record the herd at close range," proposes the vet'.

"Good idea," agrees our man. "Alan, can you manage to shoot those ponies in the background as they trot by?"

Although the mares are strangers to Roamer and me, I would enjoy meeting them, and I'll wager Roamer would love an opportunity to tell them about our deeds. Alas, we can't join them.

"Are you able to film Bill with his quad bike, too?" urges our man.

Within a minute, Cameraman has captured slickly the trot past.

"Shall we carry on?" he suggests.

"You will always sustain losses on the fell," advises the vet'. "Foals being born up there possibly could not survive the birth process for a variety of reasons; that is quite natural; that will happen with deer; it will happen with other wild animals. But breeders knew some ponies were born alive yet didn't live to weaning."

"Paul, were you involved in this from the beginning?" asks our man.

"It was the late 1980s. The trouble was that the ponies looked exactly like young, sick animals, similar to sick calves or lambs. Your first thought wasn't, 'Oh, I've found something new here.' It was, 'Why aren't my treatments working?' It was a frustrating time for veterinaries and breeders."

I guarantee those poor ponies were not high-spirited either.

"It wasn't until the early 1990s that we put the clues together," explains the vet'. "We carried out post-mortems. It was a real breakthrough. We realised it was a new disease. Affected ponies had anaemia: their red blood cells became fewer with time, which affected massively their health. A second blow was that their immune systems did not function: they couldn't mount a response to the normal challenges that were there. Consequently, they died."

"I'm upset," sobs Roamer quietly. "Our baby cousins were dying, as Stuart said, and humans couldn't help them."

"I'm angry," I retort. "I wonder whether ignorant breeding may have caused this problem – or aggravated it, at least."

"But didn't Stuart say it was a spontaneous genetic change, a genetic accident?" bursts out Roamer, still whimpering.

"Oh, yes," I reply.

"What happened next?" asks our man.

"Universities became interested. Research first focused on what was actually happening to the ponies, to determine whether this was a treatable disease or whether it was incurable. Everybody had her or his own ideas. Sometimes, the disease behaved as if it was a quite simple genetic problem. At other times it appeared there was something else involved."

"I recall," whispers Roamer. "Stuart's team realised it was an inherited disease; they developed a test to identify ponies who had the faulty gene."

"That's . . . that's right, Roamer," I utter in disbelief, thoroughly impressed by his sharp memory.

"So Paul must have toiled alongside Stuart to prevent Fell foals from dying," adds Roamer, cheerier now that he fully appreciates what the vet' is saying.

"We now know that a genetic defect is involved," continues the vet'. "Any genetic defect is a mutation. At some point, there was a mutation in one animal. For that mutation to have had a serious impact on the breed, it had to be multiplied up through various breedings until it reached the level it's at today."

"So there had to be inbreeding?" asks our man.

"Yes. At some point, related animals had to breed."

"Thorn, perhaps you are partly right," concedes Roamer. "Perhaps we might have avoided such awful consequences of the spontaneous change if humans had not allowed close relatives to interbreed."

"Well, maybe," I reply, having had second thoughts. "Should we speculate, though? After all, we're not veterinaries or veterinary scientists."

"If this is a recessive gene," presumes our man, "any foal must receive a double dose of the gene, one from his sire and the other from his dam, in order to be affected by the full-blown disease?"

"Yes," confirms the vet'. "If the foal has a solitary defective gene, it is a carrier but appears totally normal. Carriers don't have any health defects, either."

"I knew this," declares Roamer enthusiastically. "I was listening to Stuart."

"So carrier ponies should be used for all tasks, from riding to conservation?" ventures our man.

"That's right," answers the vet'.

"And they are hardy hillside grazers?"

"Just as hardy as non-carriers, yes," says the vet'.

"Why is this syndrome found in several pony breeds?" asks our man.

"I think I have figured out why," remarks Roamer.

"That's enough, show-off!" I snap gently. "Be quiet, please."

Now and then, Roamer can be intolerably clever.

"There has been continual crossbreeding of other pony groups with Fells," explains the vet'. "However, both the stallion and the mare would have to be carriers to produce the syndrome. Even then, there would be only a one in four probability you would produce a syndrome pony."

It's as well, it seems to me, that a mathematical rule of genetics means there's only a 25 per cent chance of two carrier parents giving the disease to their foal. If the disease had affected even more ponies, it might have signalled the end of our race; Roamer and I might never have existed. Even so, what do I know about genetics or statistics?

"In the test to identify whether a pony is clear or is carrying the bad gene, you pluck hairs from its mane or tail," states our man. "How many hairs are pulled?"

"Thirty would do," replies the vet'.

Our man asks him whether it would be best if all breeders knew which breeding ponies were carriers.

"There is a welfare issue," the vet' warns. "If both parents are carriers, their foal might be affected. In this case, we test it early on in its life, before it shows signs of ill health; before there's any possibility of suffering."

"Should all breeding stallions be tested?" suggests our man.

"Stuart answered that question," interjects Roamer.

"If you have clear – disease-free – mares, it doesn't matter what the stallion is," the vet' points out. "If you've got a clear stallion, it doesn't matter what the mares are. The difference between mares and stallions is that each stallion can have a far greater impact on the breed. This is most likely how the syndrome got such a grip on the breed in the first place. Presumably, an exceptionally well-liked stallion was a carrier. He quickly would have influenced the genetic make-up of the breed, especially at times when stallion numbers were down."

An awful certainty dawns on Roamer: "I've just realised something, Thorn."

"What's that?" I ask.

"This syndrome won't affect us anyway, and we can't affect it: we are geldings."

"Don't rub it in, Roamer," I respond wistfully. "I might have enjoyed having a family – a filly foal or two."

"Forget it, Thorn. We have equally important jobs – saving the breed. We couldn't accomplish that or much else by choosing to stay at home to look after families."

"True," I reply. "Even so –"

"In Holland, they keep a computerised record of all carriers," notes our man. "Would such a system benefit England's Fell Pony Society?"

"The more information you have, the better," believes the vet', "but everybody within a breed society has to be happy with it."

"I foresee another dilemma," our leader continues. "Ponies with special environmentally determined grazing characteristics will cease to exist if we lose all extensively grazing herds. Will such a scenario affect the breed's ability to graze diverse habitats?"

"It would have health implications," suggests the vet'. "Gradually removing the breed from its natural environment will produce a distinctive, changed animal. Perhaps they don't achieve their genetic size on the fell: conditions are harsher there. If you provide every need – a fully balanced, totally ad-lib, sanitised diet – you are going to produce a much bigger animal."

"Smaller ponies tend to be hardier. They are able to cope better in winter," responds our man. "They easily spot suitable natural shelter and can recognise and select a wider variety of diets. Thorn and Roamer have eaten rushes. During the last month, they've browsed maple, sycamore and ash leaves. Remarkably, I've witnessed them devouring seaweed, copious amounts of it; they obviously enjoyed it."

Our man is right. We learned from our mothers which wild foods to eat on the fell. Without their teachings, we would be incapable of surviving on hillsides, moorland, scrubland or any natural or semi-natural vegetation.

"The minerals ponies digest on the hill are completely different from what they receive in enclosed grazing situations," verifies the vet'.

"Is there any action the Fell Pony Society could undertake to prevent loss of genetic grazing characteristics?" asks our man.

"Their approach was absolutely right," insists the vet'. "They didn't say, 'We're going to devise a breeding plan; we're going to tell you which stallion you can use.' Breeders are individuals. They are producing the animal they want to produce. I think introducing an element of control could be extremely dangerous. Who will decide the rules and monitor any effects?"

"On average, is the breed becoming taller?" asks our man.

"The recent stallion show hasn't been anywhere near the cut-off point of 14 hands. A quite common height is 13¼ or 13½ hands."

"If you breed to 'type', aren't you effectively removing genes from a population?" worries our leader.

"Maybe you're not removing genes but only endeavouring to manipulate them to suit your purpose."

Our man mentions the Greenholme herd, part of which is still grazing close by: "From April to October each year, many of these ponies cannot set foot on Birk Beck Common, which, by the way, may become an addition in the not too distant future to the Lake District National Park. Government grazing scheme regulation excludes them from grazing extensively on the hill during the summer; they must stay on inbye, which eventually might affect their hefting ability and hardiness. Shouldn't we protect special characteristics like hardiness, which existed in abundance over 2000 years ago?"

"Yes," agrees the vet'. "You can't take Fells, for six months of the year, from the environment they normally live in."

"Why aren't some ponies allowed to graze on the open fell during summertime," queries Roamer. "I've forgotten."

"It's to do with overgrazing of the land, which damages habitats," I remind him. "Sheep and fewer cattle share the commons with our breed. Our man says some scientists may judge there's not enough 'desirable vegetation' for all grazing and foraging mammals, including ponies, on any particular common throughout the year. As a result, some wild plants and, therefore, some wild animal species may face extinction on that common."

"Well, I maintain that we ponies should have first say!" declares Roamer defiantly. "There are many times more sheep than ponies."

Who can argue with him?

"Protecting and enhancing remaining semi-wild, extensively grazing herds is an urgent challenge," stresses our man.

"How frequently have we heard this same plea recently?" remarks Roamer.

"They are the breed's backbone," agrees the vet'. "That backbone must be preserved if the breed is to continue as it is."

"Is there any simple solution?" wonders our man.

"No," admits the vet'. "All pressure on Cumbrian fells is to depopulate, to reduce the number of grazing animals or to change the type of grazing. While such pressure remains, ponies grazing that land will be under threat."

"The European Parliament last year recommended that we classify all 'at risk' native breeds as biodiversity," notes our man.

"This includes the Fell pony. Providing we can persuade all Government and other stakeholders to recognise formally and officially that this breed is biodiversity, farmers breeding even one or two extensively grazing ponies might be entitled to financial assistance. Is this a way forward?"

"Definitely," agrees the vet'. "It would give backing to what everybody is trying to do."

"It will give the Fell pony a chance?" suggests our man.

"Yes, it will."

"That's what's required," I tell Roamer.

"What?" he answers drowsily. "I'm falling asleep, I'm so relaxed."

"We need somebody within Government to save us."

"Well, Thorn," he murmurs, eyes half shut, "that somebody had better kick-start a rescue plan urgently: we're running out of time."

The veterinary heads towards my owner's farmhouse for a welcome, well-earned cup of tea as Cameraman packs up his filming equipment. Meanwhile, before stowing even more of his gear under Stoney Gill's lean-to, our man leads us to an inbye field.

"Boys, do you fancy some nutritious grazing right now?" he asks, opening the inbye gate wide and then unbuckling our head collars.

Roamer and I look at him silently, longingly.

"There's no carrying today," he confirms. "You two deserve a long break. I'm away with Alan tomorrow to film Carville children at their school. I'll see you both soon, I promise. Off you go."

"Bet you wish you were returning with him to Newcastle?" remarks Roamer as we stand by the now closed gate, watching our man unload equipment from his car.

"Yes," I admit, a melancholy expression etched across my face.

"Never mind," says Roamer. "Cheer up. We've exploring of our own to contemplate, here at the farm."

As we are about to examine our new surroundings, Bill's wife hails our man from Stoney Gill's back door.

"You've let your ponies into the wrong field!" she shouts. "They should be on the bottom inbye; that was Bill's instruction."

"Right, Isobel: I'll sort it out," our man calls back.

He scampers towards us to retrieve a tricky situation.

"Take it easy, boys; I'm moving you to even better, wider grazing. You'll approve."

He re-collars us easily: we'll go willingly anywhere with him.

Laid out before us are unfenced, gently rolling fields. At the bottom of a steep gully, a clump of oak trees beckons beside a babbling, bubbling stream. Higher up, towards the distant motorway, more uncluttered, tranquil land entices us to roam.

"Let's see what mischief we can get up to," I suggest.

Roamer nods rapidly thrice in approval. Before our man has closed and secured the gate, we have cantered, side by side, through two grassy fields, tails swishing, heads swaying, and are nibbling the final, fresh growth of autumn.

Revisiting

10th November – Stoney Gill, Carville School and Newcastle

Roamer:

WE have returned from our mammoth walk along Hadrian's Wall. Yesterday, after Pan left, we munched and then slept, munched again and then slept again. This morning, I am light-hearted: we came home. I am happy in this hideaway by a stream in a quiet valley, away from noisy traffic. Thorn is alongside me. We're inseparable.

It's still early, about the time Pan usually commences preparing us for trekking. I wait for his arrival, a habit I find hard to relinquish.

"I'd give anything to revisit the Wall," admits Thorn. "It was fun."

"Where is Pan?" I whinny. "Where is he? How is he?"

"I expect he and Cameraman have left Shap already to film children at Carville Primary School," Thorn reminds me. "At least, that's what they planned yesterday, and they consistently try to follow plans."

On a journey of nostalgia, I recollect our second expedition day: "Do you remember, Thorn? Alan was unable to film either the children or us at Segedunum Fort."

"That didn't bother me," he replies. "Museum staff looked after us both extremely well."

"Yes, they did" I admit. "And I loved meeting every one of those friendly children. You enjoyed their company too, didn't you, once you got used to them?"

"Our man also intends to interview the English Heritage archaeologist in Newcastle," adds Thorn, ignoring my question.

"Oh, yes," I reply. "His name's Mike. Pan mentioned him weeks ago."

"Our man said they would be filming at Castle Keep," remarks Thorn. "He also mentioned that the Keep was originally the site of the Roman fort Pons Aelius, which, I have managed to remember, means 'Hadrian's Bridge'. Is Castle Keep close to Saint Nicholas Cathedral?"

"I believe so. I think we were there 29 days ago, though I'm uncertain about the date," I tell him. "That was a saga ago, Thorn, and what a tiring journey it was through Newcastle. We weren't used to carrying, amongst other things, a tent, clothes, scientific equipment and food for Pan."

Thorn also misses Pan: I can tell.

"Is our man coming home soon?" he asks tersely.

"Didn't he tell Bill he would be away for two days, filming by the Wall?" I reply.

"Oh, of course he did. He's filming without us again tomorrow."

Thorn is distressed. I think he's slightly hurt because Pan hasn't taken us with him."

"Don't be dismayed," I reassure him. "Pan hasn't abandoned us. Possibly, he will arrange to take us back to the Wall. He and Alan are travelling along the Wall quickly in Alan's car tomorrow, en route filming scenery they had insufficient time to shoot earlier."

"As long as our man returns here, that's all right," he sighs. "Where are they filming?"

"First of all, they are off to Segedunum," I tell him. "They have sorted out their misunderstanding with museum officials."

"Where else exactly are they visiting?"

"Let me think," I reply. "They mentioned a few places: High Teppermoor; Greencarts; the Chollerford River; Stanley Plantation; and the Military Way near Errington Arms."

"Do you recall the public house?" asks Thorn, smiling."

"Wasn't that our first breakout?" I reply, smiling back at him.

We spend the rest of the day chatting about our Wall adventure.

Thorn:

"I was delighted because I was at the front, leading the way during our hike," I confess as Roamer and I relax and adjust to normality at Stoney Gill.

"Do you realise why you were chosen as the lead pony?" challenges Roamer.

"Yes. Presumably, I am the better leader," I answer triumphantly.

"You lead well, but I could lead too," asserts Roamer. "The reason was simple: Pan trusted me not to rush through gateways behind you. Rushing could have damaged me, the Military saddle and the pack."

"And I could follow," I insist.

"You probably could," he admits, though not wholeheartedly. "But Pan said I calculated sizes better at the beginning of the trek. I trained using the British saddle and the wider pack: I could estimate pack widths exactly, with millimetre accuracy."

"Don't forget," I declare, refusing to let Roamer outdo me. "You have a shorter stride length than me, so our man and I must ensure you don't overstretch. Accordingly, I may need to slow down. And I must remember not to accelerate from rest too rapidly, in case you are browsing. It takes skill to notice what's happening behind."

"That's true," admits Roamer. "Thank you for being considerate. Undeniably you carry out Pan's instructions scrupulously, but I am forced to work harder than you to maintain the team pace: you are over two centimetres taller."

"Our man sometimes gives you a slightly larger helping of high-fibre pellets than me," I point out. "So don't complain."

"I didn't realise," confesses Roamer, apologetically. "Remember, though," he adds smartly, "I carry almost three-fifths of the total load, up to 61 kilograms, which includes my saddle and our food supplies. That's about 134 pounds. You usually carry less than 45 kilograms, about 99 pounds. Even my saddle is over half a kilogram heavier than yours."

"How did you retain those numbers in your brain?" I ask, stunned once again by his amazing memory.

"I overheard Pan doing his calculations recently," reveals

Roamer. "I don't know how I managed to remember them."

"Well," I counter, though I'm not ignoring his statistics, "I have to concentrate on leading, on not making mistakes. Besides, only my spine slopes gently at the withers. Consequently, I alone can wear the Roman saddle without it rubbing against my skin. Remember, it's an attempted replica of a saddle supposedly made to fit only one particular Roman pack pony, or maybe even a mule; the pommel is set at a wide angle."

"You do handle that Roman saddle well," concedes my friend. "I'd like to try it on someday, though I won't deny that my British saddle is comfortable once you get used to it."

"And I'd like to wear your saddle," I reply. "You can carry heavier items neatly in plastic boxes. Our man must pack my Roman saddlebags in the Roman style, using canvas containers. By the way, apart from his bulky tent, high on my back, I also carry his computer. That's quite a responsibility! Our man doesn't carry much in his backpack, does he?"

"He has weighed it," recalls Roamer. "It's usually about 5 kilograms; that's 11 pounds."

"Humans are physically weak: you cannot compare them with us," I observe.

"True, though carrying a light load means Pan can assist us immediately should we get into difficulty," concedes Roamer.

At this moment, I realise we are the ultimate equine team, the perfect combination, me leading and Roamer following. Each relies upon the other equally. We are more harmonious than a nightingale's midsummer song, as smooth and unruffled in our action as silky eucalyptus honey dripping from our man's breakfast spoon.

Inevitably, particularly during those early days, there were setbacks during our expedition. Nonetheless, you won't meet a superior partnership. Our system operates flawlessly almost every time. Between us is a unique bond; a bond unlike any shared normally by living Fell ponies. Our friendship will survive time and space wherever we are, whether we remain together, on the same hill, or not.

Reunion before the final parting

13th November – Stoney Gill

Roamer:

THORN is grazing contentedly and I am daydreaming this mild, late-autumn afternoon. Suddenly, two human voices shatter a silence otherwise punctuated only by occasional breeze-carried gurgles of a distant brook and the grinding of teeth. One voice is recognisable. It's Pan!

Where is he? I can't see him. I search out his voice, whereupon I realise why I couldn't spot him immediately. He's motionless, silent, concentrating, sitting at the wheel of a stationary vehicle. The driver's door is open. Words emanate from his laptop computer.

Three days have come and gone since we last saw him. I have been anxious – and I still dream of the Wall. Now he's here again, listening intently to his recorded conversation with another man.

"Tell me, Mike. Where are we exactly?" asks Pan.

"We are in the centre of Newcastle," begins the archaeologist, "right beside Castle Keep, Newcastle's mediaeval centre, and also on the site of a Roman fort. We believe the Romans founded this fort in the third century, nearly 100 years after they built Hadrian's Wall. The Wall runs behind where your camera is set up. Saint Nicholas Cathedral is between 150 and 200 metres away."

"He-ee-ee-ee-ee!" I whinny excitedly before screaming, "Pan's back!"

"What's the commotion about?" bawls Thorn, who hates being disturbed at mealtimes.

"He's here, now!" I confirm jubilantly. "He's replaying a recording; I think it's his filmed interview with the archaeologist he and Alan visited in Newcastle recently."

"Which archaeologist?" inquires Thorn, mildly annoyed that I have interrupted his munching so comprehensively.

"Think back. Mike works on behalf of English Heritage; he protects the Roman monument – including Hadrian's Wall and the Vallum – from damage. He also liaises with landowners and tenants who work and live near the Wall."

"Now I recall," declares Thorn, collecting his thoughts. "Our man revisited Newcastle recently to gather more facts about the Wall and Roman horses. The archaeologist couldn't meet us at the cathedral last month."

Pan, alighting from a new, presumably hired, silver-grey Ford, continues to play his recording, pausing occasionally to make notes. Mike must be an expert on Roman forts.

"Are we certain where the Military Way goes?" asks Pan.

"No, not in all places," affirms Mike. "They added it sometime after the Wall's initial construction. Assuming they started building the Wall about 122 A.D., they probably added this service road in the 160s."

"We trekked by the site of that fort!" blurts out Thorn, now paying close attention.

"Your National Trail often traces the Wall line closely," suggests Pan. "In numerous locations wouldn't it have been impractical for Romans to walk right beside the Wall?"

"Plainly, we don't have Hadrian's Wall standing to its full height," observes Mike. "We don't know whether there was a walkway along the top, whether it was a defensible fighting platform, like a castle, or whether it was about control, customs and access. I suspect it had a defensive role, but Roman military functioned to defeat the enemy in the field using discipline, tactics and training, not to hide behind a wall. It most likely didn't have one specific function, which may have changed through time."

"We traced the Military Way wherever feasible," explains Pan, "otherwise using navigable channels behind or in front of the Wall. It was quite a physical feat for two laden ponies, never mind what difficulties there might have been for a large, heavily equipped cavalry contingent."

"Our man's right," remarks Thorn. "I wonder how Romans moved their gear easily along the Way."

"They were masters of logistics," insists Mike. "They were practised at going into difficult, dangerous territory to forage and deal with supply issues. Supply and logistics are vital to our understanding of the Roman military. Was it oxen, horses, ponies, mules or water transport? Logistics are difficult to grapple with archaeologically."

"What were their logistics between Tynemouth and Newcastle?" wonders Pan.

Mike reveals that the fort at Newcastle appears to have been built later than the Wall's first construction: "The bit of Wall from here to Segedunum, at Wall's End, is probably another addition, built shortly after they began the original Wall. Did they add it because they felt vulnerable on the tidal Tyne east of here? Who knows?"

"So the Wall's not chronologically constructed east to west or west to east?" concludes Pan.

"No," says Mike. "We believe they marched up Dere Street, a Roman road between York and Scotland, and hit the Wall line at Portgate. They spread out, organising the initial building of the Wall from Portgate. It was a sophisticated military operation. Of course, York was the military capital of Roman Britain."

"I'm aware that Dere Street was probably a forest route," says Pan, "and that Romans named their capital 'Eboracum' – place of the yew trees – after an ancient Celtic name."

"We camped at Portgate," I remind Thorn."

"Oh, yes. That's where we escaped from the beer garden," he chortles, an all-knowing, wide-mouthed grin stretching across his contorted face, as usual.

The computerised recording continues to play.

"How much accurate information is there about the deployment of horses and ponies near the Wall?" asks Pan.

"Recent documented evidence from Segedunum and Vindolanda indicates cavalry horses were barracked with men," explains Mike. "But understanding the wider role of equines in logistics and procurement is a key area where we have huge gaps in our knowledge."

"No acceptable hypotheses have been proposed yet to interpret all of the equine leather evidence?"

"We need to understand more," admits Mike.

"Yeah, what about the barding I wore, for example?" quips Thorn. "Has any archaeologist deciphered it completely?"

"Pan's hypothesis, that it was a heat blanket for a Roman pack pony, seems feasible," I answer, "though I suppose a mule or a ridden pony might have worn it."

Mike is answering Pan's concern about tourists walking on top of the Wall: "We desperately want people to come and enjoy walking along the Wall, see amazing landscapes and appreciate the archaeology. However, erosion issues are considerable. We rely on Natural England, which funds the Hadrian's Wall National Trail maintenance."

"Is it about education?" suggests Pan.

"Yes. We would prefer Trail walkers to spread out across the Trail, not proceed in single file down the main trod. This ensures none of the grass wears away. A team of Trail people goes up and down the Wall, carrying out day-to-day maintenance. They occasionally move the path line subtly to prevent erosion, and they can put a temporary, hexagonal, plastic latticework down in wet, winter months when the ground is most vulnerable to pounding boots. Whenever visitors have the option, they might consider visiting in spring and summer months: soils tend to be drier and the Trail is much less prone to erosion. In winter, there are circular hikes you can do, rather than end-to-end stuff. It's an 'every footstep counts' message."

"Well, we are blameless," argues Thorn. "Apart from periodically crossing Hadrian's Wall Path and going through occasional Path gates, we kept well away from the recognised National Trail – unless it coincided with the Military Way, as you might expect."

"And we didn't wear shoes," I add. "I wonder: if the National Trail followed our route instead, closer to the Way, would there be less monument erosion?"

"Possibly," concedes Thorn. "Only archaeologists and Path experts could ascertain that. One outcome would be certain: walkers would be following in the footsteps of Romans; they would be tracing an archaeologically and historically significant route. I'm not convinced Romans walked next to the Wall that much."

Pan is curious: "Over the last 1,800 years, how much soil and debris has been placed on top of the monument?"

"In some places, there is a decent layer of topsoil," confirms Mike. "In others, the archaeology effectively sprouts out of the ground. It's crucial to emphasise that no one should walk on the Wall anywhere except for a section through Housesteads Wood, to the west of Housesteads Fort. By the way, you can appreciate the Wall better by standing and looking at it, rather than by standing on top of it. It's essential for our National Trust, National Trail and Natural England partners to keep advising visitors. It's a matter of persuading people."

"Native ponies tend not to scorch the ground," argues Pan. "Is cattle scorching a serious issue along the Wall, or not?"

"Yes, in places," admits Mike. "We have tackled many of the key problem sites through Natural England's stewardship schemes. The Wall is a living landscape, owned by people who have legitimate rights and needs. Hadrian's Wall is everybody's World Heritage Site. Our new management plan emphasises 'belonging to people'."

"So you are beginning to learn from the people whose families have farmed this land for generations?"

"Many of the best ideas about consolidation measures, to avoid damage to the site, come from farmers. They are incredibly supportive of the archaeology. It's nice to be reminded that these guys sometimes know a lot more about managing their land than I, as an archaeologist, ever will."

The voices cease; it appears that Pan's recorded interview has ended.

Thorn ponders for several seconds before interrupting this new silence: "The Wall was an imposing spectacle to behold comprehensively, intact, I bet."

"The Stone Wall was likely between 12 and perhaps just over 14 feet high, and the Turf wall was about 12 feet high," I inform him, "according to an archaeological interpretation Pan has read."

"Thank goodness our man mentioned that broad hooves are less likely to damage the monument," he continues, evading my statistics.

While we are discussing the merits of our feet when compared with cattle hooves, Pan turns up at our yard gate, as if magically transported. We saunter casually over to him, attempting to disguise our eagerness.

"Hi, boys!" he begins. "I'm sorry: I've been away longer than I expected. You both appear to be in tip-top condition."

I judge him to be well too. Perhaps he has recovered fully.

"Alan and I saw the Carville children. They asked about you both. 'Did they avoid injury?' 'Did covering all those miles exhaust them?' A girl even asked whether you liked the food. I told her you raided your supplies on one occasion, so you must have."

"Carville children were lovely," I insist quietly. "Every one cared about us."

"On the subject of food, I fancy pellets right now," whispers Thorn, his eyes wide in anticipation of a potential feed from Pan.

I ignore his never-ending appetite.

"We met the archaeologist," relates Pan. "Afterwards, we filmed a few of your favourite Wall locations. Now, this is the hard bit."

Myriad nerve endings fire simultaneously within my brain, but I try not to panic. What is he going to say?

"Boys, I've decided to discontinue the expedition."

"Is he saying our adventuring is over?" whispers Thorn.

"This adventure is, anyway," I mumble solemnly. "Cheer up," I add, successfully hiding my disappointment. "We had a tremendous run. No, I mean we had a tremendous walk! What's more, we will have further adventures, possibly with Pan; you may rely on it,

Thorn."

"I truly hope so," grumbles Thorn expectedly. "If not, I'll be bored."

"Together we've achieved almost everything I intended," says Pan. "We've completed 16 of 18 planned interviews face to face, and Alan has secured much, though not all, of the film footage I sought. You've not faltered for 120 miles, not far off 200 kilometres, laden. I should expect nothing more of you at this time of year."

"Nay, nay, nay," protests Thorn almost inaudibly. "We could manage another 120 miles easily."

He's right. Our great, great, great grand dams and sires carried similar loads whatever the weather. Of course, they didn't have to contend with extremely dangerous, fast-moving vehicles or with human-made, modern enclosures and other obstacles. Furthermore, I suppose their keepers didn't camp out in late autumn, which would have been too arduous: they probably used inns.

"I've considered returning," adds Pan, "as I have completely recovered, but the days are shorter, ground conditions are poorer and the weather has worsened."

"Hai-ai-ai-ai!" cries Thorn softly. "What about those schools we visited that weren't open? Children will be sad they missed meeting us; we promised to visit them."

Thorn is surprisingly upset. I suspect Pan has noticed.

I attempt to calm my friend: "I suppose they could watch Pan's video diary once he completes it: I'm certain they'll understand then."

Thorn remains unconvinced, as am I, to be honest.

"I could continue the walk east, beyond Walby Farm Park," proclaims Pan after several seconds of silence, "if I led only one pony, which would significantly reduce preparation time each day, thus allowing faster progress and maximising safety in view of ground conditions."

"What?" wails Thorn uncharacteristically, startling me. "There's no way we'll let him split us up now, Roamer! Get ready to protest."

"Because you, Roamer, have striven hardest," explains Pan, "I contemplated resting you, cutting down the carried equipment to minimal survival gear – about 45 per cent of the original weight – and using only Thorn's packsaddle. Then I could complete the return leg easily."

"I wouldn't be keen to carry on without you," maintains Thorn.

"And I'm going where you go," I tell him.

"I'll not be requisitioning a winter tent from stores," adds Pan casually. "Upon deliberating, I've rejected the idea of splitting you up: it wouldn't be fair to either of you."

"He's not wrong there," chirps Thorn, sighing, relieved. "I wanted to carry on, but I would have been alone and lonely."

"And I would be worrying about you incessantly, Thorn," I say. "I'm confident that Pan has made the correct decision."

Thorn:

Our man returns. He is a day late: we learn that he elected to stay overnight with the farmer at Chapel House. Roamer is overjoyed to see him.

"Yesterday," relates our man in a slightly despondent voice, "I visited several campsites: Walby Farm Park; Longtown; Quarry Side; Chapel House; Greencarts; Bradley; and Vallum Farm. I collected unused supplies, duplicate maps and several reserve harness parts. And I explained to farmers that I'd decided, reluctantly, to abandon the remainder of the return trip."

We shouldn't stop now, I'm still thinking. Roamer disagrees. He says we've fulfilled our obligations. Maybe he's right. Still, making it back to where we began would have been the biggest buzz. Worst of all, I'm heavy-hearted because now we won't meet children or teachers from two schools: we'll probably have no better opportunity.

"And I visited Cawfields," adds our man, "to try to pay for one of the gates you two broke, but the farmer and his family were out."

A mischievous grin stretches across my Roman face. Even Roamer, a wild twinkle in both eyes, later admits it's hilarious.

"Boys, guess what?" declares our man, following a pause. "Finally, I have retrieved my lost boot, which the dog at Black Row

Riding Centre hid a month ago. Staff at the centre arranged for it to be posted to Walby Farm Park."

Seriously, he would have needed those boots had we carried on trekking.

"I also collected the barding from Quarry Side," he adds.

"Do you remember trying it on?" whispers Roamer.

"It was marginally undersized, especially around my ears," I remind him yet again. "It would have fitted you perfectly, though."

"And wasn't it an eventful re-enactment?" reminisces Roamer. "One of your baskets almost fell off, your headband slipped off on a tight, downhill section, and Pan narrowly avoided losing his footing during the ascent."

Our man is still chatting to us. He reveals that he considered separating us in order to carry on eastwards, but eventually he rejected this idea. I am pleased: it would have been a foolhardy decision. Instead, he has an urge to take us back to the Wall on another day, at another time, in a better season. Dare I dream of a spring reunion with him and the Wall?

He hugs each of us in turn, says goodbye and promises to visit us soon, wherever we may be.

Tonight, after chatting intently with my owner and his wife about the expedition and about how concerned humans might save free-living ponies from oblivion on the islands called Britain, our man is on his way back to his expedition base in Leicestershire. Yes, you might have guessed: almost two millennia ago, Leicester was a Roman town, Ratae Corieltauvorum, in the province of Britannia.

Our man's district is many miles and even more kilometres from us. Roamer is missing him already. Okay, I admit it: so am I.

14th November – Stoney Gill

Roamer:

It's late morning when Bill moves Thorn and me to a patchwork of empty, dying, thin-hedged fields in the vicinity of our original training ground, rough, late-autumn forage at its best. We graze freely and widely at leisure, not pestered by cars or bothered by humans.

"I am resolved," I announce to Thorn. "I shall tell our brothers, sisters and cousins, and every interested human, what we did."

"And how will you do that?" he inquires politely.

"I shall publish my diary," I explain. "At least, I'll ask Pan to publish it."

"Good idea, Roamer!" cries Thorn excitedly. "I will join you in your endeavour now that I understand our plight more clearly. At the beginning of our crusade, I felt that I was trying to solve a thousand-piece puzzle without ever glimpsing the final picture."

"Thorn, I have realised why our adventure lasted so long," I inform him. "To achieve our goal, we had to travel throughout our known world."

"It was probably the most prodigious journey of exploration you and I will attempt," agrees Thorn.

"Be honest," I implore him. "Were you ever frightened during our travels?"

"Yes, very occasionally," he admits. "Dangerous predicaments alarmed me, as they did you, but our man watched over us. He took immense care to avoid serious accidents. We were perfectly healthy at the end, and fitter."

I cherish Pan's friendship. Though he won't admit it, I believe that Thorn does too.

"I've been thinking seriously," says Thorn between mouthfuls of grass. "On the expedition, as you pointed out, I wore the lighter saddle and pack. Some equine friends might conclude that this situation was unfair."

"I didn't really mind," I reply. "Besides, you had the responsibility of leading. Honestly, I enjoyed it! As you know, there was only one practical downside: I couldn't lead."

"We covered the distance in 28 days," frets Thorn. "If you had been in front instead of me, might we have managed to travel further and in less time?"

"I sincerely doubt it," I tell him. "On reflection, I realise I couldn't have bettered your leadership."

In fact, my friend's amazing, isn't he?

"I've figured it out," I announce eventually.

"Figured out what?" he asks.

"Just this," I conclude. "We went on our expedition to help shield nearly wild, acclimatised, hefted, free-living Fell ponies from further human mistakes."

"Walking the length of Hadrian's Wall made me think about Roman ponies," admits Thorn, "our ancestors who toiled throughout the Wall's construction. Without them, we would have no saga."

"We houyhnhnms sometimes underestimate our capabilities," I confide. "Over all of the days that I walked in the shadow of the Wall, not once did I feel lost: an invisible, undying spirit of perseverance, shared by all of our kind, guided me. From now on, it will be possible for me to do anything, as long as I believe I can do it."

Thorn nods but says nothing.

I confess: I am thankful that Pan has given me such an extraordinary experience. I wonder what will happen now, however. No human shall alter my name, but much will be different; perhaps a new life, or even a new owner, is around the corner. Whatever becomes of me, I shall not forget Pan.

That's my story told. I have related it as accurately as possible, as only houyhnhnms can. I hope that you found our antics amusing. Our message is clear. What happens next is up to you.

Sincerely,

Roamer

P.S.   Solo is relieved and deliriously happy because we are safely home. He continually worried about us. We worried about him, too. He doesn't have strange dreams anymore. He jokes that this was the longest trip in which he ever participated.

Thorn:

We are continuing to relax at Stoney Gill. Though I'm enjoying the rest, already I hunger to share another quest with my great pal, Roamer. In fact, I would begin right now.

"What an exciting time we had in the shadow of the Roman Wall," I declare. "We were virtually wild until we embarked upon our voyage of exploration, an expedition into an unknown, human world."

"We've had a phenomenal adventure," agrees Roamer. "It was a unique challenge."

"At the conclusion of our quest we weren't a bit tired," I remark.

"Well, perhaps we were less tired than Pan," replies Roamer.

"I slowly adjusted to being with our man," I recall. "In future, I shall try not to be mischievous when I am with him. At least, I won't misbehave unless you get up to your old tricks again, Roamer!"

"You can rely on Pan endlessly," believes Roamer. "He is my incomparable human friend."

"We visited four distinctive schools and met scores of enchanting children on our journey, which made me think," I tell him.

"Think what?" he asks, intrigued.

"In future," I say, "I might fancy pulling carts of small children occasionally, two children at a time; it could be fun for me and fun for them."

"I knew it!" he declares. "You like mini-humans as much as I do."

"Mind you, most days I'd still prefer to roam freely," I add quickly as an afterthought.

"I've been thinking too," says Roamer.

He suggests that we record our travelogues, an idea that dumfounds me.

What's the point of it all? Well, we want to guarantee a Fell pony future in wild places; we must persuade humans to protect wilderness and our natural homes. I can speak for Roamer: I'm certain he agrees.

I may never find out whether, by relating this story of our lives alongside Hadrian's Wall, Roamer and I will help to save the future of Fell ponies and, of course, roaming ponies throughout Britain and the planet you call earth. For now, we are pleased with ourselves, knowing that we have tried our hardest to tell the world about some of England's last free-living equines. The rest depends upon sympathetic humans.

"Dare we hope to travel on another quest with Pan in months or years to come?" wonders Roamer.

"Definitely," I reply optimistically. "Who can foretell what might happen?"

Thank you for reading my version of events. Someday, we may meet: who knows?

As Roamer says, "One day, perhaps, you might enjoy walking with Houyhnhnms."

Thorn

P.S. Our man writes, "Thanks to every person who supported our expedition and to every organisation that helped 'make it happen'."

Roamer, Solo and I, too, wish to congratulate you all, not forgetting the children we met. We have learned that some humans, at least, are on the side of those who wish to roam free.

Epilogue: reflections

Roamer:

WE returned home four days ago. I have had time to reflect upon our epic journey.

It was a testing slog alongside the Roman Wall. We aimed to follow the Military Way. Thorn and I risked exposing ourselves to unknown menaces and perils. We foresaw storms, rocky terrain and marsh, yet we persevered. We attempted to accomplish whatever was necessary regardless of the weather – torrential rain, howling gale-force winds, thick fog, frost or sunshine; occasionally, the weather became surprisingly cold.

To begin with, we were frightened of unusual, ear-piercing sounds, although we never bolted or reacted impulsively in an attempt to avoid them. I usually remained calm and unruffled; Thorn was sometimes restless, even excitable. I behaved myself. So did Thorn. Well, he behaved most of the time, anyway. In the end, we weren't afraid of anything.

At the beginning, I was slightly affronted because Thorn was leading. I had to traipse behind him and Pan continuously, an outrage. When I eventually realised why I was at the back, I was no longer resentful: Thorn and I are great friends. I am proud of his clever leadership, and I am pleased and content that I could travel the same distance as Thorn whilst carrying such a bulky, heavy load.

We accepted people, regarding some highly. Contrary to our original suspicions, we decided that not all humans are biophobic. We learned why humans need our assistance to protect wild animals and plants. Humans label this wildlife "biodiversity". Furthermore, we discovered that free-living Fell ponies are biodiversity! Some of our genes and learned characteristics may be special, even unique.

We had immense fun, especially at night-times; obviously, we enjoyed cantering and rolling in long grass, and now and again we liked to escape and explore.

Thorn, Solo and I have our own website! Really, it's fascinating and quite informative. At least, we think so. Some filming, particularly during training, is hilarious.

Thorn:

Our quest took longer than I expected; at one stage, I wanted it to last for ever. Roamer and I strode a three-figure number of miles hooked up to each other whilst carrying heavy packs. In a modern world, this task isn't quite as simple as you might assume for powerful, agile and well-trained Fell ponies. Of course, as we became physically and mentally fitter, we could walk more easily together.

This was my greatest adventure, an adventure that I could barely dream of once upon a time. We travelled on ancient tracks and modern roads, and sometimes we ventured where no trail existed. We trekked, heavily laden, across rivers and moors, through woods and up steep hills. Numerous obstacles, dangerous situations and lots of threatening, dashing traffic tested us en route. However, it was possibly the finest of times.

Before we trained for the walk, no human had touched me; I wouldn't countenance the thought of being handled. I also avoided unfamiliar sounds and tastes. Virtually every step I took was a new experience. We savoured peculiar, diverse foods, even eating seaweed! And don't forget: the Roman saddle was unique; master saddlers made it specially for the trip. I am the solitary pony to have assessed it.

Roamer and I had an exhilarating, almost entirely happy time walking with our man. It was a stupendous, unforgettable experience. We visited four schools. Well, we tried to visit six, but two had closed for a holiday. I revelled in non-stop attention, never mind infrequent publicity. Of course, aided on occasion by Roamer, I was compelled to knock over several gates and fences. What's more, we are now highly accomplished escape artists.

This expedition will probably prove to be the most critical, most valuable, mission of our Fell pony lives. By the way, soon I will be seven. I cannot wait: it will be glorious. I love being a Fell pony. You would too! Humans don't know what they're missing.

Solo:

Roamer, Thorn and I trained tirelessly for our challenge. Training seemed chaotic at first. One day, my owner ferried me from my Scottish home to a Cumbrian hillside. There, two strangers coached me to walk beside roads with Thorn and to carry a heavy backpack. Humans tested me to my limit. It was a hectic, experimental, surreal time, not normal for free-living ponies.

I tried on that Roman packsaddle once, but I wasn't keen on wearing it; I kept getting into trouble.

After all, humans didn't choose me to begin the hike. I was too young to manage the whole thing: I am only three. Nevertheless, I played my part. My job was to replace Roamer or Thorn if either became injured. Upon reflection, I am glad that I wasn't needed: both of my friends have returned home perfectly fit and healthy.

We Fell ponies have an urgent message: please save our kind from extinction. There isn't much time. "Why should we bother to help you?" you may ask. As you may have concluded, we are remarkably valuable to humankind. However, the question is not whether we are worth saving. Rather, can the human race survive on this planet without free-living, wild ponies?

Illustrations

Illustrations are in chronological order.

1. Roamer: training with the British Military packsaddle on Lincoln Common
2. Thorn: training near Stoney Gill Farm, Shap
3. Solo: training at Heathlands Farm, Carlisle
4. Thorn: training near Stoney Gill Farm, Shap
5. Thorn: training with the Roman packsaddle near Stoney Gill Farm, Shap
6. Solo: training near Stoney Gill Farm, Shap
7. Roamer: resting at Rising Sun Country Park, North Tyneside
8. High Brunton Turret, west of Planetrees Milecastle
9. Roamer: Greencarts Farm
10. Sycamore Gap, Hadrian's Wall
11. Westwards along the Whin Sill, Caw Gap, Hadrian's Wall
12. Caw Gap Turret, Hadrian's Wall
13. Thorn: Cawfields Farm, Hadrian's Wall
14. Thorn and Roamer: grazing near Walltown, Hadrian's Wall
15. Walltown Crags, Hadrian's Wall
16. Wicker baskets attached to Roamer's saddle: Quarry Side, Banks
17. Thorn's right hind leg and shoeless hoof: en route between The Beck Farm and Roughlane House, Hadrian's Wall
18. Sunrise, Newtown Farm, Hadrian's Wall
19. Roamer: Campfield Marsh Nature Reserve, near Bowness-on-Solway
20. Extensively grazing Fell ponies: Birk Beck Common, near Shap

1. Roamer: training with the British Military packsaddle on Lincoln Common

He tests me severely, enticing me to execute all manner of dexterous manoeuvres whilst carrying his saddle and bags.

2. *Thorn: training near Stoney Gill Farm, Shap*

"Good boy. Steady, boy," this man gently reassures, but he's not fooling me!

3. *Solo: training at Heathlands Farm, Carlisle*

He leads me around trees and other natural obstacles, between gateposts and along farm tracks.

4. *Thorn: training near Stoney Gill Farm, Shap*

This same, persistent human one-third fills each of two large, empty, hessian bags with red sand.

5. *Thorn: training with the Roman packsaddle near Stoney Gill Farm, Shap*

Finally, they are thinking clearly. They unsaddle Solo, place his Roman saddle onto me and then reattach our connecting harness, putting me in front.

6. *Solo: training near Stoney Gill Farm, Shap*

We've swapped saddles: now I'm wearing the British saddle, which I cope
with easily.

7. Roamer: resting at Rising Sun Country Park, North Tyneside

There is a deafening crash as the gate tumbles into pieces. My monocular vision takes over, but I stay calm: it's nothing to do with me.

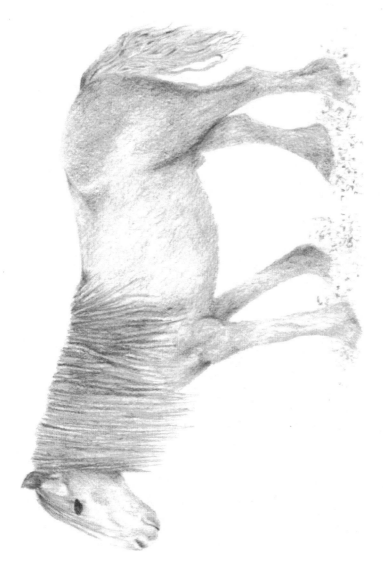

8. *High Brunton Turret, west of Planetrees Milecastle*

"Here ... the Broad Wall, which we have followed from the east, joins ... the Narrow Wall, which stretches ... westwards."

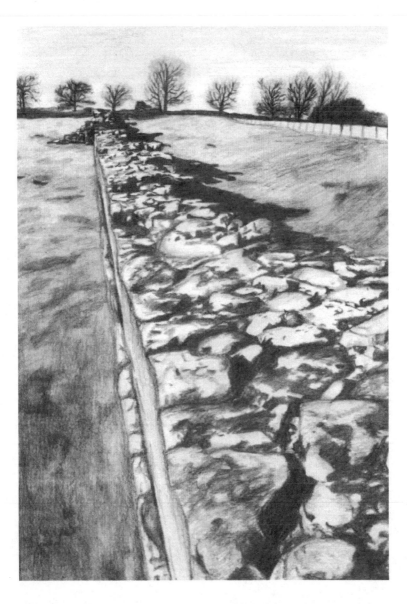

9. *Roamer: Greencarts Farm*

Our man is leaving nothing to chance. He keeps us waiting while he stalks the field's perimeter, closely inspecting every foot of wire fencing.

10. Sycamore Gap, Hadrian's Wall

From a position about 40 metres south of the turret at the summit of Highshield Crags, we are heading steeply downwards to Sycamore Gap. A solitary tree between two tall crests in the Whin Sill marks its location.

11. *Westwards along the Whin Sill, Caw Gap, Hadrian's Wall*

Our man, aided by his Lincoln guest, begins to search for the safest way down.

12. Caw Gap Turret, Hadrian's Wall

Once across the gap road, we are climbing on firmer ground, briefly west, towards Caw Gap Turret.

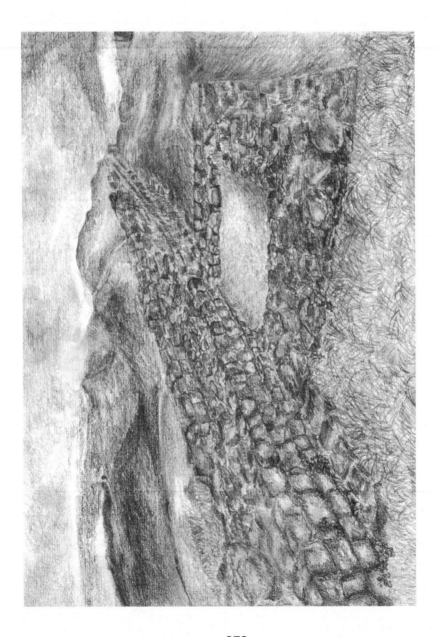

13. *Thorn: Cawfields Farm, Hadrian's Wall*

Later on, when our man ambles over to assess how we are coping, as he does habitually, he realises we have escaped.

14. Thorn and Roamer: grazing near Walltown, Hadrian's Wall

We wait. I'm content: there's tasty grass about. However, perhaps a quarter of an hour later, our master is becoming impatient.

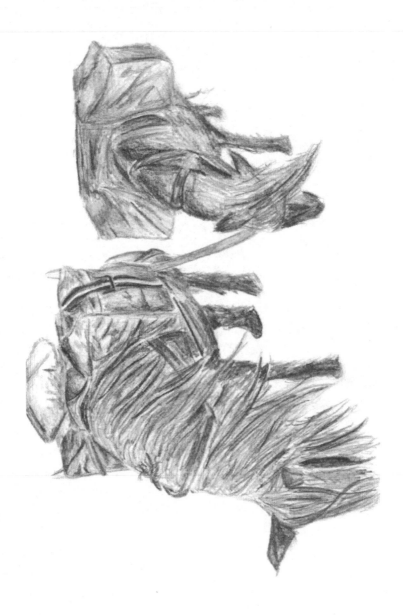

15. *Walltown Crags, Hadrian's Wall*

We follow the Way, sweeping with the contour below Walltown Crags towards a Roman Army fort where a modern museum exists.

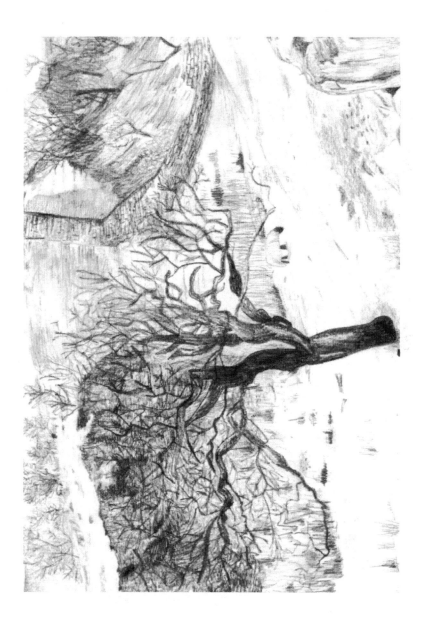

16. Wicker baskets attached to Roamer's saddle: Quarry Side, Banks

At length, Pan judges that he has attached two baskets correctly to each of our saddles using his specially made, natural fibre ropes. ... In fact, the baskets aren't secure, as he shall discover.

17. Thorn's right hind leg and shoeless hoof: en route between The Beck Farm and Roughlane House, Hadrian's Wall

The going is slow: in places, we are fetlock-deep in squelchy, liquid mud. ... This really is a rough lane.

18. *Sunrise, Newtown Farm, Hadrian's Wall*

Sunrise reveals a startling, turbulent firmament of gold and orange laced with streaks of purple.

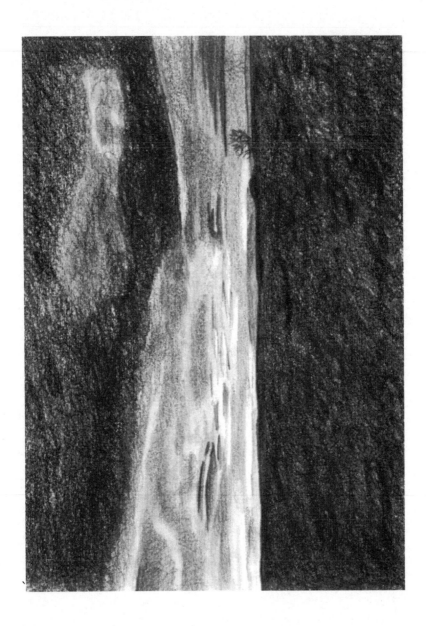

19. Roamer: Campfield Marsh Nature Reserve, near Bowness-on-Solway

Roamer is only two paces away; he has been dozing too.

20. *Extensively grazing Fell ponies: Birk Beck Common, near Shap*

"Protecting and enhancing remaining semi-wild, extensively grazing herds is an urgent challenge," stresses our man.

Itinerary maps

Key to place names shown on maps 1-4

The reader will discover the interpretation of most place names incidentally through the diary narrative. The aim of the following short list is to assist map interpretation.

In alphabetical order:

Bag-shaped hill = Codlaw Hill (Riding Centre)
Beautiful hill = Beaumont (Parish Hall)
Beside a quarry = Quarry Side (Campsite)
Broad clearing = Bradley (Farm)
Castle at a gap in the Wall = Thirlwall Castle
Castle at the outfall of the river flow = Tynemouth Castle
Church of Saint Andrew by the gushing river = Kirkandrews-on-Eden
Dark tarn = Bleatarn (Farm)
District of the people called Ligore = Leicestershire
Estuary of the ford marked by a pillar = Solway Firth
Expanse where jackdaws nest = Cawfields (Farm)
Farm on the Vallum = Vallum Farm
Grassy, rocky moor = Greencarts (Farm)
High house = High House (Farm)
Hollow ravine = Howgill (Farm)
House of the people from the bright burn (by a gate marking a gap in

the Wall) = Errington Arms Public House (near Portgate)

Hubert's hillock = Knockupworth (Farm)

Land overgrown with heather = Heathlands (Farm)

Methodist meeting house = Chapel House (Farm)

New village = Newtown (Farm)

North Plain at the bowed headland = North Plain, Bowness

(Outlying, fortified farm of an abbey) on a ridge near the fort = Drumburgh (Grange)

Outlying hamlet where flax is grown = Linstock (Castle)

Place belonging to Luguvalos = Carlisle

Place by the Wall = Walby (Farm Park)

Ridge near the fort (of Coggabata) = Drumburgh

Rising Sun = Rising Sun Country Park (previously Rising Sun Colliery)

River crossing in a gorge / Ford in a gorge = Chollerford

Rocky, narrow ravine = Stoney Gill (Farm)

Roman colony by a pool = Lincoln

Roofs by the heather-covered hill = Black Row (Riding Centre)

Rushing water = Ouseburn (Farm)

Sigewine's castle = Sewing Shields (Farm)

Itinerary map 1:

Training and
expedition locations

Land overgrown with heather

The Wall

Rocky, narrow ravine

Roman colony by a pool

District of the people called Ligore

Itinerary map 2:

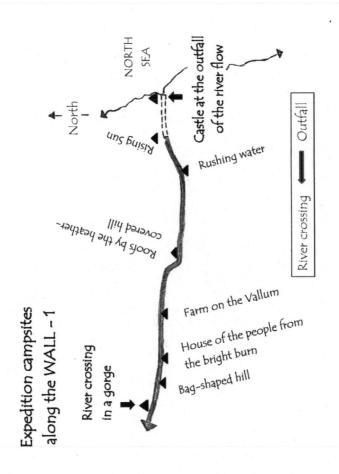

Expedition campsites along the WALL – 1

River crossing in a gorge

Bag-shaped hill

House of the people from the bright burn

Farm on the Vallum

Roofs by the heather-covered hill

Rushing water

Castle at the outfall of the river flow

Rising Sun

NORTH SEA

North

River crossing ▬▶ Outfall

Itinerary map 3:

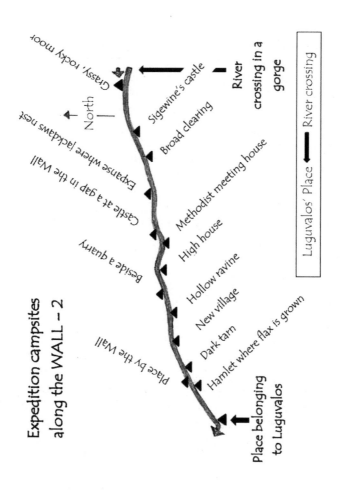

Expedition campsites along the WALL – 2

Grassy, rocky moor

Sigewine's castle

Broad clearing

North

Expanse where jackdaws nest

Castle at a gap in the Wall

Beside a quarry

Methodist meeting house

High house

Hollow ravine

New village

Dark tarn

Hamlet where flax is grown

Place by the Wall

Place belonging to Luguvalos

River crossing in a gorge

Luguvalos' Place ━━▶ River crossing

Itinerary map 4:

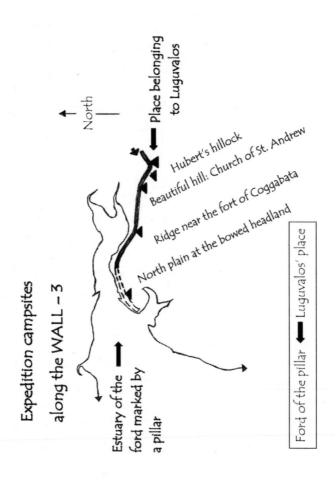

Expedition campsites
along the WALL – 3

North

Place belonging
to Luguvalos

Hubert's hillock

Beautiful hill: Church of St. Andrew

Ridge near the fort of Coggabata

North plain at the bowed headland

Estuary of the
ford marked by
a pillar

Ford of the pillar — Luguvalos' place

Acknowledgements

The author would like to thank and acknowledge the individuals and organisations who contributed to the narrative of this book.

A. Individuals / Organisations (formally recorded interviews)

Dan Boyce (Scribe), Stuart Carter (Liverpool University Veterinary Science Department), Sonia Chalmers (Burgh-by-Sands Primary School), Mike Collins (English Heritage), Ruth Dalton (Rare Breeds Survival Trust), Jamie Halbert (Farmer), David Harpley (Cumbria Wildlife Trust), Judy Hill (Fell Pony Society), Norman Holton (Royal Society for the Protection of Birds), Julian Hosking (Independent Specialist Adviser on Farm Animal Breeds, Genetic Resources Diversity Conservation and Agricultural, Horticultural and Silvicultural Biodiversity), Andrew Humphries (Federation of Cumbria Commoners), Simon Humphries (Natural England), Tom Lloyd (Fell Pony Society), Walter Lloyd (Fell Pony Society), Mark Lupton (Lincoln Fell herd manager), David Martin (Natural England), Paul May (Paragon Veterinary Group), Alison Morton (Fell Pony Society), Mandy Oliver (Ouseburn Farm), Bill Potter (Fell Pony Society).

B. Expedition Fell pony owners

Judy Hill (breeder) – Lathomdale Roamer (71051G), Bill Potter (breeder) – Huntsmans Blackthorn (70689G), Michael Rawlinson (breeder) – Thornbeck Solitaire (71126G).

C. Camera operators / Camera operator assistants / Film editors

Ernie Duncan (operator assistant: expedition), Alex McCranon (operator: pony training), Alan Scott (operator / editor: pony training & expedition).

D. College students (illustrators)

Illustrations are drawings of photographs taken by the author during either pre-expedition training or the expedition proper. Illustrators have endeavoured to represent photographs accurately. Illustrator ages are correct at the illustration creation dates.

(i) Beauchamp College

Age 15 years: Alana Deacon (*Illustr 3*). Age 16 years: Asma Alghamdi (*Illustr 17*), Nawel Hussain (*Illustr 15*), Zareena Shabudin (*Illustr 18*), Dhanika Vansia (*Illustr 12*). Age 17 years: Dharini Sachdev (*Illustr 20*). Age 18 years: Tayyaba Malik (*Illustr 6*), Isis Pinner (*Illustr 13*).

(ii) Gateway College

Age 15 years: Leah Giles (*Illustr 1, 8, 9, 10, 19*), Oliver Martin (*Illustr 2, 4, 5, 14*). Age 16 years: Elle Middleton-Evans (*Illustr 11, 16*). Age 18 years: Leona Deacon (*Illustr 7*).

E. Primary schools pupils

(a) Interviewers / Investigators:

During the expedition, children asked prepared questions and investigated pony body temperatures.

(i) Bowness-on-Solway Primary School, (ii) Burgh-by-Sands Primary School, (iii) Carville Primary School, (iv) Stanwix Primary School

Ages 4 to 11 years: 81 pupils (Anon).

(b) Storytellers:

The author's expedition website / diary and school visits with the ponies enabled children to submit drawings or short stories to the author. Where appropriate within the narrative, the author has adapted aspects of those submissions.

(i) Burgh-by-Sands Primary School

Ages 4 to 5 years (drawings): Thalia Champkins, Millie Fragouli. Ages 5 to 6 years (drawings): Honey Elliot. Ages 7 to 8 years (stories): Gemma Bell, Rachael Grey, Caitlin Hetherington, Freya Hill, Anna Holliday, Ian Jowett, Ben Miller, Emma Shannan, Natalie Sisson. Ages 8 to 9 years (stories): Poppy Elliot, Ellie Fragouli, Kiar Wilson. Ages 9 to 10 years (stories): Jonathan Hill, Joseph Knapton, Euan Read, Neve Sowerby, Charlie Walker. Ages 10 to 11 years (stories): Daniel Betts, Jonathan Davidson, Olivia Elliot, Meg Postlethwaite, Henry Walker.

(ii) Stanwix Primary School

Ages 10 to 11 years (stories): Charlotte Graham, Georgia Hodgson, Molly Hughes, Christina Kirkpatrick, Becky Miller.

(c) College / School teachers:

Teachers and others who coordinated pupil participation (see Sections D, E above).

F. Other individuals / organisations

(i) Advice on archaeological interpretation
David Breeze / Society of Antiquaries of Newcastle upon Tyne

(ii) Other contributions
Persons met – prior to, during or following the expedition – who contributed either formally or informally, including named and anonymous farmers, landowners and others.

G. Expedition management / administration assistant

Susie Goodyear

H. Observations on the accuracy of the narrative

The author's intention was to record all interviews during the expedition. Interviews with Stuart Carter, Julian Hosking and David Martin were recorded by telephone after the expedition ended. The interview with Judy Hill was recorded in person after the expedition ended. The interview with Mike Collins was recorded towards the end of the expedition but not in the presence of the ponies, and it was not played back in their presence. These five interviews were inserted into the narrative at their originally intended expedition locations. To this extent, they are not an accurate portrayal of events that occurred during the expedition. The narrative also includes additional archaeological and geographical interpretation not considered during the expedition.

I. Disclaimer

The author has attempted to represent accurately all recorded and non-recorded conversations, accepting that occasionally the narrative has been edited for the sake of brevity and to ensure clarity. The author apologises for any inadvertent error of fact that unwittingly may have occurred.

References

S Beckensall, 2012, personal communication: place-names of Northumberland

D Bennett, 2005, Bone from the Severan ditch, Area A, 2004. In: A Birley and J Blake, Vindolanda Excavations, 2003-4, Vindolanda Trust, pp 131-142

R Birley, 2009, Vindolanda: a Roman frontier fort on Hadrian's Wall, Amberley Publishing Plc

D J Breeze, 2006, J Collingwood Bruce's Handbook to the Roman Wall, 14th Ed, Society of Antiquaries of Newcastle upon Tyne

A Burton, 2003, Hadrian's Wall Path, National Trail Guides, Aurum Press Ltd & The Countryside Agency

K Cameron, 1961, English Place Names, Methuen & Co Ltd, London / Redwood Press Ltd

Cycle City Guides, 2008, Cycle North East, Newcastle upon Tyne Cycling Map, Crown Copyright

Cycle City Guides, 2008, Cycle North East, North Tyneside Cycling Map, 1st Ed, Crown Copyright

Cycle City Guides, 2009, Cycle North East, North Tyneside Cycling Map, 2nd Ed, Crown Copyright

D Dorward, 2001, Scotland's Place-names, The Mercat Press, Edinburgh

C van Driel-Murray, et al, 1993, Preliminary reports on the leather, textiles, environmental evidence and dendrochronology. In: Vindolanda Research Reports, New Series, Vol III, pp 48-53, Roman Army Museum Publications for the Vindolanda Trust

C van Driel-Murray, P Connolly and J Duckham, 2004, Roman Saddles: archaeology and experiment 20 years on. In: L Gilmour

(Editor), The Saddle – An exploration of the saddle through history, London, pp 1-20

English Heritage, 1990, Chesters Roman Fort, J S Johnson, Principal Inspector of Ancient Monuments

English Place-Name Society, 1950, The Place-Names of Cumberland, Vol XXI, Part II, B Dickins (General Editor) and A M Armstrong, A Mawer & F M Stenton (Editors), Cambridge University Press, Cambridge

English Place-Name Society, 1952, The Place-Names of Cumberland, Vol XXII, Part III, B Dickins (General Editor) and A M Armstrong, A Mawer & F M Stenton (Editors), Cambridge University Press, Cambridge

English Place-Name Society, 1967, The Place-Names of Westmorland, Vol XLII, Part I, A H Smith (General Editor), Cambridge University Press, Cambridge

English Place-Name Society, 1970, English Place-Name Elements, Vol XXVI, Part II, A H Smith (General Editor), Cambridge University Press, Cambridge

English Place-Name Society, 1971, The Place-Names of Cumberland, Vol XX, Part I, B Dickins (General Editor) and A M Armstrong, A Mawer & F M Stenton (Editors), Cambridge University Press, Cambridge

English Place-Name Society, 1987, English Place-Name Elements, Vol XXV, Part I, A H Smith (General Editor), Cambridge University Press, Cambridge

I FitzGerald, 2000, Dales Ponies, Ch 3, pp 30-40, Whittet Books Ltd, Suffolk

R Gambles, 1994, Lake District Place Names, Dalesman Publishing Co

L Gilmour, 2004, In the Saddle: an exploration of the saddle through history, Archetype Publications Ltd, London

A Goldsworthy, 2003, The Complete Roman Army, Thames and Hudson Ltd, London

P Hill, 2006, The Construction of Hadrian's Wall, Tempus Publishing Ltd, Stroud

HMSO, 1937, Manual of Horsemanship, Equitation and Animal

Transport, pp 181-191, Crown Copyright

N Hodgson, 2003, The Roman Fort at Wallsend (Segedunum), Excavations in 1997-8, Tyne and Wear Museums Archaeological Monograph, Newcastle upon Tyne

N Hodgson, 2009, Hadrian's Wall 1999-2009, Cumberland and Westmorland Antiquarian and Archaeological Society and The Society of Antiquaries of Newcastle upon Tyne, Kendal

C Howard-Davis, 2009, The Carlisle Millennium Project, Excavations in Carlisle, 1998-2001, Vol 2: The Finds, Lancaster Imprints 14

C Johnstone, 2005, A Zooarchaeological study of equids in the Roman world, unpublished PhD thesis, Dept of Archaeology, University of York

M Kasso & M Balakrishnan, 2013, Ex-situ Conservation of Biodiversity with Particular Emphasis to Ethiopia. In: International Scholarly Research Notices, Vol 2013, ID 985037, 11 pp

P Kelekna, 2009, The Horse in Human History, Cambridge University Press, Cambridge

J Lee, 1998, The Place Names of Cumbria, Cumbria Heritage Services, Carlisle / Manchester Free Press, Manchester

A D Mills, Oxford Dictionary of English Place-Names, 1998, Oxford University Press, Oxford

Naples Archaeological Museum, Inventory number 9057, Part of Julia Felix Forum Frieze, Pompeii (also: Accademici Ercolanesi, 1762, Le Pitture Antiche d'Ercolano: Tome III, p 227, Tav 43)

Ordnance Survey, 1964, Map of Hadrian's Wall, Crown Copyright

Ordnance Survey, 2001, Roman Britain, 5th Ed, Crown Copyright

Ordnance Survey, 2005, Landranger Map 86, Haltwhistle & Brampton, Crown Copyright

Ordnance Survey, 2006, Explorer Map 314, Solway Firth, Crown Copyright

Ordnance Survey, 2007, Explorer Map 315, Carlisle, Crown Copyright

Ordnance Survey, 2007, Landranger Map 87, Hexham & Haltwhistle, Crown Copyright

Ordnance Survey, 2007, Landranger Map 88, Newcastle upon Tyne,

REFERENCES

Crown Copyright

Ordnance Survey, 2008, Explorer Map 316, Newcastle upon Tyne, Crown Copyright

Ordnance Survey, 2009, Explorer Map, Outdoor Leisure 43, Hadrian's Wall, Crown Copyright

J L Petersen, et al, January 2013, Genetic Diversity in the Modern Horse Illustrated from Genome-Wide SNP Data, in PLOS ONE, Vol 8, Issue 1

B Potter / J Taylor, 2012, Beatrix Potter's Letters, Penguin UK, Literary Collections

M Richards, 2004, Hadrian's Wall Path: Two-way National Trail description, Latitude Press Ltd

C Richardson, 1981, The Fell Pony, Ch 1-2, pp 1-39, The Dalesman Publishing Co Ltd, Lancaster

D Simpson, 2015, http://www.englandsnortheast.co.uk/PlaceName Meanings KtoO.html

The English Place-Name Society, 2012, The University of Nottingham, personal communication

G Tylden, 1965, Horses and Saddlery, Ch 6, pp 179-193, J A Allen & Co (London) and Army Museums Ogilby Trust

G Watson, 1995, Northumberland Place Names, Sandhill Press Ltd, Morpeth

H Welfare, 2000, Causeways, at Milecastles, across the Ditch of Hadrian's Wall. In: Archaeologia Aeliana, 5th Series, Vol XXVIII, IN 2000, pp 19, 25.

S E Winbolt, 1941, Roman Pack Saddle, in Surrey Archaeological Collections, Vol 47, Notes, p 130, Historic Environment Record No 195, Surrey Archaeological Society

S Winterbottom & Q Mould, 2009, The Leather and Other Organic Artefacts, The Carlisle Millennium Project, Excavations in Carlisle, 1998-2001, Vol 3, Lancaster Imprints 14, pp 1401-11

About the author

D A Murray is an independent conservationist, educator and writer. A Fellow of the Royal Geographical Society, an Earthwatch Institute Fellow and a Millennium Fellow, he has completed expeditions in Australia (3), Britain (2) and Cameroon. In 1999, he walked across Britain with pack animals, a journey of 1,740 miles from Lizard Point to Dunnet Head, mostly off-road, largely through national parks. He has written widely about Britain's native ponies. His latest research considers implications of rapid climate change for semi-wild and feral ponies that help to manage British ecosystems.